In Darfur

Volume Two

Letter from the General Editor

The Library of Arabic Literature series offers Arabic editions and English translations of significant works of Arabic literature, with an emphasis on the seventh to nineteenth centuries. The Library of Arabic Literature thus includes texts from the pre-Islamic era to the cusp of the modern period, and encompasses a wide range of genres, including poetry, poetics, fiction, religion, philosophy, law, science, history, and historiography.

Books in the series are edited and translated by internationally recognized scholars and are published in parallel-text format with Arabic and English on facing pages, and are also made available as English-only paperbacks.

The Library encourages scholars to produce authoritative, though not necessarily critical, Arabic editions, accompanied by modern, lucid English translations. Its ultimate goal is to introduce the rich, largely untapped Arabic literary heritage to both a general audience of readers as well as to scholars and students.

The Library of Arabic Literature is supported by a grant from the New York University Abu Dhabi Institute and is published by NYU Press.

Philip F. Kennedy
General Editor, Library of Arabic Literature

تشحيذ الأذهان
بسيرة بلاد العرب والسودان

محمّد بن عمر التونسيّ

المجلّد الثاني

LIBRARY OF
المكتبة
ARABIC
العربية
LITERATURE

In Darfur

An Account of the Sultanate and Its People

Muḥammad ibn ʿUmar al-Tūnisī

Volume Two

Edited and translated by
Humphrey Davies

Volume editor
Devin Stewart

NEW YORK UNIVERSITY PRESS
New York

NEW YORK UNIVERSITY PRESS
New York

Library of Congress Cataloging-in-Publication Data

Names: Tūnisī, Muḥammad ibn ʿUmar, author. | Davies, Humphrey T. (Humphrey Taman), translator, editor. | Tūnisī, Muḥammad ibn ʿUmar. Tashḥīdh al-adhhān bi-sīrat bilād al-ʿArab wa-al-Sūdān. | Tūnisī, Muḥammad ibn ʿUmar. Tashḥīdh al-adhhān bi-sīrat bilād al-ʿArab wa-al-Sūdān. English.
Title: In Darfur : an account of the sultanate and its people / by Muḥammad al-Tunisi ; edited and translated by Humphrey Davies.
Description: New York : New York University Press, [2018]- | Includes bibliographical references. | In English and Arabic.
Identifiers: LCCN 2017045322 (print) | LCCN 2017045917 (ebook) | ISBN 9781479811038 (v.1 ebook) | ISBN 9781479846634 (v. 1 ebook) | ISBN 9781479876389 (hardback)
Subjects: LCSH: Darfur (Sudan)--History--18th century. | Darfur (Sudan)--History--19th century. | Darfur (Sudan)--Description and travel.
Classification: LCC DT159.6.D27 (ebook) | LCC DT159.6.D27 T8613 2018 (print) | DDC 962.7/023--dc23

LC record available at https://lccn.loc.gov/2017045322

New York University Press books are printed on acid-free paper, and their binding materials are chosen for strength and durability.

Series design by Titus Nemeth.

Typeset in Tasmeem, using DecoType Naskh and Emiri.

Typesetting and digitization by Stuart Brown.

Manufactured in the United States of America
c10 9 8 7 6 5 4 3 2 1

Table of Contents

Letter from the General Editor iii
Map 1: The Author's World: from Mali to Mecca ix
Map 2: Darfur x

IN DARFUR, VOLUME TWO 1

The Book Proper, in three chapters 2

Chapter 1: A Description of Darfur and Its People, of Their Customs and the Customs of Their Kings, and of the Names of the Positions and Ranks Held by the Latter, in five sections 4

Section 1: A Description of Darfur 4

Section 2: Customs of the Kings of the Fur 34

Section 3: On the Offices Held by the Kings of the Fur 48

Section 4: The Functioning of the Sultan's Court 64

Section 5: Garments of the Kings of the Fur 82

Chapter 2, in two sections 102

Section 1: Marriage Practices among the Fur 102

Section 2: Eunuchs (Known in Egypt as *Ṭawāshiyah*) 130

Chapter 3, in two sections 160

Section 1: Sicknesses of the Blacks; Their Dishes; the Healthiness of Their Various Climes; Hunting; and Some Animals 160

Section 2: Currency among the People of Darfur 192

A Chapter on the Plants That Grow in Darfur; on Magic, the Making of Amulets, and Geomancy; and on Other Matters 204

Colophon 252

Notes 255
Glossary 274
Bibliography 298
List of Images 303

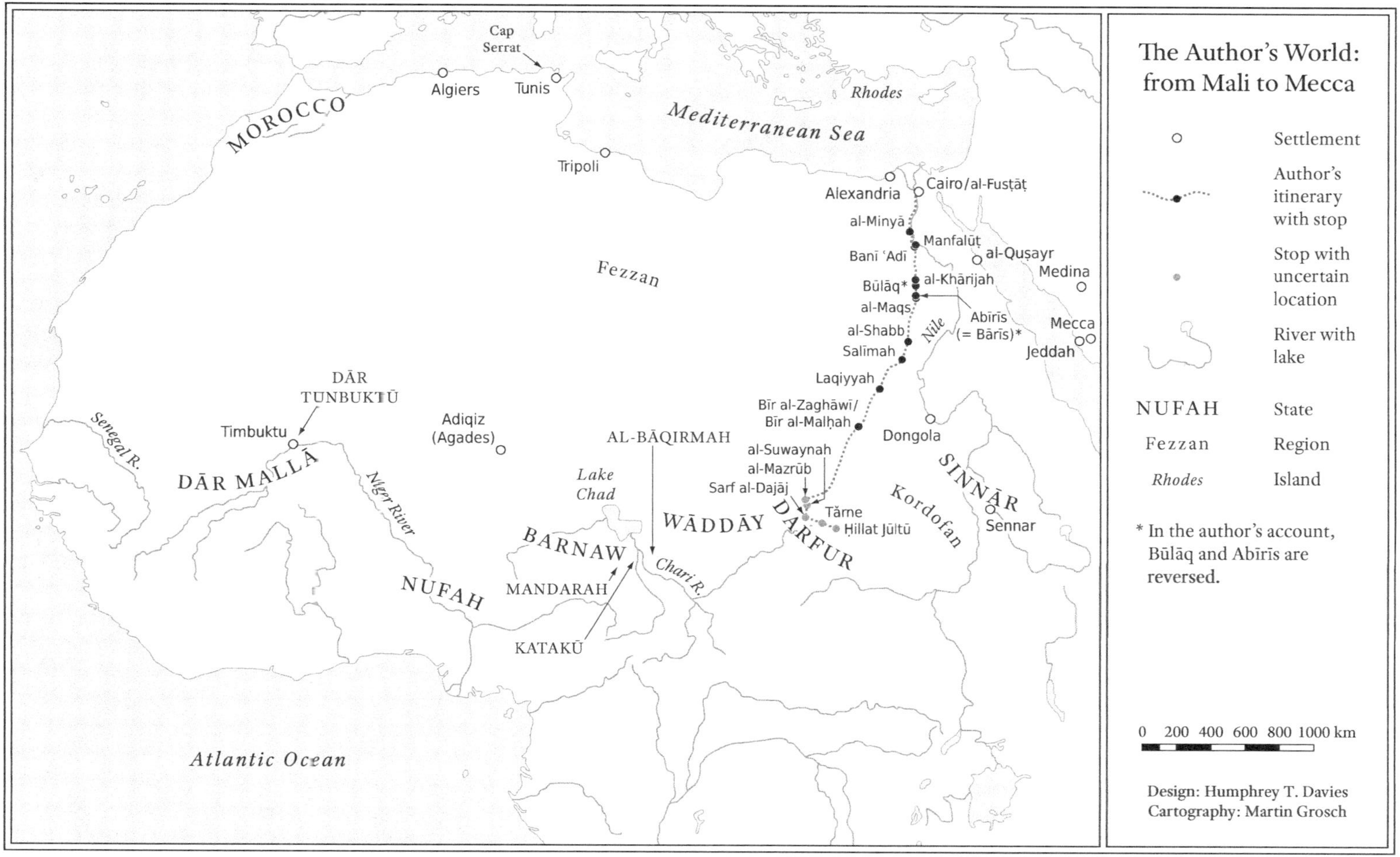
The Author's World: from Mali to Mecca
Settlement
Author's itinerary with stop
Stop with uncertain location
River with lake
NUFAH
State
Fezzan
Region
Rhodes
Island
* In the author's account, Būlāq and Abīrīs are reversed.
0 200 400 600 800 1000 km
Design: Humphrey T. Davies
Cartography: Martin Grosch
Cap Serrat
Algiers
Tunis
Rhodes
MOROCCO
Mediterranean Sea
Tripoli
Alexandria
Cairo/al-Fusṭāṭ
al-Minyā
Manfalūṭ
Banī ʿAdī
al-Quṣayr
Medina
Fezzan
Būlāq*
al-Khārijah
al-Maqs
Abīrīs
(= Bārīs)*
Mecca
Jeddah
al-Shabb
Nile
Salīmah
Laqiyyah
Bīr al-Zaghāwī/
Bīr al-Malḥah
Dongola
DĀR
TUNBUKTŪ
Timbuktu
Adiqiz
(Agades)
AL-BĀQIRMAH
Senegal R.
DĀR MALLĀ
Lake
Chad
al-Suwaynah
al-Mazrūb
Sarf al-Dajāj
Tārne
Ḥillat Jūltū
WĀDDĀY
DARFUR
Kordofan
SINNĀR
Sennar
BARNAW
Chari R.
NUFAH
MANDARAH
KATAKŪ
Atlantic Ocean

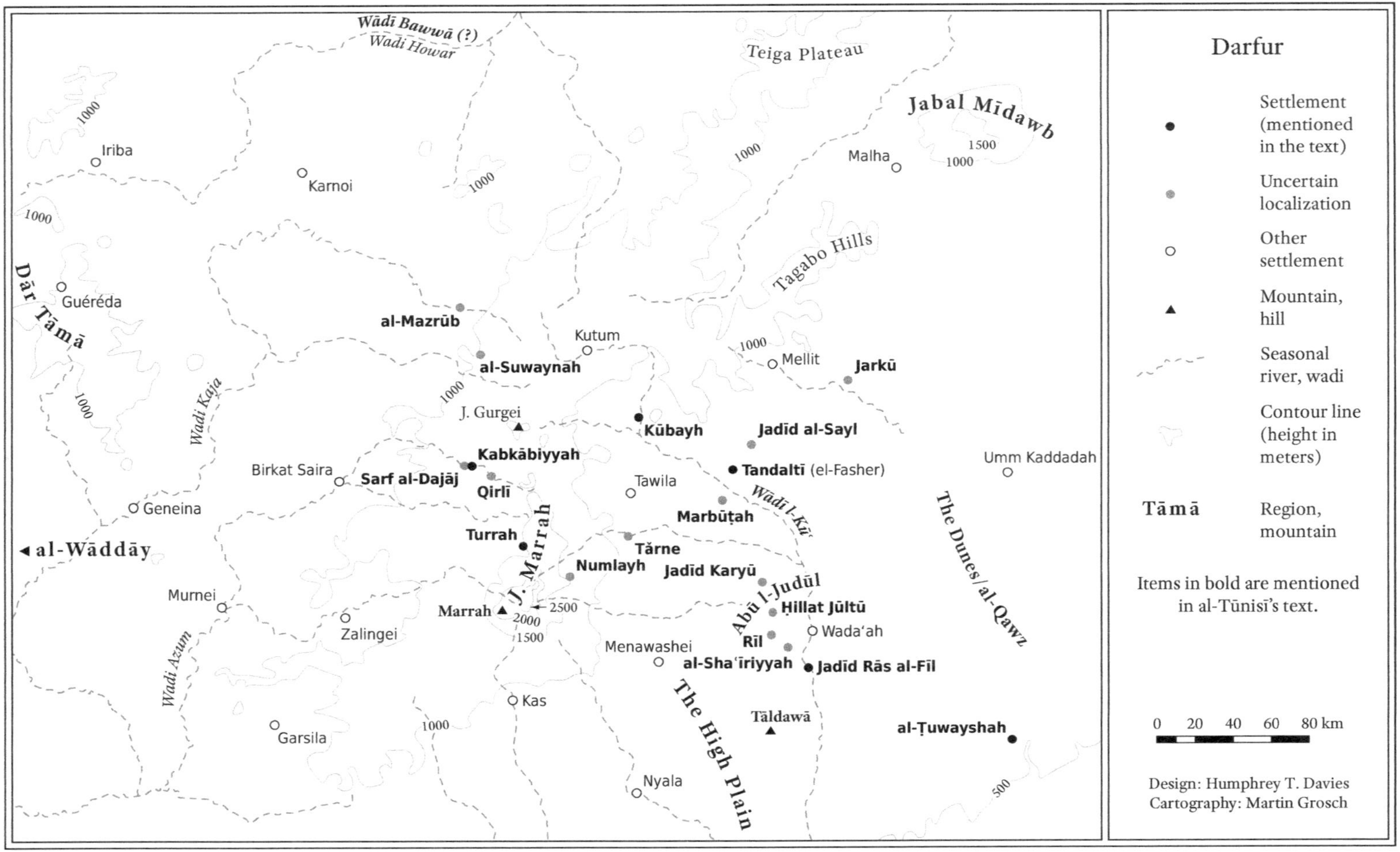
Darfur
Settlement (mentioned in the text)
Uncertain localization
Other settlement
Mountain, hill
Seasonal river, wadi
Contour line (height in meters)
Tāmā
Region, mountain
Items in bold are mentioned in al-Tūnisī's text.
0 20 40 60 80 km
Design: Humphrey T. Davies
Cartography: Martin Grosch
Wādī Bawwā (?)
Wadi Howar
Teiga Plateau
Jabal Mīdawb
Malha
Iriba
Karnoi
Tagabo Hills
Dār Tāmā
Guéréda
al-Mazrūb
Kutum
al-Suwaynah
Mellit
Jarkū
Wadi Kaja
J. Gurgei
Kūbayh
Jadīd al-Sayl
Kabkābiyyah
Birkat Saira
Sarf al-Dajāj
Qirlī
Tandaltī (el-Fasher)
Umm Kaddadah
Tawila
Wādī l-Kū'
Geneina
Marbūṭah
The Dunes/al-Qawz
J. Marrah
Turrah
Tārne
al-Wāddāy
Numlayh
Jadīd Karyū
Abū l-Judūl
Murnei
Marrah
Ḥillat Jūltū
Zalingei
Wada'ah
Rīl
Menawashei
al-Sha'īriyyah
Jadīd Rās al-Fīl
Wadi Azum
Kas
The High Plain
Tāldawā
al-Ṭuwayshah
Garsila
Nyala
2500
2000
1500
1000
500

In Darfur

Volume Two

المقصد
وفيه ثلاثة أبواب

The Book Proper,
in three chapters

الباب الأول

في صفة دارفور وأهلها وعوائدهم وعوائد ملوكهم وأسماء مناصبهم ومراتبهم وفيه خمسة فصول

الفصل الأوّل في صفة دارفور

أمّا دارفور فهو الإقليم الثالث من ممالك السودان وذلك أن للقادم من المشرق إلى بلاد السودان أوّل مملكة وإقليم يعرض مملكة سنّار ثمّ كردفال ثمّ دار الفور فظهر أنّها الإقليم الثالث وبحسب ذلك إقليم وَدَداي هو الرابع والباقِرْمَه الخامس وبَرْنَوْ السادس وأَدِقِزْ السابع ونُفَهْ الثامن ودار تُنْبُكْتُو التاسع ودار مَلاّ أو مَلّى العاشر وهي قاعدة ملك الفلاّن وهم الفلاّتا كما ذكرنا وأما الذي يأتي من المغرب فإنّه يعدّ ملاّ الأوّل وتنبكتو الثاني ونفه الثالث وهكذا ١،١،٣

واعلم أنّ القدماء يطلقون على بعض أهل السودان اسم التَكْرُور ويعنون به أهل مملكة برنو لكن الآن قد عمّ هذا الاسم على ممالك متعدّدة أوّلها دار وَدّايْ أو وَدَدايْ المعروفة أيضاً بدار صُلَيْحْ وآخرها برنو فيدخل في ذلك باقرمه وكَتَكُو ومَنْدَرَهْ فيقال لأهل كلّ منهم تكرور حتّى أنّه صار عرفاً بينهم ولقد لقيت منذ أيّام رجلاً من أهل السودان فسألته من أين أنت فقال من التكرور بل أظنّه قال تكروريّ فقلت من ٢،١،٣

Chapter 1

A Description of Darfur and Its People, of Their Customs and the Customs of Their Kings, and of the Names of the Positions and Ranks Held by the Latter, in five sections[1]

Section 1: A Description of Darfur

Darfur is the third of the territories regarded as belonging to the kingdoms of the Blacks. This is so because, when approaching from the east, the first kingdom and territory one comes to is the Kingdom of Sinnār, after which is Kordofan, then the Land of the Fūr. Thus, Darfur is clearly the third. According to this reckoning, the territory of Wadadāy[2] is the fourth, al-Bāqirmah the fifth, Barnaw the sixth, Adiqiz the seventh, Nufah the eighth, Dār Tunbuktū the ninth, and Dār Mullā or Mallā (which is the base of the king of the Fullān, who, as we have mentioned earlier, are the same as the Fallātā) the tenth. Coming from the west, however, one would consider Mallā to be the first, Tunbuktū the second, Nufah the third, and so on. 3.1.1

The ancients gave the name Takrūr[3] to certain of the inhabitants of the Land of the Blacks, meaning by it the people of the kingdom of Barnaw. Now, however, this name has come to include several kingdoms, the first[4] being the territory of Waddāy or Wadadāy, also known as Dār Ṣulayḥ, and the last Barnaw; as such, it embraces Bāqirmah, Katakū, and Mandarah, and the people of all these lands are now referred to as "Takrūr," and this has become their custom. A few days ago, I met a man from these lands and asked him, "Where are you from?" "From Takrūr," he said, or perhaps, if I remember 3.1.2

أيّ من التكارير فقال من باقرمه لكن لم يخبرني إلّا بعد مشقّة ظنًّا منه أنّي لا أعرف تلك الجهة فلمّا أخبرني وسألته عن بعض مواضع منها تعجّب تعجبًّا عظيمًا والآن القول

٣،١،٣ وحدّ الفور من جهة الشرق أقصى الطُوِيشه ومن الغرب آخر دار المساليط يعني مملكة المساليط وآخر دار قِمِرْ وأوّل دار تاما[1] وهو الخلاء الكائن بين دار صليح وبينها ومن الجنوب الخلاء الكائن بينها وبين دار فَرْتِيتْ ومن الشمال المزروب وهو أوّل بئر يعرض لمن يتوجّه لها من الديار المصريّة وتتبعها عدّة ممالك صغيرة فمن الشمال مملكة الزَغاوة وهي مملكة واسعة وبها خلق لا يحصون كثرة ولهم سلطان وحدهم ولكنه بالنسبة إلى سلطان الفور أشبه بقائد من قوّاده ومن جهة الشمال أيضاً مملكة الميدوب والبَرْتي وهما مملكتان كبيرتان إلّا أنّ أهل الثانية أكثر من أهل الأولى ومع كثرتهم أكثر انقياداً لسلطان الفور من الميدوب

٤،١،٣ وفي خلال دارفور مملكة البِرْقِد ومملكة بَرْقُو والتُنْجور ومِيمَهْ إلّا أنّ مملكة البرقد والتنجور في الوسط ومملكة البرقو والميمه من جهة الشرق ومملكة الداجو والبيقو من الجهة الجنوبيّة وكذا مملكة فَراوُجَيَهْ ولكلّ من هذه الممالك حاكم يسمّى سلطاناً لكن يولّيه عليهم سلطان الفور وكلّهم على نسق واحد في الهيئة والملبوس إلّا ملك التنجور فإنّه يلبس عمامة سوداء وسألته عن سبب سواد عمامته فأخبرني أنّ أصل مملكة دارفور لأجداده وتغلّب عليها سلطان الفور فلبس العمامة السوداء إشعار بحزنه على فقد مملكته

٥،١،٣ وقد أحاط بجانبها الشرقيّ والجنوبيّ كثير من عرب البادية كالمسيريّة الحمر والرِزَيْقات والفلّان وكلّ قبيلة من هذه القبائل لا تحصى كثرة وهم أهل بقر وخيل وأثاث وأكثرهم أهل ثروة لا يألفون الحاضرة بل يتبعون الكلأ أينما كان ويُلْحَق بهم القبيلة المسمّاة بني حَلْبَة[2] لأنّهم أهل بقر أيضاً لكنّهم يتوغّلون في دارفور ويزرعون وأمّا أهل

---

١ الأصل: تامه. ٢ الأصل: حِلْبَة.

rightly, "I'm a Takrūrī." I then asked him, "From where among all the Takrūrs?" and he said "Bāqirmah," but he only told me this after a tussle, as he thought I wouldn't know the place. When he told me, and I asked him about some places there, he was quite amazed and spoke more freely with me.

The limits of the Fur on the east are the farthest reaches of al-Ṭuwayshah, and on the west Dār Masālīṭ, meaning the kingdom of the Masālīṭ, and the last parts of Dār Qimir and the first of Dār Tāmah, which is the empty area located between Dār Ṣulayḥ and Darfur. On the south, the limit is the empty area between Dār Tāmah and Dār Fartīt and, on the north, al-Mazrūb, which is the first well one encounters when entering Darfur from Egyptian territory. Several small kingdoms belong to Darfur. On the north is the kingdom of the Zaghāwah, which is large, with countless inhabitants who have their own sultan, though in terms of his relationship with the sultan of the Fur he is more like one of his army commanders. Also to the north are the kingdoms of the Mīdawb and the Bartī, which are both large: the inhabitants of the second are more numerous than those of the first, but despite their large numbers are more submissive to the Fur sultan than are the Mīdawb. 3.1.3

Scattered around Darfur are the kingdoms of the Birqid, Barqū, Tunjūr, and Mīmah. The kingdoms of the Birqid and the Tunjūr are in the center, those of the Barqū and the Mīmah to the east, and those of the Dājū and the Bīqū, as well as the kingdom of Farāwujayh, to the south. Each has a ruler called a sultan, but he is appointed by the sultan of the Fur. These all follow the same pattern in terms of outward appearance and dress, except for the king of the Tunjūr, who wears a black turban. I asked him why, and he told me that at the beginning the kingdom of Darfur had belonged to his forefathers, so he wore the black turban as a sign of mourning for its loss.[5] 3.1.4

On its eastern and southern sides, Darfur is surrounded by large numbers of savannah Arabs, such as the Brown Misīriyyah, the Rizayqāt, and the Fullān,[6] all of them too numerous to count. They own many cattle and horses and much equipage, and most of them are wealthy. They do not mix with the settled population; on the contrary, they follow the grazing, wherever it may be. To their number should be added the tribe called the Banū Ḥalbah, who are also cattle herders; they penetrate deep into Darfur and practice agriculture there. Among the camel herders there are the Fazārah (comprising the Maḥāmīd and the Majānīn), the Banū ʿUmrān, the Banū Jarrār, the Black 3.1.5

الإبل فمنهم[1] الفَزارة وهم المحاميد والمجانين وبنو عَمْران وبنو جَرّار والمسيريّة الزرق وغيرهم وعلى كلّ من هذه القبائل ضريبة يأخذها السلطان من أموالهم في كلّ سنة

٦،١،٣ لكن في ذلك تفاوت أمّا المسيريّة الحمر والرزيقات لقوّتهم وتوغّلهم في الخلاء فلا يعطون للسلطان إلّا أقبح أموالهم ولا يقدر العامل أن يأخذ من كرائمها إلّا برضاهم وإن تاقت نفسه إلى ذلك طُرد وربّما قُتل ولا يقدر السلطان لهم على شيء ولقد بلغني أنّ الرزيقات عصوا أمر السلطان تيراب وجهّز لهم جيشاً فكسروه فخرج إليهم بنفسه ففرّوا أمامه ودخلوا في البَرَجُوب بمواشيهم فتبعهم فقتلوا منه خلقاً كثيراً ولم يملك شيئاً والبرجوب موضع يسافر فيه المسافر عشرة أيّام حتّى[2] يقطعه وهو طين ليّن مغطّى بماء يبلغ نحو عانة الرجل ومن لين طينته تسوخ فيه قوائم الدواب ومع ذلك فهو ذو شجر شائك وهذا الموضع لا ينقطع عنه المطر إلّا شهرين في السنة في فصل الشتاء

٧،١،٣ ثمّ إنّ طول إقليم دارفور من أوّل بلاد الزغاوة إلى دار رُوگَه نحو ستّين يوماً بل إن اعتبر الملحقات بها كدار روگه وفَنْقَرو ودار بَنْدَلَه وبِينگَه وشالا كانت أكثر من سبعين يوماً هذا كلّه بحسب تعريف أهل البلد لكنّ الذي أظنّه أنّها لا تصل لذلك بل نهاية مساحتها[3] تبلغ نحو من خمسين يوماً أو أقلّ وإن عُدّت ممالك الفرتيت الخمسة المذكورة وهي في ذاك الزمن الملحقات المعاهدة لسلطان دار الفور ويؤدّون له الخراج في كلّ سنة فإذا دخلت دار الزغاوة من جهة المزروب متوجّهاً على خطّ مستقيم إلى كوبيه تمكث نحو ستّة أيّام ومن كوبيه إلى تندلتي الذي هو الفاشر يومان ومن الفاشر إلى جديد كريو يومان ومنه إلى الريل يوماً ن فهذا اثنا عشر يوماً ومن الريل إلى جديد راس الفيل أربعة أيّام ومنه إلى تَلْدَوَا ثلاثة أيّام أو أربعة ومنها إلى تبلديّة ثمانية وتبلديّة على الحدود الشرقيّة للفور ومنها يدخل الإنسان في بلد الداجو والبيقو فيمشي فيها نحو من ثمانية أيّام أيضاً فهذه أربعة وثلاثون يوماً

---

١ الأصل: منهم. ٢ أضيف للسياق. ٣ الأصل: مساحته.

Misīriyyah, and others. Each of these tribes pays a tax, which the sultan takes annually in animals.

There are differences, however. The Brown Misīriyyah and the Rizayqāt, because they are strong and go far out into the desert, give the sultan only the worst of their animals, and the tax official can only acquire the good ones by paying them off. If he sets his heart on getting more, he is expelled, or even killed, and the sultan can do nothing about it. I've been told that the Rizayqāt once refused to accept the rule of Sultan Tayrāb, who sent an army against them, which they defeated. He then took the field against them himself. They fled and took their herds into the Barajūb. He followed them and they killed large numbers of his men and he could lay his hands on nothing. The Barajūb is a place that takes the traveler ten days to cross. It consists of soft mud covered with water that reaches to around the groin: the mud is so soft that the legs of riding animals sink into it. What's more, it is full of thorny trees. It stops raining there for only two months a year, during the winter. 3.1.6

It takes about sixty days to traverse Darfur from end to end, beginning at Dār al-Zaghāwah and ending at Dār Rungah. In fact, if one were to take its dependencies, such as Dār Rungah, Fanqarū, Dār Bandalah, Bīngah, and Shālā, into account as well, it would take more than seventy days—this according to information provided by the people of the country. I, however, don't believe that it extends so far, and think that at its greatest extent it may take fifty days or fewer, and then only if one counts the five kingdoms of the Fartīt referred to above, which at that time were dependencies under treaties with the sultan of Darfur and paid him an annual land tax. To be specific, if you enter Dār al-Zaghāwah from al-Mazrūb and make straight for Kūbayh, the journey takes about six days. From Kūbayh to Tandaltī, which is the sultan's seat, takes two days. From the sultan's seat to Jadīd Karyū is two days and from there to Rīl is two days. This makes twelve days. From Rīl to Jadīd Rās al-Fīl is four days and from there to Taldawā three or four days, while from there to Tabaldiyyah takes eight days—Tabaldiyyah is at the eastern limits of the Fur. Then you enter the territories of the Dāju and the Bīqū, and proceed for another eight days. This makes thirty-four days in all.[7] 3.1.7

٨،١،٣ ثمّ إذا خرجت منهما إلى جهة الشرق تجد خلاء مشحونًا بأعراب البادية كالمسيريّة الحمر والحبّانِيّة والرزيقات عالم لا يحصيهم إلّا خالقهم وإن ملت إلى جهة الغرب دخلت في دار أباديما فتقطعها في نحو عشرة أيّام ثمّ تدخل في خلاء تمشي فيه يومين وتدخل إلى دار روكه ومسافتها نحو ثلاثة أيّام ودار فنقرو مثلها أو أقلّ منها بشيء يسير ومنهما خلاء يمشي فيه الإنسان نحو يومين ومنه يدخل في دار بيكه وشالا ومسافتهما يومان فظهر لك بما ذكرناه أنّ طول دارفور بملحقاتها لا يبلغ[١] نحو خمسين يوماً

٩،١،٣ وهذه الملحقات هي البلاد الجنوبيّة التي بعد دار الفراوجيه لأنّ الفراوجيه آخره حدود ممالك الفوراويّة الحقيقيّة وما يسمّون أهل الفور بالصعيد[٢] المساحة الممتدّة من ريل لآخر دار الفور من جهة الجنوب ودار أباديما إنّما كانت مساحتها نحو عشرة أيّام، لأنّ أباديما يحكم على اثني عشر ملكاً، كلّ ملك له إيالة مستقلّة ودار[٣] أباديما هي[٤] دار تَمُورْكَهْ وأباديما اسم منصب كما سنذكره معناه الجناح الأيمن للسلطان والحاكم المسمّى بهذا الاسم يحكم على دار تموركه فسمّي لذلك دار تموركه بدار أباديما ويقابله التكنياوي الذي هو أيضاً اسم منصب معناه الجناح الأيسر للسلطان ويحكم التكنياوي على اثني عشر ملكاً[٥] أيضاً وهو حاكم الزغاوة وما يليها لجهة الشرق ولذلك أيضاً سمّي دار الزغاوة بدار التكنياوي وإن قلتَ من حيث أنّ أباديما والتكنياوي متعادلين لِمَ كان طول دار أباديما عشرة أيّام وطول دار التكنياوي خمسة أيّام قلتُ دار التكنياوي أعرض من دار أباديما لأنّ دار أباديما عرضها نحو خمسة أيّام وشيء يسير وعرض دار التكنياوي نحو سبعة أيّام فما نقص من طولها جبر بزيادة عرضها

١٠،١،٣ ثمّ اعلم أن دارفور منظّمة تنظيماً على وجه محكم لأنّنا ذكرنا أن جبل مرّة يشقّها وأنّ نصفها من جبل مرّة إلى جهة الشرق سهل وعرض جبل مرّة بقطع النظر عن ارتفاع

١ الأصل: تبلغ. ٢ الأصل: السعيد. ٣ أضيف للسياق. ٤ الأصل: هو. ٥ الأصل: ملك.

If you leave these territories going east, you find a savannah pullulating with desert nomads too many for any but their Creator to count, such as the Brown Misīriyyah, the Ḥabbāniyyah, and the Rizayqāt, and if you turn west, you enter Dār Ába Dima'ng, which will take you around ten days to cross. Then you enter a savannah that you must cross for two days before entering Dār Rungah, which takes about three days to cross. Dār Fanqarū takes the same, or slightly less. Beyond these is a savannah that takes around two days to cross, after which you enter Dār Bīngah and Shālā, which take two days to cross. In sum, you can see from what I've told you that the whole length of Darfur, from north to south, along with its dependencies, takes not more than around fifty days to cross. 3.1.8

These dependencies are the southern lands beyond Dār al-Farāwujayh, the far border of Farāwujayh being the border of the Fur kingdoms proper. The area that the Fur call the High Plain[8] stretches from Rīl to the southern limit of the Lands of the Fūr. Dār Ába Dima'ng takes as much as ten days to cross—the ába dima'ng rules over twelve petty kings, each of whom rules over an independent vassal state. Dār Ába Dima'ng is Dār Tomorókkóngá: the name, as we shall describe later, is that of an office and means "the sultan's right arm," and the governor who bears this title rules over the land of the Tomorókkóngá; Dār Tomorókkóngá is thus known as Dār Ába Dima'ng. The name is on a par with tikináwi, which is likewise the name of an office, and means "the sultan's left arm."[9] The tikináwi also rules over twelve petty kings, and is the ruler of the Zaghāwah and the lands beyond them to the east; for the same reason, then, Dār al-Zaghāwah is also known as Dār al-Tikináwi. If you were to ask, "Given that the ába dima'ng and the tikináwi are on a par, why is Dār Ába Dima'ng twelve days' riding in length, whereas Dār Tikináwi is only five?" I would respond that Dār Tikináwi is wider than Dār Ába Dima'ng: it takes a little over five days to cross Dār Ába Dima'ng from side to side, whereas Dār Tikináwi takes around seven, so what it lacks in length it makes up for in extra width. 3.1.9

Darfur is arranged in a very precise way. We have stated earlier that it is divided down the middle by Jabal Marrah, that the half that's east of Jabal Marrah is a plain, and that the width of Jabal Marrah is equal to about two days' travel as the crow flies. Behind the mountains, to the west, lies another plain. To the north, however, are the Zaghāwah and the Bartī, two mighty tribes: 3.1.10

الجبال نحو يومين ووراءه من جهة الغرب سهل أيضاً لكن من جهة الشمال الزغاوة والبرتي وهما قبيلتان عظيمتان فالبرتي من جهة الشرق والزغاوة من جهة الغرب وفي وسطها من جنوب جديد كريو يسكنها التنجور والبرقد وهما قبيلتان عظيمتان وهكذا إلى جديد راس الفيل وأزيد بل إلى تبلديّة وإن كان بينهما بلاد وقبائل صغار ثمّ من هناك إلى الخلاء من جهة الجنوب والشرق وجهة دار أباديما يسكنه الداجو والبيقو فالداجو من جهة الغرب والبيقو من جهة المشرق وشرقيّ جديد كريو يسكنه البرقو والميمه وهما قبيلتان عظيمتان

١١،١،٣ ثمّ إن جبل مرّة لا يسكنه إلّا أعجام الفور وأعجام الفور ثلاثة قبائل أحدها كُنْجارة وهي تسكن من قرلي إلى بعد الجبيل الصغير المسمّى مرّة بالخصوص وهو مرّة حقيقة وبعده بقليل إلى حدّ دار أباديما تسكنه الفور المسمّون كَراكِريت وأمّا الفور الساكنون بدار أباديما فيسمّون تموركه وبعد دار أباديما دار روگه ودار فراوجيه لكن روگه من جهة المغرب وفراوجيه من جهة المشرق ودار فنقرو بعد دار فراوجيه وبعد دار روگه دار سِلا لكن تميل إلى المغرب أكثر ولهذا يحكمها أهل الواداي

١٢،١،٣ واعلم أنّ جبل مرّة ليس جبلاً واحداً كلّه بل هو عدّة جبال كبار وصغار وقبل الدخول في دار أباديما ينقطع الجبل وتبقى أرض سهلة يسكنها الفلّان حتّى أنّهم يقربون من المساليط من جهة المغرب ويليهم بنو حلبة والمسيريّة الزرق وجميع ما ذكرناه غير البدو الحافّين بها من شمالها وشرقها وجنوبها وغير المولّدين من القبائل والفور يسمّونهم الداراويّة أي المنسوبين للدار فإنّهم في الوسط لا يعتبرون بقبيلة وإن أردت أنّ أبيّن لك كيفيّة دار الفور ووضع منازل هذه القبائل والأعراب المحتفّين بها فها أنا أرسم لك ما هو على هيئة الجدول تقريباً للفهم وهو هذا فنفرض أنّ هذه الجهة هي جهة الجنوب

the Bartī to the east, the Zaghāwah to the west. In the middle of the mountains, to the south, is Jadīd Karyū, which is inhabited by two mighty tribes, the Tunjūr and the Birqid. Moving farther south, one comes to Jadīd Rās al-Fīl and beyond; indeed, one will eventually come to Tabaldiyyah, though there are small towns and tribes between them. From there on live the Dājū and Bīqū, all the way to the savannah in the south and east and to Dār Ába Dima'ng. The Dājū are to the west, the Bīqū to the east. To the east of Jadīd Karyū live two mighty tribes, the Barqū and the Mīmah.

Jabal Marrah is inhabited exclusively by non-Arabic-speaking Fur. These consist of three tribes: the Kunjáara, who live from Qirlī to beyond the little mountain itself called Marrah, which is the true Marrah; coming soon after this and extending all the way to the border with Dār Ába Dima'ng are the Fur called the Karakiriit; the Fur who live in Dār Ába Dima'ng are called the Tomorókkóngá. After Dār Ába Dima'ng come Dār Rūngah and Dār Farūjayh, Dār Rūngah on the west and Dār Farūjayh on the east. Dār Fanqarū follows Dār Farūjayh, and Dār Rūngah follows Dār Silā, though this slopes more toward the west, which is why it's ruled by the people of Wāddāy. 3.1.11

Jabal Marrah is not one mountain, but several, both large and small. Before one enters Dār Ába Dima'ng, the mountains come to an end, and what remains is a flat land inhabited by the Fullān, up to the point where they approach the Masālīṭ on the west. Then come the Banū Ḥalbah and the Black Misīriyyah. Except for the Bedouin, all those whom we've mentioned live on Darfur's northern, eastern, and southern edges. People born neither into the tribes nor the Fur they call "territorials," meaning they are people whose origins may be traced to some territory.[10] They are in the middle and are not deemed a tribe. If you want to get from me a clear exposition of Darfur and of how the home territories of these tribes and of the Bedouin who surround it are arranged, take a look at what I've drawn—more or less in the form of a chart—to make it easy to grasp (suppose this end to be south): 3.1.12

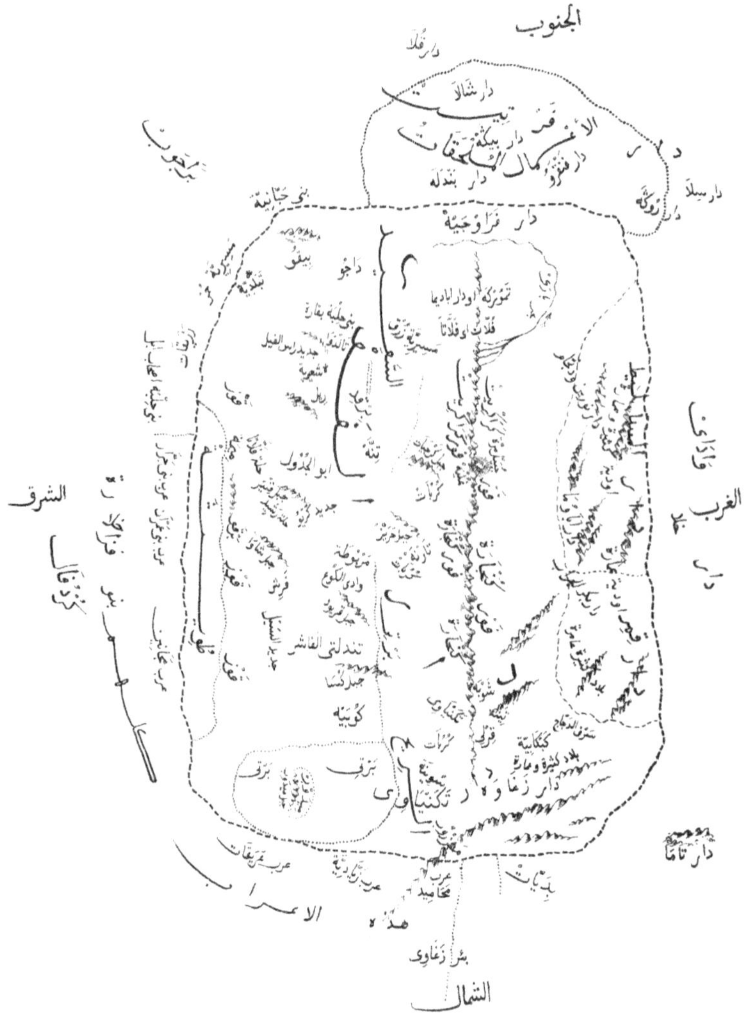

هذا وإن كنت لم أبيّن في هذا الجدول البيان الشافي لعدم معرفتي بالرسم ولضيق الورق فهي في نفسها كذلك لكنّ الماهر يستنتج منها صورة حسنة

ثمّ اعلم أنّ أعمر البلاد من جهة الشمال بلاد البرتي والزغاوة لكثرة ما فيها من العالم ١٣،١،٣
وانظر حكمة الله فإنّ القبيلتين في خطّ واحد لكنّ البرتي أرقّ قلوباً وأحسن وجوهاً

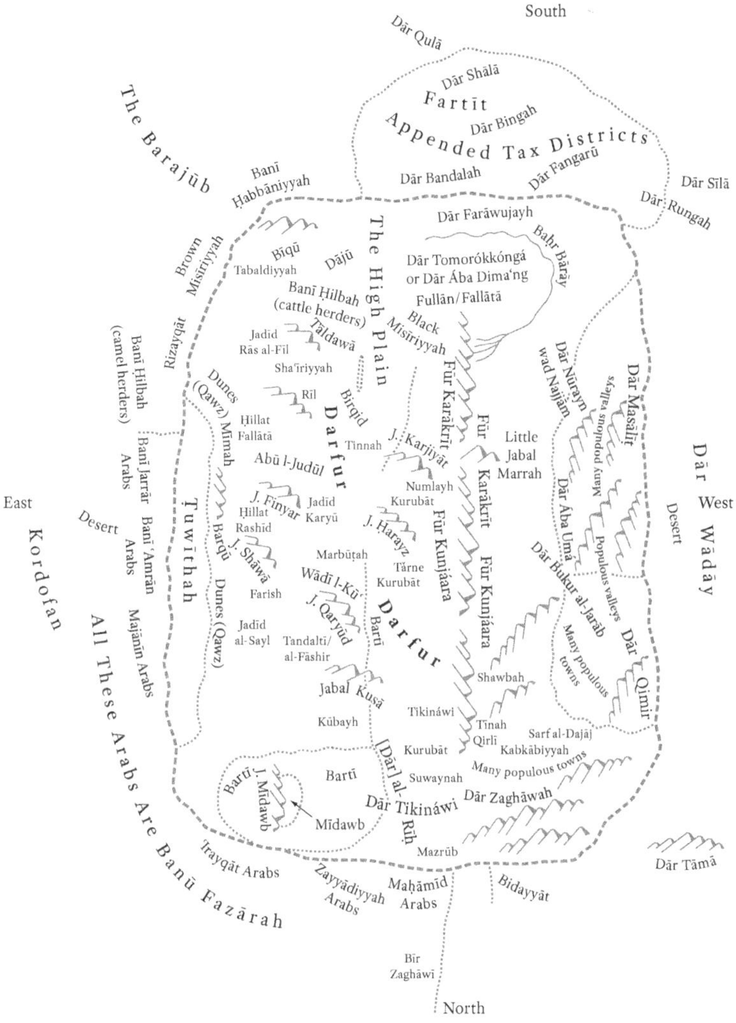

Let me add that if I have not been able to give an absolutely clear exposition, owing to my ignorance of drawing and the small paper size, it is in essence as shown. Someone with the necessary skills will be able to turn it into a better likeness.[11]

The most prosperous lands to the north are those of the Bartī and the Zaghāwah, because of the great number of people. Observe now God's wisdom, for the two tribes are on the same line of travel, but the Bartī are more 3.1.13

وأجمل نساءً والزغاوة بالعكس كما أنّ الداجو والبيقو في خطّ واحد وبنات البيقو أجمل من بنات الداجو وأمّا البرقد والتنجور فيوجد في كلّ منهما المليح والقبيح لكنّ البرقد خائنون سرّاق ليلاً ونهاراً لا يخافون الله ولا رسوله والتنجور معهم بعض دين وبعض عقل يمنعهم وأمّا أهل الجبل فكلّهم على حدّ في الوحاشة والوخاشة لكن متى جئت في دار أباديما تجد الرجال والنساء حساناً[1] فسبحان من هذا صنعه وأمّا المساليط فنساؤهم يسبين العقل ويذهبن باللبّ وأجمل النساء في دار الفور على الإطلاق نساء العرب بل ورجالهم كذلك وبين الوادي ودارفور لا يوجد ساكن البتّة ما عدا أهل جبل تاما الذي سنتحدّث عنه أنّ السلطان صابون وهو سلطان الوادي غزاه واستولى على أهله

١٤،١،٣ واعلم أنّ جميع البلاد التي في دارفور مقسومة على أكابر الدولة فكلّ منهم له فيها على قدر منصبه وحاله فأوسعهم دارأباديما والتكنياوي لأنّ كلاًّ منهما تحت يده اثنا عشر ملكاً لكلّ ملك منهم عمل مستقل ويسمّون ذلك الملك شَرْتايْ. أباديما يحكم على التموركه والتكنياوي يحكم على دار الزغاوة والبرتي وما وليهما[2] وأبا وُما ويساوي الكامَنَهْ يحكم على أربعة ملوك من المساليط وفُورَݣْ أَبا يحكم على أربعة ملوك من الكراكريت والأُرُنْدُلُنْ وهو وجه السلطان يحكم على أربعة ملوك من بلاد البرقد والأب الشيخ يحكم على أربعة ملوك أيضاً ووَرَّݣْ أبا يحكم على ملكين وهذه البلاد غير بلاد الأمناء والأشراف والفقهاء العظام والقضاة وليس للسلطان بلاد خالصة له إلّا بيوت آبائه وأجداده مثل قرلي وريل وتندلتي وغيرها

١٥،١،٣ ومحلّ حكم الأب الشيخ من أبي الجدول إلى الجنوب حتّى يأخذ أيضاً قطعة عظيمة من بلاد البرقد والأمناء يحكمون على جهة مرّة وأمّا السلاطين الصغار فإنّ كلّ سلطان منهم يحكم على بلاد جماعته كالبرقو والميمه والتنجور والداجو والبيقو والزغاوة وهؤلاء السلاطين لهم أقطاع يتعيّشون منها وإن كانت المملكة لها حاكم غيره فمثلاً

---

١ الأصل: حسان. ٢ الأصل: ولاها.

kindhearted and have handsomer faces, and their women are more beautiful, while the Zaghāwah are the opposite. Likewise, the Dājū and the Bīqū are on the same line of travel and the daughters of the Bīqū are more beautiful than those of the Dājū. As for the Birqid and the Tunjūr, both comely and ugly are to be found among them, but the Birqid are treacherous, being thieves by night and fearing neither God nor His messenger by day, whereas the Tunjūr have a modicum of religion and a modicum of reason, which prevent them from such behavior. The people of the mountain are all the same in terms of both ugliness and uncouthness, but when one gets to Dār Ába Dima'ng, one finds that the men and the women are both beautiful; glory then to Him whose work this is! The women of the Masālīṭ captivate the mind and bewitch the heart, but the most beautiful women in Darfur, without a doubt, are those of the Arabs; indeed, even their men are beautiful. Not a living soul is to be found between Wādday and Darfur other than the people of Jabal Tāmah; we shall recount later how Sultan Ṣābūn, sultan of Wādday, raided the latter and assumed power over its people.[12]

Know too that the territories in Darfur are all divided up among the high offi- 3.1.14
cers of the state, each of whom holds a portion of them according to his office and condition.[13] The largest territories are Dār Ába Dima'ng and Dār Tikináwi: each of the two office-holders in question has twelve petty kings under him, and each king an independent tax district; such petty kings are called *shartāy*s. Thus, the ába dima'ng rules over the Tomorókkóngá, and the tikináwi over Dār Zaghāwah, the Bartī, and what lies beyond them. The ába umá,[14] who is the counterpart of the kaamíne, rules over four petty kings of the Masālīṭ, and the poora'ng ába rules over four kings of the Karakiriit. The orondolong, who is the sultan's face,[15] rules over four kings of Dār Birqid, and the shaykh-father rules over four kings too. The órré'ng ába rules over two kings. These lands do not include those of the counselors, sharifs, leading men of religion, and judges. The sultan has no lands of his own except for the houses of his fathers and his forefathers, such as Qirlī, Rīl, Tandaltī, and so on.[16]

The writ of the shaykh-father runs south from Abu l-Judūl and even includes 3.1.15
a large part of Dār Birqid. The counselors rule over the area of Marrah, while each petty sultan rules over the lands of his own people, such as the Birqid, Mīmah, Tunjūr, Dājū, Bīqū, and Zaghāwah. Each of these sultans has a fief off which he lives, even though the territory may have another governor.[17] For example, the sultan of the Zaghāwah is the ruler of his people even though

سلطان زغاوة حاكم على جماعته مع أنّه في دار التكنياوي لكن له أقطاع من زمن أجداده لا يتعرّض لها التكنياوي وبقيّة البلاد يأخذ التكنياوي خيراتها وهكذا لغيره من السلاطين الصغار وبقيّة الأقاليم غير الستّة المذكورة حكّامها ملوك

٣،١،١٦ وأمّا عرض دارفور فإنّه من الخلاء الكائن بينه وبين دار صليح أي دار واداي إلى آخر الطويشة أي لأوّل الخلاء الكائن بينه وبين كردفال نحو ثمانية عشر يوماً وهذا الإقليم نصفه سهل أرض مرمّلة قليلاً إلّا آخره من الشرق فإنّه كثير من الرمل ولذلك يسمّى بالقَوْز وأمّا أراضي جبل مرّة فهي طين أسود وهو جبل يشقّ دار الفور من أوّلها إلى آخرها حتّى قيل إنّه متّصل بالمقطّم المطلّ على القاهرة لكنّه ليس قطعة واحدة بل هو متقطّع من عدّة أماكن وله طرق عديدة وفي هذا الجبل أمم وعالم لا يحصى كثرة وفيهم القبيلة المعروفة بالكنجارة التي ينسب إليها سلطان دارفور وفي هذا الجبل كهوف عديدة تحبس فيها أولاد الملوك وأخرى[1] لحبس الوزراء وفيه من الخيرات شيء كثير وذلك أنّ فيه من البقر والغنم ما لا يوجد في غيره من الأماكن ومن العجيب أنّ جميع مواشيهم ترعى وحدها بدون راعٍ ولا يخشون عليها سارقاً ولا سبعاً ولا ذئباً

٣،١،١٧ ولقد استأذنت السلطان محمد فضل سنة ١٢٢٠ في التوجّه إلى جبل مرّة للفرجة فتوقّف أوّلاً في الإذن خوفاً عليّ من غائلة أهل الجبل ثمّ أذن لي وعيّن معي خدّاماً وكتب لي فرماناً إلى جميع عمّال الجبل يقول فيه

> من حضرة السلطان الأعظم والخاقان المكرّم سلطان العرب والعجم الواثق بعناية الملك العدل الصبور السلطان محمد فضل المنصور إلى جميع ملوك جبل مرّة أمّا بعد فإنّ السيّد الشريف محمد التونسيّ ابن الشريف العلامة السيّد عمر التونسيّ التمس منّا إذناً في أن يرى الجبل وما فيه ويختبر ظاهره وخافيه وقد أذنّاه بذلك فلا يمنع من محلّ يريد النظر إليه وأأمر كلّ ملك نزل به أن يكرمه ويعظم ملقاه وقد أصحبته

١ الأصل: واخرون.

he's within Dār Tikináwi; he holds a fief that has come down to him from his forefathers, and the tikináwi doesn't oppose him in that. The yield of the rest of the lands is taken by the tikináwi, and it's the same with the rest of the petty sultans. All territories other than the six I have mentioned are ruled by petty kings.

In width, Darfur runs from the savannah that lies between it and Dār Ṣulayḥ (also known as Dār Wāddāy) to the outer edge of al-Ṭuwayshah, that is, to the beginning of the savannah between it and Kordofan, or around eighteen days' travel. Half of this territory consists of a plain of slightly sandy soil. The exceptions are its far eastern reaches, where there is a great deal of sand, which is why they are called the Dunes.[18] The soil of Jabal Marrah, on the other hand, is a black mud. Jabal Marrah is a mountain range that splits the Land of the Fūr in half from end to end. Some people even say it's connected to the Muqaṭṭam Hills that overlook Cairo but it isn't continuous; it's scattered over a number of places, and many roads lead to it. In these mountains are nations and people too numerous to count. There is a tribe there known as the Kunjáara to which the sultan of Darfur traces his origins. And in these mountains are many caves in which royal princes are imprisoned, and others for the imprisonment of viziers. Jabal Marrah produces great yields because there are more cattle and flocks of sheep and goats there than anywhere else. The amazing thing is that all their animals graze on their own, without anyone to mind them, and the people have no fear of thieves, lions, or wolves. 3.1.16

In 1220 [1805–6], I asked Sultan Muḥammad Faḍl for permission to go to Jabal Marrah, to see. At first he withheld his permission because he feared I might suffer at the hands of its inhabitants. He subsequently gave it, appointed servants to go with me, and wrote a royal order to all the district chiefs, in which he stated: 3.1.17

> From the presence of the Most Mighty Sultan and Ennobled Khāqān, Sultan Muḥammad Faḍl the Victorious, Sultan of the Arabs and the Non-Arabs, who trusts in the solicitude of the Just and Patient King, to all the petty kings of Jabal Marrah—The sayyid and sharif Muḥammad al-Tūnisī, son of the sharif Learned Scholar ʿUmar al-Tūnisī, has requested our permission to see Jabal Marrah and what it contains and to enquire as to all that is manifest and all that is hidden, and we have granted him permission to do so.

بفَلْقَنَاوِيَّيْن من خواصّ فَلاَقِتَي ليكونا واسطة بينكم وبينه لتبليغ الكلام ونيل المرام والسلام

١٨،١،٣ فتوجّهت صحبة الفلقناويين وعبدين لي ورجل من أهل البلدة التي أنا فيها فسافرنا يومين وفي اليوم الثالث أتينا أطراف الجبل فنزلنا في بلد يقال له نُمْلَيَه ولها رئيس يقال له الفقيه نَمْر وله ولد يقال له الفقيه محمّد وآخر يقال له سليمان فنزلنا في بيت رئيس البلدة وحضرهو وأولاده واستقبلونا بصدر رحب فأخبرناهم بمقصدنا وأظهرنا لهم أمر السلطان فاهتمّوا حينئذ بشأني وأعظموا ضيافتي فبتنا ليلتنا تلك ومن الغد توجّهوا بي إلى سوق نمليه وهو سوق يعمر في كلّ يوم اثنين يحضره جميع أهل الجبل رجالاً ونساء يقضون مصالحهم فرأيت أناساً شديدين السواد حمر الأعين والأسنان

١٩،١،٣ وحين رأوني اجتمعوا عليّ متعجّبين من احمرار لوني وأتوا إليّ أفواجاً أفواجاً لأنّهم لم يقع لهم رؤية عربيّ قبل ذلك وأرادوا قتلي على سبيل الاستهزاء وكنت إذ ذاك لا أعرف من لغة الفور شيئاً فما راعني إلّا أنّي رأيت من معي من الناس اختطفوا سلاحهم وجرّدوه في وجوه القوم وحالوا بيني وبين القوم فسألت عن السبب فقالوا لي إنّهم يريدون الفتك بك فقلت لماذا فقالوا لقلّة عقولهم لأنّهم يقولون إنّ هذا لم ينضج في بطن أمّه وبعضهم يقول لو نزلت عليه ذبابة لأخرجت دمه فقال أحدهم اصبروا وأنا أطعنه بحربة وأنظر مقدار ما[١] ينزل منه من الدم وحين سمعنا منهم ذلك خفنا عليك وأحطنا بك ثمّ إن الجماعة أخرجوني من السوق فتبعني خلق كثيرون فطردوهم عنّي بكلّ جهد ثمّ ذهبوا بي إلى وادٍ هناك فرأيت فيه نخيلاً وأشجار موز وبعض أشجار من الليمون ورأيت قد زرع في ذلك الوادي من البصل والثوم والفلفل الأحمر وهو قرون صغيرة رفيعة أكبر من حبّ الشعير بقليل والكمّون والكسبرة والحلبة

١ مقدار ما – في الأصل: ما مقدار.

> He must not, therefore, be barred from any place that he wishes to see. I also command every king with whom he stays to treat him hospitably and give him a warm welcome. I have provided him with two of my own royal messengers to act as intermediaries, so that they may pass on to you what he says and achieve the desired end. Farewell.

I set off in the company of the two messengers plus two slaves of my own and a man from the town where I was living. We traveled for two days, and on the third we came to the foothills. We put up in a village called Numlayh, which had a headman called Faqīh Namr, who had one son called Faqīh Muḥammad and another called Sulaymān. When we alighted at the house of the town's headman, he and his sons came and received us with open arms. We told them of our intentions and showed them the sultan's order. When they saw this, they paid me many attentions and treated me most hospitably, and so we spent the night. In the morning, they took me to the Numlayh market, which is held every Monday and attended by all the inhabitants of the mountain, men and women, who buy what they need there. I saw many extremely black people, with red eyes and teeth. 3.1.18

When the people saw me, they gathered around me, wondering at my ruddy color. Troop after troop came to see me because they had never seen an Arab before, and wanted to kill me out of contempt. At the time, I knew not a word of the Fur language and I only became scared when I noticed that the men who were with me had seized their weapons and bared them in the others' faces, placing themselves between me and them. I asked them why, and they told me that they'd wanted to murder me. "What for?" I asked, and they replied, "Because they're so stupid. Some were saying, 'This one didn't ripen properly in his mother's belly,' others, 'If a fly settled on him, it would draw blood!' and one of them said, 'Hang on a moment and I'll prick him with a spear to see how much blood comes out!' When we heard this, we feared for your life and made a circle around you." Then my men got me out of the market, pursued by a throng of people, whom they chased off only with great difficulty. After this, they took me to a wadi where I saw palm trees, banana trees, and some lemon trees, and I saw that onions, garlic, and red peppers with pods smaller and narrower than a grain of barley had been planted in the same wadi, along with great quantities of cumin, coriander, fenugreek, 3.1.19

والقِثّاء والقرع شيء كثير وكان ذلك في أيّام الخريف وقد احمرّ البلح فقطعوا لي عرجونين من البلح أحمر وأصفر وأهدوا لي بُخْسة عسل لم أر نظيره حسناً وطعماً ولذّة وبتنا في أكرم ضيافة وألذّ عيش

٢٠،١،٣ ولمّا أصبح الصباح طلبت التفرّج فأخذوني ودخلنا الأودية فصرنا نقطع وادياً[١] بعد وادٍ وبين كلّ واديين أقلّ من ميل مسافة وفي كلّ وادٍ زرع عجيب وماء يتدفّق على رمل كالفضّة وقد أحاط الشجر به سياجاً من حافتيه يتمنّى الناظر ألّا يفارقه فجلسنا على شاطئ الوادي في ظلّ شجرة هناك وذبح لنا كبش سمين وحُنِّذَ فأكلنا منه إرادتنا ثمّ ذهبنا لبلد تحت الجبل فبتنا فيها في أكرم ضيافة ولمّا أصبحنا صعدنا الجبل فمكثنا صاعدين نحو ثلاث ساعات حتّى علوناه فرأينا فيه أمما كثيرة وبلادا متفرّقة فأدخلونا على شيخ الجبل وكان حينئذ يسمّى أبا بكر وهو جالس في خلوته فلمّا دخلنا عليه وجدناه رجلا مسنّا قد ناهز الستّين وأثّر فيه الكبر فسلّمنا عليه فرحّب بنا وأجلسنا

٢١،١،٣ لطيفة: هذا الجبل لا يرتفع عنه السحاب في السنة إلّا أيّاماً قلائل ولكثرة المطر يزرعون القمح وينبت عندهم قمح لا يوجد نظيره إلّا في بلاد المغرب أو في بلاد أوروبّا لأنّه حسن جدًّا وبقيّة دارفور لا ينبت عندهم قمح لعدم الأرض الصالحة ولعدم الأمطار إلّا ما قلّ كأرض كوبيه وكبكابيّة فإنّه يزرع فيها القمح ويسقى بماء الآبار حتّى يتمّ نضجه

٢٢،١،٣ ولزيارة الشيخ المذكور يوم معلوم من السنة تذهب إليه الناس من كل جانب ويقول لهم ما يحصل في جميع العام من قحط ومطر وحرب وسلم ورخاء وشدّة ومرض وصحّة والناس يعتقدون حقيقة ذلك فاختلف أهل دارفور في ذلك فمن قائل إنّه من طريق الكشف وإنّ كلّ من تولّى شيخًا يكون وليًّا وما يقوله للناس من طريق الكشف وهذا قول أهل العلم ومن قائل إنّ الجانّ يخبره بجميع ما يحصل وهو يقول

١ الأصل: واد.

cucumber, and squash. It was fall, and the dates had turned red, so they cut me down two clusters, one red, the other yellow, and gave me a gourd full of honey the like of which I had never come across before, it was of such a beautiful color and so delicious. Then we spent the night in the lap of luxury, enjoying the most generous hospitality.

In the morning, I asked if we could see more things, so they took me into the wadis, and we crossed one after another, each less than a mile from the next. In each were amazing crops and water that gushed over the sand like silver, the trees encircling each wadi like a fence on all sides so that the beholder could only hope that he would never have to leave. We sat on edge of one wadi in the shade of a tree, and a fat ram was slaughtered for us and cooked under hot stones. After we had eaten our fill, we went on to a village beneath the mountain where we spent the night coddled in the most generous hospitality. The next morning, we went up the mountain, climbing for about three hours without stopping until we reached the top, where we found numerous peoples and widely dispersed villages. People there took us to see the Shaykh of the Mountain, who at that time was named Abū Bakr and whom we found seated inside his place of retreat. Entering, we found him to be an old man, close to sixty and showing signs of age. We greeted him, and he welcomed us and invited us to sit down. 3.1.20

A curiosity: the skies clear over this mountain for only a few days a year, and because there's so much rain, they can plant wheat. The wheat that grows in their land is of exceedingly good quality, without peer except in the countries of the Arab west and those of Europe. Wheat doesn't grow in the rest of Darfur because the soil is unsuited to it and because of the lack of rain, though there is a little good soil at Kūbayh and Kabkābiyyah, where they grow wheat that they irrigate from wells till it ripens. 3.1.21

There is a certain day, known to all, when people come from all over the area to visit this shaykh, and he tells them what will happen during the coming year regarding drought and rain, war and peace, ease and hardship, sickness and health, and the people believe what he says. The Darfurians differ over this. Some say that it is due to mystical illumination, that anyone who holds the rank of shaykh is a saint,[19] and that whatever he tells people is the result of such illumination; this is what people who know the religious sciences say. Others say that the jinn tell him everything that will happen and he passes this on to the people. I have no idea which of the two is correct. In fact, many claims have 3.1.22

للناس وكلا القولين لا أعرف صحّتهما بل قد تقوّلت عنه أمور كثيرة وحصل ضدّها فأبرزنا فرمان السلطان وقرأه عليه الفقيه محمّد فرحّب وأكرم ودعا لنا بطعام ثمّ ضرب طبلاً يقال له التنبل فجاء أناس كثيرون فانتخب من شبابهم نحو مائة نفر وأرأس عليهم رجلاً من ذوي قرابته يعرف بالشجاعة يقال له الفقيه زيد وأمره أن يكون معي هو والجماعة وأن يكونوا على أهبة وحذر من جهّال أهل الجبل

٢٣،١،٣ ثمّ ركبنا وتوجّهنا إلى مكان هناك فيه جبل صغير وهو المسمّى مرّة وسمّي الجبل كلّه باسم ذلك المحلّ فرأينا فيه مكانا أشبه بمعبد جميع أهل الجبل يعتقدون تعظيمه ويرون أن حرمته كحرمة المساجد فدخلنا فيه وقد أظلّته شجرة كبيرة بحيث صار لا تراه الشمس فجلسنا فيه قليلا ورأينا فيه خدماً لتنظيفه واستقبال النذور ممّن يأتي بها ثمّ انتقلنا من ذلك المكان ومشى العسكر أمامنا فلحق بنا عالم كثير نساء ورجالاً وجعلوني أعجوبة[١] وتكالبوا وازدحموا عليّ وأراد العسكر تفريقهم[٢] فما أمكن ذلك حتّى قال بعضهم إن السلطان أرسل لأهل الجبل رجلا لم ينضج في بطن أمّه ضيافة لهم فقال بعضهم هو آدميّ وقال آخرون هو ليس بآدميّ بل هو حيوان مأكول اللحم على هيئة الآدميّ لأنّهم ينكرون أن يكون للآدميّ لون أبيض أو أحمر وهؤلاء القوم لا يعرفون من اللغة العربيّة إلّا كلمتي الشهادة ويقولونها مقطّعتين مع العجمة القبيحة ولمّا عجز من معي عن[٣] الدفع عنّي جاءني الفقيه زيد وأمرني أن أستر وجهي بلثام لا يظهر منه إلّا الحدقتان فتلثّمت واحتاط بي العسكر وحين رأى السودان أنّي تلثّمت اختلط عليهم الأمر وسألوا أين الأحمر قالوا ذهب إلى السلطان فانكفّوا قليلاً

٢٤،١،٣ وحينئذ توجّهنا إلى محلّ الحبس أي الكهوف التي فيها المحبوسون من أولاد الملوك والوزراء فمنعنا الحرس من الوصول إليها وكاد أن يقع بينهم وبين جماعتنا شرّ فتلافى الفقيه زيد الأمر وأخذ منّي الفرمان وذهب إلى رئيس الحرس وقرأه عليه وعند ذلك امتثل وقال إن كان ولا بدّ فليأت المأمور له بالتفرّج وحده وجميع من معه يجلس على

١ الأصل: عجوبة. ٢ الأصل: تفرقهم. ٣ الأصل: من.

been made on his authority only for the opposite to happen. We pulled out the royal order, and Faqīh Muḥammad read it out to him, so he welcomed us, honored us, and invited us to eat. Then he beat a drum of the kind called *tómbol*,[20] and crowds of people arrived. He chose about a hundred young men, put one of his relatives—Faqīh Zayd, who was known for his courage—in charge of them, and ordered him and his men to escort me and to look lively and be on guard against the wild mountain people.

We now mounted and set off for a place where there is a small mountain 3.1.23
called Marrah, from which the whole range takes its name. On it we found what seemed to be a temple for all the mountain people, who believe they must honor it and hold it as sacred as any mosque. We entered. It is shaded by a tree so large that the sun never sees it. We sat inside for a little and found there servants responsible for cleaning it and for receiving votive offerings from those who bring them. Then we moved on from there, the soldiers walking ahead of us, and many people, women and men, followed us. They took me for a marvel, falling upon me and crowding around me, and the soldiers were unable to disperse them. Eventually one of them said that the sultan had sent the people of the mountain a treat in the form of a man who'd failed to ripen in his mother's belly, to which some responded, "But he's a man," while others said, "He isn't a man, he's an edible animal in the form of a man"—for they refuse to accept that a man can be white or ruddy-complexioned. The only Arabic these people know is the two phrases of the profession of faith, which they pronounce in broken fashion and with an ugly accent. When the men with me could no longer hold them back, Faqīh Zayd came and told me to cover my face with a veil through which only my eyes were visible. I put it on and the soldiers formed a circle around me. When the Blacks couldn't see me, because I'd veiled myself, they were puzzled and asked, "Where did the red man go?" The soldiers said, "He went to the sultan," so the crowd thinned out a bit.

Next, we set off for the place of incarceration, meaning the caves where 3.1.24
imprisoned royal princes and viziers are kept, but the guards barred us from reaching them. They and our men almost came to blows, but Faqīh Zayd sorted things out, took the royal order from me, and went to the commander of the guard and read it out to him. At this, the man submitted, but said, "If it must be so, then let the subject of the order come on his own and look. The rest can sit at a distance till he's done and returns to them." The faqīh came

بعد حتّى يقضي شأنه ويرجع إليهم فجاءني وأخبرني بذلك فأبيت ذلك وأدركني خوف عظيم فنأيت عن الدخول إلى الكهوف وطلبت الرجوع فرجعنا

ومن غرائب عوائدهم أنّ الرجل لا يتزوّج المرأة حتّى يصاحبها مدّة وتحمل منه مرّة أو مرّتين وحينئذ يقال إنها وَلود فيعقد[1] عليها ويعاشرها ومن عوائدهم أيضاً أنّ النساء لا يحجبن عن الرجال حتّى أنّ الرجل يدخل داره فيجد امرأته مختلية مع آخر فلا يكترث ولا يغتمّ إلّا إذا وجده عليها ومن طبيعتهم الجفاء وسوء الخلق خصوصاً إذا كانوا سكارى ومن طبيعتهم أيضاً البخل الزائد لا يقرّون ضيفاً إلّا إذا كان من ذوي قرابتهم أو لهم به علقة أو كان إنساناً يخافون منه ومن عوائدهم أنّ الصبيان والبنات الصغار لا يستترون إلّا بعد البلوغ فيلبس الصبيّ قميصاً وتشدّ الأنثى وسطها بميزل ويبقى ما زاد عن السرّة إلى وجهها بارزاً ومن عادتهم عدم الترفّه والتفنّن في المآكل بل كلّ ما وجدوه أكلوه لا يأنفون طعاماً مُرّاً كان أو نتناً بل ربّما أحبّوا أكل الطعام المرّ واللحم النتن واستحسنوه عن غيره ٢٥،١،٣

ومن عادتهم أنّ الشباب لهم في كلّ بلدة رئيس وكذلك النساء لهنّ رئيسة فرئيس الرجال يسمّى الوُرْناگ ورئيسة[2] النساء تسمّى الميْرَم فإذا كان في الأفراح والأعياد والمواسم يجمع الرئيس أصحابه ويجلس بهم في محلّ وتأتي الرئيسة وصواحبها[3] فيجلسن أمامهم على حدة فينفرد الورناگ ويدنو من الميرم ويخاطبها بكلام يعرفه هو وهي فتأمر الميرم جماعتها أن يتفرّقن على جماعة الورناگ فيأخذ كلّ فتى فتاة ويذهبان إلى محلّ يناما فيه إلى الصباح ولا عار في ذلك على إحدى منهنّ ٢٦،١،٣

وليعلم أنّ الرجال في دارفور لا يستقلّون بأمر البتّة إلّا الحرب فليس للنساء دخل فيه وما سوى ذلك فهم والنساء سواء بل أكثر الأشغال وأشقّها على النساء وللرجال اختلاط عجيب بهنّ بالليل والنهار في جميع الأعمال ٢٧،١،٣

١ الأصل: ويقعد. ٢ الأصل: ورئيس. ٣ الأصل: وصواحبتنا.

back and informed me of this, but I refused, overwhelmed by fear. I disclaimed any desire to enter the caves and asked to go back, so we went back.

One of their strange customs is that a man only gets married to a woman after he's spent some time with her as a friend and she's borne him one or two children. When they reach this point, they decide that she's fertile, and he makes a contract with her and lives with her. Another custom is that the women do not keep themselves out of sight of men. Indeed, if a man enters his house and finds his wife on her own with another man, he shows no concern and doesn't get upset, unless he finds him on top of her. By nature, they are coarse-grained and bad-tempered, especially when drunk. They are also extremely miserly and won't entertain a guest unless he's a relative, or there's some relationship between them, or he's someone they fear. Another custom of theirs is that the young boys and girls wear nothing to make themselves decent until after puberty, when the boy puts on a shift and the female ties a loincloth around her waist, leaving everything from her navel to her face exposed. Another custom is the lack of expensive ingredients and variety in their food. In fact, they eat whatever they can find and don't turn up their noses at bitter or rotten food; they may actually like bitter food and rotten meat and prefer it to anything else. 3.1.25

Another custom is that the young men in every village have a chief, as do the women. The men's chief is called the ŏrnang and the women's the mééram. At weddings, religious feasts, and holidays, the men's chief gathers his followers and seats them in a certain place, and the women's chief and her followers come and sit down in front of them separately. Then the ŏrnang goes on his own, approaches the mééram, and addresses her using words that both he and she know. Then the mééram orders her women to distribute themselves among the ŏrnang's group, each young man takes a young woman, and they go somewhere and sleep until morning. No shame attaches to any of the young women for this. 3.1.26

The men of Darfur have no independent decision-making power whatsoever, except over whether to go to war, which the women have nothing to do with. In all other matters, men and women are equal. Indeed, most kinds of labor, and the most demanding forms of it, are women's to do, and the men mix with them to an amazing degree, by night and by day, in all types of work. 3.1.27

٣،١،٢٨ ومن العجب في أهل جبل مرّة أنّهم لا يأكلون من القمح الذي يزرعونه بل يبيعونه ويستبدلون بثمنه دخنًا وأعجب من ذلك غلظ قلوبهم وجفاوتهم مع أنّهم ممتزجون بالنساء امتزاجًا كلّيًّا وهذا خلاف المشاع على ألسنة جميع أهل بلاد أوروبّا من أنّ الرجال إذا امتزجوا بالنساء تذهب غلاظة قلوبهم ويكتسبون الرقّة وحسن الطبع ومن غلاظة طبعهم أنّ الرجل يسافر الفراسخ العديدة راجلًا ويكون معه حمار فيسوقه أمامه ولا يركبه وإن سئل يقول إن ركبته أبطأ بي

٣،١،٢٩ وأمّا لغتهم فهي لغة فيها حماس. ألفاظها تشبه ألفاظ اللغة التركيّة لأنّهم إذا دعوا إنسانًا يقولون له گلا والترك يقولون گال وقولي تشبه اللغة التركيّة ليس معناه أنّهما متقاربتا[١] المعنى بل وجه الشبه في مجرّد الألفاظ وإن اختلف موضوع معنى كلّ منهما وذلك أنّ الفور يقولون للفرس يامُورْتا وعند الترك هو اسم للبيض والقبيح عند الفور اسمه ڮِتّي[٢] وعند الترك فعل ماض بمعنى ذهب ولم اسمع لغة أنقص من لغتهم لأنّ العدد بلغتهم ينتهي إلى ستّة ويكمل بالعربيّ فيقولون دِيكْ واحد أَوَّ اثنان إِيسْ ثلاثة أُونْگَلْ أربعة أُوسْ خمسة أُوصَانْدِيكْ ستّة ثمّ يقولون بالعربيّ سبعة ثمانية تسعة ثمّ يقولون وأَيَّهْ وهو لفظ يدلّ على عَشَر الأعداد

٣،١،٣٠ لطيفة: من أعجب ما سمعته بجبل مرّة أنّ الجنّ ترعى مواشيهم التي ترعى في الكلأ بدون راعٍ معهم ولقد أخبرني عدّة رجال ممّن يُظنّ صدقها أنّ الإنسان إذا مرّ بمواشيهم ورأى ألّا راعي[٣] لها ربّما طمع فأخذ منها شاة أو بقرة أو غير ذلك فإن ذبحها تلتصق يده بالسكّين على منحرها ويعجز عن فكاكها حتّى تأتي أرباب الماشية فيقبضون عليه ويغرمونه ثمنها بأغلى قيمة بعد إهانتهم له وضربهم إيّاه الضرب المؤلم ولقد تكرّر على سماع ذلك حتّى بلغ مبلغ التواتر مع أنّي لا أصدّقه

٣،١،٣١ وحين كنت في جبل مرّة توجّهت إلى دار رجل منهم في نمليه أسأل عنه فما رأيت في داره أحدًا لكن سمعت داخل الدار صوتًا غليظًا مرعبًا اقشعرّ منه جلدي

---

١ الأصل: مقاربتى. ٢ الأصل: ڮجِتّي. ٣ الأصل: راع.

A strange thing about the people of Jabal Marrah is that they don't eat the wheat they grow. Instead, they sell it and trade it for millet. Stranger still are their crude sensibilities and their rough-hewnness, even though they mix with their women without restriction. This contradicts the belief held by all Franks[21] that when men mix with women, their crudeness vanishes and they acquire refinement and good dispositions. An example of their crudeness is that a man will travel several leagues on foot, with a donkey, and will drive it ahead of him instead of riding it, and if you ask him why, he'll tell you, "It would slow me down!" 3.1.28

Their language is full of enthusiasm.[22] Its words resemble Turkish, because, when they call to someone, they say *kéla*[23] while the Turks say *gel* ("come!"). When I say they're alike, I don't mean they're close in meaning. Rather, the resemblance is just in the sounds, even when the meaning is different. Thus, the Fur call a mare *yáa murtá'ng*, which to the Turks is a word for eggs (*yumurta*).[24] To the Fur, something ugly is *jitti*, which to the Turks is a past tense verb meaning "he went."[25] I have never heard a more deficient language than theirs, because the numbers in their language end at six, after which they continue in Arabic. Thus, they say *díg* for one, *aw* for two, *iis* for three, *ongngal* for four, *oos* for five, and *oosandíg* for six. After that they continue in Arabic: *sabʿah, tamanyah, tisʿah* ("seven, eight, nine").[26] Then they say *wayye*, which is a term they use for the tens.[27] 3.1.29

A Curiosity: One of the strangest things I heard when I was on Jabal Marrah was that the jinn there look after their livestock—the ones grazing in the pastures—and these do not have shepherds. Several men whose word one would normally trust told me that if anyone were to pass by their livestock and see there was no shepherd and perhaps give in to the temptation to take a ewe or a cow or anything else and then try to slaughter it, his hand would stick to the knife at the creature's throat, and he'd be unable to let go of it until its owners came. They would seize him and force him to pay the highest price for it, after reviling him and giving him a painful beating. I heard this so often it achieved the number of independent transmitters it would need, were it a prophetic hadith, to be accepted as authentic—but I still didn't believe it. 3.1.30

When I was on Jabal Marrah, I went to the house of a local man in Numlayh to ask about this but found no one at home. However, I did hear, coming from inside the house, a terrifying, coarse voice that made my skin crawl, telling me, "*Á keeba!*" meaning "He's not here!" At that very moment, I tried to advance 3.1.31

يقول لي أبا يعني إنّه ليس هنا وفي ذلك الوقت أردت أن أتقدّم وأسأل أين ذهب فمرّ بي إنسان وجذبني وقال ارجع فإنّ الذي يخاطبك غير آدميّ فقلت وما هو فقال هذا الحارس الجنّيّ لأنّ لكلّ إنسان منّا حارساً من الجنّ ويسمّى بلغة الفور دَمَزوقَة فخفت حينئذ ورجعت من حيث أتيت

٣٢،١،٣ ولمّا رجعت من هذه السفرة وتوجّهت إلى الفاشر اجتمعت مع الشريف أحمد بدويّ الذي أخذني من مصر وذهب بي إلى دارفور فأخبرته القصّة فقال صدق وأسمعني أعجب من ذلك وقال لي يا ولدي اعلم أنّي كنت في أوّل أمري أسمع أنّ الدمازيق تباع وتشترى ومن أراد منها دمزوقه[١] يذهب إلى من يُعلم أنّ عنده دمازيق فيشتري منه واحداً بما يرضيه ثمّ يأتي بقرعة فيها لبن ويدفعها إلى ربّ المنزل فيأخذها ويدخل إلى المحلّ الذي هنّ فيه فيسلّم عليهنّ ويعلّق القرعة التي فيها اللبن في علّاقة في البيت ثمّ يقول لهنّ إنّ صاحبي فلاناً عنده مال كثير وخائف عليه من السرقة وأراد منّي حارساً فهل إحدى منكنّ تذهب إلى داره لأنّ عنده لبناً كثيراً وخيراً غزيراً وقد أتى بهذه القرعة مملوءة لبناً فيتمنّعن أوّلاً ويقلن لا أحد يذهب معه فيتحنّن لهنّ ويتملّق حتّى يرضين فيقول من أراد الذهاب منكنّ فلينزل في القرعة ويبعد عنهنّ قليلاً وحين يسمع بصوت وقوعه في اللبن يغطّي القرعة بطبق من سعف ويأخذها من علّاقتها مغطّاة ويدفعها لصاحبه المشتري فيأخذها ويذهب بها إلى داره ويعلّقها في بيته ويوكّل بالقرعة جارية أو امرأة تأتي كلّ يوم على الصباح وتأخذ القرعة وتريق ما فيها من اللبن وتغسلها[٢] جيّداً ثمّ تضع فيها لبناً آخر محلوباً في ساعته وتعلّقها وحينئذ يأمن الإنسان على ماله من السرقة والضياع

٣٣،١،٣ وكنت أكذّب ذلك حتّى كثر مالي وصارت العبيد والخدم يسرقونه فاحتلت على منع السرقة بكلّ حيلة فلم يمكنّي[٣] ذلك وشكوت لبعض أصحابي فأمرني أن أشتري دمزوقه وأنّي أُكْفَى شرَّ السرقة فحداني حبّ المال أن توجّهت إلى رجل سمعت أنّ عنده دمازيق

١ الأصل: دمزوقًا. ٢ الأصل: يغسلها. ٣ الأصل: يمكنني.

and ask, "Where is he?" but a passerby dragged me away, saying, "Get back! The one you're talking to isn't human." "What is he then?" I asked. "He's his guardian jinni," he said, "for every one of us has a guardian among the jinn, and in the language of the Fur he's called a *damsuga*." That scared me, and I retraced my steps.

When I got back from this journey and went to the sultan's seat, I met with Sharif Aḥmad Badawī, the man who had brought me from Egypt to Darfur, and I told him the story. "Believe it!" he said, and told me stranger things still: "My boy," he said to me, "when I was young I used to hear that *damsuga*s could be bought and sold and that anyone who wanted a *damsuga* would go to someone he knew had them and buy one at whatever price the other would accept. Then he'd bring a gourd of milk and hand it over to the master of the house, who'd take it and go into the room where the *damsuga*s were, greet them, and hang the gourd containing the milk on a hanger in the house. After that, he'd tell them, 'My friend so-and-so has great wealth, which he's afraid will be stolen from him, and he's asked for a guardian. Will any of you go to his house? He has much milk there and lots of good things, and has brought this gourd, full of milk.' At first, the *damsuga*s would refuse and say, 'None of us will go with him,' so he'd talk to them gently and flatter them until they agreed. Then he'd say, 'Whichever of you wants to go should get into the gourd,' and he'd remove himself from them a little. Once he'd heard the *damsuga* fall into the milk, he'd stop the gourd with palm leaves, take it, covered, from its hanger, and hand it over to his friend who'd bought it. Then the latter would take it home and hang it up in his house, where he'd put a slave girl or a woman in charge of going every morning and taking the gourd, emptying it of whatever milk it might contain, and washing it well, after which she'd put new milk in it, fresh from the cow, and hang it up. If he did so, that person could be sure that his property would be safe from theft and loss. 3.1.32

"I thought these were lies. But then my wealth increased and the slaves and servants began stealing from it. I tried everything I could to put a stop to that but couldn't, so I complained to a friend of mine and he advised me to buy a *damsuga*, saying that I'd then be protected from the evil of theft. My love of wealth prompted me to go to a man I'd heard had *damsuga*s. 'Give me a *damsuga* to guard my property for me,' I said, and gave him what he asked. Then he said, 'Go and fill a gourd with fresh milk and bring it here.' I did that and took him the gourd, filled with milk. He took it and went off and after an 3.1.33

وقلت له أعطني دمزوقه تحرس لي مالي وأعطيته ما طلبه فقال لي اذهب واملأ قرعة من لبن حليب وهاتها ففعلت وأتيته بالقرعة مملوءة لبناً فأخذها وذهب وبعد ساعة جاءني والقرعة مغطّاة وقال لي علّقها حيث مالك مخزون وعرّفني ما ينبغي أن يُفعل كلّ يوم من غسل الآنية وتجديد اللبن ففعلت ذلك ووكّلت جارية بذلك وأمنت على مالي حتّى أنّي كنت أترك بيت مالي مفتوحاً ولا يقدر أحد على الوصول إليه وفيه من العين والأمتعة شيء كثير وكلّ من رام أخذ شيء بغير إذني تكسر رقبته فقتل لي عدّة عبيد وعشت آمناً على مالي مدّة حتّى كبر لي ولد كان اسمه محمّد فلمّا شبّ واحتلم تعلّقت آماله بالبنات وأراد يهاديهنّ ببعض خرز وحليّ فترقّب غفلتي يوماً وأخذ المفاتيح وفتح خزينة الأمتعة وأراد أن يدخل فكسر الدمزوقه رقبته ومات في الحال وكنت أحبّه حبّاً شديداً فلمّا أُخبِرتُ بموته جزعت عليه جزعاً عظيماً وسألت عن سبب ذلك وأُخبرت أنّه أراد أن يأخذ شيئاً من الأمتعة فقتله الدمزوقه فحلفت يميناً أنّ الدمزوقه لا يجلس في بيتي وأردت إخراجه فأعجزني وشكوت لبعض أحبابي فأشار عليّ أن أصنع وليمة وأجمع فيها أناساً كثيرين يكون مع كلّ واحد منهم بندقيّة وبارود ويأتون كلّهم دفعة واحدة يطلقون البنادق ويصيحون بصوت واحد بكلام الفور دَمْزُوقه أَيْئِيهْ ومعناه أين الشيطان ويكرّرون الطلق ويرفعون أصواتهم بذلك حتّى يدخلون إلى المحلّ الذي فيه المال فربّما خاف وهرب منه ففعلت ذلك ففرّ ولله الحمد وخلصت من معاشرة الدمازيق أي الشياطين

٣٤،١،٣ ولقد أخبرني عدّة رجال أنّ النقاقير التي في بيت السلطان فيها واحدة تسمّى المنصورة[١] متملّكها الشياطين وأنّها ربّما ضُربت بغير ضارب فإذا وقع ذلك يحدث في دارفور أمر عظيم إمّا حرب عدوّ لهم أو حرب بينهم وسيأتي لهذا مزيد توضيح حين نتكلّم على عوائد الملوك

٣٥،١،٣ وأمّا عوائد القبائل الأخر كالبرتي والداجو والبيقو والزغاوة والبرقو والميمه وغيرهم

---

١ الأصل: منصورة.

hour returned with the gourd, covered. 'Hang it where your wealth is stored,' he said to me, and taught me what I had to do every day by way of washing the vessel and filling it with fresh milk. I did this and put a slave girl in charge of it and became so convinced my wealth was safe that I'd leave my treasury open, and no one would be able to get to it. It contained large quantities of goods and belongings, and anyone who tried to take something without my permission would end up with a broken neck. I lost several slaves that way. I lived for a while without worrying about my wealth until a son of mine called Muḥammad became a young man and, having reached puberty, started setting his sights on girls. He wanted to give them beads and trinkets, so one day he waited until I wasn't paying attention, took the keys, opened the storeroom where my property was kept, and was about to enter when the *damsuga* broke his neck, and he died on the spot. I loved him dearly. When I was informed of his death, I mourned for him greatly and asked how he had died. I was told that he'd tried to take some of my belongings, so the *damsuga* had killed him. I swore then that the *damsuga* would not stay another moment in my house and tried to expel it, but I couldn't. I complained to a friend of mine, and he advised me to hold a banquet and gather lots of men together, each with a musket and gunpowder, and have them all come at once, firing their muskets and yelling with one voice in the language of the Fur, '*Damsuga ây yé?*' meaning 'Where is the devil?' and have them keep on firing and shouting those words all the way till they entered the place where my belongings were kept. Then it might become scared and run away. I did this, and it did flee, praise be to God, and I stopped keeping company with *damsuga*s, or, to put it bluntly, with devils."

Several men told me that among the kettledrums in the sultan's house there is one called the Victorious that belongs to the jinn. Sometimes it sounds when there is no one there to strike it, and when that happens some great event occurs in Darfur, either war with one of their enemies or among themselves. This will be discussed again in more detail when we speak of the customs of their kings. 3.1.34

The customs of the other tribes, such as the Bartī, the Dājū, the Bīqū, the Zaghāwah, the Barqū, the Mīmah, and others are in some cases close to those of the people of the mountain but in others different. Insofar as they differ, it's because some of these tribes possess nobility, courage, and refined 3.1.35

فإنّ بعضها يقرب من عوائد أهل الجبل وبعضها يخالفها أمّا المخالفة فبعض هذه القبائل فيه كرم ونجدة ورقّة طبع وذلك لمخالطتهم للعرب أهل البادية وللتجار الذين يذهبون من أرض مصر وغيرها فتراهم إذا رأوا أضيافاً أقسموا عليهم وأحسنوا ضيافتهم وإن رأوا غريباً أكرموه وذلك بخلاف الفور الأعجام كأهل جبل مرّة وتموركه فإنّهم لا يكرمون الضيف ولا يألفونه ولا ينزل الضيف عندهم إلّا قهرًا عنهم انتهى

الفصل الثاني في عوائد ملوك الفور

اعلم أنّ الله سبحانه وتعالى خلق الخلائق بقدرته وميّزهم بحكمته وجعل اختلاف عوائدهم وأحوالهم عبرة لأولي الأبصار وتذكرة لذوي الاستبصار ليعلم العاقل إذا تأمّل في أحوال الممالك واختلاف عوائدها وطبائعها المتنوّعة وفوائدها أنّ القادر الخالق الأكبر جلّت قدرته وعظمت إرادته إنّما نوّع أحوال هذا العالم وخصّ كلّ قوم بمزيّة لا توجد في غيرهم ليُعلم عظم قهره وحكمته كما أنّه إذا نظر في اختلاف ألسنتهم وألوانهم وزيّهم ومعاشهم علم أنّها آية كبرى كما قال تعالى و ﴿مِنْ آيَاتِهِ مَنَامُكُمْ بِاللَّيْلِ وَالنَّهَارِ﴾ ﴿وَاخْتِلَافُ أَلْسِنَتِكُمْ وَأَلْوَانِكُمْ﴾ ثمّ إنّ الله جعل لكلّ إقليم طبيعة فمن الأقاليم الحارّ ومنها البارد ومنها المتوسّط بين الحرارة والبرودة وذلك بحسب قرب الإقليم من خطّ الاستواء وبعده عنه فسبحانه الفعال لما يريد ولو شاء لجعلهم أمّة واحدة ولكن بالاختلاف تظهر المزايا وتشتاق النفس إلى معرفة ما لم تعرفه ولولا ذلك لما ساحت السوّاح وما بُذلت في الأسفار الأموال[1] والأرواح وإذا تقرّر ذلك فنقول ٣٦،١،٣

عادة ملوك الفور مخالفة لعوائد غيرهم من الملوك ولِمَلِكِهِمْ السلطنة التامّة عليهم فإذا قتل منهم ألوفا لا يُسأل لماذا وإن عزل ذا منصب لا يسأل لماذا فهو تامّ التصرّف في كلّ أمر يريده وإذا أمر بأمر لا يُراجَعُ فيه ولو كان منكرًا إلّا من قبيل الشفاعة ٣٧،١،٣

١ الأصل: الامول.

dispositions, having mixed with the Arabs of the desert and the merchants who come from Egypt and elsewhere. You find that when such tribes see guests, they adjure them not to leave and treat them very hospitably, and when they see a stranger, they honor him. This is the contrary of the non-Arabic-speaking Fur, such as those of Jabal Marrah and Tomorókkóngá. These will neither so honor him nor behave toward him in a friendly manner, and they will not put a guest up in their houses unless forced to.

Section 2: Customs of the Kings of the Fur

God, glorified and exalted, has created all people through His power, distin- 3.1.36
guished them, in His wisdom, one from another, and caused the differences among their customs and conditions to be a lesson for those who have eyes to see and a reminder for those who have minds to ponder. He has done this so that the rational person must inevitably become aware—on contemplating the conditions of different states, their varied endowments and constitutions, their virtues, and their advantages—of the fact that the Greatest and Most Powerful Creator, of power stupendous and will tremendous, has made the circumstances prevailing in this world to be of many kinds, bestowing on this or that people some particular advantage not to be found in others, in order that the magnitude of His power and His wisdom may be known. Likewise, if the rational person observes the differences among their tongues, colors, costumes, and means of sustenance, he or she will realize that these things are a major sign of God's power: as the Almighty has said, «Among His signs are your sleep, at night or in daytime» «and the diversity of your languages and colors.»[28] In addition, God has given a particular nature to every clime. Thus, some are hot, others cold, and yet others, depending on the nearness or distance of the clime to or from the equator, occupy a midpoint. Glory then to Him who effects what He desires; "should He have wished it, He could have made them all one nation."[29] Through difference, however, virtues are made manifest, and the soul yearns to know what it did not. Were it not so, the restless would not roam and lives not be given over, in search of knowledge and wealth, to journeying far from home. With this established, we declare:

The customary practice of the monarchs of the Fur is at odds with those 3.1.37
of other countries. Their king has absolute authority over them. Should he

ولا تردّ له كلمة لكنّه إذا فعل ما لا يليق من الظلم والعسف تحصل له بغضاء في قلوبهم ولا يقدرون له على شيء

٣٨،١،٣ فأوّل عوائدهم أنّ الملك لا يكون إلّا من بيت الملك أي من سلالتهم ولا يمكن تولية أجنبيّ عنهم[1] ولو شريفاً وتحقّق نسبه عندهم وثانيها أنّ الملك إذا تولّى يجلس في بيته سبعة أيّام لا يأمر ولا ينهى ولا تقوم بين يديه دعوى[2] وكلّهم على ذلك إلّا السلطان عبد الرحمن فإنّه خرق عادتهم كما مرّ عند الكلام على توليته وثالثها أنّ لهم عجائز تسمّى الحبّوبات وهنّ طائفة عظيمة ولهنّ رئيسة تسمّى ملكة الحبّوبات فعند خروج السلطان يوم الثامن يجتمعن ويأتين إليه وكلّ واحدة منهنّ بيديها أربع

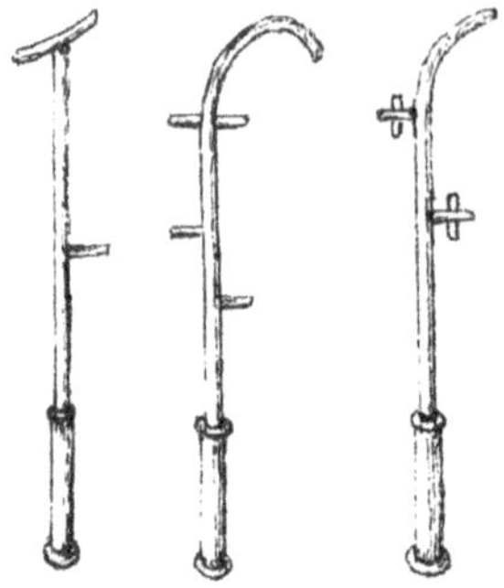

قطع من الحديد تسمّى القطعة منها كُرباجاً وصورتها إمّا هكذا أو هكذا أو هكذا وفي كلّ يد كرباجان يضربنها على بعضها فيحصل منها صوت وبيد إحداهنّ قبضة من سعف أبيض ومعها ماء اختلف أهل دارفور فيما تركب منه فتبلّ العجوز السعف من ذلك الماء وترشّ به على السلطان مع قول كلام لا يعقله إلّا هنّ ويأخذن السلطان في وسطهنّ ويطفن به البيت ويتوجّهن إلى دار النحاس وهو المحلّ الذي فيه النقاقير وهي طبول السلطان فيدخلن البيت ويأتين إلى النقاريّة المسمّاة بالمنصورة فيقفن حلقة ويجعلنها في الوسط والسلطان وحده معهنّ ويضربن الكرابج على بعضها ويقلن من كلامهنّ ثمّ يرجعن بالسلطان إلى كرسيّ مملكته وبعد جلوسه ذاك تدخل إليه الدعاوى ويتناول الأحكام

١ الأصل: منهم. ٢ الأصل: دعوة.

kill thousands, no one will ask why, and should he strip an officeholder of his office, again no one will ask why. He has total freedom of action to do everything he wishes, and if he gives a command, he may not be questioned, even if it be an abomination, other than through intercession,[30] and he may never be contradicted. If, however, he acts with an unbefitting degree of tyranny and oppression, they will come to hate him in their hearts, though they can do nothing against him.

3.1.38 The first custom is that the monarch must be from their royal house, meaning of their own line: no outsider may assume power, even a sharif whose line of descent they have verified. The second is that when the monarch takes power, he stays in his house for seven days and issues no commands or prohibitions, and no case may be tried before him. All of them have followed this practice, with the exception of Sultan ʿAbd al-Raḥmān: he broke with tradition, as mentioned when we spoke of his assumption of power.[31] The third is that there are among them old women called the Grandmothers,[32] who form a powerful faction. They have a chief who's called the Mistress of the Grandmothers, and when the sultan leaves his house on the eighth day, they assemble and go to him, each holding four pieces of iron, called "scourges." They look either like this like this or like this.

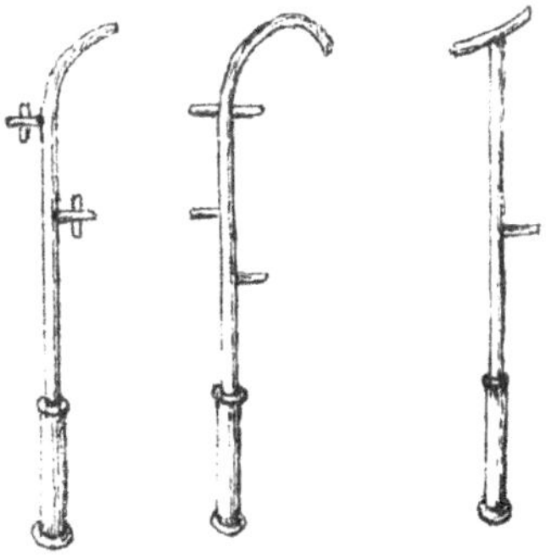

In each hand, they hold two scourges, which they strike against each other.[33] One of them has a handful of white palm leaves in her hand and carries a liquid—the people of Darfur differ on the nature of its composition.[34] The old woman wets the palm leaves with this liquid and sprinkles it over the sultan while uttering words of which only the Grandmothers know the meaning. They take the sultan into their midst, circumambulate the house, and then go to the Drum House,[35] which is where the kettledrums—the sultan's drums—are kept.[36] They enter, go to the drum called the Victorious, and stand in a circle with the drum in the middle. The sultan is alone with them, and they strike the scourges against each other and speak words in that language of theirs. Then they conduct the sultan back to the throne of his kingdom, and as soon as he's seated on it cases are brought to him and he starts pronouncing judgments.

ومن عادتهم أنّ السلطان لا يسلّم على غيره إلّا بترجمان صغيرًا كان أو كبيرًا عظيمًا أو حقيرًا وكيفيّة ذلك أنّه[1] إذا دخل عليه أناس يجثون على ركبهم ثمّ يتقدّم الترجمان ويسمّيهم واحدًا بعد واحد إلى آخرهم وهو أنّه يقول إِنَو تورًا فَلاَنْ دُوكَهْ كَنِّيجي دَارِي ومعناه إنّ هنا برًّا فلان سلام يعطي طاعة فإذا تمّ أسماء الجالسين قال كِيكِينْ دُقَلَهْ كَرِكَّهْ ومعناه معهم أولاد وراءهم حتّى أتباعهم وخدمهم فتقول العبيد الواقفون خلف السلطان المسمّون كُورْكُوَا وقد تقدّم ذكرهم دونگراي دوگه دونگراي دوگه ومعناه سلام سلام سلام فإن كان في ديوان حفل ضرب إذ ذاك طبل يقال له دِنْقَار وهو طبل عظيم من خشب مجلّد من جهة واحدة أهراميّ الشكل مقلوب هكذا  له صوت عالٍ وإن لم يكن ديوانًا لا يكون ذلك ٣٩،١،٣

ثمّ من شدّة تعظيمهم للسلطان أنّ السلطان إذا بصق في الأرض يمسحه بيده واحد من الخادمين القاعدين[2] أمامه المتطلّعين[3] دائمًا للسلطان ولأفعاله ولحركاته وإذا تنحنح قالوا كلّهم تس تس يعني يلفظون بتاء مدغمة في سين من غير حركات يكون اللسان ضاربًا للسِّنخ العلويّ للأسنان وإذا عطس لفظوا بحروف لا يلفظ بها إلّا الوَزَغ أو من يسوق دابّة وإذا جلس وأطال المجلس روّحوا عليه بمراوح من ريش النعام وإن خرج إلى الصيد يظلّلونه بشمسيّة وأربع مراوح كبار من ريش النعام مغلّفات بجوخ أحمر وهذه المراوح تسمّى بالريش وصورته هكذا 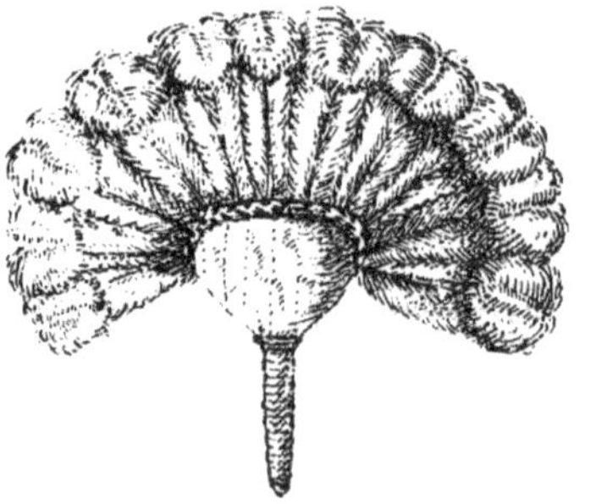 فيقفون بالشمسيّة على رأس السلطان ويجعلون المراوح اثنين عن اليمين واثنين عن اليسار فيصير على السلطان ظلّ واسع وللشمسيّة المذكورة والريش ملك مخصوص ٤٠،١،٣

[1] الأصل: ان. [2] الأصل: قاعدين. [3] الأصل: متطلعين.

Another custom of theirs is that the sultan only salutes people via an interpreter, whether the one saluted is young or old, mighty or mean. This is done as follows: when people come in to see him, they kneel; then the interpreter advances and says their names, one after another, until he's named them all. He says, "*Ínni tawrá falān dóngá kee nágí dárí*," which means "Here, outside, so-and-so, greetings, he gives obedience."[37] When he's finished listing the names of those in attendance at the assembly, he says, "*Kí kíeng dogóla kerker*," meaning "They have children behind them, even their followers and their servants."[38] Then the slaves who stand behind the sultan and are called *kóór kwa*, whom we've mentioned earlier,[39] say, "*Dóngá rǎy dóngá! Dóngá rǎy dóngá!*" meaning "Greetings! Greetings! Greetings! Greetings!" If the sultan is holding formal audience, a drum called *dinqār* is then beaten; this is a huge drum made of wood and covered with hide on one side. It has the shape of an inverted pyramid, like this: 3.1.39

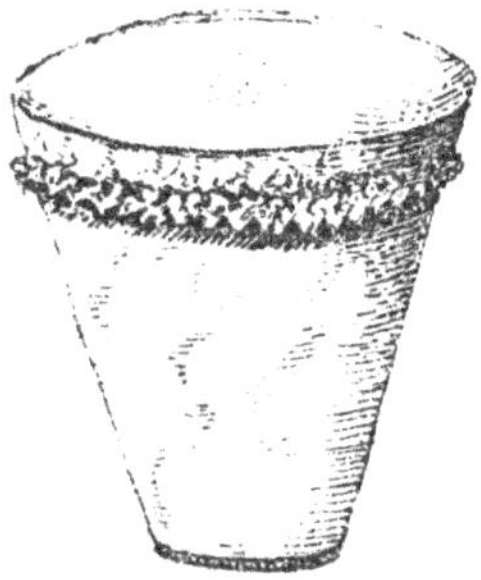

and makes a loud noise. If the audience is not that sort, then this isn't done.

Furthermore, they exalt the sultan to such a degree that when he spits on the ground, one of the servants sitting in front of him or keeping their eyes permanently trained on the sultan and his actions and movements wipes it up with his hand. When he clears his throat, they all say, "*Ts ts*," the *t* being contracted into the *s* with no vowel, the tongue striking the edge of the gums above the teeth. When he sneezes, they spit out letters that only a gecko or someone driving a donkey could pronounce. When he sits down and remains seated for a while, they fan him with ostrich-feather fans. And when he goes hunting, they shade him with an umbrella and four large ostrich-feather fans encased in red broadcloth; these fans are called "the feathers" and look like this: 3.1.40

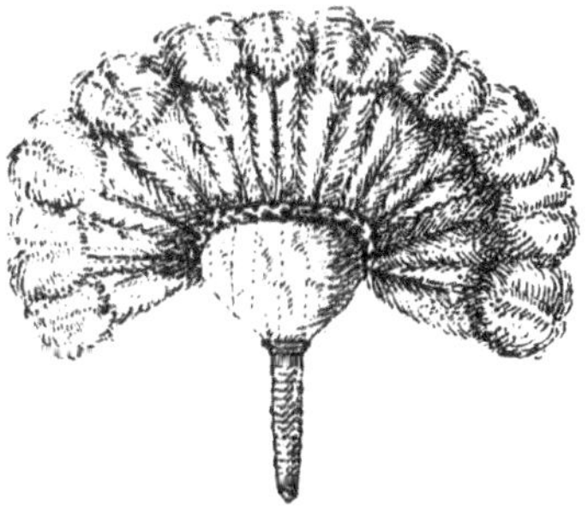

They hold the umbrella over the sultan's head and place two fans on the right and two on the left, ensuring that a large area of shade embraces him. The aforementioned umbrella and "feathers" have their own exclusive master and helpers, who take turns handling them, as they proceed on foot. Another custom relating to the sultan is that when he rides out, they roll a carpet out

وأعوان يتداولونها نوبة فنوبة ماشيين على أقدامهم ومن عادة السلطان إذا ركب أن ترفع أمامه السجّادة ولها ملك مخصوص وأعوان يتداولونها أيضاً ومن تعظيم السلطان أنّه إذا ركض جواده وعثر الجواد فرماه أو وقع من شدّة الركض أنّهم يرمون أنفسهم جميعاً من على ظهور الخيل ولا يمكن أن يثبت أحد منهم على ظهر فرسه بعد وقوع السلطان بل إن رأى الخدمة أحداً ثابتاً على ظهر جواده ولم يرم نفسه يرمونه إلى الأرض ويضربونه ضرباً مؤلماً وإن كان عظيماً لما يرون أنّ ثباته احتقار بأمر السلطان

وإذا جلس السلطان للحكم في ديوانه لا يكلّم الناس مباشرة بل بواسطة ترجمان إن ٤١،١،٣
لم يكن ديواناً عامّاً فإن كان ديواناً عامّاً كانت سبعة المترجمون أوّلهم عند السلطان وآخرهم عند الناس أصحاب الدعوى والمترجمون في الوسط والعساكر حوله والكوركوا خلفه والعلماء والأشراف جالسون وهيئة ديوانه هكذا

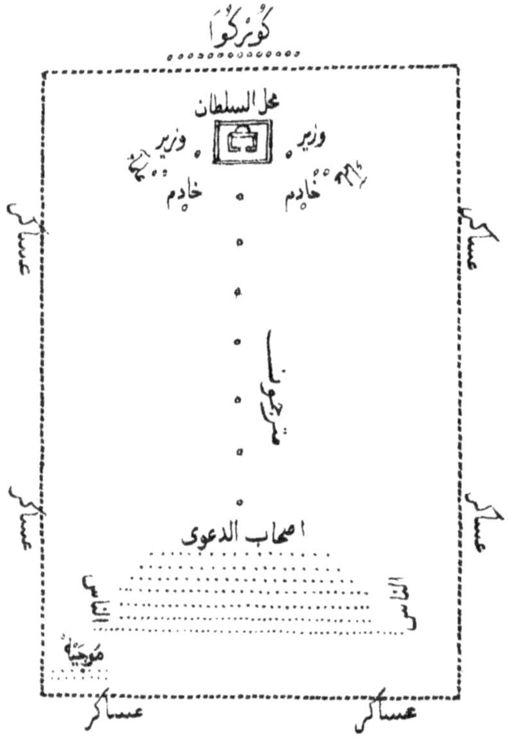

in front of him and this too has a master and helpers who manage it. Another example of their exaltation of the sultan is that if his horse gallops and stumbles and throws him, or the violence of the gallop makes him fall off, they all throw themselves off their horses' backs; it is unthinkable that any of them remain firmly mounted once the sultan has fallen. In fact, if the servants see that any of them is still firmly seated on his horse's back and hasn't thrown himself off, they throw him off themselves and beat him severely, even if he's someone important, because they think that to remain well seated is to show contempt for the sultan.

When the sultan sits in judgment in his place of audience, he doesn't address the people directly but does so through an interpreter, so long as the audience isn't public. If it's a public audience, they're seven—these interpreters—the first of them standing next to the sultan, the last next to the petitioners. The interpreters are in the middle, the soldiers around the sultan, and the *kóór kwa* behind him, while the scholars of religion and sharifs are seated. The audience space looks like this: 3.1.41

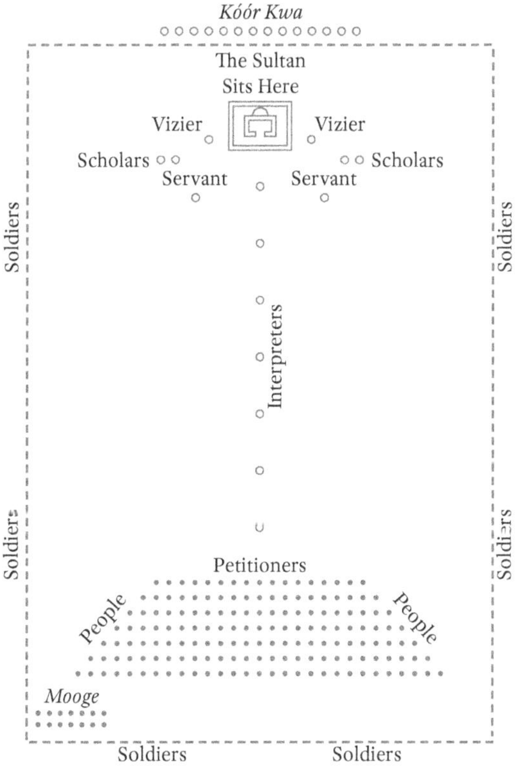

والناس جاثّون على ركبهم أمامه واضعين أيديهم على التراب والموجيه واقفون دائماً وسنذكر تعريفهم فإذا سلّم السلطان عليهم مسحوا التراب بأيديهم وإذا تكلّم أحد في مجلسه لا يبدأ الكلام إلّا بقوله سلّم على سيّدنا إن كان عربيّاً وإن كان فوراويّاً قال أباكوري دُوگَاجِني ومعناه ذلك وإذا كان السلطان هو المتكلّم يقول سلّم عليه إذا يتكلّم بالعربيّ فالترجمان يقول دُوگَايْ دَايِگْ سيدي وإذا كان بالفوراويّة يقول دُوگَاجِني إن كان عجميّاً وإن كان عربيّاً يقول سلّم عليه ولا خصوصيّة لمجلس السلطان في ذلك بل كلّ مجلس تُعمل فيه دعوى يقال ذلك حتّى في مجلس القاضي ومشايخ البلاد ولا يمكن أن تعمل دعوى بغير دُوگَاجِني ويلزم لذلك أنّ الكلام يطول وإن كان قصيراً لتكرير هذه الكلمة بعد كلّ كلمة أو كلمتين وإذا افتتح أحد دعوى بغير ذلك يعيبون عليه ويرون أنّه غير متمدّن بل إذا كان في مجلس حاكم يؤدّب بالزجر ما لم يكن غريباً فيعذر

ومن عادة ملوك الفور تجليد النحاس وهي عادة لا توجد في غير دارفور وتجليد النحاس هو تغيير[1] جلود الطبول المسمّاة في إقليم مصر بالنقاقير وهذا التجليد يعظمونه ويجعلون له موسما في السنة ومدّته سبعة أيّام وكيفيّة ذلك أنّ السلطان يأمر بنزع جلود الطبول كلّها في يوم واحد فتُنزع ثمّ يؤتى بأثوار خضر اللون فيذبحونها ويأخذون من جلودها ويجلّدون بها تلك الطبول لكن أهل دارفور يقولون في ذلك كلاماً لا يقبله عقل عاقل[2] ممارس للكتب ولكنّهم مُطْبِقون على ذلك فإنّهم يزعمون أنّ هذه الأثوار من نوع بقر معروف عندهم وأنّها حين الذبح تنام وحدها بدون من يمسكها ولا يذكرون اسم الله عند ذبحها ويقولون إنّ الجنّ هو الذي يمسكها وينيمها ٤٢،١،٣

ثمّ يأخذون لحومها وتُجعل[3] في خوابي وتُترك[4] ستّة أيّام مع الملح وفي اليوم السابع يأتون ببقر كثيرة وأغنام وتذبح كلّها ويطبخون لحومها وفي حال الطبخ يأخذون اللحم الذي في الخوابي ويقطعونه قطعا صغيرة ويجعلون في كلّ قدر منه قطعاً تخلط باللحم الجديد ثمّ تفرّق الموائد للملوك وأولاد الملوك والوزراء على حسب طبقاتهم ويقف على ٤٣،١،٣

١ الأصل: تغير. ٢ الأصل: العاقل. ٣ الأصل: ويجعل. ٤ الأصل: ويترك.

The people are on their knees in front of him with their hands on the ground, and the *mooge*, of whom we shall give an account,[40] remain standing. When the sultan greets them, they rub their hands in the dust, and when anyone speaks in his court, if he is Arab he must first say, "*Sallim 'alā sayyidnā*" ("Give greetings to my lord"), while if he is Fur, he must say, "*Ába kuri dóngá janí*," which means the same thing. When the sultan speaks, he says, "*Sallim 'alayh*" ("Give greetings to him"), when speaking Arabic, and the interpreter says, "*Dónga dáíng sīdī*."[41] If the sultan is speaking Fur, he says, "*Dóngá janí*" ("Greetings") if his addressee is not an Arabic speaker; if he's an Arab, he says, "*Sallim 'alayh*."[42] This is not peculiar to the sultan's court. The same is said at every gathering where cases are heard, even those of the judges and the village shaykhs, and no case may be heard without *Dóngá janí*! It follows that discussion is long even when substance is short, because they repeat the phrase after every one or two words. If anyone opens a case without them, they find fault with him and call him uncivilized. Indeed, if he's at the gathering of a ruler, he will be disciplined with a rebuke, unless he be a stranger, in which case he will be forgiven.

It is a custom of the Fur kings to "cover the drums," a custom found only in 3.1.42
Darfur. "Covering the drums" means changing the skins on the sort of drums that in Egypt are called *naqāqīr* ("kettledrums"). They make much of this covering and each year set a special seven-day holiday aside for it.[43] This is done in the following fashion: the sultan commands that all the skins be stripped off the drums on the same day, and this is done. Then brown bulls are brought, they slaughter them, take a portion of their hides, and cover those same drums with them. The people of Darfur have a story about this that no rational, well-read person can accept, despite which they all agree on it. They claim that these bulls are of a breed of cattle well known to them and that at the moment of slaughter they lie down of their own accord with nobody holding them and without anyone pronouncing the name of God when their throats are cut. They say it is the jinn who hold them and lay them on their sides.

They then take the meat, place it in pits, and leave it in salt for six days. 3.1.43
On the seventh day, they bring large numbers of cattle and goats, slaughter them all, and cook the flesh.[44] While it is cooking, they take the meat that was in the pits and cut it up into small pieces, a few of which they put into each cauldron, mixed in with the new meat. Then tables are allotted to the petty kings, the sons of the kings, and the viziers, according to rank, and over

كلّ مائدة منها حارس من طرف السلطان ينظر من يأكل ومن لم يأكل فإذا أخبر السلطان بأنّ فلاناً لم يأكل أمر بالقبض عليه في الحال لأنّهم يقولون إنّ من كان في قلبه خيانة للسلطان أو غدر لا يمكن أن يأكل من هذا اللحم وإن تعلّل أحد بأنّه مريض أو لا يقدر على الحضور[1] أرسلت إليه أواني منه مع حارس أمين ينظر هل يأكل أو لا فإنّ أبى يقبض عليه إلّا إذا كان معذوراً بقوّة مرضه وبعض أهل دارفور يقولون إنّه يؤتى بغلام وصبيّة لم يبلغا الحنث ويذبحان سرّاً ويقطع لحمهما ويُجعل في القدور مع لحم الحيوانات المذبوحة وبعض الناس يقول لا بدّ وأن يكون اسم الغلام محمّداً واسم الصبيّة فاطمة وإن صحّ هذا فهو غاية الكفر بالله ورسوله ولكنّي لم أشاهد ذلك ولم أقف عليه لأنّي غريب والأغراب لا اطّلاع لهم على مثل هذا الأمر أبداً لكنّي سمعته من أناس كثيرين يحلفون لي بأيمان مغلّظة أنّ هذا الكلام صحيح لا ريب فيه

٣،١،٤٤ وقبل إخراج الطعام تحضر العساكر كلّها ويقفون في بطحاء واسعة أمام دار السلطان ثمّ يخرج السلطان عليهم في زينته وأبّهته فتعرض عليه الجيوش كلّ ملك بأتباعه واحد بعد واحد وكيفيّة العرض أنّ الملك يأخذ أتباعه ويركض حتّى يصل إلى محلّ السلطان فإن كان من العظماء بـرز السلطان من جماعته إلى ملاقاته مقدار خطوتين أو ثلاثة وإن كان غير عظيم ثبت السلطان في موضعه فيرجع الملك وجماعته ويفعل ذلك ثلاث مرّات وفي الثالثة يعرضون على السلطان ثمّ يرجعون إلى محلّ وقوفهم فيخرج ملك آخر بجيشه ويفعل كذلك وهلمّ جرّاً

٣،١،٤٥ فإذا تمّ العرض خرج السلطان راكضاً وتتبع الملوك وذهب أوّلاً إلى أعظمهم ثمّ إلى مثله وإلى أقلّ منه فهكذا حتّى يمرّ عليهم أجمعين جبراً لخاطرهم وكلّما أتى قوماً صاحوا في وجهه بكلام يعظّمونه به وهو أنّهم يقولون له بصوت عالٍ برنس، حُرّ السلاطين، جنزير الملوك، أدّاب العاصي، فِرْتاك الجبال بلا ديوان، وغير ذلك فإذا تمّ العرض دخل السلطان داره ودخل وراءه جميع أرباب المناصب من الوزراء والملوك

---

١ الأصل: حضور.

each stands a guard sent by the sultan, who watches to see who eats the meat and who does not. If the guard informs the sultan that so-and-so did not eat, he immediately orders him seized, and if anyone makes the excuse that he is sick, or cannot attend, vessels containing some of the meat are sent to him with a trusted guard, who watches to see whether the man eats or not. If he refuses, he's seized, unless he is excused because of the severity of his illness. Some Darfurians say that a boy and a girl who have not yet reached puberty are brought and secretly slaughtered and that their flesh is cut up and put into the pots with the meat of the slaughtered animals. Some say that the boy's name has to be Muḥammad and the girl's Fāṭimah. If this were true it would be an extreme example of misbelief in God and His messenger. I did not witness it myself or attend such a ceremony, for I was a stranger, and strangers are not allowed to observe such things under any circumstances. All the same, I heard it from numerous people who swore mighty oaths that it was true, down to the last detail.[45]

Before the food is brought out, the soldiers all come and stand in a wide, 3.1.44
open space in front of the sultan's house. Then the sultan appears in all his finery and pomp, and each petty king, together with his followers, presents his army to him, one after another. The review takes place in the following fashion: each king takes his followers and runs until he reaches the sultan. If he is one of the notables, the sultan moves forward two or three paces from his company to meet him, and if he is not the sultan remains where he is. Then the king and his followers fall back. This is done three times, and on the third they parade before the sultan, after which they go back to where they were standing, and another king comes forward with his army and does the same, and so it continues.

When the review is over, the sultan comes out at a run and follows after 3.1.45
the petty kings, going first to the greatest of them, then to one who is like him in rank, then to one who is less than he, and so on till he has visited them all, so that none take offense. Each time he approaches a company they shout at him words extolling his might, crying out, "Mantle![46] Nobly born among sultans! Fetter of kings! Chastiser of the rebellious! Breaker and scatterer of the unlevied mountains!"[47] and so on. When the review is finished, the sultan enters his house, all the officers of state—viziers, petty kings, and sons of sultans—entering behind him, and he goes to the Drum House and takes a rod and strikes the drum called the Victorious three times.

وأولاد السلاطين فيدخل السلطان إلى دار النحاس ويأخذ قضيباً ويضرب به النقاريّة المسمّاة المنصورة[1] ثلاث ضربات والعجائز أي الحبّوبات محدّقات به بأيديهنّ الكرابج يضربنها على بعضها كما تقدّم ثمّ يمشين زوجاً زوجاً هكذا والسلطان بين الزوج الأخير حتّى يدخلن بالسلطان إلى محلّ جلوسه وأنا شاهدت ذلك

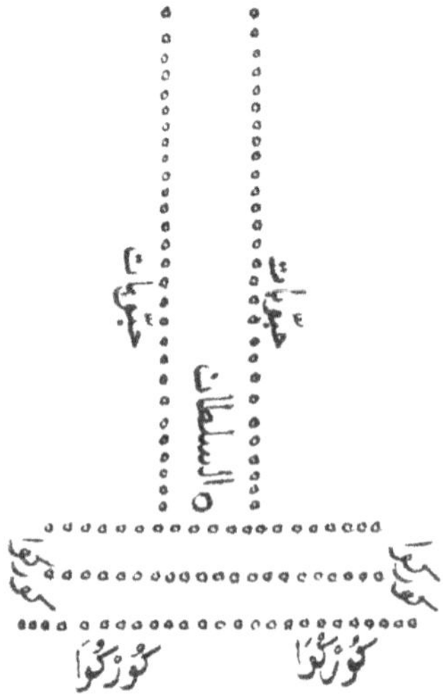

٤٦،١،٣ ثمّ تُفرّق الأطعمة كما ذكرنا وإذا كان بعض القوّاد أو الوزراء غائباً عن الفاشر في وقت تجليد النحاس ثمّ جاء بعد ذلك واتّهم بغدر أو خيانة يسقى من ماء كِيلي وهو ماء ينقع فيه ثمر شجرة مسمّاة بكيلي وثمره كالجوز تقول أهل دارفور إنّ المتهوم بشيء إذا شرب منه إن كان بريئاً يتقاياه في الحال وإن لم يكن بريئاً يشرب منه حتّى يمتلئ بطنه ولا يتقايأ حتّى أنّه ربّما شرب ملء خابية. أنا شاهدت ذلك[2] لكن في تهمة سرقة ولعلّ هذا من خواصّ النباتات لأنّ النبات في دارفور له خواصّ عجيبة سنذكرها بعد إن شاء الله تعالى

٤٧،١،٣ ومن عادة الفور أنّ السلطان له مزرعة معلومة يزرعها لنفسه في كلّ سنة وفي يوم بذر الحبّ فيها بعد الأمطار يخرج في مهرجان عظيم ويخرج معه من البنات الجميلات المتجمّلات بالحُليّ والحِلَى ما ينوف عن مائة صبيّة من محاظيه الخاصّة حاملات على رؤوسهنّ آنية فيها المآكل الفاخرة وهذه الأواني تسمّى بالعُمار مفردها عُمْرة فيمشين وراء جواد السلطان صحبة العبيد الصغار الحاملين للحراب المسمّيين كوركوا وأصحاب الصفافير وهؤلاء[3] يغنّون بغناء حال تصفيرهم وكوركوا الحاملون للحراب يغنّون معهم فحين تخرج البنات مع السلطان يغنّين[4] معهم أيضاً فيبقى لجموعهم صوت جميل جدًّا

[1] الأصل: منصورة. [2] أضيف للسياق. [3] الأصل: وهذه. [4] الأصل: تغنين.

The old women, which is to say the Grandmothers, surround him, holding their scourges and striking them against each other as previously described.[48] Then they walk two by two, as shown here the sultan between the last pair, until they've escorted the sultan to the place where he sits. I witnessed this.

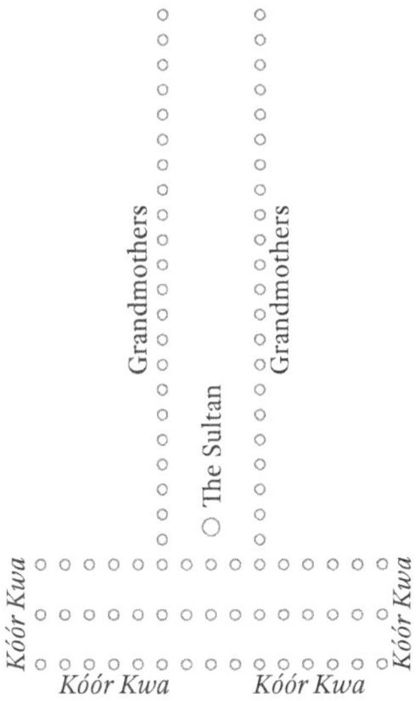

Next, the different dishes are distributed as we've described. If any vizier or army commander is absent from the sultan's seat of government at the time of the covering of the drums, and comes afterward and is accused of treachery or treason, he is given *kilí* water to drink.[49] This is water in which fruits of a tree called *kilí* have been steeped; the fruit resembles walnuts. The people of Darfur say that if the accused drinks and he is innocent, he will immediately vomit it back; if not, he will drink till his belly is full and not vomit even if he drink a caskful. I witnessed this, but the accusation was theft. This may be a property of plants, for the plants of Darfur have amazing properties, which we shall discuss later, the Almighty willing.[50] 3.1.46

Another custom of the Fur is that the sultan has a farm in a particular place 3.1.47
that he plants each year for himself.[51] On the day after the rains, when the seed is sown, he goes out in a mighty procession accompanied by beautiful girls adorned with trinkets and trappings—about a hundred maidens chosen from among his personal concubines, each carrying on her head a vessel full of costly foods, these vessels being called *ʿumār* (singular *ʿumrah*). These girls walk behind the sultan's horse, accompanied by the young spear-carrying slave boys called *kóór kwa* and by others with pipes. The girls sing while the others blow their pipes, and the spear-carrying *kóór kwa* sing along with them. In other words, when the girls go out with the sultan, they sing along with these others too, and their companies make a most beautiful sound.

وحين ما يصل السلطان إلى المزرعة ينزل عن جواده ويأخذ البذر ويأتي أحد عبيده يحفر الأرض بمسحاة معه ويرمي السلطان البذر وهو أوّل بذر يقع في الأرض في الجهة التي فيها السلطان فعند ذلك تتبعه الملوك والوزراء والقوّاد فيبذرون الحبّ ويزرعون المزرعة في أسرع وقت وبعد تمام زرع المزرعة يحضر الطعام المحمول على رؤوس البنات المذكورة فيوضع أمام السلطان فيأكل منه هو ووزراؤه ثمّ يركب في مهرجانه حتّى يصل إلى دار ملكه وهذا اليوم من الأيّام المشهورة في دارفور ٣،١،٤٨

الفصل الثالث في مناصب ملوك الفور[١]

اعلم أنّ واجب الوجود تقدّست ذاته عن المعين لمّا كان منفردًا بالقدرة المطلقة والإرادة التامّة المتصرّفة أحوج الملوك إلى الوزراء والمدبّرين والمعينين ليعلم عجزهم عن الاستقلال في تدبير ممالكهم ومصالحهم ولولا ذلك الاحتياج لطغوا وبغوا أكثر ممّا هم فيه من الطغيان بل ربّما ادّعوا الألوهيّة التي لا تليق إلّا بذاته العليّة لكن خصّ كلّ إقليم بترتيب وتنظيم فلهذا تجد أسماء مناصب وزراء[٢] الخلفاء كانت مغايرة لأسماء مناصب وزراء الملوك الآن وأسماء مناصب وزراء ملوك هذا الزمن متخالفة أيضًا ففي مملكة آل عثمان أسماء المناصب الوزير الأعظم والكَتْخُدا والخازِنْدار والسلاح دار والمُهُرْدار والديوت دار وجوخه[٣] دار وسَرْ بوّابين وقابجي باشي وغير ذلك من توتجي باشي وشُرْبَتْجي باشي وقهوجي باشي وقفطان أغاسي وبشكير أغاسي وباشات وأمراء الألوية وأمراء الألايات ٣،١،٤٩

وأمّا أهل دارفور فإنّهم لتعظيمهم للسلطان لم ينتبهوا إلّا إلى جسم السلطان فسمّوا المناصب بأسماء أعضائه فأوّل مناصبهم أُرُونْدُولُگ وهو منصب عظيم القدر صاحبه يكنّى برأس السلطان ولهذا المنصب أقطاع عظيمة وبلاد وصاحبه لا يسلّم عليه ٣،١،٥٠

١ الأصل: في مناصب ملوك في [كذا] الفور وملابسهم وكيفية مجلس السلطان وغير ذلك. ٢ الأصل: الوزراء.
٣ الأصل: خوجه

When the sultan arrives at the farm, he dismounts from his horse and takes the seed grain, while one of his slaves comes and makes a hole in the ground with a mattock he has brought with him. The sultan then throws in the grain, this being the first seed to fall on the ground in the part of the country where the sultan is. At this, the chieftains, viziers, and army commanders follow suit and sow grain, getting the farm sown in the shortest possible time. Once the whole farm has been sown, the food that was carried on the heads of the girls is brought and placed before the sultan, and he and his ministers eat. Then he rides in procession as before, until he reaches his royal seat. This is one of Darfur's most celebrated holidays. 3.1.48

Section 3: On the Offices Held by the Kings of the Fur[52]

He of Necessary Existence, whose essence, unique in the absoluteness of its power and the untrammeled nature of its perfect will, is sanctified beyond dependence on any helper, has caused kings to have need of viziers, officials, and aides, so that their powerlessness to act independently in the disposal of their kingdoms and interests may be known. Were it not for that need, they would behave even more tyrannically and oppressively than they already do. Indeed, they might lay claim to the divinity that sorts ill with any but His sublime essence. To each land, however, He has given its own particular regulation and organization, which is why one finds that the names of the offices of the viziers of caliphs differ from those of the viziers of present-day kings, and likewise that the names of the offices of the viziers of present-day kings differ one from the other. Thus, in the Ottoman state, the names of the officers are chief vizier, minister of home affairs, keeper of the treasury, keeper of the arms, keeper of the seal, keeper of the pen case, keeper of the wardrobe, and chief doorman, as well as head doorkeeper and others of the same style such as head tobacconist, head sherbet maker, head coffee maker, supervisor of the caftans, and supervisor of the towels, not to mention the pashas, brigade commanders, and regimental commanders. 3.1.49

The people of Darfur, however, so revere their sultan that their sole point of reference is his body, and they consequently name their offices after its parts.[53] The first of their offices is the orondolong, an office of great power whose holder is known as the sultan's head.[54] Attached to this office are vast fiefs and 3.1.50

إلّا بدونگاراي دونگا وترفع السجّادة أمامه كالسلطان وصاحب هذا المنصب إذا كان السلطان مسافرًا أو قانصاً وظيفته أن يمشي بعساكره أمام الجيش كلّه لا يسبقه أحد

٥١،١،٣ وثانيها منصب الكامنَه وهو في العظم والجلالة أعلى من أُروندولوگ ويكنّى عنه برقبة السلطان لكن من عادة الفور أنّ السلطان إذا قُتل في الحرب وسلم الكامنه حتّى رجع إلى محلّ الأمن يقتلونه لكن يخنقونه سرًّا ويولّون غيره للسلطان المتولّي وإذا مات السلطان على فراشه لا يقتل الكامنه وهذا الكامنه يسمّى بلغة أعجام الفور أبا فوري ومعناه أبو الفور ولصاحب هذا المنصب أقطاع جليلة وعساكر كثيرة ويفعل مثلما يفعل السلطان ووظيفته أن يمشي خلف جيش أُروندولوگ

٥٢،١،٣ وثالثها أَبَا أُومَاگْ وهو قرين الكامنه في كل شيء وهو كناية عن فقرات ظهر السلطان ووظيفته أن يمشي خلف الجيوش بجيش لا يعقبه أحد وإن أعقب الجيش عدوّ فيه كفاية لدفعه والذبّ عن الجيش حتّى يدرك ويمدّ بالجيوش

٥٣،١،٣ ورابعها أباديما وهو أعظم ممّن تقدّم جلالة وأبّهة وعساكر[١] ويحكم على اثني عشر ملكاً من ملوك الفور وله إقليم واسع يسمّى تموركه وله جميع ما للسلطان من الشارات والأبّهة ما عدا النحاس فإنّ طبله دنقار فقط[٢] وهو كناية عن ساعد السلطان اليمين ووظيفته أن يمشي هو وعساكره عن يمين السلطان

٥٤،١،٣ وخامسها منصب التكنياوي وهو قرين أباديما في كلّ شيء وهو كناية عن الساعد الأيسر للسلطان ويحكم على اثني عشر ملكاً أيضاً من ملوك الجهة الشماليّة وله إقليم واسع

٥٥،١،٣ وسادسها منصب الأب الشيخ وهو أعلى من جميع ما ذكر ولا فرق بينه وبين السلطان وأوامره تنفذ على جميع من ذكر وغيرهم وله إقطاعات جليلة وإقليم واسع وصاحب هذا المنصب مطلوق السيف يقتل بغير إذن وجميع أهل المملكة تحت يده وهو كناية عن عجيزة السلطان وقد تقدّم بعض ذلك في حديث الأب الشيخ محمّد كرّا

١ الأصل: عساكرا. ٢ أضيف للسياق.

villages. The fief holder is always greeted with "*Dóngá rǎy dóngá!*" and a carpet is taken up and carried before him just as it is for the sultan. If the sultan is on the move or hunting, it is the task of the holder of this office to march in front of the army, and no one may precede him.

The second office is that of the kaamíne, which is higher in might and majesty than the orondolong. He is known as the sultan's neck. If the sultan is killed in war and the kaamíne escapes to a place of safety, it is the Fur custom to kill him; they strangle him in secret, then appoint someone else for the incoming sultan. If the sultan dies in his bed, the kaamíne is not killed. The kaamíne is called by Fur speakers ába poor-ii, meaning "Father of the Fur."[55] The holder of the office has magnificent fiefs and many soldiers and acts just like the sultan. His task is to march behind the troops of the orondolong.[56] 3.1.51

The third is the ába ǎw mang, who is the kaamíne's opposite number in everything. The term means the sultan's spine, and it is his task to march at the armies' rear accompanied by an army behind which no one else may march. If an enemy is pursuing the main army, this army of his is sufficient to repel it and keep it at bay until it can be relieved and rendered assistance by the main armies. 3.1.52

The fourth is the ába dima'ng,[57] who is greater than all the preceding in majesty, pomp, and number of soldiers. He commands twelve of the petty kings of the Fur, has an extensive territory known as Tomorókkóngá, and all the insignia and pomp of the sultan except for the copper drums, for his drum is the *dinqār*.[58] He is known as the sultan's right arm, and his task is to march with his soldiers on the sultan's right. 3.1.53

The fifth is the tikináwi,[59] who is the ába dima'ng's opposite number in everything and is known as the sultan's left arm. He commands twelve of the northern petty kings and has an extensive territory. 3.1.54

The sixth is the office of shaykh-father. He is higher than all of the abovementioned—there is effectively no difference between him and the sultan—and his commands are obeyed by all the preceding officeholders and others. He has magnificent estates and an extensive territory. The holder of this office carries a naked sword and may kill without permission. All the natives of the kingdom are his to dispose of. He corresponds to the sultan's buttocks. I mentioned some of this earlier when speaking of Shaykh-Father Muḥammad Kurrā.[60] 3.1.55

وسابعها مناصب الأمناء وهي أربعة كلّ واحد منهم يدعى أميناً وأصحاب هذه المناصب لها أقطاع وعساكر وليس لها من شارات الملك شيء وهؤلاء الأربعة ملازمون لمجلس السلطان ٥٦،١،٣

وثامنها مناصب الكُورَايات وهي مناصب جليلة القدر إلّا أنّها أقلّ من مناصب الأمناء رتبة ومناصب الكورايات أربعة أيضاً ٥٧،١،٣

وتاسعها منصب سُومِنْدُقُلَهْ وصاحبه عظيم القدر ذو أبّهة عظيمة وأقطاع وأموال وافرة ويليه منصب كوركوا ٥٨،١،٣

وأعلى من هذين منصب وَرِيّبَايَهْ وهو منصب جليل عظيم ومن[1] عادة ملوك الفور أنّ صاحب هذا المنصب لا يكون إلّا خصيّاً لأنّه ينال منصب الأبوّة بعد موت الأب الشيخ وتقدّم لنا أنّ منصب الأب الشيخ لا يتولّاه إلّا خصيّ وصاحب هذا المنصب يحكم على جميع الخصيان الموكّلين بحريم السلطان وهو أيضاً صاحب غضب السلطان وتحت يده الحبس فكلّما غضب السلطان على إنسان أعطاه له فيسجنه في سجنه وتحت يده عساكر كثيرة ومعنى وريبايه بالفوراويّة باب الحريم وصاحب هذا المنصب تحت أمر الأب الشيخ ويليه منصب ملك وَرَّادَايَيَهْ ومعناه ملك باب الرجال ولكلّ بيت من بيوت الملوك والوزراء بابان أحدهما للرجال والثاني للنساء فباب الرجال يسمّى ورادايه وباب النساء يسمّى وريبايه ٥٩،١،٣

ويليهما منصب ملك العبيديّة وهو منصب جليل القدر صاحبه يحكم على جميع عبيد السلطان الخارجين عن داره الذين في البلاد بنسائهم وأولادهم وكذلك تحت يده مواشي السلطان وآلات السفر من خيم وقرب وغير ذلك ٦٠،١،٣

ويليه منصب ملك القَوّارين أي المكّاسين وهو منصب جليل صاحبه يحكم على جميع المكّاسين وجميع الجلّابة وله أقطاع وعساكر عظيمة ٦١،١،٣

١ الأصل: من.

The seventh is the office of counselor. There are four, each of whom bears this title. The holders of this office have estates and soldiers but none of the insignia of the king. The four of them are attached to the sultan's assembly.[61] 3.1.56

Eighth is the office of the groom, which is a position of great power but one rank lower than that of counselor. There are likewise four holders of this office. 3.1.57

The ninth is the office of the overseer of the pages' place.[62] Its holder has great power and is possessed of great pomp, estates, and abundant wealth. After him comes the office of the chief of[63] the *kóór kwa*. 3.1.58

Higher than either of the immediately preceding offices is that of órré bayyâ.[64] This is a great and powerful office. It is the custom of the Fur kings that its holder be a eunuch, because he will assume the office of the shaykh-father following the death of the holder of that title, and, as we have seen earlier, the office of shaykh-father may only be held by a eunuch. The holder of this post commands all the eunuchs in charge of the sultan's women and is also, as "keeper of the sultan's anger," in charge of the prison. In other words, when the sultan is angry with someone, he gives him to the órré bayyâ, and the latter puts him in his prison. He has many soldiers at his command. The meaning of órré bayyâ in Fur is "the women's door," and the holder of the office is under the command of the shaykh-father. He is followed by the office of "master of the órré dee," meaning master of the men's door, for every house belonging to a petty king or vizier has two doors, one for men and one for women: the men's door is called órré dee, the women's órré bayyâ. 3.1.59

Next comes the office of master of the royal slaves. This is an office of high power whose holder commands all those of the sultan's slaves who are outside his house in the villages, along with their women and children.[65] He also has at his disposal the sultan's livestock and travel equipment, such as tents and waterskins. 3.1.60

After him comes the master of the *qawwārīn*, meaning the market-toll collectors. This is a high office whose holder commands all market-toll collectors and all traders. He has large estates and numerous soldiers. 3.1.61

وأعلى منه منصب ملك الجبّايين وصاحبه في أبّهة عظيمة وملك كبير وهو ملك الجبّايين أي الذين يجبون الغلال من البلاد ومعنى الجباية أنّهم يأخذون عشرما يخرج من الحبوب ويجعلونها في مطامير لاحتياج السلطان ٦٢،١،٣

وبعد ذلك ملوك كثيرة فحكّام الأقاليم عندهم يسمّون الشَرَاتِي واحده شَرْتَايْ وحكّام القبائل يسمّون دمالج واحده دُمْلُج ولكلّ من الشراتى عساكر كثيرة ولكلّ من الدمالج أعوان وهؤلاء خلاف السلاطين الصغار الذين ذكرناهم سابقاً ٦٣،١،٣

ثمّ اعلم أن جميع من ذكرمن أرباب المناصب لا يعطيهم السلطان راتباً ولا مرتّب لهم عنده بل كلّ ذي منصب له أقطاع يأخذ منها أموالاً وما يأخذه من الأموال[1] يشترى به خيلاً وسلاحاً ودروعاً ولبوساً ويفرّقها في العساكر ٦٤،١،٣

وكيفيّة ما يأخذ هو أنّ زكاة الحبوب كلّها للسلطان كزكاة الماشية فلا ينالون منهما شيئاً وإنّما لكلّ ملك منهم أفدنة كثيرة يزرعها دخناً[2] وذرة وسمسماً وفولاً وقطناً تزرعها الرعايا وتحصدها وتدرسها له قهراً عليهم ٦٥،١،٣

وله الهامل وهو الضالّ من رقيق وبقر وغنم وحمير يبيعونها له ويأخذ ثمنها وله التقادم وهي الهدايا التي يقدّمونها له حين التولية والقدوم على البلاد وله الخَطِيّة وهي في عرفهم أموال يدفعها الجاني للحاكم ويسمّى عندهم بالحكم إذا شجّ إنسان آخر يؤخذ من الشاجّ مال ويدفع للحاكم وإذا أحبل رجل امرأة في الحرام يؤخذ من كلّ منهما مال على قدر حاليهما أيضاً وله الدم وهو في عرفهم إذا قُتل قتيل ووُدِيَ يشارك الحاكم أقارب القتيل في الدية سواء كانت دية العمد أو دية الخطأ وذلك خلاف المظالم التي يأخذونها بغير حقّ وخلاف الأعمال الشاقّة التي يكلّفونهم بها لأنّهم يبنون لهم بيوتهم ويسخّرونهم في جميع أعمالهم ٦٦،١،٣

ومن مناصب الفور ملك الموجيه وإنّما أخّرناه لطول الكلام عليه وغرابته وغرابة ٦٧،١،٣

١ الأصل: الامول. ٢ الأصل: ذخنا.

Higher than this is the office of master of the tax ollectors, whose holder has great pomp and is an important *malik*. He is master of the tax collectors, i.e., those who collect the grain from the villages, "tax" meaning here that they take one-tenth of the grain that is produced and place it in silos for the sultan's use. 3.1.62

There are many more petty kings besides. They call the rulers of the different territories *sharātī* (singular: *shartāy*) and the rulers of the tribes *damālij* (singular: *dimlij*). Each *shartāy* has many soldiers and each *dimlij*[66] has his helpers. This is not to mention the petty sultans of whom we spoke earlier.[67] 3.1.63

The sultan gives none of the abovementioned officeholders a salary, and none of them is inscribed on his payroll. Instead, every officeholder has an estate, the revenue from which he uses to buy horses, weapons, coats of mail, and clothes to distribute to his soldiers. 3.1.64

Under their tax collection system, the zakat tax on grain goes in its entirety to the sultan, as does the zakat on cattle[68]—the petty kings have no share in it. Each of them does, however, have many feddans that he sows with millet, sorghum, sesame, fava beans, and cotton, which his subjects cultivate, harvest, and thresh under threat of force. 3.1.65

The master of the tax collectors also gets "the strays," which is anything that has gone astray, whether slaves, cattle, sheep and goats, or donkeys. These are sold for him and he takes the proceeds. And he receives "the gifts," which is what they give him on his appointment and on his arrival in the villages, and "the offense," which in their custom is property forfeited to the ruler by a criminal; they also call it "the sentence." If one man gives another a sword blow to the head, money is taken from the offender and given to the ruler, and if a man gets a woman pregnant out of wedlock, money is taken from both, each according to his or her circumstances. He also gets "the bloodwite," which in their custom is when a man is killed unlawfully and blood money paid; the ruler then shares in the blood money with the relatives, whether the killing was deliberate or accidental. And this is not to mention the illegal imposts that they take without justification or the hard labor they impose on the people, who build their houses for them and whom they use as forced labor in all their works. 3.1.66

Another office of state among the Fur is master of the *mooge*, which we've kept till last because it requires such a long discussion and because of the strangeness of the *mooge*—both the office and the behavior of those who 3.1.67

المنصب وغرابة أفعال أهله وهو عندهم أدنى المناصب وأقلّها رتبة لكنّ الكلام عليه يحتاج إلى تمهيد وهو أنّ صاحب الحكمة الأزليّة والسلطنة الأبديّة واهب العقل ومانح الفضل وهب لكلّ إنسان عقلاً يميّز به الخير ليتبعه من المكروه ليحذره وأودع في كلّ إنسان حبّ رأى نفسه وعقله بحيث يرى أنّ عقله أتمّ من عقل غيره ورأيه أحسن من رأى غيره إلّا من بصره الله بعيوبه وعلّمه عجز نفسه عن تدبير جلب مصالحها ودفع مضارّها

٣،١،٦٨ وإذا تقرّر ذلك فنقول من طبيعة بلاد الفور الميل إلى اللّهو والاستهزاء واللعب والطرب يستفزّهم أدنى مطرب فتراهم لا تخلو أوقاتهم عن مطرب ملوكاً كانوا أو سوقة ولذلك استحضروا جميع ما يمكنهم من آلات الطرب فتجد كلّ ملك له غلمان صغار حسان الأصوات وهم المسمّون كوركوا ومعهم صفافير يصفّرون بها صفيراً هو في نفس الأمر غناء مع حسن أصوات الصفافير وحسن أصوات الغلمان فيسمع من جميع ذلك صوت حسن

٣،١،٦٩ وكيفيّة ذلك أنّ الملك إن كان عنده من الغلمان عشرة مثلاً يكون منهم أرباب الصفافير اثنين أو ثلاثة والرابع بيده قرعة جافّة خاوية الباطن مستطيلة أحد طرفيها غليظ والطرف الثاني رقيق يقبض عليه باليد صورتها هكذا

فيجعلون فيها بعض حصباء ويقبضها الغلام بشرط أن يكون فمها منسدّاً بالقار ويهزّها فيسمع للحصى فيها صوت يوفّق على أصوات الصفافير والستّة الباقون يغنّون وربّما أخرج السلطان بعض جواريه مزيّنات حاملات لحومها ويُجعل في خوابي ويُترك ستّة أيّام من الأطعمة للسلطان ماشيات خلفه صحبة الغلمان فيغنّين مع الغلمان والصفافير وربّما زادوا معهما طبلاً من خشب مستطيل كالطبلة المسمّاة في

hold it. It is, in their view, the lowest office and least in rank. Before speaking of it, however, we must provide some background. The Lord of Eternal Wisdom and Everlasting Power, who has given us minds and granted us His benevolence, has provided each human being with a mind with which to distinguish good, that he or she may follow it, from evil, that he or she may be on guard against it. Likewise, He has placed in each human being a love of the opinion adopted by his or her own soul and mind, with the result that every person believes his or her mind to be more perfect and his or her opinion to be better than anyone else's—exception being made for those to whom God has granted insight into their faults and taught the powerlessness of their appetites to secure what is good for them and fend off what is bad.

In view of this, we can state that a tendency to sport and levity, to play- 3.1.68
fulness and ecstasy, is in the nature of the Fur. The least stimulus to enjoyment provokes them. You find that their every moment, whether they be kings or commoners, is lived to the accompaniment of a singer. They have therefore assembled every musical instrument possible, and you find that every petty king has young boys with beautiful voices, these being what are called *kóór kwa*. They have pipes on which they make a whistling sound that is at the same time a kind of singing. The beauty of the pipes combines with that of the boys' voices to produce lovely music.

This is done in the following fashion: if a king has, for example, ten 3.1.69
of these boys, two or three will have pipes while a fourth will have in his hand a dry, hollow gourd, oblong in shape, wide at one end and narrow at the other, so that the hand can grasp it. It looks like this:

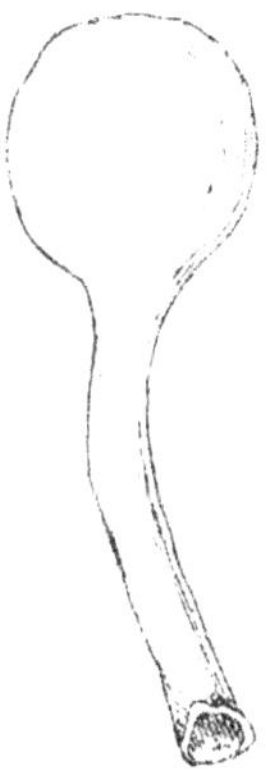

Into this they put some pebbles and the boy holds it and shakes it, the mouth having first been necessarily plugged with pitch. The stones inside produce a sound that accompanies that of the pipes, and the six remaining boys sing. Sometimes the sultan sends out some of his slave girls dressed in their finery, carrying vessels of food for the sultan. They walk behind the troupe of boys and sing along with them and the pipes. To these instruments they sometimes add elongated wooden drums like the one called in the common parlance of Egypt *darabukkah*

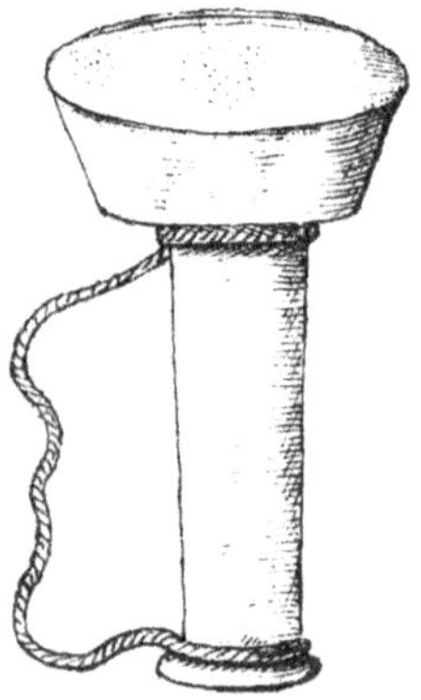

عرفمصر بالدرابّكة ويسمّى عندهم تِجِّلْ وصورته هكذا
وله علاّقة كما في الصورة فيدخل الضارب يده من العلاّقة
ويضع العلاّقة على كتفه ويصير الطبل تحت إبطه ويضرب
عليه بكلتا يديه نقرات محكمة على صوت الصفافير وما
يغنّونه يكون بلسان الفور ولهم معلّمون يعلّمونهم التصفير
والغناء والضرب على الطبل المذكور

والمشاة الذين يمشون أمامه وبين يديه يغنّون غناء ٣،١،٧٠
وحدهم وكيفيّة ذلك أنّهم يكونوا كراديس كراديس يغنّي من كلّ كردوس واحد والباقي
يردّ عليه بصوت عالٍ ولذلك إذا ركب السلطان تضرب الطبول وتغنّي جميع الناس
مُشاةً ورُكبانًا فيسمع لذلك ضجّة عظيمة مع أصوات الصفافير وغناء الغلمان يخشى
الإنسان على سمعه منه لقوّته وهذه الصفافير تسمّى طير الصعيد وذلك أنّ ببلاد
صعيدهم طيور لها أصوات حسان فاخترعوا هذه الصفافير على شكل أصواتها

وينضمّ لتلك الأصوات أصوات الموجيه وهذا اللفظ في لغة الفور يطلق ٣،١،٧١
على الواحد والجمع وهم طائفة عظيمة لها ملك مخصوص وهو في عرف الفور
كالخلبوص أو المسخرة في عرف أهل مصر أو كالسوتري في عرف الترك لكنّ الموجيه
يخالف ما ذكر لأنّه يتولّى قتل من يأمر السلطان بقتله وصفة
الموجيه أنّ يلبس على رأسه عصابة فيها صفيحة من حديد
مستديرة الشكل مع التجويف وفي العصابة المذكورة قطعة
من حديد أيضاً كالمسمار معلّقة بخيط محرّرة على التجويف
الذي في الصفيحة بحيث إذا هزّ رأسه تضرب التجويف
المذكور ويسمع لها رنّة عليه وأعلى منهما في العصابة
ريشة أو ريشتان من ريش النعام وصورتها هكذا

وعلى الطرطور ودع وخرز معلّق أيضاً وفي رجله اليمنى خلخالان

and which they call *togjêl.* It looks like this and has a strap attached, as in the illustration. The player puts his hand through the strap and places it over his shoulder so that the drum is under his arm and, using both hands, he strikes it with sharp blows that are closely matched to the sound of the pipes. They sing in the language of the Fur and have teachers who teach them how to play the pipes, sing, and beat the drum.

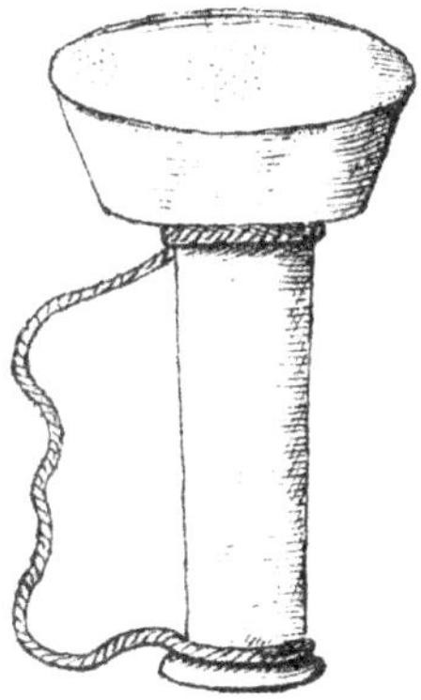

The foot soldiers who walk before and around the sultan sing on their own, forming small groups, each of which has one particular singer to whom the rest respond in a loud voice. Thus, when the sultan rides out and the drums beat and everyone, mounted and on foot, sings, a mighty clamor is heard, and this, together with the sound of the pipes and the songs of the boys, strikes fear into all who hear it because it is so loud. The pipes are called "birds of the High Plain" because in that region there are birds with beautiful voices which they call by that name, and they invented these pipes to imitate the sounds these birds make. 3.1.70

To these voices are added those of the *mooge,* a Fur word that is used for both singular and plural. The *mooge* are a mighty company, with their own master, the word corresponding in the common language of the Fur to *khalbūṣ* ("jester"), or in that of the Egyptians to *maskharah* ("buffoon"), or in that of the Turks to *soytarı* ("clown"). The *mooge,* however, is different from these because he is responsible for executing anyone the sultan orders killed. The *mooge* wears a band on his head that incorporates a round, concave sheet of metal. Inside this headband is another piece of metal like a nail, hung from a thread adjusted to fit the depression in the metal sheet. Thus, when he shakes his head, it strikes against the depression and makes a ringing sound. Placed above both of these in the headband are one or two ostrich feathers. The headband looks like this: On the tall cap he wears are shells and beads that also hang down. There are two metal anklets on his right foot and one on his left. Under his arm is a small 3.1.71

من الحديد وفي اليسرى خلخال واحد وتحت إبطه جراب صغير مستطيل إذا حلّ عصابته وطرطوره يضعهما فيه وبيده عصا معوّج أعلاها هكذا

معلّق فيه جلاجل فيقف بين يدي السلطان من الموجيه اثنان أو ثلاثة إن كان السلطان في ديوانه وإن كان في سفر أو قنص مشى أمامه أربعة أو خمسة وكلّ منهم يغنّي ويرقص ويقول كلاماً مضحكاً يضحك منه سامعه ويحاكي نباح الكلب وصوت الهرّ وغناؤه بكلام الفور لا بالعربيّ وليس في رقصه تكسّر بل يهزّ رأسه يمنة ويسرة ويضرب إحدى ساقيه بالأخرى فترنّ الحديدة التي في العصابة على رأسه وترنّ الخلخال التي في ساقيه وإذا كان السلطان مسافرًا أو قانصاً لا يغنّون بل يصيحون جميعاً صيحة واحدة بقوّة أصواتهم يقولون يا يا وهكذا مادام السلطان راكبًا

ولا خصوصيّة في ذلك للسلطان بل كل ملك من ملوك الفور الكبار له موجيه يقف أمامه في ديوانه ويمشي قدّامه في سفره والموجيه لا يخشون بأس السلطان ولا غضبه ولهم جراءة عظيمة على السلطان فمن دونه لا يكتمون السلطان أمرًا بحيث أنّهم إذا سمعوا أمرًا فظيعاً يقولونه في محفله وينسبون الكلام لقائله حقيرًا كان أو جليلاً لا يخافون لومة لائم وإذا أراد السلطان إشاعة أمر أو إعلان حكم أمر الموجيه أن ينادي به فينادي به الموجيه بعد المغرب وقبل العشاء نداء يسمعه الخاصّ والعامّ ٧٢،١،٣

ومما اتّفق أنّ السلطان عبد الرحمٰن كان يحبّ العلماء ويكثر الجلوس معهم في ليله ونهاره وقلّما يجلس مجلساً إلّا ومعه عالم أو اثنان فاغتاظ الوزراء منه وقالوا كيف يتركنا ويجلس مع هؤلاء لكن إن مات هذا السلطان لا نولّي علينا بعده رجلاً يقرأ أبدًا فسمع ذلك أحد الموجيه فأمهلهم حتّى جلس السلطان في ديوانه وحضر أولئك الوزراء فجاء الموجيه وقال بلسان الفور كلاماً معناه نحن ما بقينا نولّي علينا ٧٣،١،٣

oblong bag into which he puts his headband and cap when he's not wearing them, and he carries a stick with a crook at the top like this

to which jingles are attached. Two or three such *mooge* stand before the sultan when he holds audience. When he is on the move or hunting, four or five go ahead of him, each singing and dancing and saying funny things to make those who hear them laugh, and imitating the barking of dogs or the sounds of cats. Their songs are in the language of the Fur, not in Arabic, and there is no bending of the body in their dancing; they shake their heads right and left and strike one leg against the other, making the metal piece in the bands on their heads ring, and the anklets on their feet too. If the sultan is on the move or hunting, instead of singing they all give one great shout together at the top of their lungs, going, "*Yaa! Yaa!*" and they keep this up as long as the sultan is mounted.

This is not peculiar to the sultan: each of the more important petty kings 3.1.72
of the Fur has his *mooge* who stand before him in his court and walk in front of him when he's traveling. The *mooge* do not fear the sultan's evil or fury and are extremely daring with him and with those below him. They hide nothing from the sultan—when they hear something scandalous, they announce it in his assembly, naming the one who said it, be he lowly or mighty, without fear of censure. If the sultan wishes to spread some item of news far and wide, or announce some judgment, he orders the *mooge* to cry it. They do so between the sunset and evening prayers with a cry that reaches elite and commoner alike.

Sultan ʿAbd al-Raḥmān happened to love the company of scholars of reli- 3.1.73
gion and spent much time sitting with them by day and by night. Rarely would he sit in his assembly without a couple of them. This angered the viziers, who complained and said, "How can he shun us and spend his time with them? Once this sultan dies, however, we shall never again allow to rule over us any man who can read!" One of the *mooge* heard this and left them to their own devices until the sultan was seated in his court and these same viziers were in attendance. Then the *mooge* came and said something in Fur to the effect that "No one who knows how to read or write is ever again going to rule over us." The sultan turned to him and asked, "How so?" and the man replied, "Because you shun your viziers and spend your time with scholars." This made the sultan

من يعرف القراءة والكتابة فالتفت إليه السلطان وقال لِمَ ذلك قال لأنّك تترك الوزراء وتجلس مع العلماء فاغتاظ السلطان لذلك ونظر إليه نظرة الغضب فخاف الموجيه أن يسطو عليه فقال ما ذنبي أنا سمعت هؤلاء وأشار إلى الوزراء يقولون ذلك فقلته فالتفت السلطان إليهم ووبّخهم على ذلك وأراد القبض عليهم فما خلصوا منه إلّا بجهد ومشقّة قلت والجاهلون لأهل العلم أعداء

ومن ذلك ما حكاه لي بعض الثقات بدارفور أن السلطان تيراب السالف الذكر صنع وليمة لأمرنسيته وحين حضر الطعام تتبّعه لينظر أيّ الطعام أحسن فجاء إلى طعام صنعته إيا كري كنانة وكشف عنه فأعجبه فأمر به للعلماء فأبت عليه وقالت أأنا عندك بهذه المنزلة تعطي طعامي للمشايخ وطعام غيري للوزراء والملوك[1] فقال إنّما أمرت به للمشايخ لحسنه ولتحصل لك بركتهم فقالت دع طعامي تأكله الوزراء والملوك ولا حاجة لي ببركتهم فقال لا يأكله غير العلماء فقالت لا وحياتك لا تأكله العلماء وغلبت عليه حتّى أرسله للملوك واختار من طعام غيرها للعلماء ٣،١،٧٤

وطائفة الموجيه من أفقر أهل دارفور لأنّهم ليس لهم حرفة إلّا السؤال فإنّهم دائمًا يقصدون الأمراء ويتكفّفون الناس وتخاف الأمراء منهم ويكرمونهم لأنّهم لا يكتمون حديثًا إن أحسن إليهم أحد أثنوا عليه وأشاعوا الذكر بكرمه وإن أحرمهم أحد ذمّوه وأشاعوا ذمّه فهم في ذلك كالشعراء من أعطاهم مدحوه ومن منعهم هجوه ٣،١،٧٥

ومن مناصب الفور منصب إيا كري وقد أسلفنا ذكره ومنصب الحبّوبات وقد ذكرناه أيضًا وإن كان للسلطان المتولّي أم فلها منصب وإن كان له[2] جدّة فلها منصب أيضًا لكن هذان المنصبان ليسا مقرّرين بل يطرآن عند وجودهما ولقد رأيت أمّ السلطان محمّد فضل وهي جارية وخشاء لو بيعت في دارفور لما كانت تساوي عشرة من الفرانسا ورأيت جدّته وهي عجوز وخشاء من أقبح ما يرى في عجائز السودان وكانت ناقصة العقل ومن نقص عقلها كانت تجلس على كرسيّ وتحملها الرجال على ٣،١،٧٦

١ المكوك. ٢ أضيف للسياق.

furious and he looked at him angrily. The *mooge* feared he'd assault him and said, "What's it got to do with me?" and he pointed to the viziers. "I heard those men saying that, so I repeated it." The sultan turned to them, rebuked them, and wanted to have them arrested, and they were only saved from his anger after great effort and trouble. Truly, I observed, "The ignorant are ever the enemy of those with knowledge!"[69]

A reliable source in Darfur told me a similar story to the effect that Sultan Tayrāb, mentioned earlier, held a banquet for some reason I've forgotten, and when the food came he inspected it closely to see which dishes were best. When he came to one made by Iyā Kūrī Kinānah and took off the cover, he found it to his liking, so he ordered it be taken to the scholars. However, she objected, saying, "Is my standing with you so low that you would give my food to shaykhs and the food made by others to viziers and kings?" "I only ordered it taken to the shaykhs," he replied, "because it's so good, and so that you can benefit from their grace." "Let my food be eaten by the viziers and kings," she said. "I have no need of their grace!" "None but the shaykhs shall taste it!" he said, but she said, "I beg you, don't let the shaykhs eat it!" In the end, she had her way, and he sent it to the petty kings and chose food made by someone else for the scholars. 3.1.74

The *mooge* are numbered among the poorest people in Darfur because their only profession is begging. This is why they always target princes and leave ordinary people alone. The princes fear them and treat them generously because they disclose everything they hear. If someone treats them well, they praise him and put it about how generous he is, but if someone is stingy with them, they hold him up to scorn and make it known to all. In this they are like poets: they write eulogies to those who give them gifts and ridicule those who rebuff them.[70] 3.1.75

Among the other offices of the Fur are that of iyā kurī, to which we have alluded earlier,[71] and that of the Grandmothers, which we have also mentioned.[72] Also, if the reigning sultan has a mother, she holds an office, and if he has a grandmother, she holds one too. These offices, however, are not permanent: they come into being when these two persons exist. I saw Sultan Muḥammad Faḍl's mother, and she was an uncouth slave woman. If put on sale in Darfur, she wouldn't have fetched ten francs. I saw his grandmother too, and she was an uncouth old crone, one of the ugliest women I ever saw among the Blacks, and a half-wit to boot—witness the fact that when she went on a 3.1.76

أعناقهم[1] للسفر البعيد ومعها من العساكر خلق كثير ووشى إليها بعض الناس بأنّ أهل دارفور يقولون إنّ هذه الخادم قد طغت وبغت فحين سمعت ذلك جلست في ديوانها وأحضرت جميع أتباعها وقالت أنا الحادم الحادم جاب الفضّة وجاب الفضّة الذهب وقولها أنا الحادم بالحاء المهملة ومرادها الخادم بالمعجمة إلّا أنّها لا تقدر على النطق بالخاء المعجمة لعجمتها وهناك مناصب أخر أعرضنا عن ذكرها لحقارتها

الفصل الرابع في كيفيّة مجلس السلطان[2]

وأمّا كيفيّة مجلس السلطان فاعلم أنّ بيت سلطان الفور في بلده المسمّاة بالفاشر ٣،١،٧٧
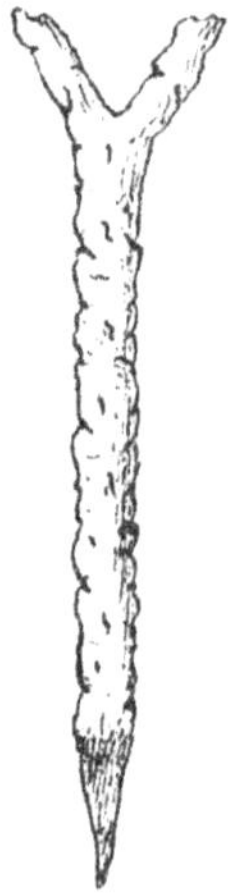
والناس حوله ولهذا جعل لبيته بابان أحدهما وهو الأعظم هو المسمّى وَرَّيْدَيَا معناه باب الرجال والثاني هو المسمى وَرَّيْبَايَا ومعناه باب النساء وفي كلّ منهما له مجلس فمجلس وريديا هو الديوان الأكبر وهو بعد أن يدخل الداخل من الباب الأوّل وهذا المجلس واسع ولا يجلس فيه السلطان إلّا في الأيّام العظيمة أو للأحوال المهمّة

وقد نذكر أنّ بناء الفور كلّه بقصب الدخن أو المَرْهَبِيب ٣،١،٧٨
ومحلّ الديوان يسمّى لِقْدابَة أو راكوبة وصورتها هي أن يؤتى بأخشاب ملساء طويلة في آخر كلّ خشبة شعبتان هكذا فيحفرون في الأرض حفرا متساوية العمق ويجعلون الأخشاب متساوية الطول ويجعلون الحفر سطوراً متقابلة لا يختلّ سطر منها عن الآخر بحيث أنّها تكون هكذا

لكن تكون كلّها على نمط واحد وخطّ واحد فيدخلون في كلّ حفرة خشبة من الأخشاب ويجعلون شعاب كلّ صفّ

---

١ الأصل: عناقهم. ٢ الفصل الرابع في كيفية مجلس السلطان – أضيف للسياق

long journey, she'd sit on a chair borne on men's necks, with a great crowd of soldiers around her. Someone whispered to her that the people of Darfur were saying, "This serving woman (*khādim*) has gone too far in her whoring."[73] When she heard this, she sat in her court, summoned all her followers, and said, "I am the *ḥādim*. The *ḥādim* brought silver and the silver brought gold"[74] (saying *ḥādim* instead of *khādim* because, not being an Arabic speaker, she couldn't pronounce the *kh*). There are other offices that we've opted not to mention because they aren't important enough.

Section 4: The Functioning of the Sultan's Court[75]

Regarding the sultan's court, his house is in his town, which is called the *fāshir*.[76] The people live around it, which is why it is built with two doors. The greater door is called the *órré dee*, meaning "the men's door," the other the *órré bayyâ*, meaning "the women's door"; the sultan has a court in both.[77] The court of the *órré dee* is the Greater Audience Chamber and is located immediately after you pass through the first door. This court is spacious, and the sultan holds court there only on great holidays and special occasions. 3.1.77

We should mention that all Fur construction is done with stalks of millet or of *marhabayb*,[78] and the place where the court is held is called a *liqdābah* or *rākūbah*.[79] It is made by fetching long, smooth poles of wood, each with a fork at the end, like this: 3.1.78

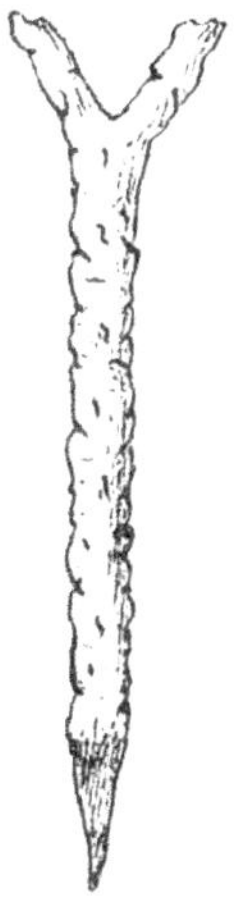

Then they dig holes of equal depth and cut the poles to equal length. The holes are in lines opposite each other, each lined up precisely with the next so that they look like this:

The holes must, however, all be of the same size and in straight rows. They put a pole in each hole, turning the forks in each row so that they face the same direction, and place on top a piece of wood called the *baldāyā* (i.e., they place

متّجهة لجهة واحدة ويضعون عليها خشبة طويلة تسمّى بَلْدَايَا أي يضعونها بين شعاب الصفّ فإذا كمل على تلك الهيئة يأتون بفروع رفيعة تسمّى مطارق فيجمعون منها كلّ أربعة أو خمسة سواء ويربطونها بلحاء الشجر حتّى تصير حزمة ويوصلونها بغيرها وهكذا حتّى تصير طول اللقدابة المذكورة ويجعلون من الفروع جملة على هذا النمط ويرتّبونها كلّها مربّعاً واحداً مستطيلاً في وسطه مربّعات فتكون صورتها هكذا

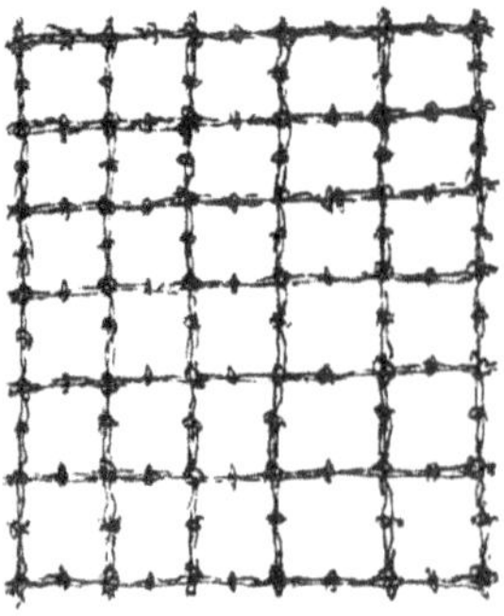

ويضعونها فوق البلدايات المذكورة ثمّ يضعون البوص عليها وهو مجعول حزماً ويربطونها مع الفروع باللحاء فيتكوّن من ذلك سقف جميل بالنسبة لبنائهم

٧٩،١،٣ فني وريديا يكون هذا المحلّ واسعاً وعلى هذه الصفة علا[1] السقف بحيث يمرّ تحته الراكب على الهجين ولا يمسّ السقف رأسه وكان قبل ذلك داني السقف لا يمرّ تحته إلّا الفارس فاتّفق أن حضر عند السلطان رجلان ممّن أتقن ركوب الإبل وادّعى كلّ واحد منهما أنّه أفرس من صاحبه في ركوب الإبل وتشاجرا ثمّ اتّفق رأيهما على أن يركبا ويمرّا ببعيريهما من تحت اللقدابة فتراهنا على ذلك وخرج السلطان والناس من اللقدابة وركبا وجاءا راكضين فلمّا وصلا إلى اللقدابة أحدهما نقز فصار على ظهر اللقدابة وترك بعيره وجرى مسرعاً فصادف بعيره وهو خارج من تحت السقف فركبه ومرّ سريعاً لم يعقه شيء والثاني حين وصل إلى اللقدابة مال إلى جانب بعيره ومسكه بيديه حتّى خرج من تحت اللقدابة فكلّ منهما جاء بشيء غريب فأحسن إليهما السلطان واعترف الناس لهما بصناعة الركوب وأنّهما كَفَرْقَدَيْ سماء وشذّ بعض فادّعى أنّ الذي ترك بعيره وجرى على ظهر اللقدابة أصنع وشذّ آخرون فادّعوا أنّ الذي مال في جنب البعير أصنع وحكم له السلطان ومن ذلك الوقت زيد في علوّ اللقدابة

---

١ الأصل: عالا.

it so that it runs between the forks in that row). When it is complete, they take thin branches called *maṭāriq*,[80] gather four or five of them, and tie them with tree bark, making them into sheaves, which they attach to one another till they reach the length of the aforementioned *liqdābah*. Then they make an assemblage from the branches in the same way and arrange them into a single elongated square [*sic*] with squares in the middle so that it looks like this:

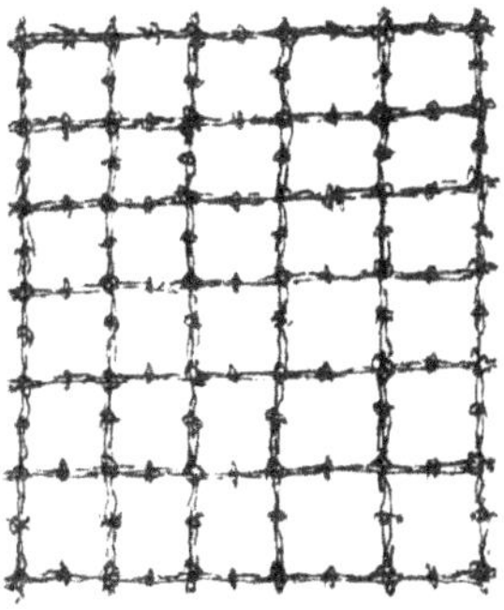

They place these frames on top of the aforementioned *baldāyā*s and on top of them they place bundled reeds, which they tie to the branches with the bark. All of it together makes an excellent roof, by their building standards.

In the *órré dee*, this *liqdābah*, or open-sided pavilion, is spacious. Made as described here, the roof is so high that a man riding a camel can pass beneath it without his head touching it. In the past, however, the roof was lower, so that only a man riding a horse could pass beneath it, but it once happened that two men who were skilled camel riders attended the sultan, each claiming to be more skilled than his companion, and they quarreled. They agreed to make bets on mounting and passing under the roof of the pavilion with their animals. The sultan and the people left the pavilion and the men mounted and came at a gallop. When they reached the pavilion, one of them leaped up and landed on the top, leaving his camel, and ran fast and caught up with his camel as it emerged from beneath the roof; then he mounted and charged ahead at high speed with nothing to impede him. When the second rider reached the pavilion, he leaned down to the camel's side, holding on with his hands until he emerged from the other end. Each of them did something extraordinary, so the sultan rewarded them well and people acknowledged that they were both excellent riders, two bright stars in a single sky. Some, however, held a minority opinion and claimed that the one who had left his camel and run over the pavilion's roof was cleverer, while others held that the one who had leaned to the side of the camel was cleverer. The sultan judged in favor of the latter, and from that time on the pavilion was made higher. 3.1.79

٨٠،١،٣ 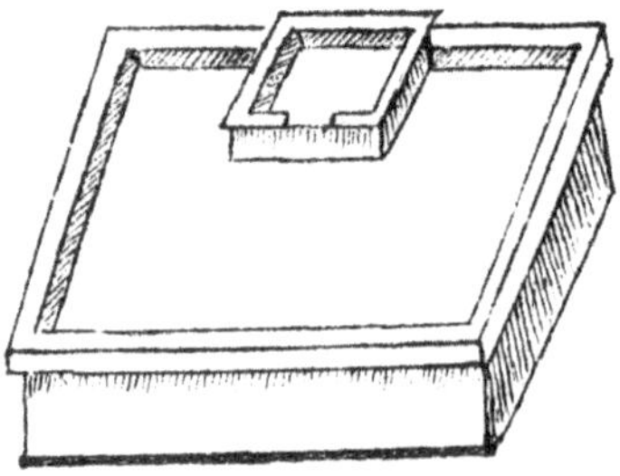

ثمّ إن السلطان إن جلس في هذا الديوان يجلس في وسطه ولذلك بنوا له فيه محلاً عالياً لكن مركزه أعلى من جانبيه هكذا فالمحلّ العالي المتوسّط هو محلّ جلوس السلطان والذي أقلّ منه من جهة اليمين هو محلّ جلوس العلماء والذي عن يساره هو محلّ جلوس الأشراف والفقهاء وعظماء الناس وأمامه رحبة واسعة فإذا أراد السلطان الجلوس لديوان عامّ أو ملاقاة بعض رسل الملوك أو يوم فرح وسرور زين محلّ جلوسه بالزردخانات والمقصّبات ووضعوا في المحلّ المذكور كرسيّاً وعليه مرتبة من الحرير فجلس السلطان في أبّهته وجلس العلماء والفقهاء والأشراف حوله ووقف وزيراه بين يديه وهما المسمّيان بالأمينين ووقف رئيس تراجمته أمامه قريباً منه ووقف التراجمة الستّة أمام الترجمان الأوّل بين كل ترجمانين مسافة قليلة بحيث كلّ ترجمان يسمع ممّن يليه سمعاً جيّداً ووقف الكوركوا بالصفافير خلفه وصاحب الدنقار معهم ووقف عبيد السلطان وأصحاب سجنه وغضبه وراء الناس وجلس الناس الباقيون كلّ واحد في المحلّ اللائق به ووقف ملك الموجيه قريبا من الترجمان الأوّل وقد انتظم المجلس وقد رسمنا كيفيّته في باب عوائد الفور فراجعه إن شئت وأمّا إن جلس السلطان في وريبايا فإنّ مجلسه يكون مختصرا وهو أشبه بمجلس سرّ لأنّ اللقدابة التي يجلس فيها صغيرة وحينئذ لا يقف أمام السلطان إلّا ترجمان واحد وموجيه واحد أو اثنان وإن كثروا فثلاثة والسلطان قد يكون جالساً وأكثر ما يكون جالساً بالليل

٨١،١،٣ وقد يكون راكبًا وأكثر ما يكون ذلك بالنهار وإن جلس في محلّ عال لكنّه غير مزيّن ولا فرش له حينئذ إلّا سجّادة واحدة وبإزائها مخدّة وقد ذكرنا سابقاً أنّ من العوائد أنّ السلطان لا يسلّم عليه إلّا بدوگراي دونگا وأنّه إذا بصق مسح التراب الذي بصق عليه في الحال وإذا تنخّم قالوا صوتاً كصوت الوزغ وبيّنّاه هناك أتمّ تبيين فلا فائدة في الإعادة.

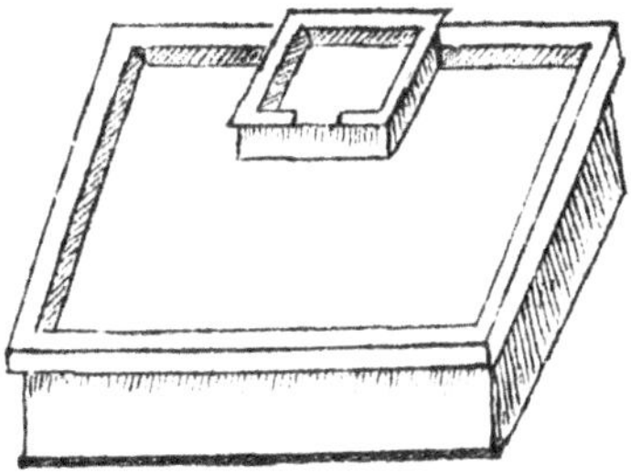

When the sultan sits in this audience chamber, he sits in the middle. They have therefore built a raised place for him within it, the center higher than the sides, like this: The high place in the center is where the sultan sits, the part that is slightly lower on the right is where the scholars of religion sit, and the part on the left is where the sharifs, the faqīhs, and the great men of the people sit, with a wide space in front of them. If the sultan wishes to sit for a general audience, receive the messenger of a petty king, or celebrate a day of festivity and happiness, his sitting place is decorated with weapons and brocades, and he is given a chair with a silk cushion. The sultan takes his seat in all his finery; the scholars, faqīhs, and sharifs take their seats around him; and his two viziers stand before him, these being the "counselors." His chief interpreter stands close by in front of him, and the six other interpreters in front of the first, with a distance between them short enough to allow each to hear the one next to him well. The *kóór kwa*, along with the player of the *dinqār*, stand with their pipes behind the sultan, while the sultan's slaves, jailers, and executioners stand behind the people. Each of the remaining persons sits in the place appropriate to him, and the master of the *mooge* stands close to the first interpreter. The arrangement of the court is thus complete. We have made a drawing of how it functions in the section on the customs of the Fur, which you may consult if you wish.[81] When the sultan takes his seat in the *órré bayyâ*, however, the court is reduced and is closer to a private court, since the pavilion in which he sits is small. On such occasions, only one interpreter and one, two, or at most three *mooge* stand in front of the sultan. 3.1.80

The sultan may be seated, mostly at night, or he may be mounted,[82] mostly by day. If he is seated, then it will be in a high place, but not one that is decorated. On such occasions, the place has no furnishings except for a single carpet with a cushion next to it. We have already mentioned that custom dictates that the sultan be greeted exclusively with the words "*Dóngá rǎy dóngá!*" and that if he spits, the place where he spat is wiped immediately, and if he clears his throat, they make a sound like a gecko. We have explained all this above, so there is no point in doing so again.[83] 3.1.81

هذه كيفيّة مجلس سلطان الفور وأمّا كيفيّة مجلس سلطان الواداي فتختلف فإنّا نذكر أن الواداي دائماً يحجبون السلطان عن أعين الناس ويشدّدون في ذلك فلا يتمكّن أحد من رؤيته جيّداً ولا تجتمع عليه الملوك كما تجتمع على سلطان الفور لأنّهم يرون أن عدم اجتماع الناس عليه أهْيَب له وأنفذ لكلمته ولمّا كان الأمر كذلك وخيفة[1] من وقوع ظلم وإجحاف رسم أن يجلس السلطان للمظالم في يوم الاثنين والخميس وجعلوا لجلوسه ذلك كيفيّة مخصوصة تقام فيها نواميس الملك وينزجر الظالم وينتصف المظلوم ورتّبوا له مجلساً بحيث يحصل المقصود من غير اختلاط بالعالم ٨٢،١،٣

وسنذكر أن بناء الواداي قد يخالف بناء الفور في أنّ الفور لا يبنون باللَّبِن إلّا قليلاً وأنّ الواداي أكثر بنائهم باللبن فجعلوا المجلس المعدّ لذلك عالياً يجلس فيه السلطان مع بعض خواصّه في يوم الاثنين والخميس ولا تراه الناس وإنّما يعرف جلوسه فيه براية يبرزونها من طاق في المجلس الذي هو فيه وبصوت البَرَدية فهما برزت الراية وضربت البرديّة وهي طبل كالكوبة المسمّاة في مصر الدربكّة لكن صوتها عالٍ شديد فيسمع الكبرتو فيبوّقون بالبوقات ويضربون بالتجل فتسمع الناس خصوصاً وأنّ من كانت له دعوى[2] يترقّب ذلك اليوم فيجلسون كلّهم في الفاشر وإنّ الكَماكِلَة دائماً جالسون في الفاشر لسماع الدعاوى وأنّ أرباب المناصب والمراتب يترقّبون في ذلك اليوم جلوس السلطان في الديوان فتحضر التراجمة المسمّون بخَشْم الكلام والعَقَدَة والملوك على طبقاتهم ويحضر القاضي وأشراف الناس والعلماء فيجلسون في ظلّ شجر في الفاشر يسمّى ذلك الشجر بالسَيَال فمتى أخرجت الراية من الطاق وضربت البرديّة دخل خشم الكلام ورقي من سلّم في داخل البيت وخرج من طاق لمصطبة معدّة لجلوسه بحيث يصير قريباً بمسمع من السلطان ووقف هناك واصطفّت العساكر وجلس القاضي والعلماء في مراتبهم وكذلك الأشراف والتجّار وجاء من له دعوى[3] رفعها إلى السلطان ذلك بعد أن يقول خشم الكلام السلطان ٨٣،١،٣

[1] الاصل: خيف. [2] الأصل: دعوة. [3] الأصل: دعوة.

This, then, is how the court of the Fur sultan functions. The court of the sultan of Wāddāy functions differently. The people of Wāddāy always screen the sultan from people's eyes, going to great lengths to do so. No one is allowed to see him clearly and the petty kings do not come and meet with him as they do with the sultan of the Fur: the Wāddāy think it more awe-inspiring and more likely to ensure that his orders are carried out if people do not meet him. This being so, and out of fear lest any injustice or injury come about, it is ordained that the sultan shall sit to hear complaints on Mondays and Thursdays. They have a special procedure for these occasions, on which the monarch's laws are applied, oppressors rebuked, and the oppressed given fair treatment. They have devised a form of assembly that allows for this without any mixing with the common people. 3.1.82

We shall describe elsewhere[84] how the building methods of the people of Wāddāy differ from those of the Fur, the difference lying in the fact that the Fur only rarely build with mud brick, whereas the people of Wāddāy use mud brick more than anything else. This has allowed them to construct an elevated room for the sultan to hold such audiences,[85] and there the sultan sits with some of his retainers every Monday and Thursday, though the people cannot see him. The only way to tell that he is holding court is that a flag is stuck through an aperture in the wall where he is seated, and the sound of the *baradiyyah* is heard. As soon as the flag appears and the *baradiyyah* (which is a drum like the goblet drum that in Egypt they call *darabukkah*) sounds, the *kabartū* hear it and they blow their trumpets and beat the *togjêl*, and the people hear. Those with petitions have, after all, all been sitting in the sultan's compound waiting for that day, as have the *kamkūlak*s, who are present on a permanent basis at the compound to hear petitions. The officeholders and persons of rank also wait on that same day for the sultan to seat himself in the audience chamber. When he does so, the interpreters known as "the language mouths," the provincial and tribal governors general,[86] and the petty kings of all ranks come, as do the judge, the sharifs, and the scholars of religion, and they sit in the shade of a *sayāl* tree inside the royal compound. When the flag appears through the aperture and the *baradiyyah* sounds, a "language-mouth" enters and climbs a ladder inside the house and emerges from an aperture onto a balcony that has been prepared for him to sit on in such a way that he can position himself to hear the sultan easily. He stands there, the soldiers form rows, and the judge and the scholars seat themselves by rank, as do the sharifs and the merchants. 3.1.83

يسلّم عليكم يأهل الفاشر السلطان يسلّم عليك يا قاضي السلطان يسلّم عليكم يا علماء وهكذا كما يفعل في يوم الجمعة

٨٤،١،٣ ولنرجع إلى ما نحن فيه من ذكر الفور[١] فنذكر نبذة في صفات تندلتي، فاشر السلطان، وفي بيته وصفة كلّ منهما حسب الإمكان

٨٥،١،٣ فنقول أمّا تندلتي[٢] فهي الآن قاعدة مملكة الفور وأوّل من نزلها وخطّها من الملوك السلطان عبد الرحمن سنة ١٢٠٦ من الهجرة وأمّا صفة أرضها فرمليّة كأحد الأقواز يشقّها وادٍ بالعرض وهذا الوادي رجل من الوادي الأكبر المسمّى الكوع ففي أيّام الخريف يمتلئ ذلك الوادي ماء فلا يعبره عابر إلّا من محلّ بعيد من جهة المشرق وفي وقت نضوب المياه وذلك تارة في آخر الشتاء وتارة في أوّل الصيف يحفرون فيه الآبار ومنها تشرب أهل الفاشر كلّها والسلطان لخوفه من السحر يشرب منه تارة وتارة يأتون له بماء من جديد السيل لأنّه قريب من تندلتي من جهة الشرق بنحو فرسخ

٨٦،١،٣ وبناء الفور كلّه من قصب الدخن وحيطان بيوتهم الخارجيّة كلّها بالشوك ويسمّون الحائط الخارجيّ زريبة والحائط الداخليّ صَرِيفاً والبيوت أعني المساكن كلّها على هيئة قبّة الخيمة فيكون الصريف لها كالطُرُنْك لكنّ البيوت أصناف في البناء فمنها[٣] بيوت المساكين وهي مساكن عندهم تسمّى بالبيوت وهي من قصب الدخن وبيوت الأمراء والملوك وهي مبنيّة من المَرْهَبِيب كما سنذكر ذلك ومنها ما يسمّى سُكَّاية ومنها ما يسمَى تُكُلْتي ومنها ما يسمّى كُرْنُك فأمّا السكّاية فصورتها هكذا

فهي كقبّة الخيمة إلّا أنها طويلة رفيعة من أعلى ويأتون ببيض النعام فيثقبونه كلّ بيضة ثقبين من

---

١ ما نحن فيه من ذكر الفور – الأصل: ما نحن بذكر الفور. ٢ أما تندلتي – الأصل: وتندلتي. ٣ أضيف للسياق.

Anyone with a petition then comes and presents it to the sultan, though only after the "language-mouth" has said, "The sultan salutes you, O people of the capital! The sultan salutes you, O judge of the sultan! The sultan salutes you, O scholars!" and so on, just as is done on Fridays.[87]

Let us now return to our primary concern, the description of the Fur. We shall give a brief notice of the characteristics of Tandaltī, the seat of the sultan, and of his house, and a description of each, to the best of our ability. 3.1.84

Tandaltī is now the base of the Fur kingdom. The first monarch to settle there and the one who laid it out was Sultan ʿAbd al-Raḥmān, in 1206 [1791–12]. Its soil is as sandy as any of the sand dunes to the east, and it is bisected laterally by a seasonal watercourse that is a spur of the larger watercourse named Wādī l-Kūʿ. In the rainy season, the wadi fills with water, and no one can cross it except at a point far to the east. When the water dries up, which is generally at the end of the winter, though sometimes at the beginning of the summer, they dig wells in it—everyone in the sultan's capital drinks from these. The sultan, because of his fear of magic, sometimes drinks from the wadi, but sometimes they bring him water from Jadīd al-Sayl, which is close to Tandaltī, about three miles to the east. 3.1.85

The Fur build exclusively with millet stalks,[88] and the outer fence around their houses consists entirely of thorns. This outer fence they call the *zarībah*, while the inner they call the *ṣarīf*. The houses, by which I mean the dwelling places, are all dome-shaped, like tents, the inner fences thus serving as a dust-break.[89] They employ various types of construction for their houses. There are the houses of the poor, which they call *buyūt*,[90] made of millet stalks; and there are the houses of the commanders and kings, built of the thin canes called *marhabayb*, as we shall mention below. There is also a type called *suktāyah*, another called a *tukultī*, and another called a *kurnug*. The *suktāyah* looks like this: It resembles a tent but is tall and narrow at the top. They bring ostrich eggs and make two holes in each, one at either end, and insert a stick. They put three or four eggs onto each stick and, between each, a ball of red earthenware (either the body of a *dullong* or of a large pot 3.1.86

محوريها ويدخلون في الثقب عودا فيجعلون في العود ثلاث بيضات أو أربعًا بينها كرة من فخّار أحمر إمّا أسفل دُلّگ أو أسفل إبريق من صناعة كِيْرِي وينصبونه على قمّة القبّة وأمّا التكلتي فهو بيت شكله هكذا من أعلى نصف كرة وقائم على دُرْزُويتَيْنِ وأمّا الكرنك فهو مثله إلّا أنّه قائم على أربع درزويات والسلطان يضع بيض النعام على سكاتيّة وتكاليّة وكرانكة ويكسو أعلاها ثيابًا حمراء وبيضاء هكذا  ليتميّز بها عن غيره وأسفل دائرة سكّايات السلطان والإياكري والسراري وكبار الدولة مبنيّ من الطين وأمّا أعلاها فمن المرهبيب وهو عزيز الوجود وهذه الدائرة تسمّى دُرْدُرْ قطره كقطر الخيمة المعتادة

٨٧.١.٣ واعلم أنّ أهل الفاشر منقسمون إلى قسمين أحدهما أهل وريديا والثاني أهل وربايا وبيت السلطان بينهما فأهل وريديا يسكنون جهة باب الرجال المسمّى بوريديا وأهل وربايا يسكنون جهة الباب المسمّى وربايا فزريبة السلطان موضوعة على شفير الوادي في العلوّ الكائن هناك فهي شمال الوادي وليس بينها وبينه إلّا خطوات قليلة وممتدّة إلى جهة الشمال مسافة بعيدة وباب الرجال يفتح جهة الشمال أمام الفضاء المسمّى بالفاشر وهو متّسع عظيم يكاد أن يكون ثلثي دائرة

٨٨.١.٣ ونذكر الآن صفة زريبة السلطان وبيوته أمّا الزريبة فهي من شوك الكِتِر والحَشَاب ثلاثة صفوف بين كلّ صفّين جذوع من خشب فيها بعض تفاريع محفور لها في الأرض حفر عميقة والشوك من أمامها وخلفها كالبنيان المرصوص علوّه أطول من قامة والجذوع بارزة منه وفي كلّ سنة يجدّد ما حصل فيه خلل وبين الشوك وبين المساكن مسافة نحو أربعين خطوة

٨٩.١.٣ ولوريديا أربعة أبواب كلّ باب عليه بوّابون يتناوبون حفظه والأبواب ليست كالأبواب المعهودة أعني أنّها من ألواح الخشب بل هي أعواد مربّطة بالقدّ

such as those made at Kīrī), and they set the stick on top of the dome. The *tukultī* looks like this: On top, it is a semicircle standing on two wooden pillars. The *kurnug* resembles it but its roof stands on four wooden pillars. The sultan puts ostrich eggs on his *suktāyahs*, *tukultīs*, and *kurnugs*, but he also dresses their topknots with red and white lengths of cloth, of the sort shown here:  to distinguish himself from others. The lower part of the circular wall that forms the *suktāyahs* of the sultan, the iyā kūrī, the concubines, and the high officers of the state is built of mud, while the upper part is made of the thin canes called *marhabayb*, which are hard to find. This circular wall is called the *durdur* and its diameter is that of an ordinary tent.

The inhabitants of the sultan's capital are divided into two halves, one 3.1.87
of which consists of the people of the *órré dee*, the other of the people of the *órré bayyâ*. The sultan's dwelling lies between them.[91] The people of the *órré dee* live on the side of the men's door that is called *órré dee* and the people of the *órré bayyâ* live on the side of the door that is called *órré bayyâ*. The sultan's *zarībah*, or outer fence, is placed on the edge of the wadi, on the rise there, which is north of the wadi, and there are only a few paces between the two. It extends for a long way to the north. The men's door opens to the north, and on the other side of it is the enclosure known as the *fāshir*, which is a huge expanse forming approximately two-thirds of a circle.

We shall now describe the sultan's outer fence and houses. The fence is 3.1.88
made of black thorn or gum arabic branches—three rows, with tree trunks on which some branches have been left between each row. Deep holes are dug in the ground for these and there are thorns in front of them and thorns behind them, put down in layers. The fence is taller than a man and the tree trunks rise above it. Each year, any gaps that may appear are repaired. Between the thorns and the dwellings is a space of about four paces.

Órré dee has four doors, each of which has doorkeepers who watch over 3.1.89
it in turns. The doors, however, are not like ordinary doors, by which I mean that they are not made of planks of wood: rather, they are made of logs lashed together with straps of rawhide, by which I mean untanned hide, and they

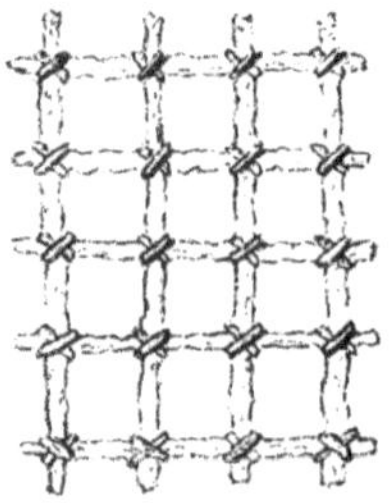

النيء أعني غير المدبوغ على هيئة شِباك هكذا وقد جُعِلَ فيه سلسلة من حديد ولكلّ[1] فجوةِ بابٍ مجعول في حافتها أعواد كثيرة من خشب فتجعل السلسلة في عود منها ويدخل في الحلقتين قفل كأقفال الصناديق ومسكن البوّابين قريب من الباب

فإذا دخل الداخل في وريدايا من أوّل باب يجد داخل الباب فضاء واسعاً وفي ٩٠،١،٣
آخره اللقدابة الكبرى التي هي ديوان السلطان فتكون على يسار الداخل وقد ذكرناها سابقاً ورسمنا صورتها فلا إعادة وعلى يمين الداخل محلّ الكورايات وهم في عرفنا سوّاس الخيل والأصابل قريبة منهم وهي لقدابة طويلة قليلة العرض مربوط فيها خيول الملك وبعد الأصابل بيت النحاس وبيوت خدمته قريبة منه والباب الثاني لسومندقلة والباب الثالث للكوركوا والباب الرابع للطواشية وبين كلّ بابين فضاء وصريف حاجز وعليه مركّب الباب وأيضاً داخل الباب الثاني لقدابة أخرى يجلس في هذه اللقدابة السلطان مع خواصّه وداخل الباب الثالث لقدابة ثالثة صغيرة يجلس فيها السلطان مع خواصّ خواصّه وداخل الباب الرابع الحرم والجوار ومحلّ سكنى السلطان كما سنبيّنه بالرسم إن شاء الله

وأمّا وريبايا فهو باب يدخل منه إلى فضاء طوله أكثر من عرضه وفي آخره لقدابة ٩١،١،٣
كبيرة تكون مثل ثلث اللقدابة الكبرى التي في وريدايا وهذه اللقدابة عن يسار الداخل وعن يمينه من بُعد أبنيّة للفلاقنة وللبوّابين وداخل الباب الثاني لقدابة أخرى أصغر منها يكون فيها السلطان بالليل مع من يحبّ من خواصّه وعن يسار هذه اللقدابة الباب الثالث وهو كأنّه في ركن [. . .][2] وقد رسمنا هنا صورة الزريبة السلطانيّة والبيوت كما ترى في الصحيفة الآتية بعد هذه لأنّك تعرف ما ذكرناه في

[1] الأصل: وكل. [2] الأصل ناقص فانظر الترجمة الأنجليزية التي تعتمد على الترجمة الفرنساوية.

are put together in the form of a grating, like this: 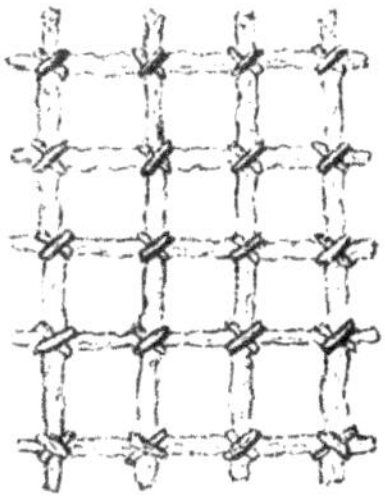 An iron chain is attached to each door and each door opening has, attached to its edge, numerous pieces of wood. The chain is attached to one of these. A lock like those used for chests is inserted through the doorpost and the door. The doorkeepers' dwelling is close to the door.

If one enters *órré dee* by the first door, one first comes to a wide space at 3.1.90
the end of which is the Great Pavilion, which is the sultan's audience chamber. This is on the left as one enters. We have mentioned this above and drawn a picture of it, so there is no need to go over it again. On one's right as one enters is the place of the *kūrāyāt,* who are what we would call grooms. The stables are close by and consist of a long, not very wide, pavilion where the monarch's horses are tethered. After the stables is the Drum House, and close by are the houses of the servitors of the drums. The second door leads to the Pages' Place, the third to the *kóór kwa*, and the fourth to the eunuchs. Between each door and the next there is a space and an inner fence, into which a door has been let. Beyond the second door is another pavilion in which the sultan sits with his intimates, and beyond the third is a third, small, pavilion where the sultan sits with those with whom he is most intimate. Beyond the fourth door are the women of the household, the slave women, and the sultan's private apartments, as we shall show in a drawing, God willing.

The *órré bayyâ* is a door through which one enters a courtyard longer than 3.1.91
it is wide and at the end of which is a large pavilion, about one-third the size of the great pavilion of the *órré dee.* This pavilion is on the left as one enters. On one's right, at a distance, are buildings for the heralds and the doorkeepers. Beyond the second door is another pavilion, smaller than the last, where the sultan spends the evening in the company of whichever of his intimates he wishes, and on the left of this pavilion is the third door, which is, as it were, in a corner[92] of the inner fence. Slave guards are posted there, as at the other doors. This last door leads directly to the women's quarters, which consist of a considerable number of houses, where the concubines live. Each has her own house, for herself and the slaves assigned to serve her. Beyond are the living quarters of the iyā kūrī and, to the right, those of the sultan. The iyā kūrī's are composed of seven or eight *suktāyah*s within her inner fence, which are occupied by the iyā kūrī herself and the women attached to her service. The living

ذلك مفصّلا وتكون كأنّك قد شاهدت ذلك عيانًا وهذه الصورة فيها صفة دار السلطان في الجملة

واعلم أنّ أهل الفاشر سواء كانوا أهل وريدايا أو أهل وريبايا كلّ منهم يحافظ على محلّ سكناه خلفًا عن سلف فكلّ من يتولّى منصبًا يبني بيته في محلّ صاحب المنصب الأوّل أو قريبًا[1] منه فمن كان من أهل وريديا لا يسكن في وريبايا وكذلك العكس ولا خصوصيّة للإقامة في ذلك لأنّهم يحافظون على أماكنهم ولو في السفر فلو انتقل السلطان بعساكره مسافرًا متى ما نصبت خيمته في بقعة نصب العساكر حسب ذلك كلّ منهم في محلّه المعلوم بحيث لا يكون بين المدينة في الإقامة وبين المنزلة في السفر فرق إلّا كبر المنازل واتّساع البيوت وأمّا الجهات فكلّ منهم يعرف محلّ البعض فكأنّهم في المدينة ومن ذلك أنّ السلطان يأتي بالليل إلى المنزلة فيعرف محلّ سكناه من غير سؤال وكذا أتباعه كلّ وزير وأمير يعرف منزله وما ذاك إلّا من المحافظة على المنازل وفي ذلك فوائد منها أنّه لو أرسل السلطان لإنسان يطلبه بالليل لا يسأل المرسل أحدا بل يعرف أنّ منزلة فلان في الجهة الفلانيّة فيذهب إليه من غير سؤال أحد وكذا لو أرسل بعض الوزراء أو الملوك لبعضهم حيث إنّ المنازل محفوظة لهم لا يتعب رسلهم بل كلّ منهم يعرف منزل صاحبه وهذا من أغرب ما يكون ٩٢،١،٣

١ الأصل: قريب.

quarters of the sultan are formed, as I have said, of two very tall *suktāyahs* within a separate inner fence that has two doors. In front of the sultan's inner fence are two buildings of mud brick, called *dinjāyahs*, which are the furniture depositories or, more accurately, the sultan's magazines. These are made of mud brick to avoid the incineration, should an accidental fire break out in the *suktāyah*, of the jewels, costumes, silver, and precious objects held in them. Finally, on the left is a very long pavilion where slave women spend the day grinding millet and wheat using hand mills. These women, whose houses are in front of their pavilion, are called *marāhīk* (singular *marhākah*), meaning "millers." Here, as you will see on the following page, we have drawn a picture of the sultan's outer fence and the houses, so that you may become as conversant with its features as if you'd seen it with your own eyes; it constitutes an overview of the sultan's abode.

Every inhabitant of the capital, whether of the people of the *órré dee* or of 3.1.92
the *órré bayyâ*, maintains the same place of residence from one generation to the next, because everyone who assumes an office builds his home in the same place as the first holder of that office, or close to it. Thus, a person from the *órré dee* will never reside in the *órré bayyâ*, and vice versa. Nor is this something peculiar to the long-term settlements, for they maintain their places even on the march: if the sultan moves with his soldiers, as soon as his tent is pitched, the soldiers pitch theirs, each, in accordance with this system, in its accustomed place. Thus, there is no difference between the city and the site where they halt when traveling, except for the size of the plots and the dimensions of the houses. As far as finding one's way around is concerned, everyone knows where everyone else is, so it's just as though they were in the city. For example, when the sultan comes to the campsite at night, he knows where his accommodation is without having to ask, and it is the same with his entourage: each vizier and emir knows the location of his campsite simply because they keep to the same positions. This has certain advantages. For example, if the sultan sends for someone at night, the messenger does not have to ask; he knows that so-and-so's campsite is in such and such a direction, so he goes there without asking anyone. Similarly, if one vizier or petty king sends a message to another, the messengers face no difficulties, as the same sites are maintained: each one knows where his friend's dwelling is. This is quite remarkable.

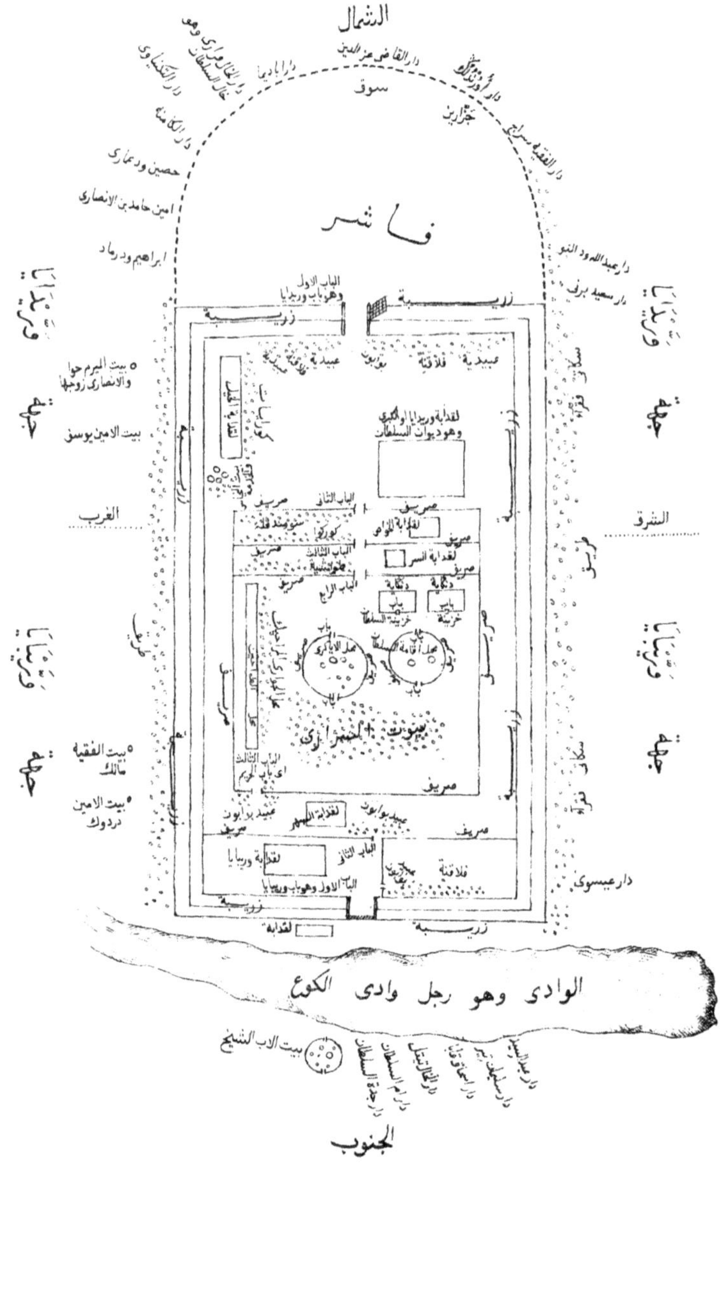
الشمال
سوق
فاشر
حصين ود عمارك
امين حامد بن الانصاري
ابراهيم ود رماد
الباب الاول وهو باب وريديا
زريبة
عبيدية
فلاقنة
لقدابة وريديا او الكبير وهو ديوان السلطان
بيت الامين يوسف
الغرب
الشرق
بيت الفقيه مالك
بيت الامين دردوك
فلاقنة
دار عيسوى
لقداية
الوادى وهو رجل وادى الكوع
بيت الاب الشيخ
الجنوب

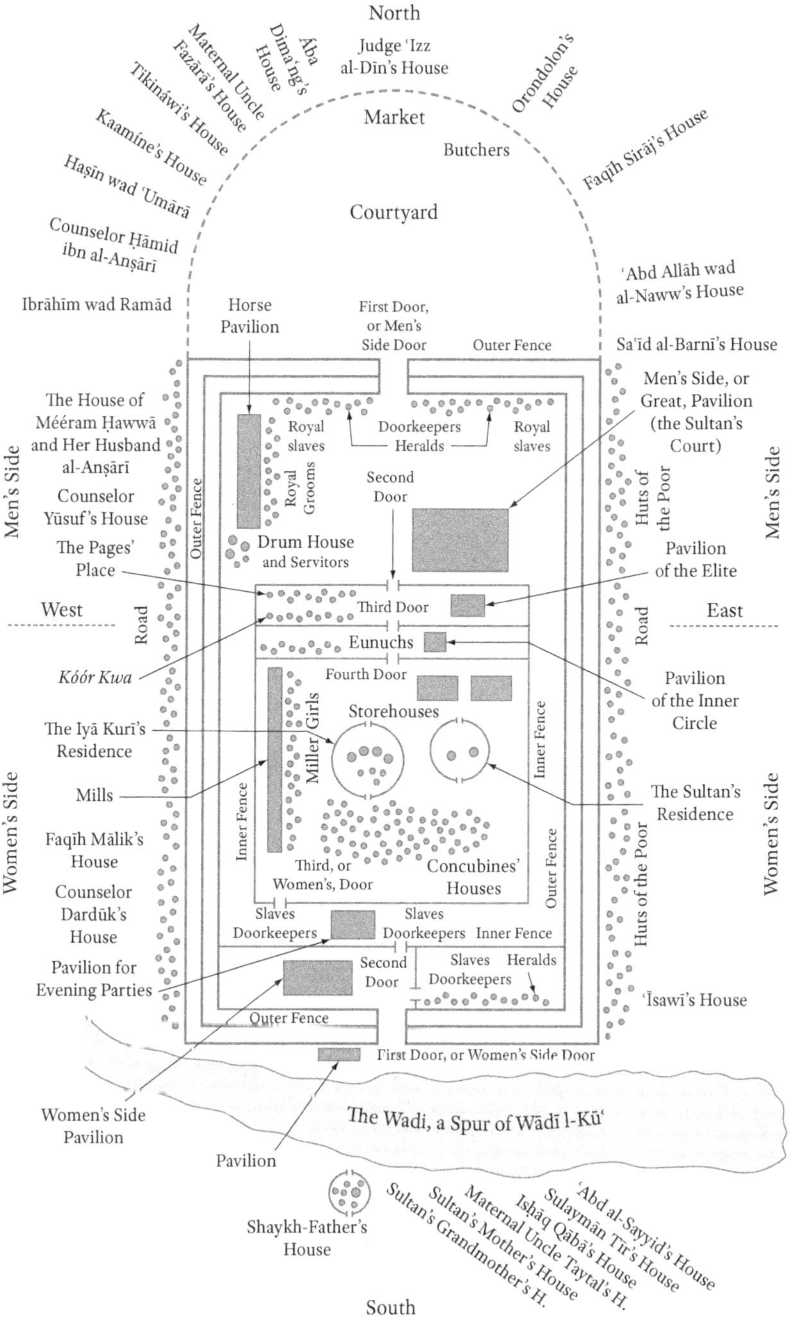
North
Judge ʿIzz al-Dīn's House
Āba Dima'ng's House
Maternal Uncle Fazārā's House
Tikináwi's House
Kaamíne's House
Haṣīn wad ʿUmārā
Counselor Ḥāmid ibn al-Anṣārī
Ibrāhīm wad Ramād
Orondolon's House
Faqīh Sirāj's House
ʿAbd Allāh wad al-Naww's House
Saʿīd al-Barnī's House
Market
Butchers
Courtyard
Horse Pavilion
First Door, or Men's Side Door
Outer Fence
Royal slaves
Doorkeepers
Heralds
Royal slaves
Royal Grooms
Second Door
Men's Side, or Great, Pavilion (the Sultan's Court)
The House of Mééram Ḥawwā and Her Husband al-Anṣārī
Counselor Yūsuf's House
The Pages' Place
Men's Side
Outer Fence
Drum House and Servitors
Huts of the Poor
Men's Side
Pavilion of the Elite
West
Road
Third Door
East
Road
Eunuchs
Kóór Kwa
Fourth Door
Pavilion of the Inner Circle
Storehouses
Girls
Miller
The Iyā Kurī's Residence
Inner Fence
Mills
The Sultan's Residence
Women's Side
Inner Fence
Faqīh Mālik's House
Huts of the Poor
Women's Side
Concubines' Houses
Third, or Women's, Door
Outer Fence
Counselor Dardūk's House
Slaves Doorkeepers
Slaves Doorkeepers
Inner Fence
Second Door
Slaves Doorkeepers
Heralds
Pavilion for Evening Parties
ʿĪsawī's House
Outer Fence
First Door, or Women's Side Door
The Wadi, a Spur of Wādī l-Kūʿ
Women's Side Pavilion
Pavilion
Shaykh-Father's House
Sultan's Grandmother's H.
Sultan's Mother's House
Maternal Uncle Taytal's H.
Isḥāq Qābā's House
Sulaymān Tīr's House
ʿAbd al-Sayyid's House
South

الفصل الخامس في ملابس ملوك الفور[١]

وأمّا زيّهم في الملابس فاعلم أنّ بلادهم في الحرارة بمكان عظيم ولشدّة حرّها لا يمكنهم أن يلبسوا إلّا الثياب الخفيفة لكن يتفاوتون في ذلك فالأغنياء يلبسون الثياب الرفيعة جدًّا بيضاء كانت أو سوداء وأمّا الفقراء فإنّهم يلبسون ثياب خشنة وأمّا السلطان والوزراء والملوك فإنّ كلّ واحد منهم يلبس ثوبين كالأقمصة رفيعين جدًّا إمّا ممّا يجلب لهم من مصر أو ممّا يعمل في دارفور لكن إن كانا من البيض فإنّهما يكونان في غاية من البياض والنظافة وإن كانا من السود يكونان نظيفين أيضاً ٣،١،٩٣

ولا يتميّز السلطان عن غيره في ذلك إلّا بما يلبسه زيادة على القميصين وذلك أنّه يضع على رأسه كشميرًا وهم لا يمكنهم ذلك والسلطان يتلثّم بشاش أبيض يضع على رأسه منه طيّات وعلى فمه وأنفه لثام منه وعلى جبينه أيضاً بحيث لا يظهر منه إلّا الأحداق لكن اللثام يشارك فيه أورondلگ والكامنه فإنّهما يتلثّمان كالسلطان وكذلك السلاطين الصغار يتلثّمون أيضاً لكنّه يتميّز بالسيف المذهّب والحجاب المذهّب وبالمظلّة إن كان راكبا وبالريش وبالسروج المذهّبة والركاب وعدّة الجواد التي لا يمكن سواه أن يجعلها على جواده وإن كان في محلّ جلوسه لا يتلثّم إلّا هو وحده ومن ذُكِرَ لا يمكنهم أن يتلثّموا بحضرته إلّا إن كانوا راكبين معه أو كان كلّ منهم في محلّ حكمه وديوانه ٣،١،٩٤

وأنواع ما تلبسه أهل دارفور الأغنياء من الملابس من المجلوب الشاش والبَفْت الإنجليزيّ والثياب الحرير في يوم المهرجان كيوم العيد ويوم تجليد النحاس ولهم ملاحف يتلفّعون بها وهي كالملاءة التي يتلفّع بها في إقليم مصر وهي إمّا من الأَلاجة أو من الشاش لكن يكون لها هُدُبٌ طويل وهذه الملحفة يُتوشّح بها أو توضع على الصدر والأكتاف وإذا حضر لابسها أمام السلطان يشدّ بها وسطه وذلك من كمال الأدب عندهم ٣،١،٩٥

---

١ الفصل الخامس في ملابس ملوك الفور – أضيف للسياق

Section 5: Garments of the Kings of the Fur[93]

Regarding their garments and how they wear them, their countries are extremely hot, and they accordingly can wear only lightweight clothes. All the same, there are differences among them. The rich wear very fine clothes, of white or black cloth. The poor, on the other hand, wear clothes of coarsely woven fabric. The sultan, viziers, and petty kings all wear two garments of very fine quality resembling shifts, either imported for them from Egypt or made in Darfur. The white ones are extremely white and clean, the black likewise. 3.1.93

The sultan is indistinguishable from others except that he wears garments in addition to the two shifts. He wears his cashmere shawl over his head, which others aren't allowed to; he also veils his face with white muslin, which he arranges over his head in folds so that it covers his mouth and nose as well as his forehead, leaving only his eyes visible. The orondolong and the kaamíne also cover their mouths, veiling themselves in the same way as the sultan, and the petty sultans do the same. The sultan is distinguished, however, by his gilded sword and gilded amulet,[94] and if he is mounted, by the umbrella, as well as by "the feathers," the gilded saddle and stirrups, and the caparison of his steed, which is of a kind no one else is allowed to use for his horse. If he is in his court, only he may be veiled. Others mentioned are only allowed to veil themselves in his presence if they are riding with him or if any of them is in his own realm and audience chamber. 3.1.94

The various imported garments worn by the rich of Darfur are made of muslin, English cotton baft, and, on festive occasions such as the Feast and the day of the covering of the drums, silk stuffs. They also swathe themselves in wraps resembling the *milāʾah* which people wrap around themselves in Egypt.[95] This is made either of a glossy, striped material of cotton mixed with silk or of muslin, but with a long fringe. This wrap is thrown loosely over the person or placed over the chest and shoulders. If someone wearing a wrap of this sort finds himself in the sultan's presence, he ties it around his waist, it being considered the acme of good manners to do so. 3.1.95

٣،١،٩٦ وإن كان من غير المجلوب فالكَلْكَف وهو ثوب من قطن غزله رفيع جدًّا طوله عشرون ذراعًا وعرضه ذراع واحد ومتوسّطهم يلبس من المجلوب الشَوْتَر وهو كناية عن العَبك المصبوغ أزرق ويجلب لهم بعض قماش من المغرب أي من بلاد الواداي والبرنو والباقرمه يسمّى التِيكَوْ والقدانيّ لكنّها غير عريضة لأنّ عرض الشقّة قيراطان لا غير فيتعبون في خياطتها والتيكو والقداني المذكوران سود لكن القداني مع أنّه أسود يرى في لونه بعض حمرة فهو كلون رقاب الحمام السود ومن عجيب ما رأيته في ذلك أنّ لابسه إذا تنخّم خرجت النخامة من صدره سوداء وذلك أنّ النيلة تدخل في مسامّ جسمه حتّى تؤثّر في صدره وبالجملة فالغنيّ سلطانًا كان أو وزيرًا أو ملكًا يلبس ثوبين وسراويل وعلى رأسه طربوش وباقي الناس لا يلبسون إلّا ثوبًا واحدًا وسراويل وملحفة إن تكن وعلى رأسه طاقيّة بيضاء أو سوداء وأكثرهم يكون رأسه عريانًا

٣،١،٩٧ وأمّا نساؤهم فإنّهنّ يلبسن مئزرًا في أوساطهنّ يسمّى في عرفهم الفَرْدة ثمّ الأبكار يلبسن فوطة صغيرة على صدورهنّ يقال لها الدُرّاعة وهي لبنات الأغنياء تكون من حرير أو ألاجة أو بفت ولبنات الفقراء تكون من التَكاكي ويربطن في أوساطهنّ أشرطة[١] يجعلن فيها الكنافيس والكُنْفوس عندهنّ عبارة عن منسوج عرضه أربع قراريط وطوله نحو من ثلاثة أذرع تأخذه الواحدة منهنّ وتدخل طرفه من الأمام في الشريط التي في وسطها وتفوّت الطرف الآخر بين فخذيها وتشبكه في الشريط من الخلف وهو كالحفاظ عند نساء المدن في أيّام الحيض إلّا أنّ الكنفوس عند نساء الفور لا يلبسنه لأجل الحيض بل يلبسنه مطلقًا وإذا تزوّجت البكر لبست إزارًا كبيرًا يسمّى في عرفهم الثوب وهو عبارة عن ملاءة تلتفّ فيها المرأة ثمّ هو على قدر مقامات الناس في الغنى والفقر فنساء الفقراء أثوابهنّ من التكاكي والأغنياء من الشوتر أو الكلكف أو التيكو أو القداني أو البفت ولا يكون من حرير ولا من ألاجة

١ الأصل: الشرطة.

If the garment isn't imported, it will be of *kalkaf*, which is a stuff made of cotton of a very fine yarn that comes in bolts of twenty cubits in length and a cubit in width. The middling people wear, among the imported stuffs, *shawtar*, which is a kind of blue-dyed camlet. Certain kinds of cloth are also imported from the west, i.e., from the countries of Wāddāy, Barnaw, and Bāqirmah. These are called *tīkaw* and *qudānī*, but aren't wide, the width of a piece being no more than a couple of inches.[96] This makes them difficult to sew. The *tīkaw* and the *qudānī* mentioned here are black, but some red may be detected in the *qudānī*, despite its dark color, so that it looks like the neck of a black pigeon. I observed a remarkable thing about this: if its wearer hawks, the sputum comes up black from his chest. This is because the indigo enters his pores and permeates his body till it affects his chest. In general, the rich man, be he sultan, vizier, or petty king, wears two layers of dress plus baggy drawers, with a tarbush on his head, while the rest wear a single layer of dress with baggy drawers, plus, on occasion, a wrap, with a white or black skullcap on their heads, though most go bareheaded. 3.1.96

The women wear an apron around their waists that they call in their parlance *fardah*. In addition, virgins wear a small piece of cloth called a *durrāʿah* over their chests;[97] for the daughters of the rich, this is made of silk, cotton mixed with silk, or coarse cotton baft; for the daughters of the poor, of lengths of raw calico. Around their waists, they tie bands to which they attach a *kanfūs*, which in their dialect is a kind of woven fabric four inches wide and about thirty cubits long. A woman takes one and passes the front end of it through the band at her waist; she passes the other end between her thighs and knots it onto the band at the back. It acts like the breechclout the city women use when they have their periods. The Fur women don't, however, wear the *kanfūs* only for the menses; they wear it all the time. When a virgin marries, she wears a large length of cloth that is called a *thawb* in their parlance, which is a sort of wrap with which the woman envelops herself. This also varies according to people's standing in terms of rich or poor: the *thawb*s of poor women are of raw calico, whereas those of the rich are of blue camlet, *kalkaf*, *tīkaw*, *qudānī*, or baft. They don't use silk or cotton mixed with silk. 3.1.97

وأمّا حليّ النساء عندهم فإنهنّ يلبسن الخزام وهو للأغنياء من الذهب وللمتوسّطين ٩٨،١،٣
من الفضة وللفقراء من النحاس وهو على نوعين حلقيّ وشوكيّ فالحلقيّ
عبارة عن حلقة فيها ثلم وهذا الثلم تجعل فيه مرجانة وهذه صورته

والشوكيّ عبارة عن حلقة نصفها غليظ ونصفها رفيع كالشوكة يجعلن
فيه أربع مرجانات بينها حبّة من ذهب أو ثلاث حبّات إحداها
ذهب ورأس طرفه الغليظ كحبّة مربّعة الأسطحة وصورته هكذا

ويلبسن في آذانهنّ أخراصاً كباراً من فضّة يزن الخرص منهنّ نصف رطل ولئلّا ٩٩،١،٣
يضرّ آذانهنّ يربطنه بعلاّقة في رؤوسهنّ تحمل ثقله عن الأذن وهو عبارة عن حلقة
واسعة أحد طرفيها شوكيّ والآخر كالحبّة المربّعة الأسطحة كالخزام ومن لم تجد خزاماً
ولا خرصاً تسدّ ثقب أنفها بمرجانة أو حبّة خرز مستطيلة وتسدّ ثقب أذنيها بقطعة
من لبّ بوص الدخن أو الذرة أو قطعة من خشب

ويجعلن في أجيادهنّ عقوداً من أنواع الخرز كالمنصوص وهو عندهم عبارة عن ١٠٠،١،٣
خرز أصفر من كهرباء وهو نوعان كرويّ ومفرطح وتختلف أفراد كلّ منهما في الصغر
والكبر والريش وهو عندهم عبارة عن خرز مستطيل أبيض فيه خطوط حلقيّة
أبيض منه وخطوط سمر وهو على أنواع أحسنها المسمّى عندهم بالسُومِيت وكلّه جامد
صلب كأنّه من رخام. يجلب من الهند وهو خرز رفيع مستطيل كثير الخطوط فيه
سمرة . والعقيق وهو عبارة عن خرز أحمر كرويّ كلّه يتفاوت في الكبر والصغر وهو
من عقيق. والمرجان وهو نوعان نوع يسمّى القصّ وهو خرز أسطوانيّ مستطيل قليلا
ونوع يسمّى المدردم وهو خرز كرويّ ودَمّ الرَعاف وهو نوع خرز أحمر داكن منه ما هو
أسطوانيّ ومنه ما هو كرويّ وهو من زجاج يجلب من بلاد أوربّا والفاو وهو مرجان
صناعيّ كرويّ وطويل كلّه فيعملون من جميع ذلك عقوداً
ويلبسنها كلّ منهن على قدر حالها في اليسار وعدمه فترى
منهنّ من يكون لها عقد واحد ومن يكون لها اثنان هكذا

Regarding jewelry, the women wear the nose ring, which is made of gold for the rich, silver for the middling, and copper for the poor. There are two types, "ring" and "thorn." The "ring" is a ring with a gap in which a piece of coral is fixed. It looks like this: 3.1.98

The "thorn" is a ring, half of which is thick and half thin, like a thorn. They attach four pieces of coral to it with a gold bead between each piece, or three beads, one of which is gold with a thick knob resembling a four-sided bead at the end. It looks like this:

In their ears, they wear large hoop earrings of silver, each weighing half a pound. So that these don't injure their ears, they tie them with a strap to their heads, thus relieving their ears of the weight. An earring of this type consists of a large ring, one of whose ends is in the form of a thorn and the other like the four-sided bead on the nose ring. The woman who can't afford a nose ring or hoop earrings stops the hole in her nose with a piece of coral or a single oblong bead and the holes in her ears with a bit of millet-cane pith, a grain of sorghum, or a bit of wood. 3.1.99

Around their necks, they wear necklaces made from beads such as the *manṣūṣ*, which in their usage is a kind of yellow bead made from amber and comes in two forms, spherical and flattened, individual specimens of both kinds varying in size. There are also "feathers," which are white elongated beads, some marked with white circular stripes, others with dark stripes. They come in various forms, of which the best is what they call *soomiit*. In all forms, it is as unyielding and hard as marble. It is imported from India—a slender elongated bead with many darkish striations. There is also the *ʿaqīq*, which is a spherical red bead no two of which are the same size and which is made of agate;[98] there is coral, which comes in two types, one of which is called "cut," which is a slightly elongated cylindrical bead, and the other "ground," which is a spherical bead; there is the *dam-l-raʿāf*,[99] which is a dark-red bead, some cylindrical and some spherical, and which is made of glass and imported from Europe; and there is the *pǎw*, which is an artificial coral, spherical and long in all cases. From all of these kinds they make necklaces, each woman according to her degree of affluence or lack thereof. Some you'll see wearing one string, others two, like this 3.1.100

ومن يكون لها ثلاثة وأغناهن لا تزيد على أربعة عقود هكذا ويرتّبن الخرز المذكور فيها ترتيباً حسناً بحيث يألفه النظر ويميل للابسه القلب

ويضعن على رؤوسهنّ تمائم من حبّ نبات يسمّى الشوش وهو حبّ صغير أحمر ٣،١،١٠١
كالجُلَّنار وفي جانب كلّ حبّة منه نكتة سوداء وهذا الحبّ رؤيته مفرحة جدّاً وودع وفول وهذا الفول عندهم ذو ألوان منه ما هو أحمر ناصع الحمرة ومنه ما هو تِبْنيّ اللون ومنه ما هو أسود ومنه عسليّ فيثقبن الشوش والودع والفول وينظمن الشوش وحده تمائم لكن يجعلن في أسفل كلّ تميمة إمّا جلجلاً أو ودعة ويجعلنها عناقيد هكذا لكن يفصلن بين كلّ تعريجة بخرز أزرق

ويلبسن في أوساطهنّ خرزاً على أنواع فنساء الأغنياء يلبسن خرزاً كبيراً مثل ٣،١،١٠٢
الجوز يسمّى عندهم رقاد الفاقة ونساء المتوسّطين يلبسن المنجور ونساء الفقراء يلبسن إمّا الحَرِش وإمّا الخَدُور وجميع ما ذُكر يُعمل في الخليل من برّ الشام لكن رقاد الفاقة أملس جدّاً وهو ما بين أخضر وأزرق وأصفر ومِشاهَرة وهو خرز أسود منقّط بنقط بيض والمنجور كذلك في الألوان إلّا أنّه أصغر حجماً منه وفيه حروشة وعدم إتقان في صناعته والحرش في لونهما لكنّه صغير كحبّ السبحة مع الحروشة الكليّة وله غضون وأمّا الخدور فإنّه حبّ أسطوانيّ وهو إمّا أحمر أو أبيض

ويلبسن في أذرعتهنّ عقداً يسمّى المَدْرَعة في المفصل بين الزند والساعد وهو عقد ٣،١،١٠٣
مركّب من خرز أسطوانيّ طول الخرزة منه[1] نحو قيراطين وهو إمّا أبيض أو أسود ويسمّى الشُوُور فينظمن خرزة بيضاء وخرزة سوداء ويفصلن بين كلّ خرزتين بحبّة إمّا من المرجان الحرّ أو من المرجان الطبخ أي الصناعيّ أو من حبّ الرعاف وذلك على قدر حالهنّ في الفقر والغناء ومن حليهنّ اللَدّاي وهو سلك غليظ من الفضّة نصف دائرة في طرفيه اعوجاج كالسنّارة فيؤخذ سلك رفيع من النحاس وينظم فيه منصوص

---

١ الأصل: من

and some three. The richest women never wear more than four, like this: They arrange the abovementioned beads prettily, in such a way as to catch the eye and draw the heart to the one wearing them.

3.1.101 On their heads, the women place amulets made from the seeds of a plant called *shūsh*[100]—the seeds are small and red, like those of the pomegranate flower; each has a black spot on its side and they are very pleasing to the eye—as well as amulets made of shells and of beans. In their country,[101] these beans are colored, some being bright red, some straw-colored, some black, some honey-colored. They bore a hole in the *shūsh*, the shells, or the beans. They also make the *shūsh* into amulets on their own, though they attach to the bottom of each amulet either a little bell or a shell, and make them into clusters, like this:

However, they separate each pedicel from the next with a blue bead.

3.1.102 The women wear various kinds of beads around their waists.[102] The women of the rich wear beads as large as walnuts that they call *ruqād al-fāqah*,[103] the women of the middle class wear *manjūr*,[104] and the women of the poor either *ḥarish*[105] or *khaddūr*. All the kinds mentioned here are made in Hebron, in the hinterland of Damascus.[106] The *ruqād al-fāqah*, however, are very glossy and the color is something between green, blue, and yellow. There is also the *mishāhrah*, which is a black bead with white spots. The *manjūr* are the same in color but smaller and somewhat rough and crudely made. The *ḥarish* are of the same color as the last two but small, the size of prayer beads, and rough all over, with corrugations. The *khaddūr* is a cylindrical bead and is either red or white.[107]

3.1.103 On their arms, at the wrist, the women wear a string of beads called a *madraʿah*. This is composed of cylindrical beads, each about two inches long and either white or black. It is also called a *shuwūr*. They string a white bead and then a black and separate each pair with one of another kind—either of genuine or "cooked" (meaning artificial)—coral, or of *raʿāf*,[108] depending on how well off they are. Another form of finery they wear is the *laddāy*, which is a thick, semicircular silver wire with a curved-over bit like a fishhook at either end. Thin copper wire is taken, *manṣūṣ*, coral, and *ʿaqīq* are threaded onto it, and the two ends are secured at the curved-over bit that is like a

ومرجان وعقيق ويربط طرفاه في الاعوجاج الذي كالسنّارة من الطرفين فيكون السلك الرفيع وما هو منظوم فيه كالوتر للقوس وصورته هكذا

فيجعلن الوتر قريبا من جباههنّ ويشبكن السلك الغليظ في شعورهنّ ويلبسن في أياديهنّ أساور[1] من عاج أو من قرن فإذا كانت من قرن سمّيت بالكِيم أو من نحاس لكنّ أساور بنات الأغنياء[2] من الفضّة والعاج معا وفي أرجلهنّ الخلاخيل وهي من النحاس للجميع لكنّ خلاخيل بنات[3] الفقراء من النحاس الأحمر وخلاخيل بنات[4] الأغنياء من النحاس المخلوط بالتوتيا فرارًا من حمرة النحاس المعروفة إلى الاصفرار القريب للون الذهب ويجعلن من أنواع الخرز الرفيع الملوّن عصابة على جباههنّ وفي أياديهنّ

وأمّا طيبهنّ فهو السنبل والمَحْلَب وكعب الطيب وهو المسمّى بعرف الفور عرق أمّ ١٠٤،١،٣
أبيض لسبب لونه الأبيض بشيء أسمر وأصفر ويعرف مصر عرق بنفسج بسبب رائحته وخشب الصندل وشيء كالمحار الصغير يقال له الظُفر وهو أسمر إلى سواد والشَيْبة والمَرْسِين وبعض الأكابر يتطيّبون بالجَلَاد وهو جلد نوافج[5] المسك وعندهم ثمر شجر زكيّ[6] الرائحة يسمّى الدايوق وهو حبّ أحمر يميل إلى الصفرة يسحقنه النساء ويخلطنه بطيبهنّ ومن عادتهنّ أن يكتحلن بالإثمد لكن لا يضعن الكحل في أعينهنّ بل يجعلنه على الأجفان السفلى والعليا من الخارج فيلتصق عليها بواسطة الدهن ويكحّلن عشّاقهنّ كذلك فترى الشباب والشابّات كلّها متكحّلة كذلك ومن عادتهم أنّ العاشق يأخذ من محبوبته شيئًا من حليّها المعروف ويلبسه افتخارًا له وتذكارًا لاسمها وإذا أصابه مهمّ أو عثر يقول أنا أخو فلانة وهي تقول كذلك أيضًا

وأكثرهم لا غيرة له على عرضه فربّما دخل الرجل داره فوجد امرأته مع غيره في ١٠٥،١،٣
خلوة فلا يغضب إن لم يجده على صدرها وأمّا إذا دخل ووجد ابنته أو أخته مع أجنبيّ لا يسوؤه ذلك بل ربّما سرّ به وظنّ أنّ ذلك يكون سببًا لزواجها ومن عادتهم

١ الأصل: اساورا. ٢ لكن أساور بنات الأغنياء – الأصل: وبنات الاغنيا. ٣ لكن خلاخيل بنات – الأصل: لكن بنات. ٤ وخلاخيل بنات – الأصل: وبنات. ٥ الأصل: نوافح. ٦ الأصل: ذكي.

fishhook, one at each end, so that the thin wire and everything that's threaded onto it are like the string of a bow. It looks like this:[109]  They place the string close to their foreheads and fix the thick wire in their hair. On their hands, they wear bracelets of ivory, horn (the latter called *kīm*), or copper. The bracelets worn by the daughters of the rich, however, are of silver and ivory together. On their legs are anklets, which are copper for everyone, but those of the daughters of the poor are of red copper, those of the daughters of the rich of copper mixed with zinc, as a way of reducing the everyday red of the copper in favor of a yellow close to gold. They also make bands from the various kinds of small colored beads, to be worn on their foreheads and wrists.

The perfumes worn by the women are spikenard; mahaleb; *kaʿb al-ṭīb* 3.1.104
(called "white root" in the parlance of the Fur because of its color, which is white with a touch of brown and yellow, and in Egypt "root of violet" because of its smell); sandalwood; something like a small mollusk, called *ẓufr*, which ranges from brown to black; artemisia;[110] and myrtle. Some great men perfume themselves with *jalād*, which is the skin of musk glands.[111] They also use the fruit of a sweet-smelling tree called *dāyūq*;[112] this is a yellowish-red berry that the women crush and mix with their perfume. It is a custom of the women to use a kohl made of antimony. However, they do not put the kohl on their eyes but on the lower and upper outer surfaces of their eyelids, and the antimony is made to adhere with fat. The women anoint their lovers' eyes this way, and one sees all the young men and women made up like this. It's also a custom of theirs for a lover to take some piece of finery from his beloved and wear it out of pride and as a memento; if any trouble befalls him, or he suffers some setback, he'll say, "I'm brother to" this or that woman, and women do the same.[113]

Most of the men aren't jealous of their honor. A man will enter his house to 3.1.105
find his wife alone with another man and not be angry, so long as he doesn't find the man on top of her. If he enters and finds his daughter or his sister with someone from outside the family, he sees nothing wrong with that. Indeed, he may rejoice and think it will lead to her getting married. Another custom of theirs is to give a girl a room of her own to sleep in when her breasts start to grow, where anyone who loves her may come to her and spend the night. Most of their daughters become pregnant as a result, but there's no shame on them for this, and a boy born out of wedlock is regarded by them as the

أنّ البنت إذا طعن ثديها يفردون لها محلاً تبيت فيه ويأتيها من يحبها فيه وتبيت معه ومن ذلك يقع الحبل بأكثر بناتهم ولا عار عليهم في ذلك وولد زناء عندهم ينسب لخاله وكذلك البنات فالبنت التي تكون من هذا القبيل يزوّجها خالها ويأكل من صداقها مالاً لا سيّما إن كانت جميلة وبالجملة لا يمكن في دار الفور أن تمتنع النساء عن الرجال ولا الرجال عن النساء بل لا يمكن الرجل أن يحرز ابنته تحت كنفه ولو كان عظيماً أمّا إن كان فقيراً فإنّه يهان ويؤذى وربّما قُتِل

١٠٦،١،٣ ومن ذلك ما اتّفق أنّ رجلاً كانت له ابنة وكان يغار عليها ولا يرضى أن يكلّمها أجنبيّ ومن شدة خوفه عليها كان يقهرها على البيات معه في المحلّ الذي هو فيه وكانت من الجمال بمكان فكان الشباب يأتون على عادتهم إلى بيت أبيها فإذا حسّ بهم زجرهم ولعنهم وطردهم فلمّا أعياهم أمره احتالوا عليه وأخذوا قرعة مستطيلة قليلا تقرب من الشكل البيضيّ تنتهي بعنق وفتحوها من أعلى وأخرجوا لبّها وملأوها غائطاً وبولاً وحرّكوه حتّى امتزج ببعضه وتوجّهوا إلى منزله ليلاً ونادوه يا والدنا مر فلانة تأت لنتحدّث معها فقام على عادته ولعن وسبّ وزجر فما أفاد ذلك بل قالوا له نحن لا نبرح حتّى تخرجها لنا فاغتاظ منهم وخرج قاصداً طردهم ومن عادتهم أنّهم كانوا إذا سمعوا أنّه خارج إليهم يفرّون منه لهيبته إلّا في تلك الليلة فإنّهم ثبتوا ومسك أحدهم القرعة من عنقها وكمن له حتّى أخرج رأسه من باب البيت فرفع يده بقوّة وضرب بها رأس الرجل بالقرعة فانكسرت على رأسه وسال الخبث الذي فيها على رأسه وثيابه ووجهه فلمّا شمّ الرائحة الكريهة صاح يشتم فقالوا له اسكت هذه الليلة فعلنا هذا معك والليلة القابلة إن عارضتنا قتلناك فأيقظ الرجل أهله وجاءوه بماء فاغتسل وتطيّب ونام وخاف منهم فلمّا أصبح أفرد لابنته حجرة لنومها قهراً عنه وجرت عليها عادتهم

١٠٧،١،٣ وإن كان غنيّاً صاحب حشمة وأبّهة وعبيد وخدم يتحيّلون في الدخول إلى الحريم بالليل ولو على زيّ النساء ومن ذلك ما اتّفق أنّ رجلاً من أكابر الناس له سبعة

offspring of his maternal uncle. A girl in the same situation will be found a groom by her maternal uncle, who benefits materially from the bride-price, especially if she's pretty. Generally speaking, in the lands of the Fur the women can't be kept from the men, nor the men from the women. In fact, no man, even if he's powerful, can keep his daughter under his wing, and if he's poor, he's regarded with contempt and may be harmed, or even killed, if he tries to do so.

For example, it happened that a man had a daughter of whom he was very protective and to whom he allowed no outsider to speak. So frightened was he for her that he used to force her to spend the night in the same room as he. She was extremely beautiful and young men used to come, as is their custom, to her father's house. When he heard them, he'd berate them, curse them, and throw them out. Fed up with this, they decided to play a trick on him and took a slightly elongated gourd, egg-shaped but ending with a neck, cut it open at the top, extracted its flesh, filled it with feces and urine, shook it so that everything was well mixed, and went at night to his house. There, they called out to him, "Hey Dad, tell so-and-so to come out and talk to us!" As usual, he got up and cursed and swore and scolded, but it did no good; in fact, they told him, "We aren't leaving till you bring her out to us." He became very angry with them and came out himself, intending to drive them away, as they usually fled in fear when they heard him coming out. That night, however, they stood their ground, and one of them took the gourd by its neck and hid out of sight until the man poked his head out of the door of the house. Then he raised his hand and brought it down hard and struck the man on his head with the gourd, which broke, and the filth inside it poured over his head, clothes, and face. When he smelled the horrible smell, he shouted curses but they told him, "Hold your tongue! Tonight we've done this to you. Tomorrow night, if you stand in our way, we'll kill you." So the man woke his family and they came and washed him with water. He bathed and put on perfume and slept, and he was afraid of them. In the morning, having no other choice, he gave his daughter a room of her own to sleep in, and things went with her as they usually do. 3.1.106

If the father is rich and a man of respectable ways and outward show, with slaves and servants, they'll try any trick to get into the harem at night, even if they have to dress as women. For example, it happened that a great man had seven sons and one daughter. She was of a unique beauty, and many had asked for her hand, but he'd refused them all. When things had gone on like 3.1.107

أولاد ذكور[1] وله بنت واحدة وكانت فريدة حسن وقد خطبها منه أناس كثيرون فأبى عليهم فحين طال الأمد على البنت تحيّلت وأدخلت شاباً لطيفاً من الشجاعة بمكان فمكث عندها ما شاء الله أن يمكث وافتقده أهله فلم يعرفوا له جهة فاتّفق أنه أُتِيَ بشراب فشرب ولمّا أخذته النشوة طلب الخروج فقالت له البنت أَصْبِرْ إلى الليل فأبى وقال لا أخرج إلّا الآن وغلب عليها وخرج وكان أبوها وإخوتها جالسين على باب بيتهم فما شعروا بالشابّ إلّا وهو خارج فصاح أبوهم على بوّاب البيت اقفل الباب فلمّا قفل الباب أمر العبيد بالقبض عليه فاجتمعت العبيد ليقبضوا عليه فجرح منهم أناساً وامتنع عليهم فخرج الأولاد السبعة مجرّدين السلاح عليه قاصدين قتله فناشدهم الله إلّا ابعدوا عنه وتركوه[2] يمضي إلى سبيله فأبوا وتراموا عليه ففرّ منهم ورماهم بالحراب فقتل واحداً منهم فكبر عليهم ذلك ورموه بالسلاح يرومون قتله فصار يذبّ عن نفسه ويرميهم حتّى قتل من الأولاد ستّة وجرح السابع جرحاً خفيفاً فحين رأى والدهم ذلك نادى يا غلام افتح له الباب ففتح له وخرج ولم يكن به جرح ولم يعرف من هو لأنّه كان متنقّباً وكانت ابنته سبباً في خراب بيته وقتل أولاده ووقائع كثيرة من هذا القبيل تذهب الدماء فيها هدراً لأنّ البنت التي يكون هذا الأمر من شأنها لا تخبر الناس باسم القاتل ولا من هو بل قصارى أمرها إذا سئلت عمّن فعل هذا الفعل أن تقول لا أعلم ولا يسلم من هذا الأمر بيت فيه أنثى إلّا إذا كانت وخشاء أو بها عاهة تنفر الناس عنها

وقد اجتهد السلطان عبد الرحمن في منع ذلك فلم يمكنه ذلك حتّى إنه جعل في السوق خصياناً كثيرين يمنعون النساء من مخاطبة الرجال والاختلاط بهم فاحتالوا في ذلك حيلاً عجيبة منها أنّ الرجل كان يمرّ بالبنت التي تعجبه فيقول لها يا بنيّة ماله راسك شين متل ديك السوكايه وماله يعني[3] لأيّ سبب وشين بعرفهم غير جميل فتقول هي وينو السوكاية الشين المتل راسي ووينو بمعنى أين هو فيقول ديكا أي ذاك وينعتها لها بإصبعه فتعرفها وبعد المساء تذهب إليه فتبيت عنده ولم ينفع الحرس بشيء ١٠٨،١،٣

١ الأصل: ذكورا. ٢ الأصل: تركوه ان. ٣ الأصل: اعنى.

this too long for the girl's liking, she played a trick and brought in a nice young man known for his courage, who spent with her what time God was pleased to allow him. His family noticed his absence and could find no trace of him. Now it happened that he'd brought with him something to drink. He drank, and when the intoxication took hold, he wanted to leave. "Wait till night," said the girl, but he refused, saying, "I have to leave right now!" and forced her to let him go. Her father and brothers were sitting at the door of their house and caught sight of the youth as he was leaving. The father shouted to the door-keeper, "Close the door!" and when he'd done so, ordered the slaves to seize the boy. The slaves gathered to do so, but he wounded some of them and kept out of their reach. Then the seven sons came out, unsheathing their weapons and bent on killing him. He beseeched them in God's name to stay away from him and let him go his way, but they refused and threw themselves at him, so he fled, throwing spears at them and killing one. This enraged them, and they threw their spears at him, intent on killing him, while he defended himself and threw his at them. In the end, he killed six of the sons and lightly wounded the seventh. When their father saw this, he called out, "Slave! Open the door for him!" which the slave did, and he left without a wound on him, and they never found out who he was because he was wearing a veil. His daughter was the ruin of his house and caused the death of his sons. Many an incident of this type has led to blood being spilled with impunity because the girl involved won't tell anyone the killer's name or who he is. Indeed, the most she'll do, if asked who did it, is say, "I don't know." Not a house with a female in it is spared such things, unless she's hideous or has some defect that makes people shun her.

Sultan ʿAbd al-Raḥmān tried to prevent the practice but couldn't. He even 3.1.108
put large numbers of eunuchs in the marketplace to stop the women from talking to the men and mixing with them, but they came up with some remarkable tricks to get around this. For example, if a man passed a girl who took his fancy, he'd say "*Yā bunayyah māluh rāsik shēn mitl dīk al-suktāyah*"[114]—*māluh* means "why?" and *shēn* in their parlance is the opposite of "beautiful"—and she'd say to him, "*Wēnu al-suktāyah al-shēn al-mitl rāsi*"[115]—*wēnu* meaning "where is it?" Then he'd say "*Dīka*"—meaning "that one"—and point it out to her with his finger. Thus, she'd know where it was, and in the evening she'd go there and spend the night with him and the eunuch guards would have been of no use.

كما أنّه اجتهد في منع شرب الخمر فما أمكنه واحتالت الناس حيلاً عظيمة حتّى ١٠٩،١،٣
كانوا يأتون لبيوت الخمّارين ويشترون منهم الخمر ويورّون لمن يراهم أنّهم يشترون خبزًا فكانوا يقولون بلغتهم تُقُرُو بَا يِنَسَا أي خبز كم عند هل أي هل عندكم خبز فإن خافوا أن يكونوا جواسيس طردوهم بقولهم اِكَبَايعني ما عندنا وإن عرفوا أنّهم أغراب يدخلونهم داخل الدار ويعطوهم ما يريدون وكان السلطان في أثناء ذلك يأمر بشمّ أفواه من حضر مجلسه من أكابر الدولة وهم أكثر الناس إدمانًا على الخمر فاستعملوا لإزالة الرائحة مضغ فروع شجر يقال له الشَعْلُوب فكانوا يشربون كفايتهم ثمّ يمضغون منه فلا تشمّ من أفواههم رائحة الخمر البتّة وهذه عوائد ارتكزت في طبائعهم وامتزجت بدمهم ولحمهم فصارت سنة متبّعة وإن كانت في الإسلام محرّمة

ومن عوائدهم أنّ الرجل إذا تزوّج وكان فقيرًا ولم يواسوه أهله الأغنياء وجاء ١١٠،١،٣
يوم الوليمة يعمد إلى مرعى المواشي حتّى يجد ماشية أقرب الناس إليه فيعقر منها ما يكفيه لوليمته ثورًا أو ثورين أو بعيرًا إن كان صاحب إبل وإن لم يكن شيء من ذلك ذبح أكباشًا على قدر كفايته فإن فطن ربّ المال له ومنعه قبل العقر ربّما قاتله إلى[1] أن يغلب وإن شحّ وطلبه للقاضي يلزمه القيمة فيدفعها له على التدريج إن لم يكن متيسّر الحال

ومن عادتهم أنّ الغلام إذا اختتن يجتمع عليه في ثالث يوم ختنه إلى سابع يوم ١١١،١،٣
جميع غلمان البلد وغيرهم ممّن له بهم قرابة أو معرفة ويأخذون السفاريك ويخرجون في بلدهم والبلاد القريبة منها فلا يرون دجاجة إلّا قتلوها وإن قدروا على ضبطها بالحياة أخذوها حتّى يجتمع عندهم دجاج كثير ولا يقدر أحد من الناس يعارضهم في ذلك وكل من عارضهم ضربوه وهم صغار لا تقام عليهم شريعة

ومن عادتهم ختن البنات لكنّهم في ذلك على أقسام فمنهم من لا يرى ذلك أبدًا ١١٢،١،٣
وهم أعجام الفور ومنهم من يخفض خفضًا خفيفًا كعادة أهل مصر وهم أكابر الناس

---

١ الأصل: الا.

He also worked hard to put a stop to the drinking of alcohol, but failed. People came up with some astounding tricks. They went so far as to go to the houses of the brewers, buy alcohol from them, and pretend to any who might see them that they were buying bread. They'd say in their language, "*Tugúra baing sá*," meaning *Bread-you-at-is*, i.e., "Do you have any bread?" If the brewers feared they were spies, they'd send them away by saying, "*Á keeba*," meaning, "We do not," and if they knew they were unknown to the police,[116] they'd admit them to the house and give them what they wanted. While this was going on, the sultan gave orders that the breath of the high officers of state who attended his court (who were the persons most addicted to alcohol) be smelled, so they'd chew the branches of a tree called *shaʿlūb* to get rid of the smell; they'd drink their fill and then chew some of it, and the alcohol couldn't be smelled on their breath at all. These ways have become integral to their natures and part of their blood and flesh, and they are now accepted practice, even though they're forbidden in Islam. 3.1.109

One of their customs is that when a poor man marries and his better-off relatives refuse to help him with the expenses on the banquet day, he takes himself off to the livestock pasture in search of animals belonging to his closest relative and hamstrings as many as he needs, be it an ox or oxen, or a camel if the relative has any. If the relative has none of these, the man will slaughter sheep of the number required. If the animals' owner is aware of what he wants to do and forbids him before he's hamstrung any, he may fight him till he beats him. If the other still refuses to help him and summons him before the judge, the latter will oblige the first to pay the value of the beasts, in installments if he's not well off. 3.1.110

Another custom is that when a boy is circumcised, the other boys in the village, as well as any others who are related to him or know him, gather, starting from the third day after his circumcision and continuing until the seventh, and they take throwing sticks, go out into their village and the nearby villages, and kill any chicken they see or, if they can, catch it alive and take it, till they've collected a large number. No one dares stand in their way, and if any does, they beat him. They're young, so no law can be applied to them. 3.1.111

Another of their customs is to circumcise their daughters, though they have different ways of doing this. Some don't think it necessary at all, these being the non-Arabic-speaking Fur. Others—the great among them—perform a light circumcision, in the same way as the Egyptians. Yet others perform 3.1.112

ومنهم من ينهك الخفاض حتّى يلتحم المحلّ ببعضه ويجعلون لمسلك البول ماسورة من صفيح وهؤلاء إذا زوّجوا ابنتهم لا يقدر الرجل على افتضاضها حتّى يشقّون له المحلّ بالموسى وهناك نساء لهذا المعنى وفي وقت الولادة كذلك أيضاً وهؤلاء أكثر بنات الفقراء المنهمكات مع الرجال دائماً ويفعلون ذلك خوف الافتضاض بالزنا ومع ذلك يقع الحبل فيهنّ وهنّ على تلك الحالة وفي خفاض البنات يعملون أفراحاً عظيمة ويولمون الولائم العظيمة ومن عادتهم أن أقارب البنت المخفوضة من الرجال يقفون خارج المحلّ الذي تخفض فيه البنت والنساء يكن عندها فإن صوّتت وقت الخفاض وصاحت لعنوها وتركوها وإن صبرت وهبها كلّ من أقاربها على قدر حاله وقرابته فمنهم من يهب لها بقرة ومنهم من يهب بقرات ومنهم من يهب لها رقيقاً ومنهم من يهب لها شاة أو شياهاً حتّى تصير من ربّات الثروة وأبوها وأمّها يهبان لها أكثر من جميع الناس إن كانوا أغنياء

ومن عادتهم أن يثقلوا مهور البنات فربّما تزوّجت البنت الوسيمة من الفقراء ١١٣،١،٣ بعشرين بقرة وجارية وعبد فيأخذ الأب والأمّ جميع ذلك ويعقدون العقد على جذعة من البقر ولذلك يفرحون بولادة الإناث أكثر من ولادة الذكور ويقولون إن الأنثى تملأ الزريبة خيرًا والذكر يخربها ومن عادتهم أنّ البنت إذا تزوّجت تمكث بعد الدخول بها في بيت أبيها سنة أو سنتين ولا يمكن خروجها لبيت زوجها إلّا بعد جهد جهيد والنفقة في تلك المدّة على أبيها وما يأتي به الرجل في تلك المدّة يكون على سبيل الهديّة ومن عادتهم أن الرجل إذا خطب بنتاً وكان قبل ذلك له اختلاط بأبيها وأمّها وكانت لها اختلاط بأبيه وأمّه أيضاً تذهب تلك المخالطة بمجرّد الخطبة ويستوحش كلّ منهم فبعد ذلك إذا رأى الرجل أبا البنت المخطوبة أو أمّها يفرّ من الطريق التي هو عليها وهما كذلك وكذلك البنت تفرّ مهما رأت أباه أو أمّه وفي أثناء ذلك إذا دخل الرجل البيت يرسل السلام لأمّ البنت إمّا مع البنت أو أختها أو جارية في البيت ونحو ذلك وهي ترسل له السلام أيضاً ولا يتلاقيان ولا يزالون كذلك حتّى يبني بها فعند سابع يوم من البناء يخرج ويقبّل رأس حماه وحماته

a circumcision so extreme that the place knits together and they have to insert a metal pipe to let the urine escape. When these marry off their daughter, the man can only deflower her after they have slit the place for him with a razor, there being women whose job it is to do this, and it's the same when she gives birth. This affects most of the daughters of the poor, who are always obsessed with men. They do it out of fear that they'll be deflowered out of wedlock, despite which they still get pregnant sometimes even in this state. They hold huge celebrations when girls are circumcised, and put on huge feasts. It's a custom of theirs for the circumcised girl's male relatives to stand outside the place where she's being circumcised, while the women are inside. If she cries out at the moment of circumcision and screams, they abuse her and leave, but if she endures, each of her male relatives gives her a gift, depending on how much he can afford and how closely related he is. Some give her a cow and others several cows, some a slave, and others a ewe or several ewes, so that she ends up a wealthy woman. Her father and mother give her more than all the rest, if they are rich.

It is their custom to demand high bride-prices for their daughters. A good- 3.1.113
looking but poor girl may marry for twenty cows plus a slave girl and a male slave. The father and mother will take all of that and seal the contract with a heifer. This is why they celebrate the birth of a girl more than that of a boy, and say, "A girl fills the homestead with good fortune, a boy reduces it to ruins." It's also their custom for a girl to remain at her father's house for one or two years after the consummation of the marriage, and she can only be made to leave and go to her husband's house with great effort. During this period, her father supports her, and anything that her husband brings is as a gift. Another custom is that if a man becomes engaged to a girl with whose father or mother he has previously been on friendly terms, and the girl too has been on friendly terms with his father and mother, that friendship comes to an end the moment they become engaged, and all behave like strangers to one another. From then on, if the man sees the father or mother of the girl to whom he is engaged, he turns around and goes another way, and they do the same. Likewise, the girl flees whenever she sees his father or mother. If the man enters her house during this period, he sends his greetings to her mother via the girl or her sister or a slave girl, or whoever is in the house, and her mother sends him her greetings by the same means, and they never meet. They go on like this till he consummates the marriage. Then, on the seventh day after the consummation, he goes

ويجتمع عليهما وكذلك البنت ومن عادتهم أنّ كلاًّ من الزوج والزوجة يرى أقارب زوجه كأقاربه فيحترم الرجل حماه ويخاطبه يا أبتي وأمّ امرأته يخاطبها بأمّي وأختها بأختي وهي كذلك ويرون ذلك من آكد الحقوق عليهم

out and kisses his father- and mother-in-law's heads and meets with them, along with the girl. Another custom of theirs is that the husband and the wife each regard the other spouse's relatives as their own. Thus, the man treats his father-in-law with respect and addresses him with the words "My dear father," while he addresses his wife's mother with the words "My dear mother" and her sister as "My dear sister," and she does the same.

الباب الثاني

وفيه فصلان[1]

فصل في اصطلاح تزويج الفور

لمّا كان المتوحّد في ذاته وصفاته وأفعاله غنيّاً عن الزوج والولد ما انفصل عن أحد ولا ينفصل عنه أحد إذ لا يحتاج لما ذكر إلّا الحادث المسكين الذي لا سند له إلّا الله ولا معين وهو سبحانه وتعالى حيّ قيّوم ﴿لَا تَأْخُذُهُ سِنَةٌ وَلَا نَوْمٌ﴾ واحد أحد فرد صمد لم يتخذ صاحبة ولا ولد ﴿وَلَمْ يَكُن لَّهُ شَرِيكٌ فِي ٱلْمُلْكِ﴾ ﴿وَلَمْ يَكُن لَّهُ كُفُوًا أَحَدٌ﴾ خلق آدم أبا البشر من التراب وخلق حوّاء زوجه من أقصر ضلع من الجهة اليسرى على الصواب ١،٢،٣

ولمّا كان سرّ خلقه أن يكون ﴿خَلِيفَةً فِي ٱلْأَرْضِ﴾ ويملأ من نسله طولها والعرض ركّب فيهما الشهوة البشريّة ليحصل التناسل وفق الإرادة السنيّة وكان آدم حين خلقت حوّاء في سنة من النوم ولمّا أفاق رآها أمامه على ترتيب منظوم فوقعت منه موقع الإعجاب وقال لها من أنت يا أعزّ الأحباب قالت أنا حوّاء وقد خلقني الله من أجلك يا آدم وقدّر ذلك من أزل تقادم فقال لها هلمّ إليّ فقالت بل أنت تعال إليّ فقام آدم إليها فصارت عادة الرجال الذهاب إلى النساء ٢،٢،٣

ولمّا أن جلس معها ومسّ بيديه جسمها دبّت فيه الشهوة الإنسانيّة وأراد مواقعتها ٣،٢،٣

---

١ الباب الثاني وفيه فصلان – أضيف للسياق.

Chapter 2

In two sections

Section 1: Marriage Practices among the Fur

Given that He who is unique in His essence, attributes, and acts—having not been disjoined from any and none having been disjoined from Him—needs neither spouse or offspring, the only one that has need of these last is that pitiful being, newly made, who has no support but God and likewise no aid, He, glory and power be to Him, being the Living, the Everlasting, whom «neither slumber nor sleep may overtake,»[117] Single, Solitary, Unique, Eternal, who has taken neither wife nor son,[118] «and who has no partner in His kingdom»[119] «and no like,»[120] who created Ādam, the father of humankind, from dust and created Ḥawwā', his spouse, from the shortest rib of his left side, as was just. 3.2.1

And given that God's intention in creating him was that he should be «a vicegerent on earth»[121] and fill it with his issue throughout its length and breadth, He instilled in them human lust, that propagation might proceed, as the Sublime Will has decreed it must. When Ḥawwā' was created, Ādam was enjoying a light sleep,[122] and when he awoke, he found her before him, limbs neatly disposed, and saw that she was pleasing. He asked, "Who are you, dearest beloved?" and she said, "I am Ḥawwā'. God has created me for your sake, Ādam, having decreed this from most ancient time." "Come to me," he said. "No, you come to me," said she. So Adam got up and went to her, which is how it came about that men go to their wives. 3.2.2

And when he sat with her and touched her body with his hands and was seized by human lust and wanted to have intercourse with her as animal nature 3.2.3

كما هو مقتضى الحيوانيّة قيل له مَهْ يا آدم لا تحلّ حوّاء إلّا بصداق وعقد نكاح ثمّ إنّ الله سبحانه وتعالى خطب خطبة نكاحهما بكلامه القديم فقال الحمد لعزّتي والعظمة هيبتي والخلق كلّهم عبيدي وإنّي أُشهِدُكم يا ملائكتي وسكّان سمٰواتي أنّي زوّجت بديعة فطرتي حوّاء أمتي لآدم خليفتي على صداق أن يسبّحني ويهلّلني فكان ذلك سنّة لأولاده

٤،٢،٣ لكن لمّا اختلفت الأقاليم واللغات وتعدّدت القبائل والاصطلاحات كان اصطلاح كلّ قوم مباينًا لاصطلاح آخرين وإن كان العقد والمهر واحدًا فمن اصطلاح الفور أنّ الشبّان إناثًا وذكرانًا ينشئون جميعًا في صغرهم يرعون الأغنام ولا حجاب بينهم على الدوام فربّما اصطحب الشابّ والصبيّة من ذلك الحين وانعقدت بينهما المودّة التي لا تبلى على ممرّ السنين فمتى أحبّها وأحبّته ركن إليها وصار يغار عليها ولا يرضاها تحادث غيره وحينئذ يرسل أباه أو أمّه أو أحد أقاربه فيخطبها فإذا انعقد بينهما الكلام ونفذ على وفق المرام جمعت الناس للإملاك وحضر الشهود للمِلاك فيذكرون شروطًا كثيرة ويطلبون أموالًا غزيرة وكلّها يأخذها الأب والأمّ أو الخال أو العمّ ويعقدون لها على شيء قليل من ذلك المال الجزيل وكنّا قد ذكرنا نبذة من ذلك فلتراجع[1] هنالك

٥،٢،٣ ثمّ بعد تمام العقد يتركون الأمر نسيًا منسيًا مدّة طويلة ثمّ يجتمعون فيما بينهم ويتشاورون فينعقد رأيهم على وقت فيه يزفّون فإن كان العروسان من ذوي البيوت الفخام والمراتب العظام ابتدأ أهلهما في تهيئة الذبائح والشراب قبل العرس بأيّام كثيرة ثمّ يرسلون الرسل إلى أحبابهم من البلاد ويقولون العرس في اليوم الفلانيّ المعتاد ويكونوا[2] قد حضروا من المِزْر والنبيذ الأحمر المسمّى عندهم بأمّ بلبل ومن البقر والغنم ما فيه كفاية فتأتي الناس في اليوم الموعود أفواجًا أفواجًا وهناك نساء معهنّ طبول صغار وكبار كلّ امرأة معها ثلاثة طبول اثنان صغيران وآخر كبير على هيئة الدربكّة تضعها تحت إبطها الأيسر أحدها وهو الكبير من أعلى والاثنان يحاذيان أسفل الكبير

[1] الأصل: فلترجع. [2] الأصل: ويكون.

requires, he heard a voice say to him, "Gently, Ādam! Ḥawwāʾ can only be yours in religion through payment of a dowry and the making of a marriage contract." Then God, glorious and mighty, pronounced them in His eternal uncreated language man and wife, saying, "My power be praised! In My majesty lies dread of Me and all Creation are My slaves. I take you, O angels and habitants of the heavens, as My witnesses that I hereby give the marvel of My creation, Ḥawwāʾ, to Ādam, My vicegerent, with, as dowry, that he glorify Me and celebrate My oneness,"[123] and this has been the practice of His children ever since.

However, given that climes and languages have diversified, tribes and conventional practices multiplied, each people's practice has come to differ from others', though the contract and the dower are the same. It is, for example, a practice of the Fur to raise their young people, females and males, together. Thus, when young, they watch over their flocks with no barrier between them, day in and day out. A boy and a girl may become friends from then on, and a bond of affection be tied that never wears, despite the passing of the years. When he loves her and she loves him, he becomes dependent on her and jealous of her and doesn't like to see anyone else talking to her. At that point, he sends his father or mother or a relative to ask for her hand. If they agree on terms and things go according to plan, people gather for the wedding, the witnesses come for the betrothal, and they set out many conditions and ask for ample assets, all of which go to the father and mother, or the maternal or paternal uncle. They conclude the contract for her on the basis of a small part of that copious wealth; we have given a brief account of this earlier to which you may refer.[124] 3.2.4

Following the conclusion of the contract, they set the matter aside, as though it were quite forgotten, for a long while. Then they meet and consult among themselves and agree when to hold the wedding. If the bride and groom belong to great houses and hold high rank, their relatives start preparing the slaughter animals and the drink many days before the wedding. Then they send messengers to their friends in the villages and say, "The wedding is on such and such a customary day." By this time, they will have assembled sufficient millet beer, the red wine they call *umm bulbul*,[125] the cattle, and the sheep; and the people arrive on the set day, troop after troop. Certain women bring with them small and large drums, each having three, two small and one 3.2.5

وتضرب بيدها على الثلاثة ومجموعها يسمّى عندهم الدلُّوكة وكلّما جاءت طائفة خرجت النساء بالطبول ويضربنها ويقلن كلاماً يمدحنها به منه قولهنّ

هَيْ باني هَيْ بَنانْ
وبَنين حِسَّ البَنانْ
يا هـزازين القَنا
أَرَيْتْ ما يجيكم فَنا
عين الحسودْ بالعمى
يا هـزازين الحِراب
أريت ما يجيكم خَراب
عين الحسودْ في التُراب

وكلّما قالت كلاماً قالت قبل أن تقول غيره

هي باني هي بنان
وبنين حس البنان

إنّما هذا الكلام لا يعني شيئاً بالحقيقة وكنت مرّة جئت إلى عرس فتعرّضت لي امرأة وقالت

الشريفْ جايْ من المَسِيدْ
الكِتابْ في إيدْ
والسيفْ في إيدْ
ومن قَبَلْ يجِيبْ
البِرقْدْ عبيدْ

وكنت أحفظ من كلامهنّ كثيرًا نسيته

large, of the same shape as the *darabukkah*, which she puts under her left arm. One, the largest, is on top, while the two smaller ones are next to it, underneath. Then she beats on the three of them with her hand, the whole set being known to them as the *dallúka*. Every time a group arrives, the women go out with the drums and beat them, singing their praises with songs such as the following:

Hay bānī! Hay banān!
Wa-banīna ḥiss al-banān!
O shakers of the lances,
Death spare you its advances!
Blinded be the eye of the envious!
O shakers of the spear,
Ruin come not near!
Dust in the eye of the envious!

Whenever she sings, she says before anything else the words

Hay bānī! Hay banān!
Wa-banīna ḥiss al-banān!

though in fact they mean nothing. Once I arrived at a wedding and a woman blocked my path and sang:

The sharif comes from the mosque,
Book in one hand,
Sword in the other.
Before, he brought
The Birqid as slaves.[126]

I used to know a lot of the words these women sing by heart, but I've forgotten them now.

٦،٢،٣ فتخرج أصحاب العرس ويتلقّون القادمين وكلّ طائفة تأتي رجال ونساء فيجعلون كلّ طائفة في محلّ ويأتون لهم بالأطعمة والأشربة على حسب مقامهم فمنهم يأتونهم بالعصائد والمزر المسمّى في مصر بالبوزة واللحم السليق والشواء[1] ومنهم من يأتون له بالفطير والشراب الأحمر الذي كالنبيذ المسمّى عنهم بأمّ بلبل وإن حضرهم جماعة من الفقهاء أتوهم بالعصائد واللحوم وبالسوبيا وتسمّى عندهم دِينْزَايَا ثمّ يقيّلون في أماكنهم حتّى يبرد الحرّ ويعظم الفيء

٧،٢،٣ فتخرج الشابّات من النساء متزيّنات والشباب من الرجال في أكمل زينة يقدرون عليه وتصطفّ النساء صفوفًا صفوفًا وكلّ صفّ[2] من النساء يقابله صفّ من الشبّان وتخرج النساء ألّلاتي[3] معهنّ الطبول فيضربن ويقلن من كلامهنّ فيبرز صفّ من صفوف النساء يمشين هَوْنًا ويرقصن بأكتافهنّ ويتقاصرن إلى الأرض حتّى يصلن إلى صفّ الرجال فكلّ شابّة تعمد شابًّا حتّى تضع وجهها في وجهه وتهزّ رأسها نحوه حتّى تضربه بضفائرها في وجهه وضفائرها إذ ذاك مدهونة بالطيب وأنواع ما يعرفونه من العطر فيهيج الشابّ ويهزّ حربته على رأسها ثمّ تلتفت راجعة فيتبعها حتّى إلى مكانها الأوّل فيقف فيه الرجل وترجع هي القهقرى حتّى تصل إلى المحلّ الذي كان واقفًا فيه الرجل فحينئذ من يتأمل يجد صفّ النساء ثبت في مكان صفّ الرجال وبالعكس وإذا كان هناك بعض شبّان لم يدخلوا في الصفّ وإحدى الصبايا تريد أن يقابلها واحد منهم تألفه تخرج من الصفّ وتذهب إليه راقصة حتّى تكبّ شعرها على أنفه فيهيج ويصيح ويهزّ حربته ويخرج وراءها وإن لم يخرج كان ملومًا وعليه وليمة للخارجة له وبعد أن يثبت كلّ صفّ في مكان الآخر تخرج النساء راقصات والرجال راقصين وكلّ منهم مقابل للآخر وكلّ شابّة مقابلة لشابّ حتّى يتلاقى الصفّان في وسط المجال وكلّ شابّة تكبّ رأسها في صدر ووجه الشابّ المقابل لها والشابّ يهزّ حربته على رأسها ويصيح صياح الفرح وهذا الصياح عندهم يسمّى الزَرْقة وكلّ من

---

١ الأصل: الشِوا. ٢ أضيف للسياق. ٣ الأصل: التى.

Then the hosts come forward and receive the guests as they arrive. Each group includes men and women, and to each group the hosts assign a place and bring food and drink in accordance with their station. Some are brought different kinds of flour-and-butter paste and the beer that in Egypt is called *būzah*,[127] as well as boiled meat and grilled meats. Others are brought rounds of layered flaky pastry and the red wine known to them as *umm bulbul*. If a group of men of religion arrives, they bring them different kinds of flour-and-butter paste and *sūbiyā*,[128] known to them as *dééng saaya*. Then everyone naps where they are till the air cools and the shadows lengthen. 3.2.6

The girls now separate themselves from the women and the boys from the men, wearing the most beautiful finery they can obtain, and the girls[129] arrange themselves in rows, with a row of boys facing each row of girls. The women who carry drums also advance, beating their drums and singing their songs, and a row of girls moves forward at a leisurely pace, shaking their shoulders and crouching close to the ground, till they reach the row of boys. Each girl now moves in on a boy till her face is right in front of his and moves her head backward and forward in his direction till her braids (which on such occasions are anointed with perfume and the various kinds of scent they're familiar with) are striking him on the face, exciting the boy and causing him to brandish his spear over her head. Then she turns around and goes back. But the boy follows her all the way to her original place, where he now stands while she retreats till she reaches the place where he was standing before. The onlooker will now observe that the girls' row has taken up position where the boys' was, and vice versa. If there are any boys who haven't joined the row, and a girl wants one of them to meet her and get to know her, she leaves the row and goes to him, dancing, and throwing her head back, she brings it suddenly forward again so that her hair falls over his nose, at which he gets excited and cries out and brandishes his spear and follows her; if he does not, he is regarded with disapproval and must put on a feast for the girl who went up to him. Once each row has taken up position where the other was, the girls and the boys come forward, dancing, each group facing the other and each girl facing a boy, till the two rows meet in the middle, and each girl moves her head back and forth in the direction of the chest and face of the boy facing her, while the boy brandishes his spear over her head and lets out cries of joy, this cry being known to them as the *raqraqah*. All the boys and girls are intoxicated from what they've 3.2.7

النساء والرجال ثمل ممّا شرب ولا يزالون هكذا حتّى يأتي الليل فترجع كلّ طائفة إلى مقرّها ويؤتى لها بالأطعمة والأشربة

٨،٢،٣ هذا ولا يخطر ببالك أنّه ليس عندهم رقص إلّا هذا النوع وهو المسمّى برقص الدَلُوكة فهناك[١] رقص آخر يسمّى باِلجيل وآخر يسمّى لَنْقي وآخر يسمّى شَكَّنْدَري ورقص العبيد والإماء يسمّى تُوزي ورقص الفور يسمّى تَنْدِگا وهناك رقص آخر يسمّى بَنْدَلَهْ وفي الأعراس كلّ أناس يرقصون نوعاً من هذه الأنواع فالنساء الجميلات بنات الأكابر يرقصن مع أمثالهنّ من الشبّان على الدلّوكة وأواسط النساء مع أمثالهنّ من الشبّان يرقصن الجيل ومن دونهم يرقصن اللنقي[٢]

٩،٢،٣ فأمّا رقص الجيل فتتقابل فيه النساء مع الرجال يرقصن بأكتافهنّ ويضربن بأرجلهنّ اليمنى على الأرض والرجال كذلك لكن في كل حلقة هناك نساء يغنين والناس ترقص على غنائهنّ وفي رقص اللنقي بعض النساء يغنّين والشابّات والشبّان يضربون[٣] بأرجلهم الأرض ويرقص كلّ منهم برجليه اليمنى واليسرى لكن الشبّان يِكِرّون كريرًا معروفًا لهم

١٠،٢،٣ وأمّا الشكندري فيجتمع الشبّان والشابّات[٤] وكلّ رجل يأخذ شابّة أمامه وتنحني هي ويمسك خصرها بيديه حتّى يكونوا كلّهم كدائرة مسلسلة أعني الأنثى تضع يديها على حَقْوَي الذكر الذي هو أمامها والذكر يضع يديه على حقوي الأنثى التي هي أمامه وكلّهم منحنيون حتّى يكونوا كدائرة تامّة ويمشون رويدًا رويدًا مع ضرب أرجلهم في الأرض لأجل أن[٥] يسمع رنين خلاخيلهنّ والبنات التي يغنّين خارجات عن الحلقة

١١،٢،٣ وأمّا البندله فهي مِن أنواع رقص العبيد وهو أنّ العبد يأتي بالنارجيل المسمّى عندهم بالدَلَيْب ويثقبه وهو أُكَر مثل كرة المدفع وينظم منه ثلاثًا أو أربعًا في خيط ويربطها في رجله كالخلخال في الرجل اليمنى وكلّ عبد يفعل ذلك وتقف جارية من الجواري خلفه ويكونون كدائرة ولهم كرير مخصوص فيخرج العبد منهم لآخر في وسط الدائرة ويحاول

١ الأصل: وهناك. ٢ الأصل: لنقي. ٣ الأصل: ويضربن. ٤ الأصل: والشبات. ٥ أضيف للسياق.

drunk, and they keep this up till night comes, when each group goes back to its assigned place and is brought food and drink.

Do not imagine for a moment, however, that this, which is called the *dallúka*,[130] is the only kind of dance they know. There is a dance called the *jêl*, another called the *lanngi*, and another called the *sangadiri*, and there is the dance of the male and female slaves, called *tawse*, and the dance of the Fur, called *tindinga*. There is also another dance, called the *bindalah*. At weddings, each type of person dances one type of dance. Thus, the beautiful daughters of the great dance to the *dallúka* with their like among the boys, the daughters of the middling class and their like among the boys dance the *jêl*, and lesser people dance the *lanngi*. 3.2.8

In the *jêl*, the women face the men, shake their shoulders, and stamp the ground with their right feet, and the men do the same, but in each circle there are women who sing, and the people dance to their singing. In the *lanngi*, some of the women sing, while the girls and boys stamp the ground, and each dances with his or her feet, right and left. The boys, for their part, make the sound known as *karīr*.[131] 3.2.9

In the *sangadiri*, the boys and girls assemble, and each boy takes a girl who is in front of him. She bends over and he takes hold of her waist, so that together they form a sort of circular chain, meaning that the female puts her hands on the hips of the male in front of her and the male puts his hands on the hips of the female in front of him and all of them are bending over so that together they form a closed circle and they move very slowly, stamping their feet so that the ringing of the girls' anklets can be heard. The girls who sing stand outside the circle. 3.2.10

The *bindalah* is a slave dance. It consists of a male slave bringing the nuts—resembling coconuts—that they call *dalayb*, making holes in them (the nuts being round, like cannonballs), stringing three or four of them on a lace, and tying this to his leg like an anklet, on the right foot; each male slave does the same and a female slave stands behind each and they make a kind of circle. They also have a special sound they make. A slave advances toward another in the middle of the circle and competes with him at this sport, which is based on bodily strength and suppleness, as though they were performing acrobatics. After they've competed for a while, one of them will strike the other with the leg to which the nuts are tied and not stop till he makes him fall or fails in 3.2.11

معه في اللعب وهذا اللعب مبنيّ على القوّة وخفّة الجسم كما يلعب البهلوان فبعد أن يتحاولا مليّاً يضرب أحدهما صاحبه برجله التي فيها النارجيل[١] فلا يخلو إمّا أن يوقعه في الأرض أو لا فالماهر هو الذي إن ضرب صاحبه أوقعه والباقي يرقصون رقصاً لا تكسُّر فيه وكلّهم يردّون على المغنّيات وهؤلاء[٢] المغنّيات خارج عن الحلقة

١٢،٢،٣ وأمّا التوزي فهو أنّ عبداً من العبيد يضرب على طبل كبير والنساء والرجال حوله حلقة وكلّ رجل واضع يديه على حقوي امرأة وكلّ امرأة واضعة يديها على حقوي رجل لكن مع الانتصاب والاعتدال لا مع الانحناء ويمشون رويداً والنساء يضربن أرجلهنّ ببعضها لترنّ الخلاخيل التي في أرجلهنّ ومشيهم كلّهم في الدائرة على نظم نقرات الطبل ويكونون أيضاً كدائرة والمغنّيات خارج الحلقة وأمّا التندگا فهي لعب البرقد والفور وهو أشبه بالتوزي وإنّما الفرق بينهما في كون أنّ التوزي يمشون فيه رويداً والتندگا بحركات عنيفة وبالحقيقة العبارة لا تفي بذلك لأنّ المشاهدة بشيء آخر فربّما يرى المشاهد شيئاً لا يمكن التعبير عنه

١٣،٢،٣ ولكلّ رقص من الأرقاص غناء مخصوص فأمّا غناء الجيل فمنه قولهنّ

يوباني هَيْ يوبانينْ
الليلْ بوبَى يالمُتْقالْ
أنا راسي إندارْ
الليلْ بوبَى يالمُتْقالْ
أنا راسي إندارْ

وهذه الكلمات يوباني هي يوبانين لا تعني شيئاً لكن واحدة منهنّ تنشد وتقول الليل بوبي يالمتقال فتقول النساء الأخر أنا راسي إندار ومنه قولهنّ

١ الأصل: النرجيل. ٢ الأصل: هذه.

the attempt, the skilled performer being the one who topples his opponent with a single kick. The rest dance a dance in which there is no bending of the body, and all respond antiphonally to the female singers, who are outside the circle.

The *tawse* consists of a male slave beating on a large drum, with the women and the men around him in a circle, each man putting his hands on the hips of a woman and each woman putting her hands on the hips of a man, but standing straight up and not bending over. Then they move ahead slowly, the women striking their feet together so that their anklets ring. They all proceed in a circle in time to the drumbeats and also form a circle, with the female singers on the outside. The *tindinga* is a sport of the Birqid and the Fur and is most like the *tawse*, the only difference being that in the *tawse* they move slowly, while in the *tindinga* the movements are violent. In truth, though, these descriptions don't get to the heart of the matter, because seeing something is quite different from hearing about it: sometimes an observer sees things words cannot convey. 3.2.12

Each of these dances has its own song. The words sung by the women for the *jêl* go: 3.2.13

Yūbānī hay yūbānīn
The night is passing, my gold piece
My head is spinning
The night is passing, my gold piece
My head is spinning[132]

The words *yūbānī hay yūbānīn* mean nothing, but one of the women sings out: "The night is passing, my gold piece," and the others respond, "My head is spinning." They also sing:

اللِيـلْ بوبَى
دارفورْ جَـفَـهْ
أنا راسي نوى

ومنه قولهنّ

فُـرَيْعْ[1] الحـانِيَّـهْ
سَبَّبْتُو الحـانِيَّـهْ
ويا فُرَيْعْ[2] الصَنْدَلْ
في بوَيْتنا قامْ رَنْدَلْ

وأمّا غناء اللنقي فمنه قولهنّ ١٤،٢،٣

يا عِيالْــــ
جيـبوا المـالْــــ
نَهيـضْ دَلْدَگْ وَدْ بِنَيَّـةْ
صَبّوا دَرِيزْ الخَيلْ في كَرْيو
نَهيـضْ دَلْدَگْ وَدْ بِنَيَّـةْ

وأما غناء التندگا عند الفور فمنه قولهن ١٥،٢،٣

باسي طاهِرٍ دُقُلا
بِي لَبا وَدُوِيگْ أَبا
كِتابْ مُصْحَفْ لَگْ حَـلْفَيْنْ فِيا[3]
تْرَيْمُدو كُبَيّ رايْلا
تارَگا مُـدُو صَـقَـلْ جُوَجِبِي

---

١ الأصل: فُرَيَعْ. ٢ الأصل: فُرَيْعَا. ٣ الأصل: حَلْفَيْنْفِيَا.

The night passes
Darfur is loveless
My head yearns[133]

They also sing:

O little branch so tender
You've made me surrender
O little branch of sandal—
Over our little house you grow and dangle.[134]

For the *lanngi*, the women sing, among other things: 3.2.14

Boys,
Get rich!
Join Daldang, son of Binayyah![135]
The pounding of hooves sounds in Karyū.
Join Daldang, son of Binayyah![136]

For the *tindinga*, the women sing, among other things: 3.2.15

Báási Tahir dogólá
Bála bá diéng ába
Kitab musab láng álpen piá,
Tárímádó kábí raaye ela.
Tarang mado sagal dió jábí.[137]

ولو تتبّعنا غناء أنواع الرقص لطال الحال

فبعد أن يأكلوا ويشربوا يزفّون العروس بالدلّوكة ويلفّون بها حول البلد ويأتون بها للمحلّ الذي أعدّ للدخول عليها فيه ثمّ بعد العشاء بكثير تجتمع الشبّان ويأخذون العريس ويزفّونه بالغناء والزرقة حتّى يأتون به إلى المحلّ المعلوم فيجلسون خارجه وحينئذ جميع الشابّات مجتمعة مع العروس والشبّان مجموعون عند العريس وقد استوزر العريس أعزّ إخوانه لأنّه حينئذ كالسلطان واستوزرت العروس امرأة وسمّوها ميرم فبعد أن يجلس الرجال مع عريسهم يطلبون الميرم فلا تخرج لهم إلّا بعد نحو ساعتين فيتقدّم لها الوزير ويسلّم عليها بلطف ويلتمس[1] منها حضور العروس فتقول لهم من أنتم ومن أين جئتم وما هي العروس التي تريدون فيقول الوزير أمّا نحن فضيوف وقد جئنا من بلاد بعيدة ونريد الملكة تؤانس ضيوفها فتقول له أمّا الملكة فمشغولة بشغل عظيم[2] وها أنا وكيلتها في ضيافتكم وقِراكم وما يلزم لكم فيقول الوزير نحن نعلم أنّ فيك البركة والكفاية لكن لنا معها كلام لا يمكن إفشاؤه لغيرها فتقول له إذا كان كذلك فماذا للملكة وماذا لي لأنّ عادتها ألّا تبرز من حجابها ولا تأتي لطلّابها إلّا بجُعل فيقول لها المال والأرواح وكلّ ما طلبته فلا يزال يحاولها وتحاوله حتّى يتراضيا وهذا كلّه والعروسة قريبة منهم وراء ستارة لكنّها لا تتكلّم بشيء والعريس أيضاً ساكت كذلك والمحاورة بين الاثنين ١٦،٢،٣

فإذا وقع التراضي رفعت الستارة فتخرج العروس فيقول الوزير أمّا الملكة فللملك وماذا لنا نحن فتنادي الميرم للبنات التي مع العروس فيحضرن وتقول لهنّ أيّتها البنات أريد منكنّ في هذه الليلة أن تؤانسن أضياف الملكة فيقلن لها حبّاً وكرامة وهي تعلم كلّ صبيّة ومحبوبها فتقول يا فلانة كوني مع فلان وأنت يا فلانة كوني مع فلان وهكذا حتّى لا يبقى إلّا التي لا محبوب لها أو الذي لا محبوبة له فيأخذ كلّ شابّ محبوبته ويبيت معها إن وسعهم المحلّ الذي هم فيه وصورة ذلك أن يبيت العريس ١٧،٢،٣

---

١ الأصل: يلتمس. ٢ الأصل: عطيم.

It would take a very long time to list all the songs that go with each kind of dance.

After they've eaten and drunk, they process with the bride to the music of the *dallúka* drums, taking her on a tour of the village and ending at the place prepared for her deflowering. Then, a long while after dinner, the young men assemble and take the groom and accompany him in procession, singing and making the *raqraqah*,[138] till they come to the place in question, where they sit down outside. By this time, all the young women will have assembled with the bride, and the young men will have assembled where the groom is, and the groom will have appointed his dearest brother as "vizier" (for at that moment he's like a sultan), and the bride will have appointed a woman as her vizier, whom they call the mééram. Once the men have sat down with their groom, they call for the mééram, but she refuses to come out to see them till about two hours have passed, at which time the vizier presents himself to her and greets her politely, requesting her to bring the bride. She asks them, "Who are you, where have you come from, and who is the bride you seek?" The vizier replies, "We are guests come from faraway lands, and we seek the queen, so that she may entertain her guests." She says, "The queen is busy with a matter of great importance, but here am I, as her representative, to offer you hospitality, entertainment, and whatever you need." The vizier responds, "We know that you are a capable person and well up to the task, but we have something to say to her that we can reveal to no other." She then says, "If that is the case, then what is there for the queen, and what for me, for it is her custom not to come out from behind what conceals her or go to those who ask for her unless there is a reward," to which he answers, "Our wealth and our lives and whatever she may ask." They continue in this way, bandying words with one another, until they agree and that's the end of things. While this is going on, the bride is close by, behind a curtain, but she says nothing, and the groom too is silent, the argument being between the other two.

3.2.16

When they reach agreement, the curtain is lifted, the bride comes out, and the vizier says, "The queen is for the king, but what is there for us?" so the mééram calls out for the girls who are with the bride, and they come, and she tells them, "Girls, I want you to entertain the queen's guests tonight," and they reply to her, "With all love and honor!" The mééram knows each girl and her boyfriend, so she says, "You, so-and-so, be with so-and-so, and you, so-and-so, be with so-and-so," and so on till only the girls who have no boyfriends and

3.2.17

وعروسه والميرم والوزير وكلّ زوجين معاً صفّاً أو صفّين على حسب سعة الموضع وإن لم يسع المحلّ جميعهم بقي من وسعه المحلّ مع العروسين وذهب الباقي فكلّ شابّ منهم يأخذ محبوبته ويتوجّه بها إلى بيتها أو إلى بيت بعض أحبابها ولا يذهب بها إلى بيته لأنّها لا ترضى ذلك لأنّ عادتهم أنّ الشابّ متى ما أحبّ صبيّة وعلمت أمّها بذلك لا تقابله أبداً ولا يقابلها وإذا رأته في طريق ولم تر لها مَخْلَصاً منه بركت في الأرض وسدلت ثوبها على رأسها ووجهها حتّى يمرّ وهو كذلك يفعل يعني إن رآها وعرفها يرجع على عقبه هارباً إن أمكنه ذلك وإلّا أدار وجهه لنحو حائط أو شجرة حتّى تمرّ ثمّ يرسل لها السلام إن كان معه أحد وكذلك هي تفعل بعد مروره إن لم يكن معه أحد ترسل له السلام إن كان معها أحد وهذا كلّه عندهم من نوع الحياء والتعظيم

١٨،٢،٣ وعندهم أهل الزوجة محترمون فأمّها كأمّه بل أشدّ احتراماً وأبوها كأبيه بل أشدّ وإخوتها كإخوته وهي مثله في ذلك إذا رأت أمّه أو أباه فرّت وسلكت طريقاً غير طريقهما وترسل السلام أو يرسل إليها ولا تواجه أحداً منهم وتعتبر أباه كأبيها وهكذا مثل ما ذكرنا في الرجل ولذلك تذهب مع محبوبها إلى محلّ آخر ولا ترضى أن تذهب معه إلى بيته بل إن ضاقت الأماكن بكثرة الناس وليس هناك دار سوى دار أبيه لا تذهب معه إليها بل يذهبان إلى الخلاء ويبيتان فيه وأمّا دار أبيها من حيث أنّ لها محلّاً معدّاً لذلك يبيت معها فيه من أرادت ولا يراها أبواها فإنّ الرجل يذهب معها إليه ويخرج عند الفجر وأبواها نائمان فلا يراه أحد منهما

١٩،٢،٣ ولنرجع إلى ما نحن بصدده فنقول ثمّ يبيتون تلك الليلة فإذا أصبح الصباح قامت كلّ صبيّة وتوجّهت إلى بيت أبويها فتصلح شأنها أعني أنّها تغسل وجهها وأطرافها بل ربّما اغتسلت ثمّ تتطيّب وتكتحل وتجدّد زينتها وكذلك العروس تدخل عند أمّها فتصلح شأنها وكذا الرجال يذهبون إلى ديارهم إن كانت قريبة فإن كانت بعيدة كأن كانوا من بلد أخرى يذهب كلّ منهم إلى دار صاحب له فيصلح شأنه هناك وكذلك

the boys who have no girlfriends are left. Each boy then takes his girlfriend and spends the night with her—right where they are, if there's enough room. This is done as follows: the bride and the groom, the mééram and the vizier, and each couple spend the night together in one or two rows, depending on how much room there is. If there isn't enough room for all of them, those for whom there's room remain, along with the bride and groom, and the rest go, each boy taking his girlfriend to her house or to the house of one of her friends. He doesn't take her to his house because she wouldn't agree, since it's their custom that when a young man loves a girl and her mother finds out about it, the mother must never meet with him nor he with her. If she sees him on the path and can find no way to avoid him, she kneels on the ground and drapes her wrap over her head and face until he has passed, and he does likewise, meaning that if he sees her and recognizes her, he turns on his heel and flees, if he can. If he cannot, he turns his face to a wall or a tree till she has passed. If there is someone else with him, he sends her his greetings via that person, and she does the same after he's passed. If there is nobody with him and she has somebody with her, she sends him her greetings via that person. All this, in their view, is a matter of modesty and respect.[139]

For them, all the members of the wife's family are taboo. Her mother is like 3.2.18
his mother, or to be treated with even greater respect; her father is like his, or more so; and her brothers like his. The same holds true for her. If she sees his mother or father, she flees and takes another path and sends her greetings, or he sends her his, and must not come face to face with either of them, and she treats his father like her own, and so on, just as we have described when referring to the man. This is why she goes somewhere else with her boyfriend and won't agree to go to his house with him. In fact, if there are too many people and too few places, she still will not go with him to his house. Instead they will go into the open countryside and spend the night there. In the case of her father's house, however, given that she has a place of her own prepared for that purpose there, anyone she likes can spend the night with her there without her father seeing her. If the man goes there with her and leaves at dawn while her parents are asleep, neither of them will see her.

But let us return to our original topic. They pass the night, and when morn- 3.2.19
ing comes, each girl gets up and goes to her parents' house and performs her toilet, by which I mean that she washes her face and limbs; indeed, she may perform the ritual ablution of her entire body. Then she perfumes herself, adorns

النساء إن كانت المرأة من بلد أخرى تذهب إلى دار حبيبة لها تصلح شأنها فيها لأنّ الشابّات اللائي حضرن للعرس مع كلّ شابّة منهنّ كحلها وعطرها وما تحتاج إليه فتصلح شأنها ويجلسن حتّى يقرب الضحى فتأتي الميرم إلى محلّ الزفاف والعريس غائب عنه أعني عند قيامه لإصلاح شأنه هو الآخر فتقمه وتنظّفه وتفرشه وتهيئ مجالسه هي وبعض صواحباتها[1] فيأتي العريس فيجده نظيفاً فيجلس هو ووزيره وتنهلّ عليه الشبّان فيجلسون معه

٢٠،٢،٣ ثمّ أصحاب العرس بالخيار إن شاءوا جعلوا السبعة أيّام كلّها بالرقص والدلّوكة وإن شاءوا اقتصروا على يوم واحد فإن ظهر اقتصارهم جلس الضيوف إلى وقت الغداء[2] وبعد تناولهم الطعام رجع كلّ منهم إلى بلده ولم يبق إلّا أهل البلد الذي هم فيه وإن لم يروا الاقتصار وعلموا أنّ أصحاب العرس يريدون أن يمتدّ عرسهم إلى السبعة أيّام أقاموا ويظهر ذلك بتجدّد الذبائح وعصر الخمور والتهيؤ

٢١،٢،٣ تنبيه: اعلم أنّ أهل كلّ بلد من البلاد الذين دُعوا إلى مثل هذه الوليمة يأتون إمّا بقرتين أو ثورين أو ثور أو بقرة أو بشياه إعانة لصاحب الوليمة وإن كان لهم أقارب خارجين عن بلدتهم ودعوا يأتون بأثوار أو بقر غير ما تأتي به أهل بلدتهم إعانة

٢٢،٢،٣ ثمّ يمكثون نهارهم كلّه في لعب وضحك وانشراح وأكل وشرب وطيب محادثة إلى العصر فتضرب الطبول التي هي الدلّوكات ويفعلون مثل ما فعلوا في اليوم السابق حتّى إلى الليل فيأتيهم الطعام والشراب وبعد فراغهم من ذلك يجتمعون رجالاً ونساء في محلّ الزفاف فيتحادثون حتّى إلى نحو نصف الليل ثمّ يأخذ كلّ شابّ حبيبته ويبيت معها حيث باتا أمسهما ويبقون على ذلك المدّة المذكورة وإذا أعوز الأمر إلى الذبائح بأن كان ما أعدّ للذبح لم يكف من حضر خرج أبو العروس أو أخوها أو أحد أقاربها

١ الأصل: صواحبتها. ٢ الأصل: الغذاء.

her eyes with kohl, and rearranges her finery. It is the same with the bride, who enters her mother's house and performs her toilet. Likewise, the men go to their houses, if they are nearby. If these are far away, as in the case of those who come from another village, each goes to a friend's house and performs his toilet there, and it's the same with the women: if a woman is from another village, she goes to the house of a friend and performs her toilet there, for each of the young women who goes to the wedding has with her her kohl, her perfume, and everything she needs. She performs her toilet and the women sit together till almost midmorning. Then the mééram goes to where the wedding festivities were held while the groom isn't there (by which I mean when he too has gone to perform his toilet) and, along with some of her friends, sets it to rights, cleaning it, spreading out mats, and preparing the places where people will sit. Then the groom comes and finds it clean, so he sits there along with his vizier, and the young men come in droves and sit with him.

After this, it's up to the hosts. If they want to, they may pass the whole seven 3.2.20
days in dancing and *dallúka*, or they may limit the celebrations to one day. If it's clear that they want to keep things short, the guests stay until lunchtime, and after eating each returns to his village and only the people of the village where the festivities were held remain. If the guests do not want to keep things short and know that the hosts want to extend their celebrations to seven days, they take up residence. This is made obvious by new animals being brought to be slaughtered, wine being pressed, and other preparations.

Note: The people invited to such feasts from each of the villages bring with 3.2.21
them either two cows or two bulls, or one bull or one cow, or ewes as a contribution for the host, and if they have relatives living outside their village who are invited, these bring bulls and cows over and above those brought by the people of their own village, in order to be of assistance.

They spend the whole of the rest of the day playing, laughing, and relaxing, 3.2.22
eating and drinking, and engaging in pleasant conversation till the late afternoon. Then the drums, those called *dallúka*s, are beaten, and they do as they did the day before till night comes, when food and drink are brought. When they're finished with those, they gather, men and women alike, in the place where the celebrations are held, and talk till around midnight. Then each boy takes his girlfriend and spends the night with her in the same place as the day before, and they go on in this way for the allotted time. If more animals have to be slaughtered, the number prepared being too small for those present, the

إلى المرعى فكلّ ما وجده من البقر أمامه عقرمنها ثورًا أو ثورين أو بقرة أو شياهًا وبعد العقر يرسل الجزّارين فيذبحون العقير ويأتون بلحمه إلى الضيوف وهكذا فإذا بلغ الخبر صاحب البقر فلا يخلو إمّا أن يطلب الثمن فيرضونه أو يسكت حتّى يبقى له عرس أو لأحد أقاربه فيعقر هو الآخر ما يريد من بقر من عقر بقره ودَقّةٌ بِدَقّةٍ ولذلك إذا عُمِلَ عرس تخاف أرباب المواشي من العقر فيأمرون رعاتهم أن يبعدوا بها في الخلاء لأنّهم لا يعقرون إلّا من الأموال القريبة المرعى وهذه سنّة جارية فيهم وفي تلك المدّة العروس كالملكة وصواحباتها معها في لعب وانشراح والعريس كذلك

٢٣،٢،٣ ومن عادتهم أنّ العريس لا يفتضّ عروسه إلّا بعد السبعة أيّام مع أنّهما يبيتان متعانقين لا حائل بينهما ويجعلون ذلك كرامة لها ولأبويها لأنّهم يقولون الليلة الأولى في كرامة أبيها والثانية في كرامة أمّها والثالثة في كرامة أخيها إن كان أو أختها وهكذا حتّى تتمّ السبعة أيّام ومن استعجل وفضّ قبل تمام ذلك عُيِّبَ عليه وقالوا قد استعجل ولكن من المحال أن يفتضّها قبل ثلاث ليال

٢٤،٢،٣ عجيبة: من عوائدهم أنّ المرأة لا تأكل أمام زوجها ولا غيره من الرجال وإذا دخل زوجها وهي تأكل قامت وفرّت وهذا عندهم من أكمل الحياء ويقبّحون على المرأة التي تأكل أمام الرجل وحين كنت هناك ورأيت ذلك قلت لهم أتستحي من الأكل مع الرجل ولا تستحي من النوم معه وأنّه يدخل بين شعبها ويولج فيها ويرى فرجها وما هي عليه قالوا ذلك لا ضرر فيه وأمّا أن[١] تفتح فاها وتدخل فيه الطعام أمام الرجل فهذا شيء قبيح انتهى

٢٥،٢،٣ ومن عادتهم أن الرجل لا يأخذ عروسه ويبني بها في بيته بل في بيت أمّها وأبيها ولا تخرج معه حتّى تلد ولدين أو ثلاثة فإن طلبها للنقلة معه قبل ذلك أبت عليه وربّما وقع الطلاق بينهما بسبب ذلك ومن عادتهم أنّها لا تذكر اسمه على لسانها أبدًا بل

---

١ أضيف للسياق.

bride's father, or her brother or a relative, goes out to the pastures and hocks whatever animals he finds before him—a bull or two, or a cow, or ewes—and, having hocked them, sends the butchers, who slaughter the hocked animals and bring the guests their meat, and so it continues. If word reaches the owner of the cattle, he either asks for the price and is compensated, or does nothing until he himself or one of his relatives holds a wedding, when he hocks whatever he wants of the cattle belonging to the man who hocked his, tit for tat. This is why, when a wedding is to be held, animal owners order their minders to take them far out into the savannah, since they only hock animals grazing nearby. Throughout this period, the bride is treated like a queen and her girlfriends are with her, playing and enjoying themselves, and it's the same for the groom.

Another custom of theirs is that the groom doesn't deflower his bride till after the seven days have passed, even though they spend the night in one another's arms with nothing between them. The grooms do this out of respect for the bride and her parents, saying that the first night is out of respect for her father, the second for her mother, the third for her brother, if she has one, or for her sister, and so on, till the seven days are up. They think badly of a man who hurries and deflowers her before then, saying, "What a hurry he was in!" That he should deflower her before three nights have passed is unthinkable. 3.2.23

A remarkable thing. It is their custom that a woman mustn't eat in front of her husband or any other man, and if her husband enters while she's eating, she gets up and flees. They see this as the acme of modesty and denounce any woman who eats in front of her husband. When I was there and saw this, I asked them, "How can she be ashamed to eat with her husband when she is not ashamed to sleep with him or let him enter her embrace, penetrate her, and see her vagina and every other bit of her?" "There's no harm in any of that," they replied, "but for her to open her mouth and insert food into it in front of her husband is an abomination." 3.2.24

Another custom of theirs is that the man doesn't take his bride and consummate the marriage in his own house: he does so in her parents' house, and she doesn't leave it and live with him till she's borne two or three children. If he should ask her to move in with him before this, she refuses, and they sometimes even get divorced over the issue. Another custom is that she never allows his name to pass her lips. Instead she will always say, "He told me such and such." If she's asked who told her, she'll say, "him"—this till such time as 3.2.25

دائمًا تقول قال لي كذا وكذا فإذا سئلت من الذي قال تقول هو حتّى يولد لهما فتى ولد لهما قالت أبو فلان أو أبو فلانة باسم من يولد إن كان ذكرًا أو أنثى

٣،٢،٢٦ ومن عادتهم أنّ الرجل لا ينفق على المرأة بعد الزفاف إلّا بعد سنة فإن جاء بشيء قبل السنة جاء به على سبيل الهديّة مع أنّه لا يأكل إلّا أعزّ ممّا يأكلون فيمكن أنّهم طبخوا شيئًا قبيحًا لهم من المآكل الرديئة ويذبحون له دجاجًا أو حمامًا أو لحمًا ومن عوائدهم أنّ الرجل مدّة ما هو في بيت أبي زوجته يصنعون له طعامًا جميلًا جدًّا غير العشاء يتناوله بالليل إمّا مرّة أو مرّتين أو ثلاث مرّات[1] ويسمّون الأوّل بلغة الفور جُرِي جَراگ والثاني تَارْگَا جِيسُو والثالث صُبحُ جَلُّو ومرادهم بذلك تقويته على الجماع وأمّا اسمه بلغتهم العربيّة وَرّانِيَّة وأكثر الأغنياء يأكلون بعد أكلهم العشاء لأنّهم ربّما جاءهم ضيف فلم يتمكّن من الشبع لحيائه من الضيف أو كان العشاء غير جيّد فلا بدّ له من ورّانيّة ومعنى قولهم جري جراگ انزع القميص فإن جري معناه قميص وجراگ معناه انزع وتارگا جيسو معناه مَسْك الرِجْل فإن تارگا معناه رجل وجيسو معناه مسك وصبح جلو معناه طلوع الفجر

٣،٢،٢٧ وأمّا الورّانيّة فهي عربيّة منسوبة لوراء ضدّ الأمام لأنّه يأكلها وراء العشاء أي بعدما يأكل العشاء ولهذا تجد بعض الناس إذا كان عنده من يعزّ عليه من الإخوان وحضر العشاء معه وأراد أن يقوم يمنعه حتّى ينفض المجلس ثمّ يدعو خادمه ويقول هل من شيء يؤكل فيأتيه الخادم بالورّانيّة فيأكلان معًا وهذا لا يُفعل إلّا مع أعزّ الأصدقاء وهذه الورّانيّة تنفع أحيانًا للضيف المفاجئ بالليل الداجي

٣،٢،٢٨ وهذا كلّه إن كان عرسًا فإن كان ختانًا فعلوا ما ذكرناه من استحضار الأطعمة والمزر وأم بلبل والدينزايا[2] ودعوا الناس ورقصوا على الدلاليك وزفّوا المطاهر وجاء المزيّن فختنه وأبوه واقف فإن بكى المطاهر نفر[3] أهله منه وتركوه ومضوا وإن صبر

---

[1] أضيف للسياق. [2] الأصل: والدنزايا. [3] الأصل: ففر.

they have children, when she'll say, "the father of . . . ," supplying the name of their child, whether a boy or a girl.

Another of their customs is that the man doesn't support the woman until a year has passed since the wedding. If he brings her anything before then, he does so as a gift. At the same time, though, he always eats better than the rest of the family: they may cook any disgusting kind of mediocre food for themselves, but for him they'll slaughter a chicken or a pigeon or prepare meat. Another custom is that, while the man is in his father-in-law's house, they prepare very good food for him once, twice, or even three times a day, in addition to the dinner that he takes at night. The first meal is called in the Fur language *juri jaráng*, the second *tarnga jíso*, and the third *subu jelló*, their hope being that this will strengthen him for intercourse. In their Arabic such a meal is called a *warrāniyyah*. Most well-off people eat again after their dinner, because a guest may have come to see them, which requires that they not eat their fill out of respect for him; or the dinner may not have been good, so they must have a *warrāniyyah*. Their term *juri jaráng* means "take off the shirt," *juri* meaning "shirt" and *jaráng* meaning "take off." *Tarnga jíso* means "grasp the leg," *tarnga* meaning "leg" and *jíso* meaning "grasp." *Subu jelló* means "the coming of dawn." 3.2.26

The word *warrāniyyah* is Arabic and is derived from *warāʾ*,[140] meaning "behind" (the opposite of "in front"), because they eat it "behind" dinner, i.e., after they've eaten dinner. This is why you will find that some people, if they have a particularly dear friend, and he's had dinner with them and is about to leave, will prevent him from doing so till all the rest of the company has left. Then they'll call their servant and ask him, "Is there anything to eat?" at which the servant will bring them the *warrāniyyah* and they'll eat together. This is done only with their best friends. The *warrāniyyah* also comes in useful for the unexpected guest who arrives in the middle of the night. 3.2.27

The above applies to weddings. If the celebration is a circumcision, they do everything we've mentioned in terms of preparing food, millet beer, *umm bulbul*, and *dééng saaya*, and invite people and dance to the *dallúka* drums, and make a procession with the boy who is to be circumcised, the barber coming and circumcising him while his father stands by. If the boy being circumcised cries, his relatives treat him with aversion and leave him. If he is patient while being circumcised and does not cry, his father says, "Be my witnesses, everyone here! I hereby give my son a cow" or a bull or a 3.2.28

حال الختن ولم يبك قال أبوه اشهدوا يا أهل المجلس أنّي أعطيت ولدي بقرة أو ثوراً أو عبداً أو أمة ممّا يقدر عليه وقالت أمّه كذلك وكلّ من حضر من أهله يهدي له شيئاً فإن كان أهله أغنياء ناله منهم شيء كثير فيصير غنيّاً وذلك كلّه بحسب غناء أهله وفقرهم ثمّ يجتمع أترابه في ثالث يوم الطهور ويأخذون السفاريك ويجوسون خلال البلد يضربون الدجاج فيقتلون دجاجاً كثيراً وفي رابع يوم إلى اليوم السابع يذهبون إلى البلاد المجاورة لهم فلا يـرون دجاجة إلّا قتلوها وكلّ يوم يتوجّهوا لبلد يقتلون دجاجها وأصحاب الدجاج لا يـرون بذلك بأساً وإن كان خفاضاً فعلوا فيه كلّ ما ذكرنا إلّا الدجاج فلا يقتلونه والخفاض لا يتغالون فيه كالختان وممّا ذكرناه يعلم الواقف على رحلتنا أنّنا استقصينا جميع ذلك لتمام الفائدة وحسن العائدة

٢٩،٢،٣ واعلم أنّ أهل دارفور لا يستقلّون بشيء في أمورهم بدون النساء بل إنهنّ يشاركنهم[1] في جميع أحوالهم إلّا في الحروب العظيمة ولذلك فإنّ[2] عرساً لا يتمّ إلّا بهنّ أو حزناً كذلك ولولاهنّ ما استقام لأهل دارفورشيء فترى النساء يحضرن في الأمور المهمّة ومن ذلك الأذكار وهي على ضربين ضرب يفعله أهل البلاد المستعربون أعني من ليسوا بعجم وضرب يفعله أعجام الفور

٣٠،٢،٣ فأمّا الأوّل فهو ما كان على طريقة شيخ من الصوفيّة أو وليّ من الأولياء وعلى كلّ فتحضر حلقة الذكر امرأة تنشد لهم والنساء خلفها وقوف لا يتكلّمن بل ينظرن أزواجهنّ وأقاربهنّ ليعلمن أيّهم أحسن ذكراً وقد ينشد رجل والنساء يسمعن كبقيّة الرجال

٣١،٢،٣ ومن ذلك ما وقع أن تلميذ الشيخ دفع الله حضر حلقة ذكر تلاميذ الشيخ يعقوب وبين تلاميذ الشيخين معاندة فلمّا حمي الذكر أراد أحد تلاميذ الشيخ يعقوب ان ينكت على تلميذ الشيخ دفع الله فقال

١ الأصل: تشاركهم. ٢ الأصل: ان.

male or a female slave, depending on what he can afford. His mother makes the same declaration, and every one of his relatives who is present gives him something. If his family is rich, he will receive much property from them, and become well off, all according to his family's access to or lack of resources. On the third day of the circumcision ceremonies, the other boys of his age get together and take their throwing sticks and roam through the village knocking down chickens and killing them in large numbers. From the fourth to the seventh day, they go to the neighboring villages and kill every chicken they lay eyes on. Each day they go to a different village to kill chickens, and the owners of the chickens see nothing wrong in that. If it's a female circumcision, they do everything we have described, except that they don't kill chickens. They don't go to as much expense over the circumcision of a female as they do over that of a male. Anyone reading this account will know that we've gone to some length to describe these things simply so that the best benefit may be provided, the greatest gain derived.

Know too that the men of Darfur undertake no business without the par- 3.2.29
ticipation of the women. Indeed, these take part with them in all their affairs, exception made for major battles. This is why no wedding or funeral takes place without them and why without them nothing would be considered by the people of Darfur to have been properly done. Thus you'll find women present on all great occasions. An example is their *dhikr* ceremonies, which are of two kinds: those performed by the Arabic-speaking inhabitants of the country, by which I mean those who do not speak one of the non-Arabic languages, and those performed by the non-Arabic-speaking Fur.

The first kind is in accordance with the practice of a particular Sufi shaykh 3.2.30
or holy man. In either case, a woman will be present at the circle of remembrance to chant to the men, and the rest of the women will stand behind her, saying nothing but watching their husbands and relatives to see which of them is the best performer: a man may chant on his own while the women, like the rest of the men, listen.

For example, a disciple of Shaykh Dafʿ Allāh once attended the *dhikr* cer- 3.2.31
emony of the disciples of Shaykh Yaʿqūb. There was tension between the two shaykhs' disciples, and once the *dhikr* had warmed up one of the disciples of Shaykh Yaʿqūb decided to make fun of Shaykh Dafʿ Allāh's disciples by singing:

ٱلْما عندو شيخًا[1] فَراجابا
لا يدخلْ دَرَقَة ونَشَّابا
ٱلْما عندو شيخْ مهيوبُ
لا يدخلْ حَلَقَةْ يعقوبُ[2]

فسمع تلميذ الشيخ دفع الله وعلم أنّه عناه بذلك فقال

نَدْخُلْ وَنُمْرُقْ مَتَعافي
بِالنِّيَّة[3] والعملْ ألصافي
دفع ٱللّهْ فوقي طوّافِ

نادرة: حضرت امرأة في حلقة ذكر وأنشدت ٣،٢،٣٢

نُصَفِّي لكمْ مَرِيسةْ دُواني
وأنا عَزَبَا بيتي طَرْفاني
يا فُقَرا ما فيكمْ زاني

فسمعها الذاكرون وكان فيهم شابّ فهم المعنى وكان يقول اللّهْ حَيّ فصار يقول أنا زاني أنا زاني

وأمّا أعجام الفور فيقفون في الذكر صفّين أو حلقة وكلّ رجل منهم خلفه صبيّة والنساء ينشدن وهم يذكرون وذكرهم كرير فمن إنشادهنّ قولهنّ ٣،٢،٣٣

كُرُّو كِرُّو يِيْ عالمَّا نِما
صِحْ لَگْ كُوِيْ جَنَّهْ
صِحْ لَگْ كُوِيْ

[1] كذا في الأصل. [2] كذا في الأصل. [3] كذا في الأصل.

He who has no shaykh to protect him, oho[141]
Shouldn't let himself get caught twixt shield and arrow
He who has no shaykh worthy of veneration
Shouldn't enter Yaʿqūb's circle of recollection

Shaykh Dafʿ Allāh's disciple heard this and understood that the man was referring to him, so he sang:

We enter and shall leave in good health
Pure in deed and intention
Dafʿ Allāh's above me at every revolution

An amusing anecdote. A woman once attended such a ceremony and chanted: 3.2.32

I'll pour you a big pot of beer
I'm single and live on the edge of town
Sufis, is none of you a fornicator?

Those performing heard her, among them a young man who understood what she meant. He'd been saying, "God lives!"[142] but he changed and started chanting, "I'm a fornicator! I'm a fornicator!"

The non-Arabic-speaking Fur stand in two lines or a circle during the ceremony, with a girl behind each man, and the women sing while the men chant, their chanting consisting of the sound called *karīr*.[143] One of the women's songs goes: 3.2.33

Kurú kirrô yé-ii áálima'ng nima-ii
Sa láng koo jánná
Sa láng koo

ومعنى ذلك كُرُو معناها شجرة وكِرُو معناها خضراء وعالمًا نما معناه ظلّ العلماء وصح لگ كويي جنه[1] صح لگ كويي معناه صحيح نمشي إلى الجنّة صحيح نمشي إلى الجنّة ومعناه إنّ الشجرة الخضراء ظلّ العلماء ونحن ندخل الجنّة حقًّا ندخل الجنّة حقًّا ومنه قولهنّ

جَبْرَاائِلَيَهْ مِيكَاائِليـهْ[2]
كُلّْ سِبا مُلْكَا الجَنَّهْ

ومعناه جبرائيل وميكائيل كلّ حسنة يملك بها الإنسان[3] الجنّة ومن قولهنّ

لله قُوَى لله
شَهَرْ رمضانْ أللهْ أنْدَوا
كَالْفَارِنْبِيَهْ

ومعناه لله يا إماء الله شهر رمضان دواء الله فافرحوا به

٣٤،٢،٣ ومثل هذا كثير لو تتبّعناه لخرجنا إلى الإسهاب وجلبنا الملل لأولي الألباب وفيما ذكرناه كفاية لكن من حيث أنّنا تكلّمنا في التزويج وما يتعلّق به عَنَّ لنا أنّنا نذكر نبذة في حُجّاب النساء وهم المسمّون في مصر بالطواشية وبأغوات الحريم وبالتركيّة قزلر أغالر لأنهم أمناء على الحريم ونقول

فصل في الخصيان المعروفين في مصر بالطواشية

٣٥،٢،٣ لمّا كان الحقّ سبحانه وتعالى غيورًا على عباده ومحارمه منتقمًا ممّن تعدّى حدوده بارتكاب مآثمه وكانت الغيرة وصفًا من أوصافه ولذا حرّم الظلم على نفسه وخلافه جعل الغيرة مركوزة في طباع بني آدم من زمن سلف وتقادم وأوّل من غار قابيل على أخته أقليما لمّا أمر آدم أن يزوّجها من هابيل ويزوّجه من أخته ذميما فكان من

[1] أضيف للسياق. [2] الأصل: جَبْرَايِيلَهْ مِيكَاايِلَيَهْ. [3] الأصل: للانسان.

The meaning: *kurú* means "tree"; *kirrô* means "green"; *áálima'ng nima-ii* means "the shade of the scholars of religion"; *sa láng koo jánná, sa láng koo* means "It's true we're going to Paradise. It's true we're going to Paradise." Thus, the meaning of the whole is "The green tree is the shade of the scholars of religion, and we'll enter Paradise for sure, we'll enter Paradise for sure." Another chant of theirs goes:

Jibraaîla Mikaaîla
Kullu sibā mulkā l-jannah[144]

which means "Gabriel! Michael! Every good deed gives one possession of Paradise." And another chant of theirs goes:

Lullá káwi lullá,
Shâr ramadaan Alla'ng dawa-ii
Kál pááreng beeng kíye

which means "Daughters of God, O daughters of God![145] The month of Ramadan is God's remedy,[146] so rejoice in it!"

The Fur have many such customs; to pursue them would be to diverge 3.2.34
into verbosity, and so induce, among the intelligent, animosity; we have said enough. Given that we have mentioned marriage and associated matters, however, it behooves us to provide a brief account of the guardians of women, namely, those persons who in Egypt are called *ṭawāshiyah* ("eunuchs") and "aghas of the harem" or, in Turkish, *kızlar ağası* ("girls' aghas"), because they have custody of the harem.

Section 2: Eunuchs (Known in Egypt as *Ṭawāshiyah*)

Given that the Truth, glorious and mighty, is jealous both of the well-being of 3.2.35
His mortal slaves and of the maintenance of His strictures, just as He is bent on vengeance against those who overstep His bounds by committing what He has declared to be offenses, and given that covetousness is one of His attributes and that He has, for these reasons, prohibited injustice to Himself and to other than Him, He has caused covetousness to be embedded in man's nature from times past and immemorial. The first man to feel covetousness was Qābīl,

الغيرة من أمرهما ما كان وقتل قابيل أخاه كما ورد بنصّ القرآن بل قد توجد الغيرة في غير بني آدم من الحيوانات فيغير الحيوان على أنثاه وتحصل المعاركات سيّما والنساء أكثر شبقًا وغلمة ولا مروءة تمنعهنّ ولا همّة

٣٦،٢،٣ وكان بعض الناس بلغ في الغيرة أعلاها وارتقى إلى منتهاها حتّى إن بعضهم لا يرون النساء إلّا كالإماء ومنهم من هو كثير الغيرة حتّى من الإخوان والأبناء بل منهم من بالغ في الغيرة فصار يغار عليهنّ من الليل والنهار ومنهم من يغار من عيون النرجس أن تراه كما قال الشاعر [كامل]

غُضِّي جُفُونَكِ يَا عُيُونَ ٱلنَّرْجِسِ مِنْكِ ٱسْتَحَيْتُ بِأَنْ أُقَبِّلَ مُؤْنِسِي
نَامَ ٱلْحَبِيبُ تَذَبَّلَتْ وَجَنَاتُهُ وَعُيُونُكُنَّ شَوَاخِصُ لَمْ تَنْعَسِ

وبالغ بعضهم حتّى إنّه غار على المحبوب من نفسه ومن المحبوب ومن الزمان والمكان كما قال الشاعر [وافر]

أَغَارُ عَلَيْكِ مِنْ عَيْنِي وَمِنِّي وَمِنْكِ وَمِنْ مَكَانِكِ وَٱلزَّمَانِ
وَلَوْ أَنِّي وَضَعْتُكِ فِي جُفُونِي إِلَى يَوْمِ ٱلْقِيَامَةِ مَا كَفَانِي

ومثله قوله [وافر]

فَلَوْ أَمْسَى عَلَى تَلَفِي مُصِرًّا لَقُلْتُ مُعَذِّبِي بِاللهِ زِدْنِي
وَلَا تَسْمَحْ بِوَصْلِكَ لِي فَإِنِّي أَغَارُ عَلَيْكِ مِنْكِ فَكَيْفَ مِنِّي

وارتقى بعضهم إلى أعلى المبالغة فغار من الضمير حيث قال [طويل]

with regard to his sister, Aqlīmā, when Ādam gave the order that she should marry Hābīl and he should marry the latter's sister, Dhamīmā.[147] Jealousy then led to the consequences that followed for each, with Qābīl killing his brother, as found in the text of the Qur'an.[148] Indeed, covetousness and jealousy are to be found in animals other than humans: animals are jealous of their females and fights occur. This is especially so given that the female has a stronger libido and carnal appetite, and no amount of manliness or zeal can hold her back.

Some people, having arrived at the pinnacle of covetousness and climbed 3.2.36
to its very peak, go so far as to consider all women slaves. Among them are those so given over to jealousy that they feel jealous of their brothers and their sons. Indeed, some men go to such extremes that they feel jealous of the day and the night, and some are so jealous that they cannot bear that even the eyes of narcissi should behold their women. As the poet says:

Lower your lids, you eyes of narcissi—
you make me too shy to kiss my sweet friend.
When the beloved sleeps, his cheeks[149] lose their color,
yet your eyes are steady, and their lids never descend.

Some go to such extremes that they feel jealous of their own contact with the beloved, of the beloved's contact with them, and even of time and place. As the poet says:[150]

With you I feel jealous of my eye and of myself
and also of you, of where you are, of Time.
If I tucked you inside my eyelids
from now till Judgment Day, it still would not suffice.

Similar are the poet's words:[151]

Should he to my destruction set his mind,
I'd say, "Torturer, I beg you, give me more
and do not grant me your embrace,
For if I'm jealous of you, then of myself how much the more?"

One poet went to such exaggerated lengths as to be jealous of his own heart, saying:

أَغَارُ عَلَيْـهِ مِنْ ضَمِيرِي فَيَـالَهُ   هَوًى رَابَنِي حتّى ٱتَّهَمْتُ جَوَارِحِي

فتحيّل الناس في حراسة الحريم لما عندهم من داء الغيرة المقعد المقيم فما رأوا أحسن من حراسة إنسان يكون مقطوع أعضاء التناسل وهو الذي تطمئنّ إليه النفوس في العاجل والآجل وأكثر الناس احتياجاً لذلك الملوك والأمراء لأنّ كلّ واحد منهم يجمع ما قدر عليه من النساء بلا مراء ولمّا كانت ملوك السودان أكثر الناس للنساء جمعاً وأبذلهم في ذلك وسعاً كان يوجد عند الملك من الخصيان عدد كثير وجمّ غفير فيوجد عند سلطان دار الفور نحو الألف أو أكثر وعليهم ملك منهم وهم له كالعساكر وهو الذي يرتّب في بيت السلطان ما يلزم منهم للحراسة ويبقي عنده ما زاد إلى وقت الحاجة ٣٧،٢،٣

والخصيان مكرّمون عند الأكابر خصوصاً في دار الفور فإن لهم فيها سطوة وأي سطوة والكلمة النافذة والقوّة ومقام ومقال وحال لا يماثله حال حتّى إن لهم هناك منصبين جليلين لا يتولاهما غير خصيّ أحدهما منصب الأبوّة والثاني منصب الباب وأقول إنّ منصب الباب غير مختصّ بدار الفور بل في تونس وفي قسطنطينيّة كذلك وأصل الخصيان الذين في دارفور من بلد روگا. يخصونهم هناك ويأتون بهم إلى دارفور على سبيل الهديّة لكنّهم كثيرون جدّاً ومنهم من يُخصى في دارفور ٣٨،٢،٣

ولقد رأيت حين كنت هناك غلاما حسن الوجه جميل الصورة في نحو الثمانية عشر خُصي في دارفور وسببه أنّه كان من خدم السلطان محمّد فضل وأحبّ غلمانه الذين رُبّوا في البيت وكان له سعد قائم تحبّه النساء لقضاء أوطارهنّ غير الخناء وكان اسمه سليمان تير فحسده أقرانه ونمّوا عليه عند السلطان فغضب عليه وأراد قتله فأشار عليه بعض وزرائه بخصيه وقال له من حيث أنّ الأمر كذلك اقطع ما يؤذيك به ولا تقتله فخصاه وعاش واجتمعت عليه وكان ذا منصب جميل وأُبّهة حسنة ٣٩،٢،٣

With him, of my own heart I'm jealous.
A love that accuses part of me—how suspicious!

Afflicted as they were by the persistent, crippling malady of jealousy, people pondered how to guard their harems and could come up with nothing better than to place them under the guardianship of a person whose organs of procreation have been cut off, a person of whom one can feel sure, in both the long and the short term. Those most in need of such things are kings and princes, for it is indisputable that each of them collects as many women as he can, and given that the kings of the Blacks are the most assiduous of men in collecting women and go to the greatest lengths in this, each one, you will find, has a large number and enormous throng of eunuchs. The sultan of Darfur, for example, has around a thousand or more, and they have their own master, who is one of them and to whom they are like soldiers to a king. It is he who organizes them as needed to act as guards within the sultan's house, keeping the surplus with him to use in time of need. 3.2.37

Eunuchs are treated with respect by the great, especially in the lands of the Fur, where they possess—and to what a degree!—authority, influence, power, standing, repute, and a station unlike any other. They even have two eminent positions that only eunuchs may occupy, one of which is that of the shaykh-father, the second that of the door.[152] I note that the door is not peculiar to Darfur; it exists also in Tunis, and in Constantinople too. The eunuchs in Darfur come originally from the town of Rūngā. They castrate them there and bring them to Darfur as gifts.[153] They are, however, very numerous, and some are castrated in Darfur. 3.2.38

When I was there, I saw a youth with a pretty face and attractive appearance, aged about eighteen, who had been castrated in Darfur. He had been a servant of Sultan Muḥammad Faḍl and was the best loved of those who'd been raised as part of his household. His star was rising, and the women were fond of him because he satisfied their innocent needs.[154] His name was Sulaymān Tīr. His peers, who were envious of him, slandered him before the sultan, who became angry with him and wanted to kill him. One of his viziers, however, advised him to castrate the youth, saying, "If it must be so, cut off the thing with which he harms you but don't kill him," so the sultan had him castrated and he survived. I met with him, and he had an excellent position and splendid clothes, though the sultan was distant with him because of what he believed 3.2.39

إلّا أنّ السلطان كان لا يألفه لعدم صلاحه[1] ولما قيل فيه ولقد سمعت من ثقات أنّه أحبل امرأة وظهر حملها فسئلت فقالت من سلميان تير فغضب عليه السلطان وخصاه وبعد أن برئ أعطاه المرأة وولدها وقد ذكرنا سابقاً أنّ الأب الشيخ محمّد كرّا كان اتّهم بما اتّهم به سليمان تير فخصى نفسه بيده دفعاً للريب فحظي عند السلطان وصار ما صار من أمره

٤٠،٢،٣ نكتة: ممّا وقع من عتوّهم وتجبّرهم أن اجتمع بعض أمراء الفور في محلّ انشراح ونزهة وانبساط وكان فيهم خصيّ فجعلوا يأكلون ويشربون والخصيّ كواحد منهم فاتّفق أنّ واحداً من هؤلاء الأمراء معه منديل من حرير فأبرزه في المجلس وقال هل تعلمون لماذا يصلح هذا المنديل فقال أحدهم هو يصلح لمسح العرق وقال الآخر هو يصلح للتجمّل والزينة وقال آخر هو يصلح لأن يجعل على صدر أنثى جميلة وطفق كلّ واحد يقول ما بدا له وصاحب المنديل يقول لا ولمّا أعياهم أمره قيل له قل لنا أنت لماذا يصلح فقال هذا يصلح للمسح بعد الجماع فاستحسنوا قوله وسكتوا فما راعهم إلّا أن قام الخصيّ من بينهم صالتاً سيفه يروم قتل صاحب المنديل وقال له أتعرّض بي أنّي مقطوع لا بدّ من قتلك فقاموا إليه وتلطّفوا به وهو لا يرجع عن قوله حتّى أرضوه بخيولهم كلّها وكان الخصيّ للخليفة ابن السلطان تيراب اللذين[2] أسلفنا ذكرهما

٤١،٢،٣ ومن عتوّهم أنّ الأب الشيخ محمّد أُورْدِكّاً كان في أيّام السلطان تيراب في منصب الأبوّة ومن عادة الأب الشيخ أن يتوجّه لبلاده ومحلّ حكمه في كلّ سنة في فصل الربيع ويجمع أهل البلاد في يوم واحد ويعرض الرجال ويرى العساكر فاتّفق أنّه جمعهم في يوم شديد الحرّ في رحبة واسعة أمام داره ولم يخرج لهم حتّى فاتت القائلة فخرج[3] في أبّهته راكباً جواده والعبيد يظلّلونه من حرّ الشمس ويجلبون له الهواء بالمراوح وخرج[4] العسكر وصفّوا الناس صفوفاً كدائرة وهو واقف ينظرهم وقد اشتدّ الحرّ وأمر الناس

١ - الأصل: لا يألف لصلاحه. ٢ الأصل: الذيْن. ٣ الأصل: فخرخ. ٤ الأصل: وخرخ.

to be his immorality and what had been said about him. I heard from trusted sources that he'd made a woman pregnant and this had shown, so she had been questioned and had said, "From Sulaymān Tīr." This was what made the sultan furious, and led to his castration. When it turned out that he was innocent, he gave him the woman and her child. We have mentioned earlier that Shaykh-Father Muḥammad Kurrā was accused of the same offense as Sulaymān Tīr, so he castrated himself with his own hand to remove any doubt. Thereafter he enjoyed the good graces of the sultan, and things went with him as they did.

A joke: an example of their effrontery and arrogance is that some Fur emirs 3.2.40
had gathered to relax, take their ease, and enjoy themselves, among them a eunuch. They set to eating and drinking, the eunuch along with them as though he were one of them. It happened that one of the emirs had a silk kerchief with him, and he showed it to the gathering and said, "Do you know what this kerchief is good for?" One of them replied that it was good for wiping off sweat, another that it was good for looking attractive and adorning oneself, another that it was good for attaching to the bosom of a beautiful female, and so it went, each saying what he thought, while the owner of the kerchief kept saying no. When they grew tired of the business, they told him, "You tell us what it's good for." He replied, "It's good for wiping yourself off after sex," and they all thought this was a good answer and said no more. All of a sudden, they found that the eunuch had stood up and drawn his sword, with the intention of killing the owner of the kerchief, to whom he said, "Are you hinting at my having been cut? I shall certainly kill you!" They leaped toward him and spoke to him gently but he refused to take back his words until they'd mollified him by giving him all their horses. He was a eunuch belonging to the Successor, son of Sultan Tayrāb, both of whom we have spoken of earlier.

Another example of their effrontery is that in the days of Sultan Tayrāb, 3.2.41
Muhammad Órré Dungo[155] held the office of shaykh-father, and it is customary for the shaykh-father to go to his lands and seat of government every year in the spring.[156] There he gathers all the people together on the same day and reviews the men and inspects the soldiers. One extremely hot day, Muḥammad Órré Dungo had everyone assemble in a wide space in front of his house and didn't emerge to see them until the hottest part of the day had passed. Then he came out in all his splendor, riding his horse, his slaves shading him from the heat of the sun with parasols and fanning him. The soldiers now also came out and the people formed rows, making a circle, while he sat there watching

بالجُثيّ على ركبهم وسلاحهم ودرقهم في أيديهم فكان الإنسان منهم لا يستطيع الجثيّ لشدّة حرّ الرمضاء وسال العرق وكثر القلق ومكث مليّاً لا يأمر بأمر ولا ينهى عن شيء وعطش الناس وأخذ منهم حرّ الشمس أكبر مأخذ وهم صابرون على ما قضاه الله عليهم حتّى مات بعضهم من العطش ولمّا رأى قلق العالم وتحيّرهم أعجبه ذلك وضحك وقال بلسان الفور نَتُو نتو نتو ﴿يوماً عَبوساً قَمْطَرِيرًا﴾ وكرّرها مرّتين أو ثلاثاً وكان العالم المجتمع في تلك الجَلْدَگا أي العرض ما ينوف عن زهاء عشرين ألفا وكان فيهم رجل صالح يقال له الشيخ حسن الكَوْ فبرز وقال بأعلى صوته اسكت يا كافر ثلاثاً فأخذه الرعب من الشيخ المذكور وولّى هارباً ورفع الشيخ يديه إلى السماء وقال اللّهمّ ارحم عبادك فما تمّ كلامه حتّى ارتفع السحاب مثل الجبال ونزل المطر وتفرّق الناس وكان يوماً مشهوراً وسبب[1] غضب الشيخ أنّه مثّل نفسه بالإله ومثّل عرض الناس عليه بعرضهم للحساب ومثّل شدّة حرّ الشمس بشدّة حرّ يوم القيامة ولذلك استشهد بقوله نتو بالآية الكريمة ونَ بمعنى هذا وتُو بمعنى يوم والباقي هو[2] نصّ الآية الكريمة

٤٢،٢،٣ نادرة: حُكي أنّ الأب الشيخ محمّد أوردكا المذكور كان قليل العقل ومن قلّة عقله أنّه لمّا تولّى في منصب الأبوّة أمره السلطان تيراب أن يقرأ ليتعلّم القراءة والكتابة فأحضر فقيهاً يعلّمه فكتب له حروف الهجاء وصار يقرأ عليه في كلّ يوم واستمرّ على ذلك مدّة أيّام ثمّ إنّه ذات يوم طلب المصحف فجيء به له فتصفّحه ونظر في السطور فرأى واواً مفردة فعرفها وقال للفقيه إنْماگ وَاوِ يعني أليس هذه واو فقال الفقيه نعم فقال قد ختمت القرآن وأمر بذبح الذبائح وضرب الطبول وصنع وليمة عظيمة فعُدّت هذه من طيشه وخفّة عقله

٤٣،٢،٣ ولنرجع إلى ما كنّا بصدده فنقول ومع كثرة الخصيان في دار السلطان لم يسلم من الدنس لأنّ النساء شياطين لا يغلبهنّ غالب سيّما وقد قام عذرهنّ بداعي كثرتهنّ في

---

[1] الأصل: وبسبب. [2] الأصل: هي.

them. The heat was intense, but he ordered the people to go down on their knees, still holding their weapons and shields. The ground was so hot it was hard to kneel, and the sweat flowed and the suffering intensified, but he just stood there awhile without telling them what was expected of them. The people grew thirsty and the heat took a great toll on them, but they endured what God had ordained for them, to the point that some died of thirst. When he saw how thirsty and dismayed everyone was, he was pleased, laughed, and said in the Fur language, "*Na-tū, na-tū, na-tū*[157]—«a frowning day, inauspicious!»"[158] and repeated the phrase two or three times. The number of people gathered for this *galanga*, or review, was around twenty thousand and included a righteous man called Shaykh Ḥasan al-Kaw. He now stepped forward and cried out three times at the top of his voice, "Silence, you infidel!" and the man was seized with terror at the shaykh, and turned and fled. Then the shaykh raised his hands to the skies and said, "O God, have mercy on Your slaves!" and before he'd stopped speaking, clouds had reared up like mountains, and the rain fell and everyone scattered. It became a celebrated day. The shaykh was angry because Muḥammad Órré Dungo had likened himself to God and the presentation of the people to him for review to that of their presentation for Judgment, while he'd likened the extreme heat of the sun to that of the Day of Resurrection, which is why he used the word *na-tū* to introduce the Noble Verse (*na* means "this," *tū* means "day," and the rest is the text of the Noble Verse).

An amusing anecdote: it is reported that the Shaykh-Father Muḥammad Órré Dungo of whom we speak was of limited intellect. By way of example, when he assumed office, Sultan Tayrāb ordered him to study so that he could learn to read and write. He engaged a man of religion to teach him, and the man wrote out the letters of the alphabet for him and began giving him daily lessons. This went on for a few days until the day came when the shaykh-father asked for a copy of the Qur'an. One was brought and, leafing through it, he saw a freestanding letter *wāw* and recognized it and asked the man of religion, "*A mang waawi*?" meaning "Isn't that a *wāw*?" "It is," said the man. Órré Dungo said, "I've finished the Qur'an!" and he ordered that animals be slaughtered and drums beaten and he held a great banquet. This was considered an example of his silliness and lack of brains. 3.2.42

Let us return to our original topic. Given the large number of eunuchs in the sultan's house, the place has not escaped defilement, since women are devils whom none can control, and especially since the excuse may be made 3.2.43

بيت السلطان وهنّ في سنّ الشباب والراحة وحسن المأكل والملبس فللشهوة فيهنّ نصيب أوفر ولمّا سُجِنَّ في هذا السجن تحيّلن على دخول الرجال بكلّ حيلة فمنهنّ من تصاحب من الرجال من الخدمة الذين بالباب ومنهنّ من لها عجائز يأتينها بالرجال بحيلة وهي أنّ العجوز تتأمّل في الفتيان حتّى ترى الشابّ الجميل الذي لا نبات بعِرْضَيْه[1] فتتحيّل عليه بلطف حتّى تأخذه إلى دارها ومن المعلوم أنّ شبانّ السودان لا يحلقون رؤوسهم بل يوفّرونها فتصير الوفرة لهم كشعر النساء وتجعل وفرته ظفائر كظفائر النساء وتلبسه حليًا كحليّهنّ من عقود وتمائم ومدارع ومنجور وتلبّسه درّاعة وفردة وثوبًا بحيث لا يشكّ رائيه أنّه امرأة وتدخله دار السلطان بين نساء فمتى ولج ذهب خوفها وسلّمته لمن أدخلته برسمها فيمكث ما شاء الله أن يمكث فإن ستر الله عليه خرج كما دخل وإن عثر عليه قُتل ولا يُعثر عليه إلّا بأسباب منها أن تعلم أمره إحدى ضرائرها فتطلبه منها فتأبى هي بخلاً به أو لا يرضى هو أن يذهب فحينئذ يحملها الغيظ على أن تَفْتِنَ عليه فيعثر عليه ومنها أنّ السلطان يأمر بالتفتيش فيحضر الطواشية كلّهم ويفتّش معهم البيوت ومن وجدوه قتلوه ومنها أنّه يزهق من طول المكث فيخرج وحده فيعثر عليه البوّابون وهو خارج فيقتلونه وإن ستر الله عليه خرج وأغلب من يدخل بالصفة التي ذكرناها لا يخرج إلّا بالليل أو مع نساء كثيرة وهو في وسطهنّ

ومن العجائز من يتحيّلن[2] في خروج النساء من بيت السلطان بأن ينكّرن المرأة منهنّ ٤٤،٢،٣
بثياب مهنة قذرة ويخرجنها أمام الناس جهارًا فإذا عثر بها البوّاب أو أحد الخصيان قيل له هذه امرأة مسكينة كانت دخلت معنا تلتمس معروفًا ومنهنّ من يدلّس عليها الخصيان وذلك لا يكون إلّا إذا علم الخصيّ أنّه إن عرض انفتح له مهوى فقتل فيه فحينئذ يسكت قهرًا عنه وتدخل المرأة وتخرج وتدخل من شاءت ولم تخش بأسًا ومن

[1] الأصل: بعَرَضَيْه. [2] الأصل: يتحيل.

for them that many of those in the sultan's house are young and at leisure, and eat and dress well. This gives greater rein to their appetites, and, being prisoners there, they spend their time thinking of how to bring men in by any means possible. Some of them make friends with one of the male servants at the door. Others have old women who bring them men using the following stratagem: the old woman watches the young men until she sees one who is beautiful and has no down in his armpits and she works on him gently and eventually takes him to her house. Now—it being well known that the young Blacks do not shave the hair on their heads but let it grow so long that their tresses are like a woman's—she takes these tresses and braids them like a woman's and dresses him in women's finery such as necklaces and amulets, with *madraʿah* beads at his wrists[159] and *manjūr* beads around his waist,[160] and she dresses him in a pinafore, an apron,[161] and a body wrap, so that any who sees him will have no doubt that he's a woman, and she introduces him into the sultan's house along with other women. Once he's in, she loses all fear and hands him over to the woman who commanded her to get him. After that, he stays as long as God wills. And as long as God continues to provide cover for him, he will leave as he came in; if discovered, however, he will be killed. A number of things may lead to his discovery. One of the girl's co-wives may learn of his presence and ask her for him. The girl may then refuse, being too miserly to give him up, or the youth may not agree to go to her. Anger will then drive the other woman to inform on him, leading to his discovery. Or the sultan may order a search: then all the eunuchs come, he searches the huts with them, and they kill anyone they find. Another is that the young man may grow tired of staying there so long and leave on his own, but the doormen come across him as he's leaving and kill him. If God provides cover for him, though, he will escape. Most of those who enter in the way I have described leave only at night, or in the middle of a large group of women.

Some old women find ways to get women out of the sultan's house by dis- 3.2.11
guising them in the clothes of some squalid profession and then taking them out right under people's noses. If the doorman or a eunuch happens upon her, they're told, "She's just a poor woman who came in with us to beg for a handout." In other cases, the eunuchs connive with the old woman; this occurs when the eunuch in question realizes that an abyss may open into which he could fall and be killed if he gets involved. In such cases, he says nothing, despite himself, and the woman comes and goes and takes in whomever she

ذلك ما وقع من بعض محاظي السلطان صابون مع تُرْقُنَكْ محمّد بن عمّها وسنذكر ذلك في سيرة السلطان صابون سلطان دار الوَادَاىْ إن شاء الله تعالى

٤٥،٢،٣ واعلم أن نساء السودان كثيرات الشبق والغلمة أكثر من غيرهنّ لأمور. الأوّل لفرط حرارة الإقليم. الثاني لكثرة مخالطتهنّ للرجال. الثالث لعدم صونهنّ واستقرارهنّ في البيوت فمن ذلك ترى المرأة منهنّ لا تقنع بزوج ولا بخليل واحد على حدّ قول الشاعر [هزج]

أَيَا مَنْ لَيْسَ يُرْضِيهَا خَلِيلٌ وَلَا أَلْفَا خَلِيلٍ كُلَّ عَامِ
أَرَاكِ بَقِيَّةً مِنْ قَوْمِ مُوسَى فَهُمْ لَا يَصْبِرُونَ عَلَى طَعَامِ

الرابع لعدم اقتصار أزواجهنّ عليهنّ لأنّ الرجل منهم إن كان ذا قدرة نكح من الحرائر أربعاً وتسرّى بغيرهنّ من السراري وكلّ ذلك على قدر حاله والنساء شقائق الرجال والنفس واحدة في الشهوة والطبع خصوصاً وعندهنّ من الغيرة ما لا مزيد عليه فيتحيّلن على الاجتماع بغير زوجهنّ وتأخذ[1] كلّ منهنّ في ضروب من الحيل تتوصّل بذلك إلى مرغوبها وإن كان لا يقدر على التسرّي طمح نظره إلى غير امرأته فمتى علمت امرأته بذلك حداها حادي الغيرة على الاجتماع بغيره. الخامس العادة لأنهنّ من صغرهنّ قد تعوّدن الاجتماع مع أترابهنّ من الذكور حتّى كبرن على ذلك والعادة إذا استحكمت صارت طبعاً فلذلك إذا تزوّجت لا يمكنها الاقتصار على زوج واحد إلّا من رحم الله ومن حيث أنّ هذا الطبع مركوز فيهنّ يصدر منهنّ ما يصدر فلذلك لا يرى منهنّ من اقتصرت على بعلها إلّا القليل وكلّما تقادم الزمن كلّما كثر الفساد عندهم

٤٦،٢،٣ نادرة: ومن المجرّب في دارفور أنّ النار إذا اشتعلت في دور واشتدّ وقدها وعجزوا عنه نادوا هل من طاهرة فتأتي امرأة عجوز لم تَزْنِ قطّ فتَخْرُج كفوسها وتشير به للنار

[1] الأصل: وياخذ.

pleases, fearing no ill. Something of this sort happened involving a concubine of Sultan Ṣābūn's and her cousin Turqunak Muḥammad; we will mention this when we tell the history of Sultan Ṣābūn of Wāddāy, the Almighty willing.[162]

The women of the Blacks are more lustful and libidinous than other women for several reasons. The first is the region's excessive heat. The second is that they mix so much with men. The third is the lack of surveillance over them and the fact that they don't keep to their houses. It follows that these women are never satisfied with one husband or lover, as alluded to by the poet when he says:[163] 3.2.45

You whom just one lover cannot please,
 nor even two thousand in a single year,
I think you must be what's left of Mūsā's folk,
 for they won't put up for long with the same old fare.[164]

The fourth is that their husbands don't limit themselves just to them: if a man has the means, he'll marry four freeborn women and take concubines as well, depending on his social condition. However, women are the female counterparts of men and the appetitive soul is the same for everyone where lust and physical nature are concerned, especially since there is no one more jealous than a woman. Thus, they come up with ways to meet with men other than their husbands, each using a different stratagem to achieve what she wants. If a man can't afford to take concubines, he'll set his sights on some woman other than his wife, and when his wife finds out, her jealousy will drive her to meet with other men. The fifth is habit, for they are accustomed to mix with their male peers from their earliest years, so they grow up that way, and habit, if it takes hold, becomes a deep-seated trait. It follows that when she marries, she cannot limit herself to a single husband, unless God has mercy on her. As this trait is embedded in them, they get up to what they get up to. Thus, only a few can be found who limit themselves to their husbands, and as time passes, so corruption among these people increases.

An amusing fact. It is a tried and true fact that if a house catches fire in Darfur and the fire takes hold and they can't put it out, they cry, "Is there a chaste woman here?" and an old woman who has never committed adultery comes, pulls out her breechclouts,[165] and waves them at the fire, which will then be extinguished, if the Almighty wills. This is one of those things they've learned from experience. When I was there, a fire broke out and took hold in 3.2.46

فتطفأ[1] بإرداة الله تعالى وهذه من مجرّباتهم وحين كنت هناك وقع حريق في بيت جدّة السلطان واشتدّ وحضر السلطان بنفسه وأرباب دولته فما أمكنهم إطفاؤه ونادى منادي السلطان هل من طاهرة وتكرّر النداء في البلد فما قدرت امرأة تأتي لذلك الحريق ومن هنا يعلم أنّه لا يوجد الآن فيهنّ طاهرة لكن سمعت بأنّ ذلك قد يوجد في نساء أعراب باديتهم وأمّا نساء السودان فقلّ أن يوجد فيهنّ طاهرة لأنّ المرأة منهم حيث لا عقل يردعها ولا خوف يزجرها ولا دين تراعيه تفعل ما أرادت بل قد تفتخر بكثرة الأصحاب وتقول لو كنت قبيحة ما جاءني أحد ولولا أنّي من الحسن بمكان ما ألفني الرجال وارتكبوا من شاني الأهوال

٣،٢،٤٧ ومن العجب أنّ في بلاد العرب إذا أسنّت المرأة وكان لها ولد جليل ذو شهرة يمنعها ذلك عن ارتكاب الزنا وعن التطلّع للرجال إمّا لعلمها بعدم الرغبة فيها إن كانت مسنّة أو لخوفها على مقام ولدها وجلالة قدره إلّا نساء السودان فقد حكى لي من هو أعزّ أصحابي وصونًا لصحبته لا أذكر اسمه أنّ خال السلطان محمّد فضل المسمّى محمّد تَيْتَل زوّجته أخته وهي أبنوسة[2] أمّ السلطان وعمرها بنحو خمس وثلاثين سنة بامرأة من بيتها وصنعت له مهرجانًا عظيمًا هرع الناس للفرجة عليه

٣،٢،٤٨ فأخبرني أنّه كان من جملة المتفرّجين قال بينما أنا واقف إذ جاءت أمّ السلطان ومعها سرب من النساء كأنهنّ الغزلان وهي تمشي أمامهنّ وهنّ خلفها وهي كانت جارية بشعة المنظر مشوّهة الخلق دنيّة الأصل لأنّه لا يوجد في سكّان دار الفور أدنى أصلا من البيقو الذين هي منهم فصار كلّ من الواقفين يتعجّب من صنع الله تعالى أن قدّم هذه المرأة مع ما هي عليه من قبح الذات والأصل على من هنّ أحسن وجهًا وأصلاً وذاتًا وبهاءً وجمالاً قال فدخلت على أخيها تيتل وكان وقت بنائه بعرسه فمكثت عنده برهة ثمّ خرجت قال فلم نشعر إلّا برنين الخلاخل والحليّ وعبق الطيب فعلمنا أنّها خارجة فوقفنا صفًّا حتّى إذا خرجت لم أشعر بها إلّا وقد قبضت على

---

١ الأصل: فتطفى. ٢ الاصل: أنبوس.

the sultan's grandmother's house, and the sultan himself came along with the high officers of the state. They were unable to put it out, and the sultan's crier called out, "Is there a chaste woman here?" The cry was repeated throughout the town and not one woman could go to the fire, showing that there isn't a single chaste woman in the place these days, though I've heard that some such are to be found among their desert Bedouin. Rarely, though, is a chaste woman to be found among the Blacks, for such women—given that they have no brain to restrain them, no fear to hold them in check, and no religion to observe—do whatever they want. Indeed, women boast of how many lovers they have, saying, "If I were ugly, no one would have come to me, and if I were not so beautiful, men wouldn't have been my intimates and performed doughty deeds for my sake."

It is an amazing fact that, in the Arab lands, if a woman grows old and has a son who is well-respected and well-known, this prevents her from committing adultery and running after men, either because she's aware that no one wants her, if she's old, or because she fears for her son's standing and the respect with which he is viewed. Not so the women of the Blacks. Thus my dearest friend (I won't mention his name so that I can keep his friendship) told me that the maternal uncle of Sultan Muḥammad Faḍl, who was called Muḥammad Taytal, was married off by his sister, called Anbūsah, who was the sultan's mother and aged about thirty-five, to a woman of her household, and held a great celebration for him that everyone hurried to watch. 3.2.47

My friend told me that he had been an onlooker. He said, "I was standing there when the sultan's mother came, along with a herd of women as lovely as gazelles. She was walking in front, they behind. She was a slave woman of hideous appearance, deformed physique, and base origin, for there are none in Darfur of origin baser than the Bīqū, to whom she belonged. All the onlookers marveled at the doings of the Almighty, that He should give this woman who was ugly in both person and origin precedence over those better favored in physiognomy, origin, pride, and beauty. She went in to see her brother Muḥammad Taytal, who had just consummated his marriage, stayed with him awhile, and then came out again. No sooner did she do so than we heard the ringing of anklets and jewelry, smelled a waft of perfume, and realized she was leaving. We stood in a line, but no sooner had I set eyes on her than she grabbed me by the hand and pulled at me to make me go with her. I tried to hold back but it looked as though I was refusing, so the women behind her 3.2.48

يدي وجذبتني للذهاب معها فأردت الامتناع وكأنّي تعاصيت فدفعني النساء اللائي خلفها وكرهت أن يشعر الناس بذلك فمشيت معها محاذيًا لها وهي بجانبي قابضة عليّ

فلمّا كنّا في أثناء الطريق قالت أنا تعبت مع أنّه لم يكن بين بيت أخيها وبيتها أكثر من مائة خطوة وقد بلغني أنّها قبل اتّصالها بالسلطان كانت من أقلّ الجواري المبتذلات للمهنة فكانت تأتي بالماء والحطب على رأسها من الخلاء والآن تتعب من مشي[1] مائة خطوة قال فقلت لها من كثرة ما عانيت في هذا اليوم قال ثمّ دخلنا الدار والخصيان واقفون على الباب لا يجترئ أحد منهم أن يتكلّم وقد عرفوني معها ٤٩،٢،٣

فلمّا وصلت إلى حجرتها دخلت فدخلت معها فأطلقت يدي فجلست على فراش هناك وانطرحت هي على سريرها تتقلّب يمنة ويسرة وتهزّ منجورها بيديها ثمّ قالت لي إنّ بي صداعًا فقلت لها لا بأس عليك قالت فاقرأ لي عليه لعلّه يذهب فجئت إليها وقد علمت أنّ ذلك حيلة منها لمقصودها وأنّ الكبر يمنعها أن تقول لي هيت لك مع أنّ جميع من كان معها من النساء ذهب ولم يبق إلّا أنا وهي وهناك جارية جالسة خارج الباب إن احتاجت إلى شيء دعتها له ٥٠،٢،٣

قال فلمّا أكثرت من التقلّب ولم ترمني ميلا إليها دعتني لأقرأ على صدغها فحين وضعت يدي على صدغها وابتدأت القراءة ارتعشت تحت يدي وصارت تضطرب اضطراب المذبوح وتتأوّه فشممت منها رائحة الطيب فأنعشتني وأخذني ما يأخذ الرجل من النشاط فهممت أن أعلوها فأدركني خوف من ابنها السلطان لأنّه متى وجد مع أمّه أحدًا قتله وقد تكرّر منه ذلك مرارًا ويهجم عليها بغير استئذان لكنّها قد رصدت له أناسًا يخبرونها بمجيئه فإن كان عندها أحد تحيّلت في إخراجه قال وخفت أيضًا لي لأنّي كنت سمعت أنّها مصابة بداء الحَصَر وهو المعبّر به عند الحكماء بالسيلان الأبيض أعني أنّ كلّ من واقعها ابتلي به سيّما وقد شاهدت من مرض به منها قال فحين أدركني الخوف من هاتين الجهتين برد ما بي قليلًا وكانت قد اطّلعت ٥١،٢،٣

---

[1] الأصل: شي.

pushed me. I didn't want people to notice, so I walked with her, side by side, her grip on me never loosening.

"On the way she told me, 'I'm tired' (even though it wasn't more than a hundred paces from her brother's house to hers, and I'm told that before her relationship with the sultan she'd been one of the lowest of the slave girls, and with a lowly job too, as she used to bring water and firewood from the countryside—and now she was tired out after walking a hundred paces?). Anyway, I told her, 'It must be from everything you've had to put up with today!' Then we entered her house, the eunuchs who were standing at the door not daring to say anything, even though they could see me with her. 3.2.49

"When she reached her room, she went in, so I went in with her. She let go of my hand, so I sat down on some cushions that were there while she flopped onto her bed, twisting and turning right and left and flapping her *manjūr* beads with her hands. She told me, 'I have a headache,' so I said, 'I'm sorry to hear that.' 'Recite some verses from the Qur'an over it,' she said. 'Maybe that'll make it go away.' So I went over to her, though I knew it was a trick to get what she wanted and that only her pride in her status prevented her from telling me, 'Get over here!' even though all the women who'd been with her had gone, and only she and I were left, plus a female slave sitting outside the door whom she could call to if she needed anything. Having twisted and turned a lot, but finding no sign that I was attracted to her, she called on me to recite verses from the Qur'an over her temple. 3.2.50

"When I placed my hand on her temple and began reciting, she started trembling and thrashing about like an animal being slaughtered, and moaning. Then the smell of perfume wafting off her reached my nose and this stimulated me and the vigor of the male seized me and I set about mounting her—but then I was overcome by fear of her son, the sultan, because every time he found a man with his mother he killed him; he'd done so many times before, when he'd burst in on her unannounced. She, however, had positioned men to watch for him and inform her when he was coming, and if anyone was with her she'd work out a way of getting him out. I was afraid for myself too, because I'd heard she suffered from *al-ḥaṣar*, which doctors call 'leucorrhea,' meaning that anyone who had sex with her caught it—especially as I'd seen men who'd caught it from her.[166] Overcome by fear on both these counts, I cooled off a bit. She'd taken a look at my state straight away, and when she saw how limp I'd become, she thought I must be hungry, so she called a slave called 3.2.51

على حالي أوّلاً فلمّا رأت منّي الفتور ظنّت أنّي جائع فدعت بجارية لها اسمها ذراع القادر وقالت لها ائت بطعام جميل فأتت الجارية بإناءين في أحدهما حمام مقلوّ في السمن وفي الآخر فطير بالعسل وقالت لي كل قال فأبيت واعتذرت بأنّي غير جائع فحلفت عليّ فتناولت من الطعام وأعجبني وكنت في تلك الليلة محتاجاً للطعام[1]

٣،٢،٥٢ وبينما أنا آكل إذ سمعت حركات عنيفة وكركبة وجاء الخدم يهرعون ويقولون إنّ السلطان قد أتى فقالت خذوا هذا وأخرجوه من الباب الثاني فأخذني الجوار وأسرعوا في المشي حتّى أخرجوني من الزريبة ومن لطف الله تعالى أنّ السلطان لم يدخل عليها من الباب الذي عادته الدخول منه بل من[2] الباب المذكور وأوقف عليه حرساً ودار حتّى أتى للباب الذي خرجت منه لأنّي بمجرّد خروجي وانفصالي عن الباب رأيت نواصي الخيل قد أقبلت فوقفت على بعد أرى ما يكون فسمعته يقول للبوّابين من خرج الآن من هنا فقالوا لا أحد فقال أحد الفرسان أنا رأيت إنساناً انفصل من هنا وأظنّه كان هنا فقال جميعهم ما رأينا أحداً كلّ ذلك وأنا واقف أسمع وحمدت الله الذي أخرجني قبل وصولهم وإلّا لو وصلوا إلى الباب قبل خروجي كنت أوّل قتيل

٣،٢،٥٣ فحين سمعت منه هذه القصّة تعجّبت غاية العجب وعلمت أنّ الخصيان لا ينفعون إلّا مع عدم غرض النساء ومتى كان للمرأة غرض لا يقدر الخصيّ أن يصنع شيئاً فانظر يا أخي كيف وقعت هذه القصّة من هذه المرأة مع أنّها أمّ ملك ولو وقعت من غيرها لكان للكلام فيها مجال فكيف بهذه وبالجملة فالنساء لا خير فيهنّ إلّا من حفظها الله ورحم الله من قال [طويل]

[1] أضيف للسياق. [2] الأصل: الى.

Dhirāʿ al-Qādir[167] and told her, 'Bring some good food!' So the slave brought two vessels, one of them holding pigeons fried in clarified butter, the other a round of flaky pastry with molasses, and she said, 'Eat!' I refused, making the excuse that I wasn't hungry, but she swore I had to, so I took some of the food, which I liked, and I was in fact in need of food.

"While I was eating, I heard violent activity and confusion outside, and the 3.2.52
servants rushed in saying that the sultan had come. 'Take him away,' she said, and they got me out through the other door. The slave women led me at a fast pace till they'd gotten me out of the house enclosure. It was only through the grace of the Almighty that instead of going in to see her through the door he usually used, the sultan went in through the one I just referred to, leaving a guard at the first and going around till he came to the door through which I'd exited, for no sooner had I gotten out and moved away from the door than I saw the heads of the horses that had arrived. I stopped at a distance to see what would happen. I heard him saying to the doormen, 'Who came out this way just now?' and them replying, 'No one.' Then one of the horsemen said, 'I saw someone moving away and I think he may have been here.' All the others repeated, 'We didn't see anyone.' All this was going on as I stood there listening, and I thanked God I'd gotten out before they arrived, because, if they'd gotten to the door before I did, I'd have been done for."[168]

When I heard this story from him, I was quite astounded and realized 3.2.53
that eunuchs are of use only if women have nothing in mind, but if they do, a eunuch avails nothing. Observe, my friend, how these goings-on were the doings of this woman, even though she was the mother of a monarch. If it had been anyone else, there would have been no end of talk, so how much more in her case? By and large, women have nothing good in them, with the exception of those whose chastity God has preserved. May He bless the poet who said:[169]

فَفِيهِنَّ مَنْ تَسْوَى ثَمَانِينَ بَكْرَةً وَفِيهِنَّ مَنْ تَغْلُو بِجِلْدِ حُوَارِهِ
وَفَفِيهِنَّ مَنْ تَأْتِي ٱلْفَتَى وَهْوَ مُعْسِرٌ فَيُضْحِي وَكُلُّ ٱلْخَيْرِ فِي صَحْنِ دَارِهِ
وَفَفِيهِنَّ مَنْ تَأْتِي ٱلْفَتَى وَهْوَ مُوسِرٌ[1] فَيُصْبِحُ لَمْ يَمْلِكْ عَلِيقَ حِمَارِهِ
وَفَفِيهِنَّ مَنْ لَمْ يَسْتُرِ ٱللّٰهُ عِرْضَهَا إِذَا غَابَ عَنْهَا ٱلزَّوْجُ رَاحَتْ لِجَارِهِ
فَلَا رَحِمَ ٱلرَّحْمٰنُ خَائِنَةَ ٱلنِّسَا[2] وَأَحْرَقَ كُلَّ ٱلْخَائِنَاتِ بِنَارِهِ

وليعلم أنّ كلّ مصيبة تقع أصلها النساء فكم بسببهنّ قتلت ملوك وخربت ممالك وسفكت دماء فهنّ لنا شياطين على حدّ قول الشاعر [بسيط]

إِنَّ ٱلنِّسَاءَ شَيَاطِينٌ خُلِقْنَ لَنَا نَعُوذُ بِٱللّٰهِ مِنْ شَرِّ ٱلشَّيَاطِينِ

٥٤،٢،٣ غريبة: مقتضى أنّهم جعلوا الخصيان لصيانة الحريم عن الرجال أنّ الخصيان أمناء عليهنّ من طرف السيّد والأمر يخالف ذلك فقد رأينا منهم من عنده عدّة نساء يتمتّع بهنّ وأوّل من رأيت عنده ذلك محمّد كرّا الذي أسلفنا ذكره وحكى لي من أثق به أنّه لمّا رأى الغلب عليه في قتال السلطان محمّد فضل كان عنده امرأة من أجمل النساء فذبحها بالليل قبل موته لئلّا يُحظَى[3] بها غيره وهذه نهاية الغيرة ورأيت في دارفور وفي الواداي كثيرًا من الخصيان كلّ منهم حائز نساء عديدة وسألت من أهل الخبرة ما يصنعون بهنّ وهم كهنّ من حيث إن أعضاء التناسل مفقودة فقيل لي إنّهم يساحقون النساء ويشتدّ بهم الحال وقت المساحقة حتّى إنّه يعضّ الأنثى وقت الإنزال عضًا مؤلمًا وكنت إذ ذاك لجهلي بعلم الطبّ أصدّق ذلك لكنّ الآن لا أصدّقه لأنّ وظيفة العضو قد فقدت بفقده والعلّة تدور مع المعلول وجودًا وعدمًا

---

١ الأصل: مؤسر. ٢ الأصل: النساء. ٣ كذا في الأصل.

Among them are some worth eighty young she-camels;
for others one newborn calf's too much to pay.
Some become a young man's bride when he's still poor,
but he finds his courtyard stuffed with wealth one day.
Some become a young man's bride when he's living high
but finds one morn that for donkey fodder he can no longer pay.
Among them are those whose honor God does not protect:
when her husband's away, she goes to his neighbors to play—
So let the Merciful show no mercy to an unfaithful woman
and burn in His fire any who would her spouse betray!

Women are at the root of every disaster that occurs. How many a king has been killed for them! How many a kingdom ruined! How much blood spilled! They are devils made for us, as says the poet:

Women are devils created for us—
God save us from those devils' ways!

A strange thing: a concomitant of the fact that they've made eunuchs to preserve their womenfolk from other men ought to be that the eunuchs deal honestly with their masters regarding them, but that's not how things are. We've seen eunuchs who keep a number of women for their pleasure, the first I observed doing so being the Muḥammad Kurrā of whom we've spoken earlier. Someone in whom I have every confidence told me that when the latter saw he was about to be defeated in the fighting with Sultan Muḥammad Faḍl, he had a woman of exceptional beauty with him, and he cut her throat the night before he was going to die so that no one else might enjoy her. There is no jealousy more extreme than that. In Darfur and Wādday, I saw many eunuchs, each of whom possessed many women, and I asked men of experience what they did with them, given that the eunuchs were just like the women, in the sense that their organs of procreation were missing. I was told that they ground their bodies against the women and that when they did so they would become so excited that they would bite the woman painfully on ejaculating. At the time, because of my ignorance of medical science, I believed this, but now I do not, because the function of the member is lost with the loss of the member itself, and cause goes with effect whether we're talking about what is or what is not. 3.2.54

٥٥،٢،٣ وكنت سألت أهل الخبرة عن كيفيّة الخَصْي فأخبرني بعضهم أنّه يؤتى بمن يراد الفعل به فيضبط ضبطاً جيّداً وتمسك المذاكير وتستأصل بموسى حادّ ويوضع في ثقب مجرى البول أنبوبة صغيرة من صفيح لئلاّ ينسدّ ويكون قد سُخّن السمن على النار تسخيناً جيّداً حتّى غلى ثمّ يكوى به محلّ القطع وبعد أن يكون محلّ القطع جرحاً حديدياً ينقلب جرحاً نارياً ثمّ يداوى بالتغيير عليه بالتفتيك والأربطة حتّى يشفى أو يموت ولا يشفى منه إلّا القليل فإن قيل إنّ في هذا تعذيباً للحيوان الناطق وقطعاً للتناسل المأمور بكثرته شرعاً فهو حرام قلت نعم قد صرّح غير واحد من العلماء بحرمته خصوصاً جلال الدين السيوطيّ رحمه الله فإنّه صرّح بالتحريم في كتابه الذي ألّفه في حرمة خدمة الخصيان لضريح سيّد ولد عدنان لكن الحرمة على الفاعل وإنّما يخصي الخصيان قوم من المجوس ويأتون بهم إلى بلاد الإسلام فيبيعونهم ويهادون بهم ولا يخصى على يد المسلمين منهم إلّا القليل النادر وأمّا استخدامهم بعد الخصي فلا ضرر فيه بل فيه ثواب عظيم لأنّهم لو لم يستخدموا لحصل لهم الضرر من وجهين الأوّل ممّا وقع عليهم من الخصي الموجب لفقد اللذّة العظيمة وقطع التناسل والثاني من ضيق المعيشة

٥٦،٢،٣ فإن قيل إن كان الأمراء كالملوك ومن يجري مجراهم يجمعون كثيراً من النساء في دورهم وكلهنّ شابّات ومن المعلوم أنّ الغيرة موجودة فيهنّ كما هي موجودة في الرجال لأنهنّ شقائقهم فكيف يعاشرن بعضهنّ خصوصاً إذا أحبّ الرجل واحدة منهنّ وأعرض عن غيرها قلت إنّ العداوة واقعة بينهنّ على قدر أحوالهنّ فكلّ منهنّ تتمنّى أن يخلو[١] لها وجه زوجها ولا يألف سواها لكن لمّا كنّ تحت قهر الزوج خصوصاً إن كان ملكاً يخفين البغضاء ويظهرن المودّة وهذه عادتهنّ في إخفاء ما يُبْطِنَّ وإظهار ضدّه ولا يظهر ما أخفت المرأة منهنّ إلّا إذا زال[٢] خوفها وملكت رشدها وحينئذ تظهر ما كان كامناً في صدرها

[١] الأصل: يخل. [٢] الأصل: زاد.

I also asked men of experience how the castration was carried out. One of them told me that the subject is brought and bound tightly, then the testes are grasped and removed with a sharp razor and a small metal cylinder is inserted into the urinary canal so that it doesn't become blocked. Clarified butter will have been heated over the fire till it's boiling and the site of the incision is cauterized, transforming the cut into a burn instead of a metal-inflicted wound. Thereafter, it's treated with changes of cotton pads and bandages until the man either recovers or dies, though only a few recover. If it be said that this constitutes the torture of a rational being and a disruption of the procreation whose increase is commanded by religion and should therefore be forbidden, I would reply, "Indeed, more than one scholar has made it clear that this is so, above all Jalāl al-Dīn al-Suyūṭī, God have mercy on his soul. He states that it is forbidden in his work *The Prohibition on Using Eunuch Attendants at the Tomb of the Prophet and his Descendants.* However, the prohibition applies to the one who carries out the act, and eunuchs are castrated by a certain Magian people[170] who bring them into the lands of Islam for sale or in payment of tribute, and only a rare few are castrated by Muslims. As far as employing them after castration is concerned, there is no harm in it; on the contrary, it brings with it great divine reward, for if people did not employ them, they would suffer from two perspectives, the first the fact of castration itself and the loss of great pleasure and disruption of procreation that that entails, the second that they would find it hard to make a living." 3.2.55

If it be said, "Emirs are like kings, and any who imitate them will gather many women into their homes, all of them young, and at the same time it is a known fact that jealousy is as much present in them as it is in men because the former are the latter's counterparts, so how can these women be friends with one another, especially when the husband loves one of them and avoids the others?" I would reply that enmity occurs among them in keeping with their circumstances. Each would like her husband's face to be hers alone and that he be intimate with none but her; however, given that they are at the mercy of their husbands, especially when these are kings, they conceal their hatred and display affection, and this is the way of women—they conceal what is inside and display its opposite. What a woman is hiding will appear only when she is no longer afraid and has regained her capacity to judge wisely. Only then will she reveal what has been lurking in her breast. 3.2.56

٥٧،٢،٣ فإن قيل ما رتبة نساء السودان في الجمال قلت اعلم أنّ نساء السودان على أقسام في ذلك ومن المعلوم أنّ كلّ قبيلة يوجد فيها الجميل والقبيح لكنّ هناك قبائل يوجد فيها الجمال أكثر وأخرى يوجد فيها الشوه أكثر وأقلّ قبيلة في دار الفور معروفة[١] بالجمال هم التموركه لأنهم وحشيّون أهل جبال وسوء معاش وكذا الكراكِرِيت وقد ذكرنا سابقاً أنّ قبيلة البرتي والميدوب أجمل نساء من غيرهما ويليهما قبيلة البيقو والبرقو والميمه والتنجور وأشوه قبائل الفور نساء أعجام الفور ويليهم الداجو والبرقد والمساليط كما أنّ في دار الوادي قبيلتي أَبْ سَنُونْ ومَلَنْقا أو مَنَنْقا أجمل الوادي نساء ويليهم الكوكه والميمه وكَشْمِرَة وأقبحها نساء التاما ويليها البرقد والمساليط والداجو ولا يقدر الإنسان أن يساوي بين جمال أهل السودان وغيرهم من أهل بلادنا لاختلاف اللون

٥٨،٢،٣ تنبيه: أجمل أهل بلاد السودان عموماً من مشرقها لمغربها نساء عَفْنو ويليهم باقرمه وبرنو وسنّار وأوسطهم الوادي ويليهم الفور وأقبحهم التُبُو والكَنْكو وبالجملة فالجمال يوجد في كلّ قبيلة لكن قد يقلّ في واحدة ويكثر في أخرى وسبحان من خصّ من شاء بما شاء لا ربّ غيره ولا معبود سواه فما كلّ أسمر مسكًا ولا كلّ أحمر ياقوتًا ولا كلّ أسود زبادًا ولا كلّ لمّاع ماسًا وإن شئت قلت ما كلّ أسود فحمًا ولا كلّ أحمر لحمًا ولا كلّ أبيض جيرًا فقد يوجد في الأسود والأسمر من الجمال ما لا يوجد في الأبيض الشاهق وكأنّي بقائل يقول وهل تستوي الظلمات والنور أو الظلّ والحرور لكن من الناس من تعشق في السمر حيث قال [طويل]

وَفِي ٱلسُّمْرِ مَعْنًى لَوْ تَأَمَّلْتَ حُسْنَهُ لَمَا عَشِقَتْ عَيْنَاكَ بِيضًا وَلَا حُمْرَا

٥٩،٢،٣ وأحبّ بعضهم السواد وبالغ حتّى قال من الوافر

---

١ أضيف للسياق.

If I were asked how the women of the Blacks rank in terms of beauty, I'd 3.2.57
say, "They fall into different classes. It's an acknowledged fact that the beautiful and the ugly are to be found in every tribe, but there are tribes among whom beauty is more common, and others among whom misshapenness is more common. The tribe in the lands of the Fur least known for beauty is the Tomorókkóngá, because they are a savage mountain people, and live roughly. The Karakriit are the same. We have stated before that women of the Bartī and Mīdawb tribes are more beautiful than those of other tribes.[171] The Bīqū, Barqū, Mīmah, and Tunjūr tribes come next, and the most misshapen women are those of the non-Arabic-speaking Fur. Next come the Dājū, the Birqid, and the Masālīṭ. By the same token, in Dār Wāddāy, it is the two tribes of the Ab Sanūn and the Malanqā (or Mananqā) that have the most beautiful women, followed by the Kūkah, the Mīmah, and Kashmirah, while those with the ugliest are the Tāmā, and after them the Birqid, the Masālīṭ, and the Dājū. One cannot draw comparisons between the beauty of Blacks and of others because of the difference in color."

Note: generally speaking, the most beautiful inhabitants of the lands of the 3.2.58
Blacks, be they of the east or the west, are the women of ʿAfnū, followed by Bāqirmah, Barnaw, and Sinnār; those of middling beauty are the Wāddāy, followed by the Fur; and the ugliest are the Tubū and the Katakū. In summary, beauty is to be found in every tribe but may be less in one or more in another—glory be to Him who allocates what He wishes to whom He wishes and other than Whom there is no lord or object of worship! Thus, not everything that is brown is musk, not everything that is red a ruby, not everything that is black civet, not everything that shines a diamond, and you might, if you wish, add that not everything black is charcoal, not everything red flesh, and not everything white lime, for as much beauty may be found in brown and black as in shining white.[172] Now methinks I hear a voice saying, "Can dark and light, or shade and a hot wind, be equal?"[173]—and yet there are people who fall passionately in love with the brown-skinned, as when the poet says:[174]

> The dusky-skinned have something, whose beauty, once gazed upon,
> will never let your eye love white or red again.

Someone once loved black so much that he went overboard and said: 3.2.59

أُحِبُّ لِأَجْلِهَا ٱلسُّودَانَ حتّى أُحِبَّ لِأَجْلِهَا سُودَ ٱلْكِلَابِ

وكنت قديماً مغرماً بهذا المذهب فقلت [وافر]

يَلُومُونِي عَلَى حُبِّي بِسَوْدَا[1] وَمَا عَلِمُوا ٱلسِّيَادَةَ فِي ٱلسَّوَادِ
فَقُلْتُ لَهُمْ دَعُونِي لَا تَلُوموا فَإِنَّ ٱلسُّودَ سَادُوا بِٱلسَّوَادِ
وَجُلُّ ٱلْبِيضِ لَوْلَا ٱلحَاجِبَانِ وَخَالُ ٱلْخَدِّ حَالِكُ فِي ٱلسَّوَادِ
لَمَا عُشِقُوا وَلَا نُظِرُوا بِعَيْنٍ وَلٰكِنَّ ٱلْفَضِيلَةَ فِي ٱلسَّوَادِ

وفي الأوّل السواد بمعنى السُودَد وفي الثاني بمعنى المال وفي الثالث بمعنى السواد الحقيقيّ وفي الرابع العالم الكثير أنتهى

وقال بعضهم [بسيط] ٦٠،٢،٣

قَالُوا تَعَشَّقْتَهَا سَوْدَا فَقُلْتُ لَهُمْ لَوْنُ ٱلْغَوَالِي وَلَوْنُ ٱلْمِسْكِ وَٱلْعُودِ
إِنِّي ٱمْرُؤٌ لَيْسَ حُبُّ ٱلْبِيضِ مَكْرُمَةً عِنْدِي وَلَوْ خَلَتِ ٱلدُّنْيَا مِنَ ٱلسُّودِ

وقال الفاضل الشيخ عبد الرحمن الصَفَتيّ [كامل]

بِٱلرُّوحِ أَسْمَرَ نُقْطَةٌ مِنْ لَوْنِهِ تَكْسُو ٱلْبَيَاضَ مِنَ ٱلْجَمَالِ شِعَارَا
وَلَوِ ٱسْتَقَلَّ مِنَ ٱلْبَيَاضِ بِمِثْلِهَا لَٱعْتَاضَ[2] مِنْ ثَوْبِ ٱلْمَلَاحَةِ عَارَا
مَا مِنْ سُلَافَتِهِ سَكِرْتُ وَإِنَّمَا تَرَكَتْ سَوَالِفُهُ ٱلْعُقُولَ[3] حَيَارَى
حَسَدَ ٱلْمَحَاسِنُ بَعْضَهَا حتّى ٱشْتَهَتْ كُلُّ ٱلْمَحَاسِنِ أَنْ تَكُونَ عِذَارَا

١ الأصل: لسودا. ٢ الأصل: لا اعتاض. ٣ الأصل: القول.

For her sake, I love blacks—
for her I even love black dogs!

I myself was once so taken with women of this persuasion that I declaimed:

They censure me for loving a black-skinned girl (*sawdā*),
Unaware that nobility (*siyādah*) lies in glory (*sawād*),
So I told them, "Let me be and be not censorious,
For the blacks (*sūd*) have become rulers (*sādū*) through their wealth (*sawād*)
And most whites, were it not that their eyebrows
And their cheek moles are of the darkest black (*sawād*),
Would be neither loved nor looked at—
But good qualities were ever the preserve of the masses (*sawād*)."

In the first line *sawād* is used to mean "rule, lordship" (*sūdad*), in the second to mean "wealth," in the third in its true meaning, and in the fourth to mean "a large number of people."

Another poet has said: 3.2.60

"You've fallen for a girl who's black!" said they, so I replied,
"'Tis the color of galias,[175] of musk, and of aloeswood!
I'm the type to whom love of whites would seem no virtue
even if there wasn't a single black left in the world."

And Learned Shaykh ʿAbd al-Raḥmān al-Ṣaftī says:

My soul I'd give for a brown-skinned boy, one spot of whose color
would invest white skin with beauty's name[176]
While one white spot upon his face would
transform the cloak of cuteness into shame.
It's not from his wine[177] that I've become drunk—
it's his sidelocks that drive us men insane.
His charms so envy one another that each
to be the down on his cheeks lays claim.

وكنت عارضته بقصيدة منها قولي [كامل] ٦١،٢،٣

اَلْحَقُّ أَبْيَضُ دَعْ مَقَالَةَ مَعْشَرٍ   قَدْ عَانَدُوا وَٱسْتَكْبَرُوا ٱسْتِكْبَارَا

وقال الصفتيّ أيضاً [بسيط]

قَالُوا تَعَشَّقْتَهَا سَمْرَا فَقُلْتُ لَهُمْ   لَوْنُ ٱلْغَوَالِي وَلَوْنُ ٱلْمِسْكِ وَٱلْحَدَقِ
وَمَا تَرَكْتُ بَيَاضَ ٱلْبِيضِ عَنْ غَلَطٍ   إِنِّي مِنَ ٱلشَّيْبِ وَٱلْأَكْفَانِ فِي فَرَقِ

وتغالى بعضهم في مدح البياض وذمّ السواد بكلام يطول وقال من عاند في ذلك ٦٢،٢،٣
عميت بصيرته عن قوله تعالى ﴿فَمَحَوْنَا آيَةَ ٱللَّيْلِ وَجَعَلْنَا آيَةَ ٱلنَّهَارِ مُبْصِرَةً﴾
﴿وَلِكُلٍّ وِجْهَةٌ هُوَ مُوَلِّيهَا﴾

وَلِلنَّاسِ فِيمَا يَعْشَقُونَ مَذَاهِبُ

I countered[178] this with a poem of my own, which goes in part: 3.2.61

The truth is white! Forget a certain tribe
of obstinates and swollen heads who claim it's not!

Al-Ṣaftī also says:[179]

"You've fallen for a girl who's brown!" said they, so I told them,
"'Tis the color of galias, of musk, and of nightshade!
I've not abandoned the whiteness of white-skinned girls in error—
white hairs and shrouds make me so afraid!"

Some people go to great lengths in their praise of white and dispraise of black, claiming that the discernment of any who oppose this point of view has been blinded to the words of the Almighty: «We have blotted out the sign of the night, and made the sign of the day to see.»[180] The fact is that «Each man has a direction to which he's turned»[181] 3.2.62

for one man's meat, in love, is by another spurned.[182]

الباب الثالث

وفيه فصلان[1]

فصل في أمراض السودان والمأكولات وصحّة الأقاليم والصيد وبعض الحيوانات

١،٣،٣ يجب على العبد أن يعلم أنّ الله خصّ كلّ إقليم بما لا يوجد في غيره وجعل في كلّ قبيلة خاصيّة لا توجد في غيرها ولذا إذا تغرّب إنسان من بلده لأخرى يكون هواؤها مخالفاً[2] لهواء بلده تحصل له مشقّات فيمرض حين يتغيّر عليه الهواء فربّما مات وإن لم يمت يطول مرضه ولا يصحّ جسمه حتّى يعتاد بهواء البلد التي سكن فيها بعد طول المدّة

٢،٣،٣ ولمّا كان الأمر كذلك كان الأولاد الذين يتناسلون من أمّ وأب فوراويّين مثلاً أطول أعماراً وأقوى بنية ولذلك ترى الرجل له عشرة من الولد وأكثر أقوياء أصحّاء وكذا أعراب البادية هناك لا يموت الرجل منهم حتّى يرى من ولده عدداً كثيراً فلو انعكس الأمر بأن تزوّج فوراويّ عربيّةً أو عربيّ فوراويّةً ترى سلالته ضعيفة نحيفة لا يعيش منها إلّا ما قلّ وندر وهذا ممّا يدلّ على أنّ في البلد والجنس خاصيّة لا توجد في غيرهما لأنّ كلّ ولد يوجد من أبوين من نوع واحد وبلد واحد كان أقوى بنية وأعدل صحّة وترى من العكس فيه الأمر ضعيفاً فاسد اللون نحيفاً

---

١ الباب الثالث وفيه فصلان – أضيف للسياق. ٢ الأصل: مخالف.

Chapter 3

In two sections

Section 1: Sicknesses of the Blacks; Their Dishes; the Healthiness of Their Various Climes; Hunting; and Some Animals

Mortal man should be aware that God has made specific to each territory things to be found in no other and allotted to each tribe a peculiarity to be found in no other. Thus, if one leaves his country for another whose air differs from that of his own, afflictions will beset him: he will become sick when the change of air has its effect on him and may die, or if he does not die, his sickness may be prolonged and his body not become well until, at length, it accustoms itself to the air of the country in which he has come to reside. 3.3.1

This being the case, children who are born of a father and a mother who are both Fur, for example, live longer and are more strongly built than others. This explains why one may find a man with ten or more children, all of whom are strong and healthy. The same applies to the Bedouin of the deserts there: none of them ever dies without first having looked on large numbers of offspring. Conversely, if a Fur man marries a Bedouin woman, or a Bedouin man a Fur woman, you will find that his offspring are weak and thin and only a rare few of them survive. This is one of those things that indicates that each country and race has something special not to be found in any other, for any child born of parents of one and the same type and one and the same country is better built and has better health; if the converse is the case, you will find that he is weak, of a bad color, and thin. 3.3.2

٣،٣،٣ ورأيتهم في دارفور ودار واداي يستعينون على صحّة الطفل بأخذ الدم فيأخذون الطفل حين يستكمل أربعين يوماً من ولادته ويشرطون بطنه من الجهتين أعني اليمنى واليسرى تشاريط كثيرة وينزل منه دم غزير وحين يستكمل ثلاثة أشهر يفعلون به ذلك وإن لم يفعل به ربّما هاج عليه الدم فقتله

٤،٣،٣ وأكثر أمراض الأطفال عندهم المرض المسمّى أبو لسان وهو داء يعتري الطفل في غلصمته أي عند اللّهاة فتحدّث له فيها زائدة كلسان العصفور عند أصل اللسان فيعالجونها بالقطع وصورة الآلة التي يقطعونها بها هكذا

وهي حديدة مركّبة في يد من خشب ومعها قطعة خشبة ناعمة فيدخل الطبيب الخشبة أوّلا حتّى يوصّلها إلى المحلّ الذي فيه الزائدة ويكون العليل قد ضبط ضبطاً جيّداً ثمّ يدخل الحديدة حتّى يصل رأسها المعوّج إلى أصل الزائدة من الجهة الأخرى وتبقى الزائدة بين الحديدة والخشبة ويتّكئ عليهما معا فتنقطع الزائدة بينهما فيخرج الحديدة والخشبة معا فيرى على الخشبة قطعة لحم صغيرة ويكون قد استحضر على قليل من النطرون وسُحِقَ جيّداً بين حجرين ثمّ يبلّ الرجل إصبعه ويجعله على المسحوق فيلتصق به ويدخله في فم العليل بعد أن يكون قد أدخل الخشبة إن كان الطفل قد أثغر لكن لا يوصلها إلى محلّ الألم بل حتّى تتجاوز أسنان العليل ثمّ يدعك محلّ القطع بالمسحوق الذي على إصبعه دعكاً جيّداً فيبرأ العليل بذلك وإذا ترك أبو اللسان المذكور أنحل جسم الطفل ونشأ عنه إسهال عجيب فيكون سبباً في قتله

٥،٣،٣ ويليه مرض آخر يسمّى عندهم أمّ صُقُع ولا يعتري إلّا الأطفال أيضاً وهي استرخاء يقع في اللّهاة وبثرة تحدث فيها فلا يشرب العليل اللبن ولا يأكل ويصفرّ لونه فيدعون له بالطبيب فيأتي ويسحق النطرون كما تقدّم ويضع الخشبة وحدها في فم العليل ويدخل إصبعه فيرفع لهاته ويفقأ البثرة التي توجد فينزل منها دم وقيح ثمّ يغمس إصبعه مبلولاً

In Darfur and Wādday, I saw that people resorted to bloodletting to protect their children's health. Once the child had completed forty days from the time of birth, they'd take it and make incisions on both sides—by which I mean on the right and the left—of its belly, making it bleed copiously. When it had completed three months, they'd do the same again; if they didn't, the blood was liable to rise up against it and kill it. 3.3.3

The childhood disease most widespread there is that called *abū l-lisān* ("tongue disease").[183] It afflicts the child in its epiglottis, i.e., in its uvula. This acquires an excrescence like a sparrow's tongue at the base of the tongue, which they treat by excision, using an instrument that looks like this  and consists of a blade mounted on a wooden handle. It comes with a smooth piece of wood, and the doctor first inserts this piece of wood until it reaches the site of the excrescence, the patient being tightly secured. Then he inserts the blade till its curved end reaches the base of the excrescence on the other side, the excrescence thus being between the blade and the piece of wood, and compresses the two of them, resulting in the excision of the excrescence. Then he removes the blade and the piece of wood together, and a small piece of flesh may be observed on the piece of wood. The doctor will previously have prepared a little natron by grinding it finely between two stones. The man wets his finger and puts it into the powder, which sticks to it, and inserts the finger into the patient's mouth, having first inserted the piece of wood, if the child's teeth have grown in. However, he does not let the latter intrude all the way to the site of the pain but rather until it intrudes just beyond the patient's teeth. Then he rubs the site of the excision well with the powder on his finger and the patient is cured. If this "tongue disease" is left untreated, the child's body will become emaciated and it will cause terrible diarrhea, possibly leading to death. 3.3.4

This is followed by another disease, which they call *umm ṣuquʿ*,[184] which also afflicts only children. It consists of a softening in the uvula and the appearance on it of a pustule. This leads to the patient not drinking milk or eating, and a paling of the complexion. They therefore call in the doctor, who comes and grinds natron as previously described, places the piece of wood, on its own, in the patient's mouth, inserts his finger, and raises the uvula, bursting the pustule, from which blood and pus discharge. Then he wets his finger with his saliva, dips it in the natron, and rubs the pustule with it, along with 3.3.5

بريقه في النطرون ويحكّ به البثرة واللّهاة لكن يفعل ذلك ثلاثة أيّام فيبرأ العليل

وقد يقع الإسهال المفرط لكن يُنظَر في الطفل فإن كان ابن سنين ووجدوا المقعدة تبرز من محلّها حكّوها بشقفة حتّى فقأوا ما فيها من البثور وينزل منها دم كثير وقلّلوا مأكله فيبرأ وإن كان صغيراً كابن سبعة أشهر أو ثمانية أو نحوها كووه حول السرّة أربع كيّات هكذا ٦،٣،٣

أعني تكون السرّة في الوسط ويكون الكيّ أعلاها وأسفلها وأيمنها وأيسرها

وقد يعتري الأطفال المرض المسمّى بالغُزَيِّل وهو مرض ناشئ عن إصابة في المخّ يترك الطفل يعبث بيديه ورجليه على غير الحالة المألوفة وأهل مصر كأهل تونس يقولون إنّه من الجانّ حين يترك الصبيّ وحده في محلّ يعتريه هذا الحادث فيقتل في مصر وتونس وبلاد العرب أطفالاً كثيرة فأمّا أهل مصر فيستعينون[1] في علاجه بالكتّابات لاعتقادهم أنّه من الجانّ فيأتون بمن له شهرة في الرُقَى والعزائم والأقسام فيكتب للعليل[2] ويَرقي وهذا قد يصادف أنّ العليل يخفّ ألمه وقد لا ينجع وأمّا أهل السودان فيعالجونه بالكيّ في الجبهة بأنّ يأتوا بلبّ قصبة من قصب الدخن ويلامسون بها النار حتّى تأخذ فيها وتبقى لها زهرة كزهرة الشمعة التي تُقَطّ فيكوون العليل بها فيبرأ لوقته ومن أمراض الأطفال هناك أبو صفّير وهو مرض يعتري الطفل فيفسد لونه ويصفرّ صفرة ظاهرة وهو المسمّى في كتب الطبّ باليرقان الأصفر ٧،٣،٣

وهناك أمراض عامّة الصغير والكبير فيها على حدّ سواء فمنها الوِرْدة وهي الحمّى ولا يكاد ينجو منها أحد في كلّ سنة وتتسلطن عندهم في أيّام الخريف وأوّل الربيع المسمّى عندهم بالدَرَتّ وهو وقت خريفنا وتتنوّع فمنها حمّى الوِرْد التي تأتي في كلّ يوم في ساعة معيّنة ومنها حمّى الغِبّ وهي التي تأتي يوماً وتغيب[3] يوماً ومنها حمّى التثليث وهي التي تأتي بعد كلّ يومين ومنها حمّى الربع وهي التي تأتي بعد كلّ ثلاثة أيّام وهي أقوى أنواع الحمّى وأقلّ منها بدرجة حمّى التثليث ومنها الحمّى المُطبِقة وهي التي لا ٨،٣،٣

---

١ الأصل: يستعينون. ٢ الأصل: العليل. ٣ الأصل: ويغيب.

the uvula. This time, however, he does this for three days in a row, after which the patient recovers.

Severe diarrhea may occur, but in this case the child should be examined; 3.3.6
if it's more than two years old and they find that its backside protrudes too much, they scrape it with a pottery shard, producing much blood, and reduce the child's food, after which the patient recovers. If the child is very young, say seven or eight months or so, they cauterize it around the navel, making four brands, in the following fashion: I mean that the navel should be in the middle, the brands above and below it and to its right and left.

Children may be afflicted by the disease called *al-ghuzayyil,* which is caused 3.3.7
by an injury to the brain that leaves the child waving its hands and feet about in an abnormal manner. In Egypt and Tunis, people say it comes from the jinn. This disorder afflicts a child who is left alone somewhere. It kills many children in Egypt, Tunis, and the Arab countries. To treat it, the Egyptians have recourse to written amulets[185] because they believe that it's caused by jinn. Thus, they fetch someone well known for spells, incantations, and conjurations and he makes written amulets for the patient and performs his spells. This may or may not coincide with the patient's pain being cured. The people of the Lands of the Blacks treat the disease by cauterization of the forehead and by obtaining some millet-cane pith, which they pass back and forth over a fire until it catches and forms a flame like that of a trimmed candle, with which they cauterize the patient, who recovers immediately. Another children's disease found there is *abū ṣuffayr*; it's an affliction that spoils the child's skin color and produces a distinctive yellow. It is what's called in medical books "yellow jaundice."

There are also nonspecific diseases that affect young and old alike. Among 3.3.8
these are *wirdah,* which is a fever, from which almost everyone suffers at least once a year. It is at its peak there during the rainy season and at the beginning of the spring, which they call *darat* and which is the same as our autumn. This fever is of different kinds: there is time-specific fever, which comes every day at a certain hour; quotidian fever, which comes every second day; tertian fever, which comes every third day; and quartan fever, which comes every fourth day, this last being the strongest; tertian is a shade less strong.[186] There is also total fever, which leaves the sufferer only upon recovery or at death and which in Egypt is called *al-nōshah*; doctors now refer to it as

ترتفع عن صاحبها إلّا بالشفاء أو بالموت وتسمّى في مصر بالنوشة وهي في عرف الأطبّاء الآن التهاب معديّ معويّ وكلّها عند أهل السودان تسمّى بالوردة. لا يميّزون فيها. ومن الأمراض العامّة الوبائيّة عندهم الجدريّ وهو عندهم كالطاعون في مصر ويشتدّ خوفهم منه لأنّه قتّال جدًّا وكلّ من مرض به منهم أخرجوه من البلد إلى محلّ آخر في الخلاء وبنوا له عشّة تسمّى عندهم بالكَرَّابة وتركوا عنده من يخدمه ممّن يكون قد مرض بالجدريّ وكلّما مرض آخر نقلوه إليه وهكذا وهذا هو الكرنتينة بعينها. تنبيه: أخوف أهل السودان من الجدريّ أعراب باديتهم لأنّ الجدريّ إن دخل في حيّ من أحيائهم أفناه فلذلك تراهم أخوف الناس منه

٩،٣،٣ ولقد أخبرني رجل من أكابر البرقد يقال له عثمان ود عَلَوَ أنّه كان مرض بالجدريّ وقاسى ما قاسى ثمّ شفاه الله فلمّا قشر جدريّه وقبل أن يندمل صار يؤذيه الذباب فكان يتلثّم لأجل ذلك قال بينما أنا ذات يوم متلثّم واقف على باب داري إذ رأيت أعرابيًّا قد جاء يمشي مشية الخائف فلمّا رآني أقبل عليّ حتّى دنا منّي وسلّم عليّ ثمّ قال أمانة عليك هل في حلّتكم هذه جدريّ فقلت كفانا الله شرّ الأمانة ورفعت اللثام عن وجهي فحين رآني صاح صيحة عظيمة وسقط إلى الأرض فجاء لصيحته إخوانه من الأعراب فرفعوه وذهبوا به وكنت أنا حين جاء إخوانه فررت لئلّا يقتلوني فبلغني بعد ذلك أنّه مات بعد ثلاثة أيّام

١٠،٣،٣ ومن خرافات أهل السودان أنّهم يقولون إنّ الجدريّ حيوان لا يُشاهد إلّا أثره يعلق بالإنسان فيقتله وسمعت من كثير منهم أنّه رأى أثره ويتواطأون على ذلك ويصدّق بعضهم بعضاً وسألتهم عن أثره كيف هو فقالوا[1] أثره نُكَت مستديرة متوالية هكذا ○○○○○○ على سطر واحد فكلّ بيت أصبحنا ورأينا ذلك الأثر دخل فيه نجد أهله قد أصيبوا

١١،٣،٣ عجيبة: أخبرني القاضي الدليل قاضي القضاة بمملكة الواداي حين جاء إلى

---

١ الأصل: فقال.

"gastrointestinal inflammation."[187] All these types are known to the people of the Lands of the Blacks, without distinction, as *wirdah*. Among the non-specific epidemic diseases is smallpox, which to them is as the plague is to Egypt, and which they fear since it is often very deadly. If anyone contracts it, they remove him from the village to somewhere in the countryside and build him a reed hut, called a *karbābah*, leaving someone who has already had the disease to tend to him. Each time another falls sick they take him there and so it continues, this being precisely the same as quarantine. Note: The people of these lands who most fear smallpox are the desert Bedouin, because once it enters a tribe it decimates it. Thus, they fear it more than anyone else.

A prominent man of the Birqid tribe, called ʿUthmān wad ʿAllaw, told me 3.3.9
that he had once been sick with smallpox and suffered through it. Then God cured him. When the papules formed scabs, and before these had healed over, he was greatly bothered by the flies, so he used to veil his face. He told me, "One day, I was wearing my veil and standing at the door of my house when I saw a Bedouin coming along, walking as though terrified. When he saw me, he approached till he was close and saluted me. Then he said, 'Tell me the truth! Is there smallpox in this village of yours?' 'God preserve us from the evil of hiding the truth!' I said and I lifted the veil from my face. The moment he saw me he let out a great cry and fell to the ground. At his cry, his Bedouin brothers came and picked him up and took him away. I fled the moment his brothers arrived, so they wouldn't kill me. I heard afterward that he died three days later."

The people of the Lands of the Blacks claim, among other superstitions, 3.3.10
that the smallpox is a creature of which nothing is ever seen but the tracks, which stick to the person and then kill him. I heard many of them say that they had seen its tracks; they connive with one another over this and believe one another. I asked them what its tracks looked like and they said, "Its tracks are round spots that follow one another, like this oooooo in single file. In any house where we see these tracks of a morning, we find its inhabitants have been stricken."

An Amazing Thing. When he came to Cairo in 1257 [1841–42],[188] Judge 3.3.11
al-Dalīl, chief judge of the kingdom of Wādday, told me that the disease called *al-hayḍah*—known as "the yellow air" to the Egyptians—[189]which came to

القاهرة سنة ١٢٥٧ أن المرض المسمّى بالهَيْضة وأهل مصر سمّوه الهواء الأصفر الذي كان أتى إلى مصر من الحجاز سنة ١٢٤٧ ذهب إلى بلادهم وأخربها وقتل منها عالماً كثيراً كنّا نظنّ أنّه لا يصل إلى هناك فسبحان الفعّال لما يريد لا معقّب لحكمه

١٢،٣،٣ ومن الأمراض العامّة الكثيرة الحصول عندهم المرض الإفرنجيّ ويسمّى عندهم بالجِقّيل وكثرته بينهم لكثرة الفساد وليس له عندهم دواء إلّا الكيّ وصفة هذا الكيّ أنّهم يأتون بحديدة وهي المسمّاة عندهم بالحَشّاشة وهذه الحديدة مستطيلة مفرطحة عرضها بنحو قيراطين وطولها بنحو خمسة قراريط أو ستّة فيحمّوها بالنار حتّى تحمرّ ولها صورة أنبوبة مركّبة في وسطها عرضاً فإذا احمرّت الحديدة أخرجوها من النار وصبّوا على الأنبوبة ماء قليلا ثمّ يدخلون في تلك الأنبوبة عوداً يرفعونها به ويكوون به المحلّ الذي ظهر فيه الداء من غير استثناء ومتى ما شهد هذا الداء على أحد وله أهل كووه ولو قهراً عنه وبهذه المعالجة شفاه الله بأقرب زمن

١٣،٣،٣ وهذا المرض في كردفال أكثر من دارفور ودارفور أكثر من الواداي حتّى إنّه في الواداي لا يسمع بإنسان مرض بهذا الداء إلّا نادراً وسبب كثرته في كردفال أنّ من أصيب منهم به يعتقد أنّه كلّما أعدى غيره به يخفّ عنه ما هو فيه ولم يدر أنّه لو أعدى مائة ألف لم ينقص ممّا هو فيه شيء فترى المريض منهم سواء كان امرأة أو رجلاً يعدي خلقاً كثيراً فلذلك كثر عندهم وفي دارفور وإن كان كثيراً لكنّه لمّا كان منهم من لا يستحي أن يراه الناس مريضا فيعدي غيره وهو قليل ومنهم من يستحي من ذلك فيجلس في بيته حتّى يبرأ وهو كثير فقلّ عندهم وأمّا في الواداي كلّ من مرض به لزم محلّه حتّى يبرأ فكان وجوده نادراً

١٤،٣،٣ ومنه الحصر وهو السيلان الأبيض ومثله الهَبُوب وهو ريح ينعقد في البطن السفلى من المرأة أو الرجل وأكثر ما يوجد في النساء ويقولون إنّهما معديان ومن الأمراض الفاشية عندهم الجُذام وهو تأكل مارن الأنف وأطراف الأصابع وكذلك البَرَص إلّا أنّه أقلّ ومنها أبو الصفوف وهو ذات الجنب وعلاجه عندهم بالتشريط على

Egypt from the Hejaz in the year 1247 [1831–32], spread to their country and devastated it, killing large numbers of people, "though we'd never thought it could spread so far—so glory to Him who effects what He desires; nothing can stand in the way of His wisdom!"

Another nonspecific disease that occurs frequently among them is the Frankish disease,[190] which they call *al-jiqqayl*, whose prevalence is due to the prevalence of depravity and for which the only cure they have is cauterization. They do this by fetching an iron instrument that they call a *ḥashshāshah*.[191] The instrument is elongated and flat, about two inches wide and five or six inches long. They heat this in the fire till it turns red. It has something in the form of a cylinder mounted in the middle, crossways. When the instrument has reddened, they take it out of the fire and pour a little water over the cylinder and insert into it a length of wood by which they can lift it, and with it they cauterize the place where the disease has appeared. No exceptions are made. When the disease is observed on anyone, they cauterize him—assuming he is married—using force if necessary. With this treatment God cures him very quickly. 3.3.12

This disease is more common in Kordofan than in Darfur and more common in Darfur than in Wādday, so much so that one only rarely hears of someone becoming sick with it in Wādday. The reason it's so frequent in Kordofan is that those who contract it there believe that the more people they infect, the better they'll get. They have no idea that even if they infect a hundred thousand, it will in no way alleviate their own condition. You find that anyone who has it, man or woman, will infect many more, which is why it's common among them. It is less common in Darfur, though it is widespread there, because, while they have people who are not ashamed to let everyone know that they are sick and therefore infect others (though these are few), they also have people who are ashamed to do so and therefore stay at home until they get better (these are numerous). In Wādday, however, everyone who contracts the disease keeps to his house until he recovers, so it is of rare occurrence. 3.3.13

Another such disease is *al-ḥaṣar*, which is leucorrhea.[192] Similar is *al-habub*, which is wind trapped in the lower part of a woman's or a man's belly (though more often found in women).[193] Both, they claim, are infectious.[194] Another disease widespread among them is leprosy, which eats away the fleshy part of the nose and the ends of the digits. Vitiligo is also widespread, though less so. Another disease is *abū l-ṣufūf*,[195] which is pleurisy, which they treat by 3.3.14

الأضلاع فيشرّطون أربعة صفوف أو خمسة كلّ صفّ أربع شرطات أو خمس هكذا  ويدعكون المحلّ بعد التشريط بمسحوق النطرون فينزل من الفتحات دم كثير فيبرأ المصاب ومنها الفَرَنْدِيتْ وهو كثير عندهم ويسمّى في مصر بالفَرِنّيت وهو ورم يحدث في الساق أو اليد أو في محلّ آخر فيتكوّن فيه قيح فيُبعَج ويخرج من محلّ البعج خيط أبيض طويل أشبه بالعصب إلّا أنّه غير متين كالعصب والظاهر أنّه حيوان لأنّه يخرج ويدخل وعلاجه البعج والتدفئة بورق العُشَر المدهون بالسمن المسخّن على النار

ومن الأمراض العضويّة عندهم السُوتيّة وهي مرض يخصّ الركبة وهو ورم كالفرنديت إلّا أنّه لا يظهر له خيط ويتكوّن داخله قيح كثير ولا يبرأ حتّى يبعج المحلّ بعجًا غائرًا ثلاثة صفوف في كلّ صفّ ثلاث بعجات أو أربع فينزل منها قيح كثير وبالتدهين بالسمن والتدفئة يبرأ العليل ومنها الدُقّري وهو مرض يخصّ الساق على طولها وهو ورم كورم السوتيّة إلّا أنّ هذا يمتدّ على قصبة الساق وذاك مقصور على الركبة وعلاجه كعلاج السوتيّة إلّا أنّ البعج يكون صفّين من وَحْشِيَّة الساق وصفّين من إِنْسِيَّتِها ومن الأمراض عندهم التي تصيب الأطفال الحصبة[1] والبُرْجُك وهي القرمزيّة ومن الأمراض العامّة وجع الطحال أعني كبره والاستسقاء بأنواعه وأغلب الأمراض عندهم إلّا الطاعون والسلّ فلا يوجدان وإن وجد السلّ فنادر ١٥،٣،٣

وأمّا الجراحة فمتقدّمة بينهم لكثرة الفتن والحروب فتراهم يخيّطون الجروح حتّى إن من خرجت أمعاؤه يردّونها ويخيّطون عليها ويبرأ وكذا يداوون الشجاج بأنواعها[2] وهناك ناس يسمّون الشَلّاكين يعملون عمليّة الكَتَرَاتَا من العين مع المهارة التامّة ولكن لا أعلم كيفيّة العمليّة ولا الآلات المستعملة عندهم لذلك وأعرف منهم رجلًا شهيرًا يسمّى الحاجّ نور غير أنّهم لا يستعملون البتر ولا القطع ولا الاستئصال وأمراض الأُدْرة قليلة عندهم هذا ما انتهى إليه علمي في ذلك ١٦،٣،٣

١ الأصل: الحصْبا. ٢ الأصل: بانواع.

scarification of the ribs; they cut four or five rows, each row consisting of four or five cuts, as here,  rubbing the place after scarification with natron powder; a large quantity of blood comes out of the openings and the afflicted person gets better. Another is guinea worm (*al-farandīt*), which is widespread among them; in Egypt it is called *al-fartīt*. It consists of a swelling that occurs in the leg or the hand or some other place. Pus forms in it so they slice it open and a long white thread like a sinew but softer emerges from the place where it has been sliced. It would seem to be an animal because it goes in and out. The treatment is to slice open the swellings and warm them with leaves of Sodom apple daubed with clarified butter heated over the fire.

Diseases of the limbs from which they suffer include *al-sūtiyyah*, which is a 3.3.15
disease that affects the knee and consists of a swelling like *al-farandīt* but does not produce a thread. Much pus is formed inside the swelling and it only gets better if three rows of deep incisions are made at the affected place, each row consisting of three or four incisions from which copious pus will then emerge; following daubing with clarified butter and warming, the patient will recover. Another is *al-duqrī*,[196] which is a disease that affects the leg along its length. It consists of a swelling like that of *al-sūtiyyah* except that the former extends along the shin while the latter is limited to the knee. It is treated the same way as *al-sūtiyyah*, except that the incisions are made in two rows at the back of the leg and two at the front. Other diseases that affect children are measles and *al-burjuk*, which is scarlet fever. Other nonspecific diseases are pain in (by which I mean enlargement of) the spleen, and dropsy in all its forms. Most epidemic diseases occur among them except for the plague and tuberculosis, which are not present (tuberculosis may occur, but is rare).

Surgery is well advanced among them because of the frequency of con- 3.3.16
flicts and wars. They sew up wounds; if someone's guts come out they can even put them back in place and sew over them so that the man recovers. They also know how to treat head wounds of all types. There are people, called *shallangīns*, who are able to operate with great skill on eye cataracts, though I was unable to find out how the operation is performed or what instruments they use for it. I knew one such celebrated individual, a man called Hajj Nūr. They do not, however, employ amputation, scission, or excision, and scrotal hernias are rare. That is all I know about the topic.

وأطبّاؤهم مسنّوهم فلا تجد فيهم طبيباً شابّاً إلّا نادراً ومن برع في صناعة الطبّ تهرع إليه الناس ولو من مسافة أيّام ويكرمونه إكراماً تامّاً وأكثر علاجهم التشريط والكيّ ولا يستعملون من الباطن إلّا التمرهنديّ والعسل النحليّ[1] والسمن البقريّ ١٧،٣،٣

عجيبة: أخبرني شيخي الفقيه مدنيّ الفوتاويّ عليه سحائب الرحمة أنّه كان أصيب بالنقرس الذي هو وجع المفاصل وهو المسمّى في كتب الطبّ بداء الملوك وأنّ أعرابيّاً من البادية وصف له الوقوف في السمن البقريّ فقال أمرت بإحضار كثير من السمن البقريّ وسُخِّنَ على النار حتّى ذاب ذوباناً تامّاً فنُزِّلَ عن النار وترك إلى أن هدأ وصار يتحمّله الإنسان ورُبِطَ لي حبل في سقف البيت وصار[2] طرفاه بيدي وأفرغ السمن في قصعة كبيرة وغسلت رجلي ووقفت في السمن ومَسَكْتُ الحبل المذكور فكان معيناً لي على طول الوقوف قال فلم أشعر إلّا والسمن يسري في جسمي كسريان السمّ غير أنّه أوّلاً صعد إلى ساقيّ ثمّ إلى ركبتيّ ثمّ إلى فخذيّ ثمّ سرى في النصف الأعلى فصرت أحسّ به يصعد في جسمي شيئاً فشيئاً حتّى وصل إلى عنقي فأخذني دوار وغشي عليّ وكدت أسقط فتلقّاني الخدم ودثّروني في ثيابي وأضجعوني على فراشي وأنا لا أشعر بشيء من ذلك فِقلْتُ نهاري كلّه وليلي كذلك ثمّ أفقت عند الصباح وأنا ناشط كأنّما حللت من عقال ورأيت أنّه خرج منّي عرق كثير كريه الرائحة وبذلك شفاني الله وأخبرني غير واحد أنّ أهل البادية كذا يفعلون حتّى بلغ هذا الخبر مبلغ التواتر ولكونهم يتعاطون السحر كثيراً يتداوون بالكتابة وعندهم أناس مشهورون بذلك وأكثرهم شهرة فَلاّتا ١٨،٣،٣

وكيفيّة الولادة عندهم أنّه إذا أخذ المرأة الطلق أتاها بعض العجائز من النساء وربطوا لها حبلاً في سقف البيت فتمسكه وهي واقفة وتعتمد عليه كلّما اشتدّ بها الوجع وتفرج بين رجليها حتّى يسقط المولود فتتلقّاه إحدى النساء الحاضرات وتقطع سرّه وتضجِعن النفساء على فراشها فإذا تمّ للولد أسبوع عملوا له عقيقة كلّ إنسان على قدر حاله فتجتمع النساء عند النفساء والرجال مع الرجل ويكون قد ذبح شاة فتأكل النساء ١٩،٣،٣

Their doctors are their old men; one rarely finds a young man among them. People flock to those who are masters of the craft of medicine, even traveling for days, and they respect them utterly. The treatments they use most often are scarification and cauterization, and the only things they use for internal treatments are tamarind, honey, and clarified butter made from cows' milk. 3.3.17

An Amazing Thing. My teacher, Faqīh Madanī al-Fūtāwī, may clouds of mercy hover above him, informed me that he was afflicted with gout—pain in the joints, called in medical books "the disease of kings"—and that a Bedouin man prescribed standing in clarified cow butter. "So," he said, "I ordered a large quantity of clarified cow butter brought and it was heated over the fire till it was completely melted. Then it was taken off the fire and left till it had cooled enough for a person to be able to stand it and they hung me a rope from the ceiling of the house with its two ends in my hands and emptied the butter into a large wooden bowl. I washed my feet, stepped into the butter, and took hold of the rope, which made it possible for me to stand for all that time. Suddenly I felt as though the butter were running through my body like a poison, ascending first to my legs, then my knees, and then my thighs, after which it flowed into the upper half of my body. I could feel it climbing through my body little by little till it reached my neck, and then I started to feel dizzy and fainted, and would have fallen but the servants caught me and wrapped me in my clothes and laid me down on my bed, though I was unaware of all that. I slept on through the rest of the day and that night too, and in the morning woke up feeling as lively as if I had been released from shackles. I could see that a great quantity of foul-smelling sweat had come out of me, and that was how God cured me." So many people told me that the desert dwellers do this that it was as though the information had achieved the status of common wisdom. Because they practice magic so much, they use written charms a lot and they have people who are well known for that, the most famous being Fallātā. 3.3.18

They manage childbirth as follows. When a woman is taken by birthing pangs, old women come and tie a rope for her from the roof of the house, which she grasps, standing, and leans on every time the pain becomes intense. She also keeps her feet wide apart until the newborn falls, whereupon one of the women attending her catches it and cuts its umbilical cord. The women then lay the mother on her bed. When the baby is one week old, they prepare a meal to celebrate, each according to his means, the women gathering with 3.3.19

والرجال لحم الشاة ويسمّون المولود ثمّ يتفرّقون ويطعمون النفساء في ذلك الأسبوع عند الصباح المديدة وهي الحريرة بلغة أهل مصر والحسو بلغة أهل المغرب والكَرِيمْ بلغة الإفرنج وعند الظهر لحم دجاجة إن كانوا أغنياء فإن كانوا فقراء فالمديدة أيضه وهي مركّبة من دقيق الدخن ودقيق التبلدي أو الهِجْلِيج فإن كانت من الهجليج كان بها مرار وإن كانت من التبلدي كانت حامضة فإن تمّ للمولود شهران أو ثلاثة حملته أمّه على ظهرها وربطته بثوبها ويسمّى ذلك الحمل قوقو فتحمله كذلك وتذهب إلى شؤونها من زرع وماء وحطب حتّى يشبّ

ومن عادتهنّ أنّهنّ يرضعن أولادهنّ حولين فأقلّ كالإسلاميّين ولا يزوّجن بناتهم إلّا إذا بلغت البنت الحلم وعرفت منفعة الرجل ولقد مكثت عندهم سبع سنين ما رأيت عروساً تزوّجت قبل بلوغها وإن عقد عقدها قبل البلوغ لا يبني بها الرجل إلّا بعد بلوغها لأنّ عادتهم أنّ الرجل يملك ويترك مدّة فمنهم من لا يبني بعرسه إلّا بعد سنتين ومنهم بعد ثلاث والمستعجل منهم يبني بعد سنة لأنّهم لا يُملّكون عليها إلّا إذا نهزت البلوغ. هذا في البكر وأمّا الثيّب فيبني بها الرجل يوم ملاكه أو غده ٢٠،٣،٣

وأمّا قراءة القرآن فمتأخّرة جدّاً لأنّهم لا يُقرِئون القرآن إلّا بالليل في المكاتب فيكون الصبيّ في النهار سارحاً بماشيته من غنم أو بقر وبعد أن يرجع في المساء يأخذ لوحه ويذهب إلى المكتب وعلى كلّ صبيّ الإتيان بالحطب يوماً فيقيدون النار ويحيطون بها فيستضيئون بضوئها وعلى ذلك الضوء يحفظون ويكتبون وحفظهم غير جيّد فلذلك قلّ من يحفظ القرآن منهم حفظاً جيّداً وأمّا قراءة العلوم فمتأخّرة أيضه لعدم العلماء وأكثر قراءتهم للفقه والتوحيد وأمّا المعقول فقليل جدّاً ومع قلّته لا يقرءون إلّا قليلاً من النحو وأمّا المعاني والبيان والبديع والمنطق والعروض فلا يعرفون منه إلّا الاسم ومن يعرفه منهم يكون قد تغرّب لبلد آخر كمصر وتلقّاه فيه فإذا رجع إلى ٢١،٣،٣

the new mother, the men with the father. They will have slaughtered a ewe, and the women and men eat the meat and name the baby; then they disperse. During that week, in the mornings, they feed the mother *madīdah*, which is what Egyptians call *ḥarīrah*, the people of the Maghreb *ḥasūw*, and Franks *crème*. At noon, they give her chicken to eat, if they are well-off; if they are poor, *madīdah* again. This is composed of millet flour and *tabaldī* or *hijlīj* flour. If made with *hijlīj*, it is somewhat bitter and if with *tabaldī* it's sour. Once the newborn is two or three months old, the mother starts carrying it on her back, tying it there with her wrap; this way of carrying the child is called *qūqū*. She puts the child there and goes about her business, be it farming or bringing water or fuel, till it is grown.

Another of their customs is that the women suckle their children for two years or less, as elsewhere in the Islamic world. And they do not give their daughters away in marriage until they have attained puberty and learned the value of a man. I lived seven years among them and never saw a bride marry before she had grown to maturity, and if she were betrothed before that, the man would only consummate the marriage after she had done so, as it is their custom that the man should marry and then leave the girl alone for a period. Some of them only consummate their marriage after two years, others after three; if one of them is in a hurry, he will consummate it after a year. In any case, they are given possession of their brides only after the latter have reached maturity. The preceding applies to virgins; if the woman has been married before, the man consummates the marriage the day of the wedding, or the following day. 3.3.20

They memorize the Qur'an very late in life because they read it only at night, in the schools, since by day a boy is out in the countryside with his flocks or cattle; he takes his tablet when he returns in the evening and goes to the school. Each boy also has to bring firewood one day a week. They light a fire and sit around it, making use of its light. By this light they memorize and copy out the Qur'an, but they memorize it poorly, which is why only a few of them know it well by heart. The study of the sciences also occurs at an advanced age since there are few scholars. Most of what they study is religious law and theology. The rational sciences[197] are very rarely taught, though that's more than one can say for grammar, which they hardly study at all. Of the sciences of rhetoric relating to motifs, metaphors, and figures of speech, and of logic and 3.3.21

بلده كان هو العالم وأكثر ما يعانونه الروحانيّ والسحر ويسمّون علم السحر علم الطبّ ومن مهر فيه سمّي طَبَّابِيّ وهذا العلم يوجد عند الفلاّن أكثر من غيرهم وقد نذكر ما وقع من الفقيه مالك في أولاد السلاطين وسحره إيّاهم حتّى رجعوا إلى الفاشر بعدما هربوا منه وما وقع من الفقيه تَمُرُّو

٢٢،٣،٣ تنبيه: اعلم أنّ دارفور وإن كانت كلّها إقليماً واحداً ومملكة واحدة هواؤها مختلف وأصحّها القوز فلذلك تجد من فيه من أعراب البادية أقوياء أجرياء لسلامة أرضه من العفونات والوَخَم لكنّ ماؤه قليل فقد ذكرنا سابقاً أنّ منهم من بينه وبين الماء مسافة يومين وأكثر ويليه في الصحّة بلاد الزغاوة المسمّاة بدار الريح فلذلك تجد الزغاوة والبِدَيات القاطنين بها في غاية القوّة وسلامة الأعضاء وأردأها هواء الصعيد لكثرة مياهها خصوصاً جبال مرّة ووخمها وعفونتها لكن لا تكون أرضه وخيمة إلّا على من لم يعتدها وأمّا المولودون فيها تراهم أصحّاء أقوياء لكن عندهم الحمى كثيرة وأردأ من الصعيد المدن وأقواها الفاشر ويليه كوبيه وكبكابية وأمّا سلا وفنقرو وبيگا وشالا فأوخم الأماكن كلّها لكثرة الرطوبة عندهم واستمرار الأمطار لأنّها لا تنقطع في السنة إلّا مدّة شهرين أو ثلاثة

٢٣،٣،٣ ومع ما في دار الفور ممّا ذكرناه من الأمراض كلّ منهم يحبّ وطنه ويألف سكنه وإذا تحوّل إلى غيره يبكي عليه ويتمنّى الرجوع إليه وهذه غريزة جبل عليها الإنسان وانطبع عليها الجنان من قديم الزمان فلذلك كان المصطفى صلّى الله عليه وسلّم يحنّ إلى مكّة حنين المشتاق ولولا أنّ الله أمره بسكنى المدينة لأقام بمكّة بعد الفتح باتّفاق لكن من حيث أنّ أمراض بلاد السودان لم تكن وبائيّة قتّالة كانت أعمارهم أطول من أعمار غيرهم فلذلك تجد فيهم المسنّين حتّى تجد من تجاوز المائة وعشرين وأمّا أبناء السبعين والثمانين والتسعين فلا يكاد أن يحصرهم العدّ ولا يوقَف لكثرتهم على حدّ. هذا مع ما ابْتُلِيُوا به من الفتن والحروب والمحن لأنّ كلّ قبيلتين منهم بينهما دم مسفوك

prosody, they know nothing but the names. Anyone who knows that much will have traveled to another country, such as Egypt, and come by their knowledge there. On returning to his country, he becomes the scholar of his locality. They pay the greatest attention to the spirit world and to magic, calling the science of magic the science of *ṭibb* and the one who practices it a *ṭabbābī*.[198] This science is found mostly among the Fullān. We may describe later what Faqīh Mālik did with the sons of the sultans and how he bewitched them so that they returned to the sultan's capital after first fleeing from it,[199] and the doings of Faqīh Tamurrū.[200]

Note: Darfur, though a single territory and realm, varies in terms of its air. 3.3.22
The healthiest part of it is the Dunes, which is why one finds that the desert Bedouin there are strong and bold, their land being free of rottenness and impure air. It has, however, little water; as we have mentioned earlier, some of these Bedouin live two or more days from any water.[201] The next healthiest is the country of the Zaghāwah, known as Dār al-Rīḥ, which is why one finds that the Zaghāwah and the Bidayāt who live there are extremely strong and sound of limb. The worst part of Darfur in terms of air is the High Plain, because of the copiousness of its waters, especially in the mountains of Jabal Marrah. The strongest part is the sultan's capital, followed by Kūbayh and Kabkābiyyah. Silā, Fanqarū, Bīngah, and Shālā are the places with the foulest air because of their high humidity and continuous rainfall, which lets up for only two or three months a year.

Despite all the sicknesses I've described as being found in the lands of the 3.3.23
Fur, they all love their homeland and feel at ease there. If one of them is transported to another country, he weeps for it and wishes he could return. This is an instinct that has been created in humans and with which the heart has been imprinted from time immemorial. Because of this the Chosen One, may God bless him and give him peace, longed for Mecca like a lover; had not God commanded him to live in Medina, he would, for sure, have stayed there. However, given that the diseases of the Land of the Blacks are not epidemic and fatal in nature, their lifespans are longer than others'. This is why you find so many old people among them, even some who have passed one hundred and twenty. Seventy-, eighty-, and ninety-year-olds are almost too numerous to count, too many to render in account, and this despite the conflicts, wars, and trials with which they have been afflicted. There are no two tribes among them who in

وثأر مطالب به غير متروك كما بين البرتي والزيادية وبني عمران والميمة وفلاّتا والمساليط والمسيريّة الحمر والرزيقات والمجانين وبني جرار والزغاوة والمحاميد ممّا لا يكاد يحصى. هذا خلاف فتن الملوك وخلاف ما يصير من القتل في مجلس الشراب أو في المعاندة على الكواعب الأتراب ولولا ذلك لكانوا في الكثرة كياجوج وماجوج وضاق بهم الفضاء والمروج

٢٤،٣،٣ فإن قلت إذا كان الأمر كما ذكر فما بال النساء العجائز قليلة مع أنهنّ لا يقاتلن ولا يحضرن حروباً فلو كان ما ذكر صحيحاً في عدم كثرة الرجال كان وجود النساء المسنّات كثيرًا مع أنهنّ مثلهم أو أقلّ قلت لمّا كنّ يحزن على من قتل لهنّ من الرجال ويتحمّلن بعدهم الضرّ والنكال كنّ عرضة للأمراض المردية الجالبة للمنيّة بسبب ما يحصل لهنّ من الانفعالات النفسانيّة ومع ذلك هنّ أكثر من الرجال المسنّين ولقد كنت في بلدة أقلّ عماراً وسكّاناً وهو أبو الجدول ورأيت فيها من المسنّين والمسنّات كثيرًا وكلّما دخلت حلّة أرى فيها أكثر من ذلك مع أنّ معيشتهم في غاية الانحطاط لو تناول منها أحد من أهل بلادنا مرّة واحدة لذهب منه النشاط لأنّ أكثر مآكلهم إمّا مُرّة أو متعفنة ويرون أنّ هذه هي النعمة المستحسنة

٢٥،٣،٣ وكنت حين حللت ببلادهم ولم أعتد باعتيادهم صنعوا في الدار ويكة ودعوني أن آكل منها فأبيت ولمّا سمع والدي بذلك قال لي حيث لم ترض أن تأكل من هذه الأُدُم لِمَ جئت هنا وصار متحيّرًا فكان يتكلّف ويصنع لي أرزًا بلبن ولمّا توجّهت إلى الفاشر ونزلت في بيت الفقيه مالك الفوتاويّ حضر العشاء فرأيت الأدم مرًّا فسألت ما هذا فقيل لي هذه ويكة الهجليج فأبيت أن آكل منها فجاءوني بأدم آخر فشممت منه رائحة منتّنة فقلت ما لهذا منتّن فقيل لي هذه ويكة الدَوْدَري وهي جيّدة عندهم فأبيت أن آكل منها فأخبر الفقيه مالك بذلك فأرسل لي لبناً حليباً عليه عسل فأكلت منه ولمّا حضر في ديوانه للسمر قال لي لِمَ لم تأكل من ويكة الهجليج أو الدودري فقلت له

bloodshed have not been involved and between whom no feud is ongoing, unresolved, including feuds between the Bartī and the Zayādiyyah, the Banū ʿUmrān and the Mīmah, the Fallāta and the Masālīṭ, the Brown Misīriyyah and the Rizayqāt, the Majānīn and the Banū Jarrār, the Zaghāwah and the Maḥāmīd—feuds too many to number. And this is not to mention the conflicts between their petty kings that erupt out of rage, or the killings that occur when they're in their cups or during quarrels over maidens with "swelling breasts, like of age";[202] absent these, they'd be as numerous as Yājūj and Mājūj and their race, and fill to overflowing every meadow, every open space.

Were you to say, "If things are as you describe, how is it that old women are few, even though they don't fight one another or go to war, and if what's been said regarding the small number of men is true, elderly women should have a significant presence, while in fact they are similar in number to men, or fewer?" I would reply, "Given how much they mourn for the men who've been killed for their sake, and given the harm and suffering they put up with when these die, they are vulnerable to terrible, fatal diseases resulting from their psychological reactions. That said, there are still more of them than of elderly men. I was in a town that was relatively poorly developed and held relatively few inhabitants, namely, Abū l-Judūl, and I saw many elderly men and women there, and every time I entered a village I would see even more, even though they live in conditions that are extremely debased—so much so that were someone from our country to suffer them even once, he'd lose all vigor, for most of what they eat is either bitter or rotten, though they believe it to be the best food anyone could wish for." 3.3.24

Once, after I'd had just arrived in their country and before I'd become used to their ways, they made *waykah*[203] at home and invited me to eat some, but I refused. When my father heard, he said, "If you aren't ready to eat that kind of food with your bread, why did you come here?" and he didn't know what to do. He'd go to great lengths to please me, and would make me rice puddings. When I went to the sultan's seat and stayed at the house of Faqīh Mālik al-Fūtāwī, dinner was brought. I thought the dish accompanying the bread was bitter and asked, "What's this?" and was told, "It's *waykah* made from *hijlīj*." I refused to taste it so they brought me another dish, but it smelled rotten to me so I asked, "Why is this rotten?" and they told me, "It's *dawdarī waykah*," which they find very good. Again, I refused to taste it. Faqīh Mālik was told of this so 3.3.25

إحداهما مرّة وثانيتهما متعفّنة فقال هذا هو الطعام الذي يصلح في بلادنا ومن لم يأكل هكذا يخشى على نفسه من الأمراض

٢٦،٣،٣ والدودريّ ويكة تتّخذ من عظام الغنم والبقر وسائر الحيوانات وهو أنّهم يأخذون عظم الركبة وعظم الصدر ويجرّدون ما عليها من اللحم ثمّ يضعون العظام في خابية ويتركونها أيّاماً حتّى تعفن فيخرجونها ويهرسونها في هاون حتّى ينهرس العظم في اللحم ويصنعونه كرات في جرم البرتقان الكبير فإذا أرادوا الطبخ أخذوا قطعة من كرة وذوّبوها في الماء فإن كان فيها قطع من عظم صفّوها من مصفاة ثمّ صبّوا ذلك الماء في القدر ووضعوه على النار حتّى يصير له قوام فيأتون بقدر صغير يقطعون فيه قليلاً من البصل ويقلونه في قليل من السمن ويضيفونه لذلك ويضعون فيه شيئاً من الملح والفلفل والكُمّا إن وجدت وهذا طعام لا يوجد إلّا في بيوت أمراء الفور

٢٧،٣،٣ وأمّا ويكة الهجليج فلا يخلو إمّا أن تكون من الورق أو من الثمر فالتي من الورق هي أنّهم يجنون الوريقات الطريّة الحديثة ويدقّونها وتوضع في القدر على النار وتحرّك بالمسواط حتّى تمتزج مع ما فيه من الماء والدهن وإن كانت من الثمر فكيفيّتها أنّهم يأخذون الثمر وينقعونه في الماء ثمّ يهرسونه باليد حتّى يذهب لحمه كلّه في الماء ويأخذون ذلك الماء ويصفّونه في قدر فإن كانوا فقراء وضعوا عليه قليلا من الشحم وأكلوا وإن كانوا أغنياء قادوا النار حتّى يصير له قوام ثمّ عملوا تقلية كالتي ذكرناها في الدودري وأضافوا لها لحماً مدقوقاً من القديد وصبّوا فيها الماء وتركوا الجميع على النار حتّى يحصل الامتزاج التامّ فتنزل عن النار وهذه من أعظم وِياكِهم. هذا طعام أغنيائهم

٢٨،٣،٣ وأمّا فقراؤهم فقد ذكرنا سابقاً أنّهم يأكلون الدخن بغير تقشير وأنّ أدمهم قبيح جدّاً لأنّه إمّا كَوَل أو ورق الهجليج الصغير الطريّ المسمّى عندهم بالنِيَلْمو أو ثفل السمسم أو ثمر الهجليج الأخضر المسمّى عَنقَلُو أو ثمره الناضج ومِلح كَلّ ممّا ذُكِرَ الرمادُ المسمّى بالكنبو لقلّة الملح وغلوّه وأترف الفقراء من تكون له شياه أو بقرة يحلب لبنها ويأخذ زبده ويأتدم

he sent me fresh milk with honey and I ate some. When he came to his reception room to pass the evening with his friends, he asked me, "Why wouldn't you eat either the *hijlīj* or the *dawdarī waykah*?" I said, "One was bitter and the other rotten," and he said, "This is the food that suits our country. Anyone who doesn't eat such things should worry about falling ill."

Dawdarī is *waykah* made from the bones of sheep, cattle, or any other animal. They take the knee and chest bones, strip them of the meat, put the bones in a vat, and leave them for a few days till they become putrescent. Then they take them out and grind them up in a mortar until the bones and meat have turned into a paste and make them into balls the size of large oranges. When they want to cook, they take a bit from a ball and dissolve it in water, removing any pieces of bone that may remain with a strainer. Next, they pour the same water into a cooking pot and put it on the fire and leave it till it has thickened. They now fetch a small pot into which they've put a little chopped onion and they fry this in a little clarified butter and add it to the large pot, along with a certain amount of salt, pepper, and *kumbā*, if available. It's a dish found only in the houses of the Fur emirs. 3.3.26

The *waykah* made with *hijlīj* may be made from either the leaves or the fruit. To make the kind that is made from leaves, they harvest the fresh young leaves and pound them. These are then put into a pot over the fire and stirred with a stick till well mixed with the water and fat already there. If made from the fruit, the method is to take the fruit and steep them in water. Then they crush them by hand until the flesh is all transferred to the water. They take that water and strain it into a pot. The poor add a little fat to it and eat it. The rich leave it over the fire till it thickens, then make a fried garnish like the one we described when speaking of *dawdarī*, adding pounded jerked meat, and pour the water onto it and leave it all on the fire till completely blended. It is then taken off the fire. This is one of their most splendid *waykah*s. It is the food of their rich. 3.3.27

The poor, as noted above, eat unhusked millet, and the food that goes with it is quite disgusting, consisting of either *kawal*[204] or small fresh *hijlīj* leaves, which they call *nyúlmá*, or sesame lees, or green *hijlīj* fruit, called *ʿanqallū*, or its mature fruit. For all of these they use *kumbā* ashes instead of salt, as real salt is scarce and expensive. The best-off among the poor are those who have sheep or a cow they can use for fresh milk, whose butter they can take, and 3.3.28

بمخيضه ولا يعرفون اللحم إلّا بعد أشهر إن ذبحت في البلد بقرة أو ثور واقتسموها فيأخذ الفقير منهم قسماً على قدر حاله بأمداد من الدخن لا بشيء آخر ولذلك تجد أكثر شبّانهم يعانون القنيص

٢٩،٣،٣ وقد ذكرنا سابقاً أيضاً أنه في كلّ سبت يضرب الوَرْناگ طبله ويخرج[١] الشبّان كلّهم معه للصيد فكلّ منهم يأتي في المساء بما تيسّر معه لأنّ غاباتهم فيها كثير من الحيوانات الوحشيّة فأكثر ما يصيدونه الأرنب ثمّ الغزال ثمّ أبو الحُصَيْن ثمّ بقر الوحش وإن وجدوا تيتلاً مريضاً أو أخذوه على غرّة قتلوه واقتسموا لحمه والتيتل حيوان وحشيّ على صورة البقر الأهليّ إلّا أنّه أصغر جرماً فأعظمه كالعجل وله قرنان صاعدان مائلان قليلاً إمّا للخلف أو للأمام طولهما بنحو شبرين وأقلّ ومع وحشيّته فيه نوع بلادة فلا يفرّ إلّا من ناس كثيرين وأمّا من رجلين أو ثلاثة رجال فلا يفرّ بل يثبت مكانه وينظر إليهم نظر المتأمّل ومن عادة الفور أنّهم إذا رأوه ينادونه بصوت عال يا تيتل يا كافر فيصير شاخصاً إليهم كأنّه غير مكترث بهم فلا يبرح من مكانه إلّا إذا يدنون إليه دنوّاً كلّيّاً فحينئذ يمشي رويداً رويداً فإن رآهم جدّوا في طلبه هرول والفرق بين التيتل وبقر الوحش المعتاد أنّ التيتل وإن كان نوعاً من بقر الوحش إلّا أنّه أصغر حجماً وقرونه تنبت معتدلة كقرن الغزال وبين القرنين من أعلى انفراج كثير ولون التيتل أصفر كلّه وأمّا البقر الوحشيّ فمنهم الأسود والأصفر والأبلق الذي لونه مختلط ببياض كثير وقرونه كقرون البقر الأهليّ في الغلظ والاعوجاج وحجمه كحجم البقر أيضاً وبهذا تعلم أنّ التيتل نوع من البقر وبينه وبين البقر الفروق المذكورة

٣٠،٣،٣ وهناك أناس مشغولون بصيد الحيوانات لا حرفة لهم سواها وكلّ منهم قد أعدّ لذلك عدّة فأمّا الشبّان فيستعينون على الصيد بالكلاب والسفاريك لا غير وأمّا الحدّادون فيحتالون ومنهم طائفة الصيّادين المذكورين لا حرفة لهم سواها وهم على قسمين

---

١ الأصل: وتخرج.

whose buttermilk they can use as an accompaniment to food. They see meat only once every few months, if a cow or bull is slaughtered in the village and they divide it up, in which case the poor man may buy a portion, depending on his means, paying in *mudd*s of millet, nothing else. It follows that most of their young men are keen hunters.

We've mentioned earlier too that every Saturday the ŏrnang beats his drum and all the young men go off with him on a hunt.[205] All of them return in the evening with at least something, as their forests are full of wild animals. The animal they hunt most is rabbit; after that gazelle, then fox, then wild cattle. If they come across a *taytal* that is sick or they happen upon one inadvertently, they kill it and divide up its meat. The *taytal* is a wild animal that looks like the domestic cow but is smaller in size, the largest being the size of a calf. It has two horns that incline slightly as they rise, either backward or forward, and that are two handspans or less in length. Though wild, it is somewhat sluggish; it runs away only when faced by a large number of people. If there are only one, two, or three men, it stands still and looks at them placidly. When they see one, the Fur customarily call out to it, "*Taytal*, you infidel!" and it trains its eyes on them as though quite unconcerned and only moves if they get very close. When this happens, it walks away slowly, and only trots off if it sees they're serious in their pursuit. The difference between the *taytal* and ordinary wild cattle is that the *taytal*, though a form of the latter, is smaller and its horns grow straight, like the horns of the gazelle, with a large space between them at the top, and it is yellow all over. The term "wild cattle" includes the black, yellow, and piebald forms, the color of the latter being mixed with a lot of white. Its horns are as thick and curved as those of the domestic cow and it is the same size as a cow too. This shows us that the *taytal* is a kind of cow, with differences as noted.[206] 3.3.29

Certain people devote themselves to hunting animals and have no other profession. Each kind of hunter equips himself appropriately. The young men rely entirely on dogs and throwing sticks. The smiths use special equipment. The hunters we mentioned as having no other profession are smiths, and fall into two groups.[207] 3.3.30

٣،٣،٣١ منهم من يتمحّض لصيد ذوات الأربع كالغزال وبقر الوحش والفيل والجاموس والضباع والسباع والخرتيت ونحوها وهؤلاء يجتمعون فرقًا فرقًا كلّ فرقة منهم خمسة أنفار أو ستّة فيأتون للطريق التي يمرّ عليها الفيل وغيره حين وروده على الماء ويحفرون فيها حفرة عميقة أطول من قامة ويدقّون في مركزها وتدًا مدبّب الرأس حادّ السن كالرمح ويصلّبون على الحفرة أعوادًا ضعيفة ويغطّونها بالحشيش ثمّ يغطّون الحشيش بالتراب فيأتي الفِيَلة أو السباع أو بقر الوحش أو الجاموس أو الخرتيت واردة للماء فتمرّ على تلك الحفرة فمتى ما ثقل على الأعواد الوطء تكسّرت تحت أرجلهم وسقط في الحفرة منها حيوان أو اثنان فمتى نزل الحيوان بثقله على الوتد الذي في المركز دخل ذلك الوتد في لحمه فلا يقدر أن يتحرّك حتّى يأتي صاحب الحفرة فيتمّم قتله ويأخذ لحمه بعد سلخ جلده فيعملون اللحم قديدًا وهو المسمّى عندهم بالشراميط لأنّهم يشرمطونه أي يقطعونه سيورًا ويأكلون منه طريًّا

٣،٣،٣٢ فإن كان فيلًا أخذوا سنّه وجلده وقدّدوا لحمه وإن كان خرتيتًا أخذوا قرنه وجلده وقدّدوا لحمه وهذا القديد يأكلون منه ويبيعون منه وكلّ فرقة لها جماعة في البلد يفتقدونهم في كلّ أسبوع ويأتونهم بما يحتاجونه من الزاد وغيره ويكون معهم جمل يحملون ما يجدونه عندهم من القديد والجلود والقرون وسنّ الفيل فيأتون بالجلود فيعملون منها الدرق والسياط ويبيعون العاج وقرن الخرتيت والسياط للتجّار ويبيعون الدرق للعسكر وهم قوم لا عهد لهم ويسمّون الدرامدة فلا يناكحونهم أبدًا ولا يتزوّج الدرموديّ إلّا من جنسه

٣،٣،٣٣ ومنهم من يتحيّل على الصيد بأن يأتي لمحلّ الوحوش ويأتي بحبل من قِدّ متين يجعله خُرْتة واسعة فإذا مرّ عليه شيء من الوحش ودخلت رجله في الخرتة وهي دائرة أشبه بالعروة فرفع الوحش رجله انخرطت عليه وهي ماكنة الأوتاد فلا يقدر الوحش على قطعها ولا قلعها فيمكث حتّى يأتوا[١] إليه فيقتلوه[٢] ومنهم من يعلو على شجرة يقيّل تحتها

---

١ الأصل: فياتون. ٢ الأصل: فيقتلونه.

One group devotes itself exclusively to the hunting of quadrupeds, such as gazelle, wild cattle, elephant, buffalo, hyena, lion, rhinoceros, and so on. These hunters band together in teams of five or six persons. They go to the track along which the elephant or whatever will pass on its way to water and dig in it a pit deeper than a man's height. In the middle of the pit they hammer a stake with a pointed end, sharp as a spear at the tip, and lay a latticework of thin sticks over it, and cover these with grass. Then they cover the grass with soil. The elephants, or lions or wild cattle or buffalos or rhinoceroses, come to drink and pass over this pit, so when their weight becomes too much for the sticks to bear, they break beneath their feet and one or two animals fall in. When the weight of the animal comes down on the stake in the middle, the spike enters its flesh and the animal is immobilized until the one who dug the pit comes and finishes it off, and takes its meat after removing its skin. They make the meat into jerky, which they call "shreds" because they shred it, meaning they cut it into strips. Some of it they also eat undried. 3.3.31

If the animal is an elephant, they remove its tusks and hide and make the meat into jerky. If it's a rhinoceros, they remove its horn and hide and make its meat into jerky, some of which they eat and some of which they sell. Each team has a group of people in the village who each week go and look for them, bringing them what they need by way of supplies and so on. These people have a camel, which they load with whatever jerky, hides, horns, and elephant tusks they find with the hunters. The hides they make into shields and whips; they sell the ivory, rhinoceros horns, and whips to the merchants and the shields to the soldiery. They are a people who recognize no law and are called Darmūdīs; others never contract marriages with them, and the Darmūdīs will marry only their own kind. 3.3.32

Others use traps, as follows. They go where the wild animals are, bringing a tether of strong leather that they make into a large loop. When a wild animal passes over it and its foot enters the loop—which is circular and resembles a noose—and the animal raises its foot, it becomes caught in it. The loop is well secured with pegs, so the animal can neither break it nor pull it out, and it remains trapped like that till they come and kill it. Others climb trees beneath which wild animals nap, having with them one 3.3.33

الوحش ويكون معه حربة أو حربتان من الحراب الواسعة الحادّة التي هي هكذا
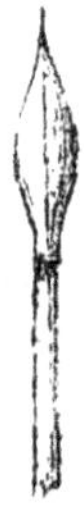
فيمكث في أعلى الشجرة حتّى يأتي الوحش ويقيّل ويهدأ فينظر لمن هو قريب منه ويطعنه وهو نائم في بطنه فتنفر باقي الوحوش التي معه ويمكث المطعون فينزل إليه الصيّاد ويتمّم قتله

٣٤،٣،٣ ومنهم من يتمحّض لصيد الطير وأحسن طير يصاد عندهم الحبارى وهو طائر عظيم أكبر من الدجاج الروميّ لونه أبيض يميل إلى الاصفرار والخضرة يسمن في أيّام الدرت سمناً مفرطاً ويكون لحمه طريّاً لطيفاً وهذا يألف دوداً معروفاً عندهم وحشرات صغيرة فيأتي الصيّاد بذاك الدود والحشرات ويكون معه خيط قد فتله من العصب فتلاً جيّداً وهو رفيع لا يكاد أن يرى للطائر ويقصد المحالّ التي يصيد فيها فمتى رأى الصيّاد الحبارى في محلّ ربط حشرة أو دودة في خيط وربط الخيط في أسفل شجرة ويذهب إلى الحبارى فيسوقها وفي الحبارى بلادة لا تكاد تطير حتّى يقرب الإنسان أن يمسكها فيسوقها لجهة الحشرة أو الدودة حتّى تراها فمتى ما رأتها هرعت إليها وابتلعتها ولمّا صارت الحشرة في حوصلتها وأرادت تذهب يمنعها الخيط من الذهاب فيأتي الصيّاد فيذبحها ويضعها معه ويربط في الخيط حشرة أخرى إن كان هناك حبارى ويوجد أيضه طير آخر يسمّى أبا طَنْطَرَة وهو أبيض وهو طائر أكبر من الحبارى بقليل وله في عنقه كيس طويل مخروطيّ الشكل أسفله واسع وأعلاه ضيّق يبتلع الحشرات أيضاً كالحبارى

٣٥،٣،٣ ومنهم من يصيد الطيور الصغيرة بالشباك وهذا أقلّ الدرامدة كسباً لكونه يغرم حبّاً إذ العصافير وأبو موسى وأمثالها لا تقع إلّا على الحبوب فيأتي في المحلّ الذي يريد الصيد فيه بحيث يكون قرب نهر أو بركة وينصب شبكته وهي شبكة مربّعة وصورتها هكذا

or two of the spears of the broad, sharp kind, as in the illustration: The hunter stays at the top of the tree until the animal arrives, naps, and settles down. He fixes his eye on one that is close to him and stabs it in the belly as it sleeps. This causes the rest of the animals to run away, but the one that has been stabbed stays put and the hunter descends to finish it off.

Some devote themselves exclusively to hunting birds, the best of 3.3.34
those hunted there being the bustard. This is an enormous bird, larger than a turkey, in color white shading into yellow and green. It grows extremely fat during the hot season, and its meat is tender and delicate. It feeds on a certain kind of worm that is common there, as well as small insects. The hunter brings some of these worms and insects and will have on him some line that he's carefully made out of well-plaited sinew so fine the bird can scarcely see it. He goes to the places where these birds are hunted, and when he sees bustards in a particular place, ties an insect or a worm onto the line, ties the line to the bottom of a tree, goes toward the bustards, and drives them (bustards being so sluggish that they can hardly fly even when a person is close enough to catch them) in the direction of the insect or worm, till it sees it. As soon as it does so, the bird rushes toward it and swallows it. When the insect is in its craw and the bird wants to leave, the line prevents it from doing so. The hunter comes, cuts its throat, sets it beside him, and if there are more bustards there ties another insect to the line. There is another bird also to be found there called *abū ṭanṭarah*:[208] it is white, slightly larger than the bustard, and has a long conical sac on its neck that is wide at the bottom and narrow at the top. Like the bustard, it eats insects.

Another group hunts small birds with a net. These are the Darmūdīs who 3.3.35
earn the least, because they have to cover the cost of grain, as sparrows, whydahs,[209] and the like alight only on grain. Such a hunter goes to the place where he wants to hunt, such as close to a river or pond, and sets up his net. The net is square and looks like this:

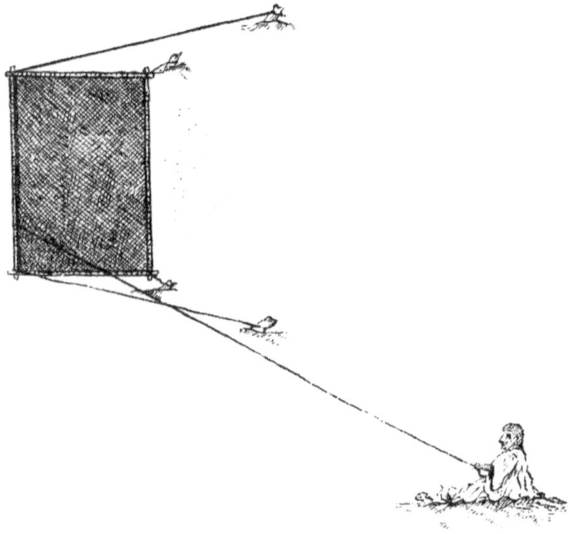

ولها أربعة أوتاد وتدان منها مربوطان لصق ركنيها ووتدان مربوطان في حبلين طويلين في ركنيها الآخرين[1] فيدقّ الأوتاد في الأرض وفي قرب أحد أركانها الوحشيّ حبل متين طويل جدّاً فينصب الشبكة ويبذر الحبّ أمامها ويأخذ طرف الحبل الطويل ويمكث بعيداً عنه فمتى نزلت الطيور وكثرت على الحبّ كفأ الشبكة عليها بالحبل الذي في يده وعيون الشبكة ضيّقة جدّاً فلا يخرج منها عصفور ولا يفلت منها شيء فيأتي صاحب الشبكة ويأخذ الطيور منها فإن كان فيها ما هو غالي الثمن كالدُرّة أو الببغاء ونحوه أخذ ريش جناحيه وتركه في مِكَّله وإن لم يكن فيها ذلك ذبحها كلّها وبذر حبّاً آخر وحين كنت هناك كانت لي شبكة وكنت أصطاد بها في بيتي فطالما شبعت من العصافير بصيدي بها وهناك من هو مغرم بصيد القرود والنسانس في الجبال ولا أعرف كيفيّة اصطيادهم بها

وأحسن من ذلك كلّه الصيد بالبارود لأنّ الإنسان هناك متى ما كان معه بندقة جيّدة يشبع من لحوم الحيوانات بغير مشقّة ومن الأغنياء من يشتري من الدرامدة ٣٦،٣،٣

[1] في الأصل: الاخريين.

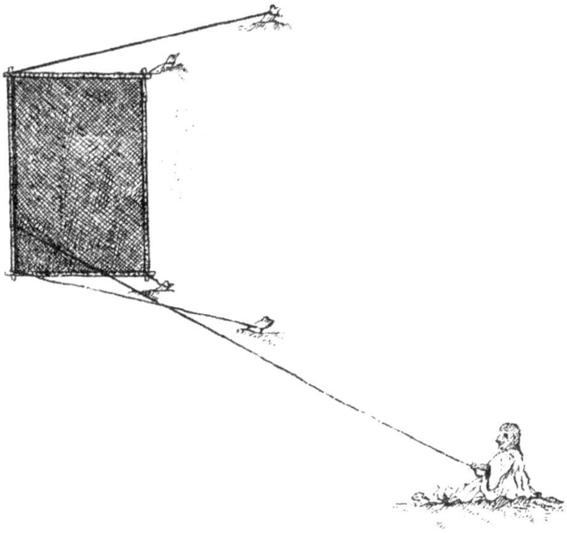

It has four pegs, two of which are tied directly to two of its corners while two are tied to two long ropes attached to its two other corners. The pegs are hammered into the ground, and close to one of its upper corners is a strong, very long rope. Then the net is set upright and grain scattered in front of it. The hunter takes the end of the long rope and stays there, at a distance. When the birds have come down in large numbers on the grain, he pulls the net down on them using the rope in his hand. The interstices of the net are very narrow so no birds can escape and nothing can get through. The owner of the net then goes and extracts the birds. If it contains anything of high value, such as a parakeet or a parrot or the like, he takes out its wing feathers and leaves it in his basket; if it doesn't, he cuts the birds' throats and scatters more grain. When I was there I had a net, and used to hunt with it at home. Often, I was able to satisfy my appetite with the birds I caught. There are others who are fond of hunting apes and monkeys in the mountains, but I don't know how they catch them.

Better than all the above is hunting using gunpowder, for anyone with a good musket can eat as much meat as he likes with no effort. Some of the wealthy buy a Darmūdī slave and use him just for hunting; if the slave is clever, his master will never go without meat. At the home of my teacher Faqīh 3.3.36

عبداً ولا يكلّفه إلّا بالصيد فلمّا نصح ذلك العبد أشبع سيّده من اللحم ولقد رأيت عند شيخنا الفقيه مدنيّ عبداً يسمّى سعيداً مسنّاً فأخبرني أنّه صيّاد وأطعمني لحم غزال وذكر أنّه من صيده وأنّه لا بدّ له في كلّ جمعة أن يأتي له باللحم مرّتين أو ثلاثاً فصرت أتمنّى أن يكون لي عبد مثله فما عثرت عليه

٣٧،٣،٣ وقسم متمحّض لصيد الزراف والنعام وهم أعراب البادية كالمحاميد والزَبَدَة والعريقات بدار الواداي والمجانين والزَيَاديّة وبني جرار والعريقات بدار الفور وكلّ من هؤلاء يصطاد على الخيل فأكثرهم صيداً أسبقهم جواداً ثمّ إنّ الإنسان منهم إذا رأى صيداً وتبعه لا يقفو أثره بل يباريه حتّى يحاذيه ومتى تمكّن من فريسته عقرها فأمّا النعام وإن كان شديد العدو فيوجد من يلحقه وأمّا الزراف فلا يكاد يلحقه في العدو فرس ولذلك لا يلحقه إلّا الفرس الذي يمرّ كالريح وأعراب البادية في دارفور ودار واداي منعّمون فيما يشتهون لا يحتاجون إلّا إلى الدخن والذرة والملبوسات لكن يشترون ما يحتاجونه من ذلك بما زاد عن كفايتهم من السمن والعسل والمواشي وجلود الصيد والبقر والإبل حتّى إنّهم يجلبون لدار الواداي ولدار الفور الأجربة والقرب والبُطَط والحبال المصنوعة[1] من سيور الجلد ويسمّون هذه الحبال الجلديّة بالوَجّ والسياط وغير ذلك

٣٨،٣،٣ وأمّا السمن فمن أنعامهم والعسل فمن الأشجار لأنّ النحل يعشّش فيها وهم يجتنونه والصيد كثير فلذا ترى ريش النعام عندهم لا قيمة له وكذا قرن الخرتيت وحين كنت في دار الواداي جاء بعض التجّار من فزّان يطلب ريش النعام وطلب من الشريف أحمد الفاسيّ الذي توزّر بعد أبي أن يكتب له كتاباً إلى الشيخ شوشو شيخ المحاميد بالوصيّة عليه وأن يأمر الأعراب بالصيد له برفق في الثمن وكان معه خمسون ريالاً فرانسا[2] فكتب له الشريف بذلك فأخذ الكتاب وتوجّه إلى المحاميد بدليل من العرب ومكث هناك ما شاء الله أن يمكث ولمّا جاء أخبرنا بأنّه حين وصل إلى حيّهم وسأل عن بيت الشيخ دلّ عليه فنزل في أكرم ضيافة وأرحب نزل ولمّا أراهم كتاب الشريف زاد

١ الأصل: وبطط وحبال مصنوعة. ٢ الأصل: من الفرانسا.

Madanī, I saw a slave called Saʿīd, who was advanced in years. Faqīh Madanī told me Saʿīd was a hunter and fed me gazelle meat, mentioning that it was Saʿīd who had shot it, and that Saʿīd had to bring him meat two or three times a week. I started looking for a slave like him but couldn't find one.

One group devotes itself exclusively to hunting giraffe and ostrich, namely, the Bedouin of the savannah, such as the Maḥāmīd, the Zabadah, the ʿIrayqāt in Dār Wāddāy, the Majānīn, the Zayādiyyah, and the ʿIrayqāt and Banū Jarrār in Darfur. They all hunt on horseback. The best hunter is the one with the fastest horse—when one of them catches sight of his prey, he doesn't track its spoor but chases it till he comes alongside it. When the prey is within reach, he hocks it. Though ostriches run fast, there are those who can out-gallop them. As for giraffes, however, a horse can only barely outrun them, so it takes a horse that runs like the wind to actually catch up with one. The Bedouin of the savannah in Darfur and Wāddāy are blessed with every comfort they could wish for, except millet, sorghum, and clothing. Their requirements in terms of these, however, they buy with whatever clarified butter, cattle, wild-animal skins, cows, and camels they do not need for themselves. They can even afford to import into Dār Wāddāy and Darfur scabbards, waterskins, leather butter flagons, ropes made from leather strips (which they call *wajaj*), whips, and other things besides.

3.3.37

Their clarified butter is from their own cattle, and their honey from trees— the bees nest there and they harvest it. Hunting is widely practiced, which is why you'll find that ostrich feathers have no value for them, and the same goes for rhinoceros horn. When I was in Dār Wāddāy, a merchant came from Fezzan looking for ostrich feathers and asked Sharif Aḥmad al-Fāsī, who was vizier after my father, to write him a letter of recommendation to Shaykh Shūshū, shaykh of the Maḥāmīd, and order the Bedouin to hunt for him at a reasonable price. He brought with him fifty French dollars. The sharif wrote him a letter to that effect, and the merchant went to the Maḥāmīd with a Bedouin guide. He stayed there awhile and when he came back told us that when he reached the place where the tribe had settled and asked after the shaykh's tent, he was shown the way, received with the most lavish hospitality, and put up in the grandest style. When he showed Shaykh Shūshū the sharif's letter, the shaykh became yet more generous in his hospitality and treated him with extraordinary kindness and charity, allocating him a tent with its furnishings

3.3.38

الشيخ في إكرامه وبالغ في التلطّف والبرّ[1] به وأفرد له بيتاً من الشعر بفرشه وجميع ما يحتاجه ووكّل وصيفاً ووصيفة لقضاء مهمّاته

٣٩،٣،٣ وكان ذلك التاجر أخذ معه هديّة للشيخ المذكور فقدّمها له فقبلها منه وأثاب عليها ثمّ إنّ التاجر سلّم للشيخ الخمسين ريالاً فطلب الشيخ العرب وقال لهم هذا رجل غريب أضافني والتجأ إليّ ويريد ريش النعام فمن كان له أرب في الريالات فليغد للصيد من الصباح وكلّ من أتى بجلد ظليم فله نصف ريال ومن أتى بربداء فله ربع ريال فاهتزّ العرب لمطلبه وأصبحوا قانصين ففي يوم واحد جاءوا بنحو عشرين ظليماً فمكث عندهم نحو من عشرين يوماً فجمع فيها نحو مائة جلد ظليم وحملها له الشيخ على إبله وزوّده بزاد كثير وكان من جملة ما جاء به دهن النعام فإنّه جاء منه بكثير وأتى ومعه من العسل والكَنَيْكَنْيا[2] والسَرَنة والكَرْنُوشيء كثير وباع في وارة الظليم بثلاثة ريالات ولم يبق معه إلّا نحو عشرة من الجلود وربح ربحاً كثيراً

٤٠،٣،٣ وأمّا الزراف لا نفع في المتجر إلّا بجلوده يبيعونها وأمّا لحمه فيأكلونه طريّاً وقديداً ويوجد عند العرب من الأرز والدفرة والكوريب والهجليج والتمر هنديّ والعسل والكرنو والسرنة ما لا يوجد عند غيرهم وأمّا اللبن فلا قيمة له عندهم لكثرته. يأخذون منه السمن ويرمون رائبه حتّى إنّ من أتى إلى أحيائهم وخصوصاً أحياء الرزيقات والمسيريّة[3] الحمر والحبّانيّة يجد الغدران والبرك القريبة منهم كلّها لبناً

فصل في معاملة أهل دارفور

٤١،٣،٣ قد تقرّر في علم التوحيد أنّ الحق تعالت أسماؤه غنيّ عن المحلّ والمخصّص فهو صاحب الغناء المطلق لا يحتاج إلى أحد من خلقه وجميع الخلائق لفضله محتاجون ولنواله سائلون وعلى أبواب رحمته مزدحمون فنظر إليهم بعين رحمته ووهب لكلّ منهم

١ الأصل: واكبر. ٢ الأصل: والكَنْياكَنْيا. ٣ الأصل: ومسيرية.

and everything he needed, and appointing a senior male and female servant to see to his needs.

The merchant had brought with him a gift for the shaykh, which he presented to him and which the latter accepted and requited with gifts of his own. Then the merchant handed the fifty dollars over to the shaykh, and the shaykh summoned the Bedouin and told them, "This man is a stranger who has claimed my hospitality and sought my protection, and he desires ostrich feathers. If any of you would like some of these dollars, let him go hunting tomorrow morning. For each *ẓalīm* ostrich he brings he will receive a half dollar, and for each *rabdā'* ostrich a quarter dollar."[210] The Bedouin leaped to obey his request and set off to hunt the next morning—in one day they brought around twenty *ẓalīm*s. The man stayed with them for some twenty days, during which he collected about one hundred *ẓalīm*s. The shaykh had loaded these onto his camels, and gave him a large stock of provisions. Among the items he provided was ostrich fat, of which the merchant brought a large quantity. He also arrived with large quantities of honey, *kenykenya* candy, *hijlīj* kernels, and yellow jujube fruits. He sold the *ẓalīm*s in Wārah for three dollars apiece and was left with only around ten skins. He made a large profit. 3.3.39

Giraffes have no value as a trade item, except for their skins, which they sell. They eat the meat fresh and jerked. The Bedouin also have more rice, sawa millet,[211] *kūrayb*, *hijlīj*, tamarind, honey, yellow jujube fruits, and *hijlīj* kernels[212] than anyone else. Milk is so abundant among them that it has no value: they take the clarified butter and throw away the curds. It's so plentiful that anyone who goes to their settlements, especially those of the Rizayqāt, the Brown Misīriyyah, and the Ḥabbāniyyah, will find the nearby streams and ponds awash with milk. 3.3.40

Section 2. Currency among the People of Darfur

It is acknowledged in theology that the Truth, may His names be exalted, has no need of place or particularity. He possesses absolute sufficiency and is in no need of any of His creation, while all creatures need His bounty, plead for his charity, and crowd together at the gates of His mercy. He has therefore bestowed on them the gaze of His benevolence, granting to each that which will support him and his family, while favoring some over others 3.3.41

ما يقوم به وبعائلته وفضّل بعضهم على بعض في الرزق فجعل منهم الملوك ومنهم الغنيّ ومنهم الصعلوك وجعل لهم أسباباً يتبعونها في طلب الأرزاق وأمر بالسعي والاجتهاد خوف الإملاق

٤٢،٣،٣ ومن عظيم مِنّتِهِ أن جعل البيع والشراء حلالاً بين الناس لينالوا ما في نفوسهم ويذهب عنهم الباس فجعل في البلاد المتمدّنة النَقْدَيْنِ قرّة للعين ينالون[١] بهما ما يحتاجونه من أمور معاشهم ويضطرّون إليه فى ارتياشهم وخصّ سبحانه وتعالى كلّ مملكة بسكّة معروفة ودراهم ودنانير بينهم مألوفة

٤٣،٣،٣ لكن لمّا كانت أهل السودان في بون عن التمدّن العظيم وفي ظلمة وحشيّة كالليل البهيم كان أغلبهم لا يميّز الذهب من النحاس ولا القصدير من الرصاص حتّى من كان في بلادهم معدن الذهب يبيعونه تبرًا ويرون أنّ بيعه كذلك أحرى وسيّما مملكة دارفور ليس بها شيء من المعادن إلّا ما جلب إليها من الأقطار حتّى إنّ أعظم حليّ نسائهم كما تقدّم من أنواع الأحجار فهم جديرون أن يكونوا بمعزل عن المعاملة بالفضّة والنُضار لكن لمّا وطئت بلادهم التجّار وتمصّرت بالمتاجر فيها الأمصار احتالوا إلى سكّة بها يتعاملون ويشترون بها ما يشتهون فانقسموا في ذلك أقساماً وأذهب كلّ قسم منهم بما اصطلح عليه من المعاملة يِواماً[٢]

٤٤،٣،٣ فأوّلها الفاشر وهو مقرّ السلطنة وتخت المملكة. جعلوا من القصدير خواتيم يشترون بها ما يحتاجونه من لحم ودجاج وطيب وحطب وخضراوات وغير ذلك وتسمّى بالفوراويّة تَارْنَيَهْ وهي على قسمين غليظة وتسمّى تَارْنَيَهْ تُونْقَانَيَهْ ورفيعة وتسمّى تَارْنَيَهْ بَيَّيَا يتعاملون بها فى سفاسف أمورهم كما ذكرنا والأمور المهمّة يتعاملون فيها بالتكاكى جمع تُكِّيَة وهي شقّة من غزل قطن طولها عشرة أذرع وعرضها ذراع وهي على نوعين شِيكه وهو منسوج خفيف غير مندمج وكَتْكات ومنسوجها ثقيل مندمج فمن الأوّل كلّ أربع تكاكى بريال فرانسا ومن الثاني كلّ اثنين ونصف بريال فرانسا وما عدا ذلك

١ الأصل: يتنالون. ٢ الأصل: أوامًا.

in terms of the livelihood they receive, making some kings, others rich men, and yet others paupers. He has created for them means to use in pursuit of their livelihoods and commanded them to strive and struggle lest they fall into poverty.

As a part of His vast favor, He has made buying and selling permitted to men, so that they can obtain what they hanker for and be relieved of misery. Thus, in civilized countries He has made the two forms of specie[213] sources of consolation by means of which men may obtain the things needed for their daily lives and necessary for them to accumulate wealth. Likewise, He has in His glory and exaltedness assigned to each realm a recognized mintage and gold and silver coins they recognize. 3.3.42

Given that the people of the Lands of the Blacks are so far from civilization and its might, and live in a darkness as savage as the blackest night, most of them, it must be said, cannot tell gold from brass or tin from lead. Even those whose lands contain gold as a mineral sell it as ore, believing that to sell it that way is more proper. This ignorance is particularly characteristic of Darfur—it has no metals other than those imported from other lands,[214] so that even the most splendid of its women's jewelry consists, as noted above,[215] of different kinds of stone. Predictably, then, these people do not have the benefit of silver and gold as currency for their use. Despite this, given that merchants have set foot in their country and that their cities have grown because of the presence therein of commercial establishments, they have come up with equivalents of minted currency with which to carry on commerce and to buy what they want. For this purpose, they are divided into different areas, and each area has adopted the currency it finds appropriate for daily use.[216] 3.3.43

The first area is the *fāshir*, the headquarters of the sultanate and seat of government. The people there have made rings of tin with which they buy whatever meat, chicken, perfumes, fuel, vegetables, and so on they need. In the language of the Fur these rings are called *tarne* and come in two forms, thick (called *tărne tonga nia*) and thin (called *tărne bayyâ*). They use these as currency in their small-scale transactions, as stated earlier.[217] For larger transactions, they use *takākī* (plural of *tukkiyyah*), which are pieces of cotton cloth ten cubits in length and one cubit in breadth. This cloth is of two types: *shīkah*, which is of a light, loose weave, and *katkāt*, which is of a heavy, compact weave. Four *takākī* of the former are equivalent to one French dollar, as are two and a 3.3.44

فبيعهم كلّه استبدال شيء بشيء والأمور العظام عندهم تباع بالرقيق فيقال هذا الفرس بسُداسيَّيْن أو بثلاثة سداسيّاً والسداسيّ عندهم العبد الذي إذا قيس بالشبر من كعبه إلى شحمة أذنه كان طوله ستّة أشبار والسداسيّة كذلك وقيمة السداسيّ من التكاكى ثلاثون تكّيّة ومن الشواتر الزرق ستّة والبيض ثمانية ومن البقرستّة ومن الريالات فرانسا عشرة ريالات وكل إنسان يشتري بما عنده ولا يعرفون المحبوب ولا القرش ولا الفرانك ولا الخيريّة ولا شيء من معاملات أهل المدن سوى الريال الفرانسا المسمّى عندهم أبا مدفع

٤٥،٣،٣ وأمّا أهل كوبيه وكبكابيّة وسرف[١] الدجاج فإنّهم يتعاملون بالخَرَش وهو خرز ليس بالغليظ ولا بالرفيع منه أخضر ومنه أزرق. يعمل سبحاً كلّ سبحة مائة حبّة وقد قدّمنا الشرح عليه في حليّ النساء وزينتهنّ فيتعاملون به في سفاسف الأمور عوضاً عن التارنيه في الفاشر ومن العجائب أن التارنيه في هذه الأسواق الثلاثة لا تسقي شربة ماء بل المعاملة بالخرش من خمسة[٢] حبّات إلى مائة ومن سبحة إلى عشرة إلى ما لا نهاية له وقيمة التكّيّة عندهم ثماني[٣] سبح وبقيّة الأحوال كالفاشر

٤٦،٣،٣ وأمّا قرلي وما وليها[٤] فيتعاملون بالفلقو وهو ملح صناعيّ مستخرج تراباً من الأرض ويصبّون عليه الماء على غالب ظنّي لرسوب الأوساخ والأتربة ويصفّي ويقطرون ماءه لنقص هذا الماء ويتلقّون المقطّر منه في قوالب كالأصابع فيجمد بعد برودته ويصير كالأصابع وقد شاهدت محالّ استخراج هذا الملح ورأيت أواني التقطير ويشابهون البرام الأفرنجيّة ولا نعلم من أوصل هذه الصناعة إليهم وأهل البلد لا يعلمون أيضاً بل قصارى أمرهم إذا سئلوا وقال لهم قائل من علّمكم هذه الصناعة أن يقولوا شيء وجدنا آباءنا يفعلونه ففعلناه ولا نعرف أوّل من صنعه ولقد عاملت بهذا الملح واشتريته وله لذّة عجيبة في طعمه تخالف لذّة الملح الطبيعيّ إلّا أنّه غير شفّاف وفيه سمرة

٤٧،٣،٣ وأنواع الملح في دارفور ثلاثة: زغاويّ وهو ملح طبيعيّ يخرج من بئر الزغاويّ وفلقو[٥]

١ الأصل: صرف. ٢ كذا في الأصل. ٣ الأصل: ثمان. ٤ الأصل: ولاها. ٥ أضيف للسياق.

half of the latter. For all other transactions, they barter. For major transactions, they price things in slaves. Thus, they may say, "This horse is for sale for two, or three, *sudāsīs*," the *sudāsī* being, in their parlance, a slave who, when measured from heel to earlobe, is six handspans tall; *sudāsiyyah* is used for females. A *sudāsī* is equivalent in value to thirty *takākī* of six blue, or eight white, lengths of camlet, or to six head of cattle, or to ten French dollars. People make their purchases using whichever of these currencies they possess. They know nothing of the sequin, the piaster, the franc, the *khayriyyah*, or any other currency used by the people of the cities, with the exception of the French dollar, which they call "the cannon coin."[218]

The people of Kūbayh, Kabkābiyyah, and Sarf al-Dajāj use *ḥarish* as currency. These are beads that are neither thick nor thin, some of which are green, some blue. They gather these beads into strings of one hundred; we've already described them in the section on women's finery and adornment.[219] They use these as currency for their small-scale transactions in place of the *tǎrne* used in the *fāshir*. It is remarkable that in these three markets one can't buy even a sip of water with *tǎrne*—all exchange is in *ḥarish*, in quantities from five to a hundred beads, and in anything from one to ten to countless strings. Among them the *tukkiyyah* is worth eight strings, and everything else is the same as in the *fāshir*. 3.3.45

In Qirlī and its dependencies they use *pôlgo*, which is manufactured salt extracted from the ground in the form of dirt. They pour water on it, or so I imagine, so that the impurities and soil particles settle, then strain, filtering the water, which is small in quantity, and put the filtrate into finger-shaped molds. On cooling, this hardens and turns into finger-shaped pieces. I saw the places where they extract this salt and saw the filtering vessels, which resemble Frankish cooking pots. I have no idea who introduced this craft to them, and the people of the country don't know either. The most they are likely to come up with if any were to ask, "Who taught you this craft?" would be, "Our fathers used to do it, so we do it too; we don't know who first practiced it." I have used this salt as currency myself and bought it; it has a remarkably delicious taste, different from that of natural salt, but is cloudy and brownish. 3.3.46

There are three kinds of salt in Darfur—*zaghāwī*, which is a natural salt taken from Bīr al-Zaghāwī, *pôlgo*, which we have just described, and *mīdawbī*, which is also a natural salt but bloodred in color. *Mīdawbī* is extracted in pieces 3.3.47

وقد قدمنا ذكره وميدوبيّ وهو ملح طبيعيّ أيضاً إلّا أنه لونه أحمر كالدم وقد يستخرج قطعاً كباراً كأحجار[1] الطاحون في العظم والاستدارة وثقله لا يحمل الجمل منه إلّا حجرين وله طعم لذيذ أكثر من النوعين الآخرين وأغلى ثمناً منهما ولا نعلم ما سبب احمراره وبالجملة فأغلى الأملاح الميدوبيّ وأوسطها الفلقو وأدناها الزغاويّ فأهل سوق قرلي وما وليها[2] يتعاملون بالملح الفلقو في سفاسف أمورهم كالحرش في كوبيه والتارنيه في الفاشر ولا يباع عندهم الملح بكيل ولا وزن بل بالأصابع فيباع هذا الشيء بفلقويه بفلقويتين[3] بثلاثة فلقويّات وهكذا وباقي الأمور هم كغيرهم

وأمّا سوق كُسَا فيتعاملون فيه بالدخان ويسمّى بلغتهم تابا كما يسمّونه الإفرنج وهذا الاتّفاق من العجائب ولا خصوصيّة لأهل دارفور بل جميع السودان يسمّون الدخان تابا وأما أهل فزّان وأهل طرابلس المغرب فيسمّونه تبْغاً وفي سنة ١٢٣٢ رأيت قصيدة لبعض البكريّين في حلّ شرب الدخان وأظنّ تاريخ كتابتها في وسط القرن التاسع من الهجرة يقول فيها [طويل] ٤٨،٣،٣

وَقَدْ أَظْهَرَ ٱللهُ ٱلْقَدِيرُ بِمِصْرِنَا نَبَاتًا يُسَمَّى ٱلتَّبْغَ مِنْ غَيْرِ مُرْيَةِ
بِتَاءٍ مُثَنَّاةٍ وَبَاءٍ مُوَحَّدٍ وَغَيْنٍ وَضَبْطُ ٱلْغَيْنِ فِيهَا بِفَتْحَةِ

ومنها

وَمَنْ يَدَّعِي ٱلتَّحْرِيمَ جَهْلًا فَقُلْ لَهُ بِأَيِّ دَلِيلٍ أَمْ بِأَيَّةِ آيَةِ
وَلَيْسَ بِهَا سُكْرٌ وَلَا ٱللهُ ذَمَّهَا[4] فَقَوْلُكَ بِٱلتَّحْرِيمِ مِنْ أَيِّ وِجْهَةِ

ومنها

فَإِنْ تَنْتَشِقْ دُخَّانَهَا فَتَرَى ٱلشِّفَا فَلَا تَنْسَ بِٱسْمِ ٱللهِ أَوَّلَ مَصَّةِ
وَقُلْ بَعْدَ ذَاكَ ٱلْحَمْدُ للهِ وَحْدَهُ فَحَمْدُكَ لِلْمَوْلَى زِيَادَةُ نِعْمَةِ

١ الأصل: كالحجار. ٢ الأصل: ولاها. ٣ الأصل: بفلقويه بفلقوتين. ٤ الأصل: زمها.

as large and round as millstones and so heavy that a camel can carry only two. It tastes delicious, more so than the two other kinds, and is more expensive. We have no idea how it comes to be red. To summarize: the most expensive kind of salt is the *mīdawbī*, the middling is the *pôlgo*, and the cheapest the *zaghāwī*. The people who fall within the market area of Qirlī and its dependencies use *pôlgo* as currency for small-scale transactions in the same way that in Kūbayh they use *ḥarish*, and in the sultan's capital *tǎrne*. Salt isn't sold among them by volume or weight, but by finger. A given item may be sold for one finger of *pôlgo*, two fingers of *pôlgo*, three fingers of *pôlgo*, and so on. All other transactions they conduct the way the others do.

In the Kusā market area, they use tobacco—which is called *tābā*, in their 3.3.48
language as in the languages of the Franks[220]—as currency. This is a remarkable coincidence, and not something peculiar to the people of Darfur: all the Blacks call tobacco *tābā* (the people of the Fezzan and Libyan Tripoli call it *tabgh*). In 1232 [1816–17], I saw a poem by a member of the Bakrī family on the permissibility of using tobacco; I think it was written in the middle of the ninth century [late 14th/15th c. AD].[221] He says:

God, All-powerful, has caused to appear in this Egypt of ours
a plant called *tabgh*, let no one this gainsay,
Written with *t* and two dots, an undoubled *b*,
and *ghayn* (the *ghayn* being voweled with an *a*).

And from the same poem:

To any who claims, in his ignorance, that it's forbidden,
to him "On what evidence and per what Qur'anic verse" say,
And "It intoxicates not and neither has God forbidden it
so whence your claim that God says nay?"

And still from the same poem:

If you inhale its smoke, you'll find yourself cured,
So forget not "In God's name!" before you puff away,
And say thereafter, "Praise is due to God alone,"
for when you praise the Lord, more grace will come your way.

٣،٣،٤٩ انتهى. وهذا التابا هو أقماع أهراميّة الشكل مصنوعة من ورق الدخان بعد دقّه وهو أخضر في مهراس من خشب حتّى يصير كالعجين ويجعلونه أقماعًا ويجففّونها في الشمس وبعد جفافها يبرزونها إلى سوقهم ويتعاملون بها في سفاسف أمورهم وهذا الدخان قويّ الرائحة يكاد إذا شمّه إنسان أن يأخذه الدوار وهذه[1] الأقماع منها ما هو كبير ومنها ما هو صغير فكبيرها كأكبر الكمّثرى وصغيرها كصغيرها

٣،٣،٥٠ وأمّا كريو والريل والشعيريّة فإنّهم يتعاملون فيها بالرُبَط وهي ربط غَزْل من قطن طولها عشرة أذرع وفيها عشرون فتلة لا غير فيتعاملون بالربط في سفاسف أمورهم ويتعاملون في الأمور التافهة جدًّا بالقطن كما يُجتنى من شجرته أي بغلافته التي خرج منها فيتعاملون بقطع منه كأوقيّة وأوقيّتين وثلاث أواقٍ على سبيل الحدس والتخمين لا بالوزن والأمور المهمّة كباقي الأسواق

٣،٣،٥١ وأمّا سوق نمليه وما والاها فمعاملتهم بالبصل يشترون به جميع أمورهم التافهة والقطن أيضه والربط وباقي أمورهم بالتكاكي ولا يعرفون الشواتر ولا الريالات

٣،٣،٥٢ وأمّا سوق راس الفيل فبالحشّاشات وهي قطع من حديد مصنوع صفائح ولها أنبوبة وصورتها هكذا  فيدخلون في طرفها الأنبوبيّ قضيباً ويحرثون بها الزرع فتقطع الحشيش الذي في الزرع ولذلك سمّيت الحشّاشة فيتعاملون بها في سفاسف أمورهم وتافهها من حشّاشة إلى اثنين إلى عشرين وما زاد على ذلك فبالتكاكي والشواتر كباقي الأسواق

٣،٣،٥٣ وأمّا تموركه فمعاملتهم بدمالج النحاس وهي في مهمّات أمورهم وبالخدّور في سفاسف أمورهم وقد تقدّم تعريف الدمالج والخدّور في حليّ النساء فلا إعادة

٣،٣،٥٤ وأمّا أهل القوز فيتعاملون بالدخن في سفاسف أمورهم كلّها كقبضة وحفنة وحفنتين إلى نصف مُدّ وباقي أمورهم المهمّة بالتكاكي والريالات كباقي الأسواق وأكثر

---

١ الأصل: ومن هذه.

3.3.49 This *tābā* consists of pyramid-shaped cones made of tobacco leaves pounded while still green in a wooden mortar till they achieve a doughlike consistency. They make this into cones, which they dry in the sun. Once the cones have dried out, they take them to their market and use them as currency for small-scale transactions. This kind of tobacco has such a strong smell that one almost faints on smelling it. The cones come in two sizes, large and small; the large are the size of a large pear, the small the size of a small pear.

3.3.50 In Karyū, Rīl, and al-Shaʿīriyyah, they use skeins of spun cotton yarn as currency, each skein being ten cubits in length and containing precisely twenty strings. They use these skeins for small-scale transactions. For trivial transactions they use cotton harvested from the bush, i.e., still in the boll out of which it has burst; they use small amounts of this cotton, such as one, two, or three ounces, by rough estimation or guesswork, without weighing. Major transactions are as in the other markets.

3.3.51 The market area of Numlayh and its dependencies use onions as currency; they make all their trivial purchases with these, as well as with cotton and cotton skeins. For other purchases, they use *takākī*. They are unfamiliar with both *shawātir* and dollars as currency.

3.3.52 In Rās al-Fīl, they use hoes, which are pieces of iron hammered flat and with a cylindrical attachment, as in the picture:  They insert a handle into the cylindrical end and use the hoe to dig around the plants; they cut the weeds that are among the plants, which is why one such hoe is called a "weeder."[222] They use these as a currrency for their small-scale and trivial transactions ranging from one to two to twenty hoes.[223] For larger transactions they use *takākī* and *shawātir* as in the other markets.

3.3.53 The Tomorókkóngá use copper bracelets as currency. This is for their major transactions; for their small-scale transactions, they use *khaddūr* beads. Descriptions of their bracelets and of *khaddūr* beads appear earlier[224] in the section on women's finery, so there's no need to repeat them here.

3.3.54 The people of the desert use millet as currency for all their small-scale transactions, in quantities such as a handful, or enough to fill the cupped palms, or twice that amount, up to half a *mudd*. Their other, major, transactions are made with *takākī* and dollars, as in the rest of the markets. What they most

ما يتعاملون به البقر فيقولون هذا الفرس بعشر بقرات أو بعشرين

فانظر أيّها المتأمّل إلى أهل مملكة واحدة كيف تنوّعت معاملاتها واختلفت أحوالها فترى هؤلاء يرون شيئاً حسناً وهؤلاء يرونه قبيحاً والملك لا يحكم عليهم بإجراء معاملة واحدة في جميع الأسواق بل أبقى كلّ قوم على ما اعتادوا فسبحان الفعّال لما يريد ولنمسك عنان القلم عن الركض في ميدان المعاملات لأنّ ما ذكرناه فيه كفاية في الاعتبارات ٥٥،٣،٣

commonly use as currency, though, is cattle. They say, "This horse costs ten head of cattle" or "twenty head of cattle."

Behold, dear observer, how diverse are the currencies used by the people 3.3.55
of a single realm, and how varied their conditions: one finds that some people believe a certain thing to be an object of value, while others believe that same thing to be worthless! The monarch doesn't insist they use one currency in all markets; on the contrary, he has left each group to follow the system to which it has become accustomed. Glory to Him who effects what He desires! Let us now rein in the pen from its canter over the parade ground of currencies and commercial transaction, for what we have stated is enough by any consideration.

باب فيما ينبت في دارفور من النبات وفي السحر والتعزيم وضرب الرمل وغير ذلك

اعلم أنّ الغنيّ عن المتى والأين والكيف والمنزّه عن الجور والظلم والحيف قسم الأشياء وعدّلها وأنزل كلاًّ منها منزلها فجعل في البلاد الشماليّة البرد الشديد وفي الجنوبيّة الحرّ الذي ما عليه من مزيد لكن لرحمته بعباده منّ على أهل الشمال بالدفء بالملابس وبالأكنان التي لا يبرد فيها المجالس ونظر لأهل الجنوب بعين الإسعاف والتلطيف فجعل المطر ينزل عليهم وقت اشتداد المَصِيف ١،٤

ولمّا كانت أرض الفور من هذا القبيل وفي وقت الصيف يشتدّ فيها الغليل كان مدرار الوبل مطفئاً لوهج ذلك الحُرور لطفاً من العزيز الغفور فيزرعون على مطر الصيف ويسمّون ذلك الفصل بالخريف فلذلك على ظنّي لا يزرعون بُرًّا ولا شعيرًا ولا فولاً ولا عدساً ولا حمّصاً ولا ينبت عندهم المشمش ولا الخوخ ولا التفّاح ولا الرمّان ولا الزيتون ولا البرقوق ولا الكمّثرى ولا الترنج ولا الليمون الحلو ولا «البرتقان» ولا اللوز ولا البندق ولا الفستق ولا الجوز ولا الزعرور ونحو ذلك ٢،٤

بل يزرعون الدخن وهو حبّ صغير أصفر منه يقتاتون هم ودوابّهم ومواشيهم فهو الغذاء الرئيس عندهم ويزرعون الذرة على اختلاف أنواعه ويسمّى عندهم الماريق وهو أنواع فنوع منه يسمّى العزير وهو الذرة الحمراء ونوع يسمّى أبا شَلَوْلَوْ وهو الذرة البيضاء ونوع يسمّى أبا أَباط وهو الذرة المعروفة في مصر بالذرة الشاميّ ولا يزرع القمح عندهم إلّا في جبل مرّة لكثرة الأمطار فيه أو في كوبيه وكبكابيّة ويسقونه من الآبار حتّى يتمّ نضجه كما تقدّم ذلك والدخن عندهم نوعان نوع معتاد و[1]نوع يسمّى ٣،٤

---

١ نوع معتاد و – أضيف للسياق.

A Chapter on the Plants That Grow in Darfur; on Magic, the Making of Amulets, and Geomancy; and on Other Matters

Know that He who is without need of any when, where, or how and is devoid of any tyranny, injustice, or prejudice has divided things up, arranged them in order, and sent them down, each to its appointed place. He has put extreme cold in the lands of the north and the hottest possible heat in those of the south. He has also, however, out of His mercy for His mortal slaves, bestowed warmth on the people of the north through the agency of clothes and of homes where men may gather without feeling the cold, and has turned on the people of the south the gaze of succor and mitigation by causing rain to fall on them when the summer is at its height. 4.1

Given that the territory of the Fur is of this second type, and that in summer thirst becomes extreme, the downpours that extinguish the blazing fire of that heat are an act of kindness from the Mighty, the Forgiving—for they sow at the coming of the summer rains and call that season the "autumn." It is for this reason, or so I imagine, that they cultivate neither wheat nor barley nor fava beans nor lentils nor chickpeas, and grow no apricots, peaches, apples, pomegranates, olives, plums, pears, citrons, sweet lemons, oranges, almonds, hazelnuts, pistachios, walnuts, medlars, or the like. 4.2

Instead, they grow millet, which is a small yellow grain they use as food for themselves, their mounts, and their cattle. It is their primary means of subsistence. They also grow sorghum in its various forms, calling it *mārīq*. It consists of different types. There is a kind called *ʿazīr*, which is red sorghum; a kind called *abū shalawlaw*, which is white sorghum; and a kind called *abū abāṭ*, which in Egypt is called Syrian sorghum.[225] Wheat is grown only in Jabal Marrah, where there is abundant rain, and Kūbayh and Kabkābiyyah, where they water it from wells until it matures, as already mentioned.[226] The millet that they have is of two kinds, an ordinary kind and a kind called *dinbī*,[227] 4.3

دِنْبي وهو ما يزرعه أعجام الفور في الجبال وغيرها وهو حبّ كالدخن المعتاد إلّا أنّه يميل إلى البياض وسنبله أغلظ منه وينضج زرعه قبله بنحو عشرين يوماً وهو قليل في سهل دارفور ولا يألفونه كالدخن الأصفر وأمّا أنواع الذرة فلا يألفون منها إلّا الأبيض ومع ألفتهم له لا يكثرون من تناوله وأمّا أبو أباط فيزرعون منه قليلاً للشهوة فيأكلونه مشوياً ولا يخزنون منه حبّاً وأمّا العزير فهو مبغوض عندهم لا يأكله إلّا الفقراء وعند الاضطرار وينبت عندهم في البرك والغدران أرزّ ينبت بدون زارع فيجمعون منه ما قدروا عليه في أيّام الربيع فيطبخونه باللبن من قبيل الترفّه وعندهم نوع آخر يقرب من الأرزّ وليس بأرزّ ويسمّى بالدِفْرة وهو حبّ صغير أصغر من حبّ الأرزّ وفيه بعض فرطحة شديد البياض يألفونه أكثر من الأرزّ

٤،٤ ويزرعون من السمسم شيئاً كثيراً ومن العجب أنهم لا ينتفعون منه بزيت بل يأكلونه حبّاً ويطبخون منه في أطعمتهم. كما أنّ العسل النحليّ كثير عندهم ولا ينتفعون بشمعه بل يأخذون العسل ويرمون الشمع وهم أحوج الأنام إليه وإلى زيت السمسم لأنّهم يستصبحون في بيوتهم بالحطب ومع كثرة الحطب عندهم لا يفحمون منه فحماً ينفعهم ولا يعرفونه

٥،٤ ويزرعون اللوبيا والبطّيخ مع الدخن سواء فأمّا اللوبيا فهي كاللوبيا بأرض مصر إلّا أنها أكبر لأنّها عندهم تقرب من حبّ الفول المصريّ وأمّا البطّيخ فأكثره صغير الحجم كالبطّيخ الذي يكون فى آخر فصل البطّيخ فى المقثأة وإذا كسر يكون غير نضيج لكن الذي في دار الفور مع صغره نضيج ولهم في البطّيخ ثلاث منافع الأولى أنهم يأكلون منه حال نضجه كما نأكل بطّيخنا ويشربون ماءه كذلك الثانية أنّهم يأخذون البطّيخة وينزعون قشرها بالسكّين ثمّ يقطعونها أربع قطع ويتركونها حتّى تجفّ فيخزنون منه من هذا القبيل شيئاً كثيراً وفي وقت الاحتياج يدقّونه في مهراس من خشب حتّى يصير دقيقاً فيعملون منه حَسُوًّا يشرب وتسمّى عندهم مديدة وهي المسمّاة بعرف الأوروبّا بالكريمة وربّما أكلوا منه بغير دقّ ولا طبخ الثالثة أنهم يجمعون من البزر شيئاً كثيراً ويخزنونه

which is what is grown by the non-Arabic-speaking Fur in the mountains and elsewhere. It is a cereal like ordinary millet but whitish in color and with larger ears; it also ripens some twenty days before the latter. It is little found in the Darfur plain, where they are less familiar with it than they are with yellow millet. Of the different kinds of sorghum, they are familiar only with the white and don't eat much of that, despite their familiarity with it. The kind called *abū abāṭ* they grow in small quantities because they find it tasty; they eat it grilled and don't store it as grain. They dislike the kind called *ʿazīr*; only the poor eat it, or others when they have no choice. Rice grows wild there in ponds and watercourses without being sown; they gather as much of it as they can during their spring[228] and cook it with milk as a luxury dish. They have another kind of cereal too that is similar to rice but isn't rice, called *difrah*; it has a small grain, smaller than rice, slightly flattened and extremely white. They are more familiar with this than they are with rice.

They cultivate a great deal of sesame but, remarkably, don't use it to make 4.4
oil. They eat it as a grain and use it in their cooked dishes. Honey is also plentiful there, though they make no use of the wax; in fact, they take the honey and throw the wax away, though no one is in greater need of it, or of sesame oil, than they, since they use dry fuel to light the lamps in their houses. Similarly, despite the plentiful supply of fuel wood, they don't use it to make charcoal, which would be of use to them; in fact, they don't even know what it is.

They also grow black-eyed peas and watermelons alongside the millet. 4.5
The black-eyed peas are like those found in Egypt but larger, growing to nearly the same size as fava beans in Egypt. The watermelons are of a smaller size, like those found in the melon patch at the end of the season, which, if one breaks them open, turn out to be unripe; the ones in Darfur, however, are ripe, despite their small size. They have three different uses for watermelon. First, they eat them as soon as they ripen, as we do our melons; they also drink the juice. Second, they take the melon, remove its rind using a knife, and cut it into four pieces, which they leave till dry. They store it, treated this way, in large quantities, and when they need it, pound it in a wooden mortar till it turns to flour, which they use to make a broth that they drink called *madīdah*, which is what the Franks call *crema*.[229] Sometimes they eat the dried watermelon unpounded and uncooked. Third, they gather large quantities of the

ويدقّونه وقت الاحتياج وينسفون قشره ويأخذون اللبّ فيطبخونه في أدمهم أو يعملون منه الكريمة أيضاً

٦،٤ ويـزرعون البصل والثوم والفلفل وهو حبّ صغير والكسبرة وحبّ الرشاد في كوبيه وكبكابيّة وفي أودية جبال الفور كما تقدّم ويـزرعون القرع بأنواعه ويـزرعون نوعاً من القثّاء وفي كوبيه وكبكابيّة يـزرعون الخيار والفقّوس الطويل والباذنجان والملوخيّة والبامية وفي غيرهما لا وهناك واد بين البلد المسمّاة[1] بمربوطة والفاشر يسمّى وادي الكوع يفيض وقت الخريف من كثرة الأمطار فلا يعبره إلّا من يعرف السباحة وفيه تيّار شديد فإذا فاض هذا الوادي وطفا الماء على شاطئيه ثمّ نضب ينبت فيه من البامية شيء كثير فيهرعون إليه من الجهات القريبة له ويجمعون تلك البامية ويجفّفونها ويدّخرونها لأدمهم العام كلّه[2] وهذا الوادي يشقّ دارفور بالعرض من أوّلها إلى آخرها ونشاؤه من جبال مرّة وعلى شاطئيه سياج من شجر السنط وإذا فاض يعمّ من كلّ جهة من جهتيه ما ينوف عن فرسخين إلّا في بعض المحالّ ضايقته الرمال وسعته في بعض المحالّ كخليج مصر وفى بعضها أوسع بمرّتين. يسافر المسافر على شاطئه نحو خمسة عشر يوماً وإنّما ذكرت أنّه بين مربوطة والفاشر لأنّي مررت به كثيراً من هناك وإلّا فهو ممتدّ كما ذكرت ويـزرعون فولاً قرونه تكون تحت التراب وليس كالفول المسمّى في مصر السنّاريّ الآن لأنّ ذاك فيه ألوان عجيبة من أحمر ناصع وأصفر وأبيض وبنّيّ كما تقدّم ذلك

٧،٤ وأمّا الأشجار فليس عندهم من الأشجار المعروفة إلّا النخل وهو في كوبيه وكبكابيّة وسرف الدجاج ونمليه كما تقدّم ذلك في التكلّم على جبل مرّة وفي نمليه بعض شجر من الموز وفي قرلي شجرات من الليمون الحامض وبقيّة الأشجار الموجودة هناك كلّها نابتةٌ طبيعةً في الخلاء فأعظمها منفعة الهجليج وله نوعان الهجليج الأصفر والهجليج الأحمر وذلك بحسب لون ثمرها وهذا الثمر كالبسر الغليظ والهجليج شجر يعظم كما يعظم الجُمَّيز

[1] الأصل: المسمة. [2] الأصل: كلها.

seeds, which they store and pound as needed. They also pulverize the rind, remove the flesh, and cook the rind to be used as a condiment or, again, make *crema* from it.

4.6 In Kūbayh, Kabkābiyyah, and the valleys of the Fur mountains, they grow onions, garlic, pepper (which has a small grain), coriander, and cress, as mentioned earlier.[230] They also grow different varieties of squash and a type of cucumber. In Kūbayh and Kabkābiyyah, they also grow cucumber, long cucumber, eggplant, Jew's mallow, and okra; elsewhere they do not.[231] There is a seasonal watercourse between the village called al-Marbūṭah and the sultan's capital that is called Wādī l-Kūʿ. It is flooded during the autumn due to the copious rains, and only those who know how to swim can cross it, as it has a strong current. When the wadi floods, and the water overflows its banks and soaks into the ground, okra sprouts in large quantities and they rush there from nearby parts and gather it, dry it, set it aside, and use it as something to eat with their bread for the rest of the year. This wadi traverses Darfur from beginning to end breadthwise, and has its origin in Jabal Marrah. It has a belt of acacia trees on either bank, and when it overflows it covers approximately two miles in either direction, except in a few places where the sands constrain it. In some places it's as wide as the Khalīj in Cairo,[232] in others twice as wide. One traveling along its bank can go for fifteen days. I describe it as being between al-Marbūṭah and the *fāshir* simply because I passed it so often at that point; in fact, it runs a long way, as I've explained. They also grow a kind of bean whose pods grow below ground; it is not the same as the bean now called in Egypt the Sinnār bean, because the first has remarkable colors, including bright red, yellow, white, and brown, as mentioned above.[233]

4.7 As far as trees are concerned, they have none that are well-known, with the exception of the date palm, which is found in Kūbayh, Kabkābiyyah, Sarf al-Dajāj, and Numlayh, as mentioned in the course of the earlier discussion of Jabal Marrah.[234] At Numlayh there are some banana trees, and at Qirlī bitter lemons. All the rest of the trees in Darfur grow naturally in the countryside. The most useful of these is the *hijlīj* tree, of which there are two kinds, yellow and red, the names according with the colors of the fruit, which are the size of large unripe dates. The *hijlīj* is a tree that grows to a great size, like the

في أرض مصر أوراقه بيضيّة قليلاً وله ثمر حلو الطعم ببعض مرارة وله رائحة خاصّة به ولهذا الثمر غلاف يكون عليه وهو قشرة ليست بالغليظة ولا بالرفيعة فينزعونها ويمصّون الثمر مصّاً لأنّه خشب مكسوّ بشيء كالطلاء يمتصّ أو يبلّ بالماء فإذا ذهب صار الخشب أي نواه أبيض وهو غلاف لشيء كالصنوبر هيئةً وبياضاً وهو بزر إلّا أنّه أكبر منه حجماً لكنّه مرّ الطعم فيعطنونه في الماء نحو ثلاثة أيّام ويغيّرون ماءه في كلّ يوم فتذهب مرارته وحينئذ بعضهم يملّحه بالملح وبعضهم يقلوه وبعضهم يطبخه بالعسل وإذا كان مملوحاً كان طعمه كطعم اللوز المملوح وهناك نوع ثاني من الهجليج وهو الهجليج الأحمر فيأخذون لبّه بعد نضجه ويضيفون عليه الصمغ ويعجنونه به فيصير حلواً مرّاً لذيذاً وعلى الإطلاق يأكلون ثمر الهجليج على كيفيّات مختلفة

٨،٤ ولشجر الهجليج هذا منافع لا توجد عندهم في غيره من الأشجار. لا يرمون منه شيئاً بل ينتفعون بجميع أجزائه فأمّا ورقه[١] فإنّهم يطبخون الطريّ الغضّ منه في أدمهم وإذا كان بإنسان جرح[٢] فيه دود يمضغون من هذا[٣] الورق حتّى يصير كالعجين وينخونه في الجرح فينقى من الدود وينظّف من اللحم النتن ويأخذ في البرء وإذا أخذ ثمر الهجليج وهو أخضر وهُرس في مهراس حتّى صار كالعجين نفع كالصابون في غسل الثياب فإنّ له رغوة كالصابون يُنقي الأوساخ وينظّف الثياب المغسولة به إلّا أنّه يصفّرها قليلاً وإذا لم يكن وقت الثمر تؤخذ جذور الشجرة وتُدقّ ويُغسل بها فتفعل ذلك وخشبه يستصبح به في البيوت بالليل عوضاً عن السراج لأنّه لا دخان له ومن خشبه تعمل ألواح القراءة ومن رماده يعمل الكنبو وهو ملح سائل يؤخذ من الرماد المذكور ويطبخ به إلّا أنّ به مراراً وذلك عند إعوازهم للملح لقلّته وغلوّه

٩،٤ والنبق وهو نوعان عربيّ وكَرْنو والثاني أكبر حجماً من الأوّل وأكثر لحماً ويخالفه في اللون فإنّ النبق المعتاد العربيّ إذا نضج احمرّ لونه والكرنو إذا نضج اصفرّ وهذا أنفع من الأوّل ومن منافعه أنّ الثمر عجينه يمسك إطلاق البطن وقبل ما يدقّ ويعجن

١ الأصل: ورق. ٢ الأصل: جراح. ٣ الأصل: هذه.

sycamore-fig in Egypt. Its leaves are slightly rounded, and its fruit tastes sweet, with a hint of bitterness, and has a distinctive smell. The fruit also has an outer covering around it, a rind that is neither thick nor thin and which they peel off to better suck on the fruit, the latter consisting of a woody piece covered in a kind of coating that they either suck off or soak in water. When that is gone, the woody piece, which is to say the kernel, turns white. This is itself a covering for something like a pine nut in shape and in whiteness, which is a seed, albeit larger than most seeds. This, however, is bitter in taste, so they steep it in water for around three days, changing the water every day. This removes its bitterness. At this point, some salt it, others roast it, and yet others stew it with honey. Salted, it tastes like salted almonds. There is another kind of *hijlīj*, which is the red *hijlīj*, the flesh of whose ripe fruits they take, adding gum and then kneading the two together, producing something deliciously sweet and sour. In sum, they eat the *hijlīj* fruit prepared in a variety of ways.

The *hijlīj* has useful properties not to be found in any other of their trees. They throw none of it away; on the contrary, they use every part of it. 4.8
The leaves they cook when fresh and juicy as a condiment for bread. If someone has a worm-infested wound, they chew some of these leaves till they turn into a kind of paste and spit this into the wound. This cleanses it of the worms and cleans out the rotten flesh, so that it starts to heal. The fruit of the *hijlīj* can be taken when green and pounded in a mortar till it turns into a paste and can be used like soap for washing clothes; it makes a foam like soap that removes the dirt and cleans clothes washed in it, though it does make them slightly yellow. If it is not the fruiting season, the roots of the tree are taken and pounded and used to wash clothes, for they act in the same way. The wood is used for lighting in the houses at night in place of oil lamps because it makes no smoke. From its wood, too, reading tablets are made, and from its ash *kumbā* is made, a liquid salt extracted from the aforementioned ash; it is used for cooking but is bitter. They use it when they have no ordinary salt, which is costly and hard to come by.

There is also the jujube,[235] which comes in two forms, "Arabic" and *karnū*, 4.9
the second being larger than the first, having fleshier fruits, and differing from it in color, the fruits of the ordinary "Arabic" jujube being red when ripe, while

ينحت جلدته الظاهرة ثمّ يعملون منه أقراصاً ويجففونها ويأكلونها وإذا كسر نواه يوجد فيه بزرتان في مسكنين والعرب يأخذون هذا البزر الصغير ويجففونه في الشمس ثمّ يطبخونه بالعسل فيصير لذيذاً ويبيعونه في دار الفور ويسمّى كيكنيا فيؤكل كالحلوى وإذا مضغ من به دود القرع[1] من ورق النبق الكرنو وازدرد ريقه قتل دود القرع[2] وأخرجه ميتاً

١٠،٤ والتبلدي وهو شجر عظيم ضخم أجوف الجذع ينبت في الفيافي وأهل البادية إذا اشتدّ بهم العطش في غير وقت الأمطار يأتون إلى التبلدي فيجدون في تجويفه ماء مجتمعاً من المطر فيشربون منه ويذهب أوامهم ولهذا الشجر ثمر مستطيل كبير كالألواز في باطنه بزر أحمر كحبّ الترمس في الحجم وكبزر الخرّوب في اللون إلّا أنّه فيه دقيق أبيض حامض الطعم يستفّ منه فيوجد مرّاً والاستفاف منه على الريق يقبض إطلاق البطن وتعمل منه الكريمة مع الدقيق فتصير لذيذة

١١،٤ وشجر الدُلَب وهو المسمّى في عرف مصر بالجوز الهنديّ إلّا أنّ هذا الشجر لا يوجد في جميع دارفور بل لا يوجد إلّا في الجهة الجنوبيّة منها ويسمّى في عرف الفور بالدَلَيْب وهو شجر طوال كالنخل أو أطول وينتج جوزاً كبيراً إذا كسر غلافه وجد ماء في باطنه في غاية اللذّة لا سيّما قبل تمام نضجه فإنّه يكون كاللبن مع الحلاوة واللذّة

١٢،٤ ومن أشجارهم الحُمَّيْض وهو شجر شائك كأضخم ما يكون وله ثمر كالتفّاح الكبير إلّا أنّ له عَجَماً وفيه حموضة لذيذة ولونه أبيض يميل إلى الصفرة ومن أشجارهم الدوم وهو شجر معروف في صعيد مصر ويسمّى بالمُقْل أيضاً ومن أشجارهم العَنْدُراب وهو شجر متوسّط في الطول والغلظ يحمل ثمراً أشبه بعنب الذئب إلّا أنّه أحمر قانئ الحمرة ولا عجم فيه وهذا الثمر حلو[3] الطعم جدّاً ينضج في أوّل فصل الدرت أي الربيع بلغتهم وهو أوّل فصل الخريف عندنا

١٣،٤ ومن أشجارهم القِدّيم وهو شجر أشبه بشجر[4] الرمّان يحمل ثمراً صغيراً ذا فلقتين عليه

١ الأصل: القرح. ٢ الأصل: القرح. ٣ الأصل: حلوا. ٤ الأصل: شجر.

those of the *karnū* are yellow. The former also has more useful properties than the latter, one of which is that a paste made from its fruit prevents defecation. Before it is pounded and kneaded, its outer skin is scraped off. Then they make it into disks, which they dry and eat. When its kernel is broken open, two seeds will be found inside, each in a pocket of its own. The Bedouin take this small seed and dry it in the sun. Then they stew it with honey, and it turns into something delicious called *kenykenya*, which they sell in Darfur and which is eaten as candy; also, if anyone with roundworm chews *karnū* leaves and swallows his saliva, it kills the worms and expels them dead.

There is also the *tabaldī*, which is a vast, mighty tree with a hollow trunk 4.10
that grows in the deserts. When desert dwellers grow extremely thirsty in the dry season, they go to the *tabaldī* and find rainwater that has collected in its cavity. They drink and their thirst goes away. The tree has large oblong fruits like almond trees, and inside these are red seeds like lupine seeds in size and carob seeds in color. These contain a white flour with a sour taste that people eat by the handful. They taste bitter, and eating them on an empty stomach prevents defecation. They make a *crema* using the flour, which makes it delicious.

There is also the *dulab*, which the Egyptians call *al-jawz al-hindī*. This tree 4.11
isn't found throughout Darfur, however, only in the south. In Fur parlance it is called *dalayb*.[236] The trees are as tall as date palms, or taller, and produce a large nut, inside which is an extremely delicious juice, especially before it is fully ripe; it is almost as sweet and tasty as milk.[237]

Also among their trees is the *ḥummayḍ*, which is a huge thorny tree that 4.12
has a fruit like a large apple but with a pit. It is deliciously sour and is white in color, shading to yellow. Another is the doum palm, well-known in Upper Egypt and also called *muql*. Another is the *ʿandurāb*, a tree of medium height and girth that bears a fruit resembling black nightshade, though it is deep red and seedless. This fruit is very sweet and ripens at the start of the *darat*, which is to say, in their language, the spring, which is the beginning of autumn in our country.

Another is the *qiddīm*,[238] which is a tree very like the pomegranate. It bears 4.13
a small fruit that is divided into two halves and covered with a bright-red skin

جلدة حمراء ناصعة الحمرة في غاية الحلاوة وعجمه كبير ولا أجد له شبيهاً في فواكهنا أمثّله به

١٤،٤ ومن أشجارهم شجر المُخَيِّط وهو شجر صغير يحمل ثمراً كالنبق فيه مرار فيؤخذ وينقع في الماء أيّاماً فتذهب مرارته فيرشّ عليه الملح ويطبخ ويؤكل ومن الناس من يجفّفه بعد النقع ويسحقه حتّى يصير دقيقاً وتعمل منه عصيدة وهذا الفعل خاصّ بأيّام الغلاء واشتداد الكرب

١٥،٤ ومن أشجارهم اللُولُو وهو شجر يقرب من شجر الجوز المسمّى بعين الجمل. يحمل ثمراً كثمر أبي فروة إلّا أنّ ثمر أبي فروة فيه تفرطح وهذا كحبّ البندق لكنّه أكبر من البندق في الحجم يساوي حجم أبي فروة وأبو فروة هو المسمّى في بلاد الترك بالكاستنا وفي تونس بالقَصْطَل ولهذا الثمر لبّ دسم ولا يوجد إلّا في الجهة الجنوبيّة في آخر دارفور أي في جهة بلاد الفرتيت وأهل تلك الناحية يعصرون منه زيتاً ولقد رأيته ووجدته أكثر شبهاً بالشيرج في الهيئة وبزيت الزيتون في الطعم فيدهنون منه ويجعلونه أدماً في أطعمتهم ويوجد الخرّوب والجمّيز لكنّهما رديئين لا ينفعان بشيء

١٦،٤ ويزرعون القطن بنوعيه البلديّ ويسمّى عندهم بالعربيّ والهنديّ ويسمّى عندهم بلَوِيّ وينتفعون عنه أتمّ المنافع لأنّ منه كساويهم وبه معاملتهم كما قدّمنا ذلك في باب المعاملات

١٧،٤ وأمّا الأشجار التي لا يؤكل لها ثمر فكثيرة جدّاً تكاد ألّا تدخل تحت حصر ولكن نذكر أشهرها وأنفعها فنقول من أنفعها العُشَر وهو شجر قصير متعدّد الفروع جذعه مكسوّ بشيء أبيض كالشحم إذا ضغط بين الأصابع يتفتّت وورقه كبير وإذا كسر يخرج منه عصارة بيضاء كاللبن وله ثمر كالكرة باطنه ممتلئ بشيء كالزغب أو الوبر يتطاير في الهواء لخفّته ولهذا الشجر منافع منها أنّ عصارته إذا وضعت على جلد حيوان أزالت شعره ويلحون لحاءه فتوجد فيه خيوط رفيعة كالحرير فتجمع ويفتل منها خيوط تنفع لخرز القرب ويفتل من اللحاء حبال فتنفع للربط والحمل والوبر الذي في الثمر تسدّ به

and is extremely sweet. The pit is large, and I can't think of another fruit we know that resembles it enough to compare it to.

Another is the *mukhkhayṭ*, which is a small tree that bears a fruit like that of the jujube but bitter. It is taken and steeped in water for several days, which rids it of its bitterness. Then it's sprinkled with salt, stewed, and eaten. Some people dry it after the steeping and pound it until it turns into flour, from which they make a thick paste with clarified butter. This they do only during times of high prices and extreme hardship. 4.14

Another is the shea, which resembles the tree that produces the nuts called walnuts. It bears a fruit like the chestnut, though the chestnut has a flattened shape whereas this one looks like a hazelnut, though larger, about the size of a chestnut (the chestnut is what in Turkish lands is called *kestane* and in Tunis *qaṣṭal*). The fruit has a fatty flesh and is found only in the southern extremity of Darfur, i.e., toward the country of the Fartīt, where the people extract an oil from it. I've seen this and it seemed to me that it was most like sesame oil in appearance and olive oil in taste. They use it as a rub and also make it into a condiment to eat with their various dishes. Carob and sycamore-fig are also found, but are of poor quality and have no useful properties. 4.15

They grow cotton in both its local variety, which they call "Arabic," and its Indian variety, which they call *lawī*. They make the most complete use of it because they not only get their clothes from it but also use it as currency, as we have described in the chapter on such things.[239] 4.16

The number of trees whose fruit is not eaten is large, almost too large to count, but we shall mention the best known and most useful. One of the most useful is the Sodom apple, which is a low, many-branched tree whose trunk is coated with something white resembling grease. Its large leaves crumble when pressed between the fingers and emit a white, milk-like juice when torn. It has fruit like a ball that is filled with something like down or nap that's so light it flies about in the air. This tree has useful properties, one being that its juice, if placed on an animal's hide, removes the hair. They peel off its bark, and inside are found fibers as fine as silk; these are gathered and threads are spun from them that they use to sew waterskins. Ropes are also spun from the fibers, and are good for tying things and securing loads. The nap inside the fruit is used for stopping up holes in waterskins. If they steal a donkey or a horse, 4.17

خروق القرب ومن عادتهم إذا سرقوا حماراً أو فرساً وأرادوا تغيّر شعر موضع منه يدهنون المحلّ الذي يريدون تغيّره بهذه العصارة فيذهب الشعر ويخلفه شعر أبيض فيشتبه على أربابه لكن منهم من يعرف ذلك للاعتياد به وخشبه خفيف كخشب القَفَل ورأيتهم يسوّدون البارود بفحمه وفي اسبتاليّة أبي زعبل شجرة منه وفي الصعيد كثير منه أيضه

١٨،٤ منها شجر يسمّى الحَشَاب وهو شجر ذو شوك ومنه يؤخذ الصمغ العربيّ ولقد رأيته واجتنيت منه الصمغ ليناً يمتدّ كالعلك وينبت في الأماكن المعطّشة الرمليّة ومنها السَنْط وهو شجر القَرَظ وهو شائك ضخم ومنها الطَلْح وهو من فصيلة السنط والطلح شجر يعلو أكثر من قامة ولحاؤه أحمر وله شُوَك طويلة كالإبر وورقه مركّب من وريقات صغيرة. السَيَال[1] شجر طويل يعلو أكثر من قامة لكن أصغر من الطلح ولون قشره أخضر يضرب إلى البياض وله شوك أبيض وأوراقه مركّبة كلّ ورقة من وريقات صغيرة ومنها الكِتِر وهو شجر ذو شوك وفروع كثيرة وشوكه كالسنّارة وله صمغ يجتنى منه لكنّ صمغ الحشاب أغلى وأحسن منه

١٩،٤ ومنها اللَوُوت وهو شجر صغير ذو شوك صغير وفروع كثيرة فيه اخضرار لا يفارقه وإن جف. إذا قشر لحاؤه تشمّ[2] منه رائحة كريهة خاصّة ومنها القَفَل وهو شجر ليس بالكبير ولا بالصغير لكنّ أكثره ينبت في الجبال ومنها الحَرَاز وهو شجر هائل الضخم والكبر ذو شوك يعظم جذعه حتّى لا يعتنقه الرجلان إذا مدّا باعيهما ظلّه ظليل حتّى إنّ منه ما يجلس في ظلّه مائة رجل وأكثر

٢٠،٤ وبالجملة فالأشجار التي لا يؤكل لها ثمر تنفع في أمور أخر فإنّهم يقطعون منها الأخشاب لبيوتهم أمّا السنط فقرظه للدِباغ وشعبه الطويلة عمد لبيوتهم وأمّا اللؤوت فلحاؤه يربطون به سقف البيوت وفروعه يجعلونها في السقوف وفي الصريف والصريف عندهم عوض عن الحائط عندنا وأمّا الكتر والحشاب فيأخذون منهما

١ الأصل: السَيّل. ٢ الأصل: وتشم.

and want to change the color of part of its hair, they anoint with its juice the place they want to change; the hair disappears, and white hair grows back in its place. In such cases, there will be doubt as to who is its owner, though some owners are familiar with the ruse, having been subjected to it before. Its wood is as light as that of the *qafal* tree. I've seen them blackening gunpowder with the charcoal made from it. There's a specimen at the Abū Zaʿbal hospital, and many are to be found in Upper Egypt too.

There is also a tree called *ḥashāb*. It is thorny and gum arabic is extracted from it. I've seen it and gathered the gum from it while it was still soft and stretchy like mastic. It grows in arid, sandy places. There is also the sant tree, which is the tree that produces *qaraẓ* pods. It is huge and thorny. And there is the *ṭalḥ*, which belongs to the same species as the sant. *Ṭalḥ* grows taller than a man, its bark is red, and it has long thorns like needles. Its leaves are made up of smaller leaves. The umbrella thorn acacia is a tall tree that grows higher than a man but is smaller than the *ṭalḥ*, while the color of its bark is whitish green. It has white thorns and each leaf is made up of smaller leaves. Another such tree is the *kitir*. This is a thorny tree with many branches; its thorns are like hooks. It also produces a gum that is harvested, though *ḥashāb* gum is more expensive and of better quality. 4.18

Another tree is the *laʾūt*,[240] which is a small tree with small thorns and many branches that have a greenish tinge that never disappears even if the wood dries out. When its bark is peeled off, a distinctive, unpleasant odor may be smelled. Another is *qafal*, which is a tree that is neither large nor small but grows mostly in the mountains. Another is the *ḥarāz*. This is a thorny tree of enormous size whose trunk grows so large that two men cannot put their extended arms around it. It provides extensive shade; some are so large that a hundred or more may sit in its shade. 4.19

In general, the trees whose fruit is not eaten are useful for other purposes. They cut timber from them for their houses. The pods of the sant are used for tanning, and its long branches as pillars for their houses. They use the bark of the *laʾūt* to tie the ceiling beams of their houses together and use its branches to make ceilings and *ṣarīf*s, which serve the same function as enclosure walls around our houses. From *kitir* and *ḥashāb* they take gum, and sometimes they cut off their thorns and make them into hedges for pens for their animals, 4.20

الصمغ وأحياناً يقطعون شوكهما يجعلون منه الزرايب لمواشيهم ولبيوتهم لأنّ لكلّ بيت زريبة غالبا وهى كناية عن السور وصريفاً وهو كناية عن الحائط والبيوت فى الوسط أشبه شىء بالخيم والطُورْلُك المضروب حولها والبيوت إمّا من قصب الدخن أو من قصب رفيع يسمّى المرهبيب والثاني لا يعمل إلّا للأغنياء وأكابر الدولة وهو قصب ناعم قليل الكعوب رفيع كالسمار أبيض يميل إلى الصفرة زكيّ[1] الرائحة خصوصاً بعد نـزول المطر

٢١،٤ واعلم أنّ النبات في بلاد السودان كثير لا يحصى أفراده العدّ ولا يوقف له على نهاية ولا حدّ ولا أعرف منه إلّا ما اشتهر وذاع وملأت شهرته البقاع لأنّي كنت إذ ذاك في سنّ الشباب والجهل سابل عليّ جلباب لكن لكثرة مخالطتى بهم وأسفاري معهم عرفت ما عرفته بالاسم ولا أقدر أن أميّزه تمييزاً[2] كليّاً

٢٢،٤ فمنه شجر الشاو وهو شجر كبير وصغير وصغيره أكثر من كبيره وهذا الصغير أطول من القامة وقشوره خضراء بالنسبة للكبير لأنّ قشرة كبيرِهِ مغبّرة أعني أنّ لونها أغبر وهو اللون الذي يقرب للبياض وليس أبيض ناصعاً ويحمل في إبّان حمله عناقيد تأكل منها أهل السودان وهذه العناقيد فيها حبّ كأصغر العنب. ما نضج منه يكون أسود وما قرب للنضج يكون أحمر وما لم يقرب منه يكون أخضر وطعمه حلو فيه بعض حرافة وورقه يغلب على ظنّي أنّه بيضيّ أو يقرب من أن يكون بيضيّاً أخضر الظاهر والباطن

٢٣،٤ والبَطُّوم شجر كبير هائل المنظر أغبر اللون غليظ الساق صلب الخشب أوراقه صغيرة بيضيّة في حوافيها تسنّن وترى قشرة الساق من أسفل مشقّقة شقوقاً غير منتظمة وثمره كثمر الشاو وعناقيده أيضاً إلّا أنّ هذا لحبّه أذناب طويلة ولا يؤكل ثمره وهو أصغر من ثمر الشاو وتعلو ساقه أكثر من قامتين ويتفرّع فروعاً كثيرة

٢٤،٤ وأمّا الأَبَنُوس فهو شجر متوسّط وقشرته خضراء داكنة والأبنوس قلبه فإذا لُحِيَتْ القشرة انكشفت عن عود أسود إلّا أنّه يكون سواده خفيفاً وهو أخضر فكلّما يبس

١ الأصل: ذكي. ٢ الأصل: تميزا.

because generally speaking every house has a *zarībah*, which is a kind of outer wall, and a *ṣarīf*, which is a kind of inner wall, with the houses in the middle, much like tents with dust-breaks erected around them.[241] The houses are made either of millet canes or of thin canes called *marhabayb*, the second being used only by the rich and the great men of the state. It is a cane with few knots, and is as thin as a reed, yellowish white, and sweet-smelling; the smell is strongest after rainfall.

The plants found in the Lands of the Blacks are so numerous that the differ- 4.21
ent species are too many to count, and to their number no end or limit can be found. I am acquainted only with those that are well-known and widespread and whose fame has filled the globe, for at the time I was but a youth, ignorance my very robe. Despite this, and because I mixed so much with the Blacks and made so many journeys with them, I learned many by name, though I can't distinguish each and every one of them.

Among them are the *shāw*, a tree that occurs in large and small varieties, 4.22
the small being more plentiful than the large. The small variety is taller than a man, and its bark is green compared to that of the large variety, because the bark of the large form is "dusty," by which I mean gray (which is a color close to white but not as bright). When it puts forth fruit these come as clusters of berries resembling small grapes, which the inhabitants of the Lands of the Blacks eat. Those that ripen are black, and those not quite ripe are red, while those that are unripe are green. They taste sweet, with a certain piquancy, and the leaves, if I remember correctly, are ovoid, or almost so, and green both above and below.

The *baṭṭūm* is a large tree, impressive to look at, grayish in color, with a 4.23
thick trunk, hard wood, and small ovoid leaves with teeth around their edges. At the bottom, the bark of the trunk appears irregularly cracked. Its fruits resemble those of the *shāw*, as do its clusters, but the *baṭṭūm* has long tails to its berries, and its fruits, which are smaller than those of the *shāw*, cannot be eaten. Its trunk reaches more than twice a man's height and divides into many branches.

The ebony tree is a medium-sized tree with a dark-green bark. Ebony is its 4.24
heartwood: when the bark is peeled off, a black wood is exposed, though the black is not very intense when the wood is green; the more it dries, though,

ازداد سوادًا وأحسن الأبنوس ما أخذ من الجذور وهذا النبات لا يوجد في دار الفور وانّما يجلب من دار الفرتيت إليها والجُوخان أو الجُوغان كذلك إلّا أن الجوخان له ثمر كالبندق في الجم حلو الطعم فيه بعض يبوسة كالغضروف وأمّا الجَنجَع فهو شجر متوسّط أيضاً ولون ساقه يميل إلى الحمرة وفروعه ليست كثيرة التفرّع وفيه شوك طويل وأذناب أوراقه قصيرة فربّما ظنّ أنّها ملتصقة بالفروع لقصر أذنابها وهذه الأوراق مستديرة مسنّنة تسنّنًا غائرًا وثمره كثمر الزعرور وفيه مساكن إلّا أنّه غضروفيّ أو فيه خشبيّة وأغلب ظنّي أنّ في كلّ ثمرة أربعة مساكن بينها حواجز

٢٥،٤ وأمّا دار فرتيت وهم مجوس السودان المحاذون لجنوب دارفور فينبت فيها القنا ومنها يصنعون أعواد حرابهم وأكثر أعواد حراب أهل الدولة فى دارفور من القنا وهو جميل جدّا ويجلب من دار فرتيت

٢٦،٤ وأمّا النباتات التي فيها الخواصّ فمنها شجرة كِيلِي وهي شجرة متوسّطة لا شوك فيها تثمر ثمرًا كالزعرور إلّا أنّه خشبيّ. يؤخذ الثمر وينقع في الماء ويسقى المتهوم ولون هذا الثمر كلون الرمّان الحامض إذا جفّ والشَعْلوب وهو شجر نصف خشبيّ كثير الفروع لينها ورفيعها تمتدّ فروعه وتشتبك ببعضها متراكمة حتّى تصير الشجرة وحدها كالأكمة وله ثمر كالبلح الكبير الأخضر ولا عجم ولا نوى فيه وفيه عصارة لبنيّة ببعض لزوجة.[١] لطعمه بعض حلاوة ابتداءً وحرافة انتهاءً. أخضر لا يفارقه لون الخضرة ولو جفّ إذا مضغه شارب الخمر أزال ريحتها وقد تقدّم ذلك

٢٧،٤ ومنها دَقَرَة وهو نبات حشيشيّ ينبت في الأراضي الصلبة أوراقه رقيقة فيها نوع استدارة إذا دقّ الورق في هاون وعصر ماؤه في العين الرمداء المتورّمة بالتهاب حادّ ثلاثة أيّام صباحاً ومساءً أبرأه ولقد كنت في سوق نمليه في غير رؤية الجبل ومسكت بيدي الفلفل وصرت أعبث به ثمّ هبت ريح فقذيت عيناي فدعكتهما بيدي ونسيت أمر الفلفل فتألّمت ألمًا عظيمًا والتهبتا[٢] في الحال وورمتا[٣] فركبت وسافرت

١ الأصل: لزوحة. ٢ الأصل: والتهبا. ٣ الأصل: وورما.

the blacker it becomes. The best ebony is that taken from the roots. It is not found in Darfur but imported from Dār Fartīt. The jackalberry tree is the same, but the jackalberry has fruit like hazelnuts in size, sweet tasting, with a certain toughness, like gristle. The *jaʿjaʿ* is another medium-sized tree, with a reddish trunk and branches with few bifurcations.[242] It has long thorns and the stalks of its leaves are so short one might think they were stuck straight onto the branches; these leaves are round and deeply indented. The fruits resemble medlars and contain compartments, but are gristly and have a certain woodiness. To the best of my recollection each fruit contains four compartments with walls between them.

In the lands of the Fartīt (who are the Magians among the Blacks[243] and who live south of the borders of Darfur) grows *qanā*, from which they make the shafts of their spears; most of the shafts of the spears of the officers of state in Darfur are of this bamboo, which is very beautiful and is imported from Dār Fartīt. 4.25

Plants that have special properties include the *kilí* tree, which is of medium size, without thorns, and bears a fruit like a medlar but woody. The fruit is steeped in water, and given to one charged with a crime to drink.[244] The color of the fruit resembles that of sour, dried pomegranates. The *shaʿlūb* is a semi-woody tree with numerous soft, thin branches, which spread out and interweave with one another until the tree, when standing alone, ends up looking like a hill.[245] It has fruits like large green dates with neither pit nor kernel that contain a milky, somewhat viscous juice. The fruits taste sweet at the beginning and piquant at the end; it is green, the green never disappearing, even when they dry out. If someone who's been drinking wine chews them, they get rid of the smell, as noted earlier.[246] 4.26

Another is the *daqarah*,[247] which is a grassy plant that grows in hard soils. Its leaves are delicate and somewhat rounded. When the leaves are pounded in a mortar and their juice squeezed for three days, morning and evening, into a diseased eye that is acutely inflamed and swollen, it will cure it. I was in the market at Numlayh once (not the time I went to see the mountain)[248] and I picked up some pepper with my hand and toyed with it for a moment. Then there was a gust of wind and my eyes got dust in them so I rubbed them with my hand, forgetting about the pepper. It hurt terribly and my eyes immediately 4.27

فلم أقدر على الركوب من شدّة الألم فدخلت في بلدة وبتّ عند امرأة عجوز فيها فلم أكتحل بنوم وبتّ بأقبح ليلة وانقلب الجفنان وغلظاً حتّى خشيت على عينيّ من العمى وصرت لا أعرف ما ينقذني من ذلك

٢٨،٤ فلمّا أصبح الصباح جاءتني عجوز ونظرت عينيّ وتوجّعت لي ثمّ قالت هذا أمر سهل ثمّ دعت بابنة لها صغيرة تكاد أن تكون ابنة سبع سنين أو ثمانية وقالت لها بلغة الفور اذهبي إلى أسفل الجبل وائتيني بأوراق من النبات المسمّى دقرة فذهبت الصبيّة وغابت قليلاً ثمّ جاءت ومعها أوراق كثيرة فأخذتها العجوز ودقّت بعضها بين حجرين حتّى صار كالعجين وأمرت بفتح عينيّ ومسك يديّ ثمّ عصرت في عينيّ من عصارة النبات المذكور فنزل في عينيّ بارداً ثمّ ابتدأ يأكل بغير ألم حتّى كأنما في عينيّ دود وأريد أدعكهما بيدي فلا أستطيع للضبط عليّ فعانيت من ذلك مشقّة حتّى اضمحلّ الأكلان وجاءني النوم فنمت واستغرقت في نومي مدّة عظيمة فلم أفق إلّا قرب العصر فأحسست في عينيّ خفّة وذهب الألم ولمّا كان من الليل جاءت وعصرت لي من تلك العصارة وبتّ بأنعم ليلة وفي الصباح عصرت لي منها أيضاً فانفتحت عيناي وكأنّي لم أرمد بهما فذبحت إذ ذاك كبشاً سميناً وليمة لشفائي وأعطيت العجوز جدياً سميناً

٢٩،٤ وغالب النبات والشجر يثمر في آخر زمن الخريف وهو الصيف عندنا لأنهم يسمّون صيفنا خريفاً وخريفنا درتاً وفي عرفهم يعنون به الربيع وربيعنا صيفاً ولم يوافقونا إلّا في الشتاء فإنّ الشتاء عندهم هو الشتاء عندنا وفي الصيف الحقيقيّ تمطر السماء عندهم ويزرعون لأنّ أوّل سقوط المطر عندهم في الجوزاء ويسمّونه الرُشاش وفي السرطان تنفتح عزالي السحاب ويكثر المطر وتمتلئ الأودية وبذلك تعلم سبب زيادة النيل المبارك وممّا يؤكّد أنّ كثرة الأمطار عند أهل السودان هي السبب في كثرة نيل مصر ما وقع من الاتّفاق أنّ سنة ١٢٥٣ هجريّة وقع في مصر غلاء عظيم حتّى أبيع الأردبّ من القمح بمائة وخمسين غرشاً بل أكثر وسببه عدم فيضان النيل كعادته وحينئذ كنت متشكّكاً هل وقع ذلك بأرض السودان أم لا وبقيت على الشكّ إلى سنة ١٢٥٧ فجاء القاضي

became inflamed and swollen. I mounted and left but couldn't go on riding because of the terrible pain, so I entered a town and spent the night in the house of an old woman. I was unable to sleep and spent a horrible night, my eyelids inverting and emitting a viscous liquid. I feared I might go blind and had no idea what could save me.

In the morning, the old woman came and saw my eyes and felt sorry for me. 4.28
"That's easily dealt with," she said, and she called a young daughter of hers, aged perhaps seven or eight, and told her, in the language of the Fur, "Go to the foot of the mountain and bring me some leaves of the plant called *daqarah*." The girl went off and was away awhile. Then she came back, bringing a large quantity of leaves, which the old woman took and some of which she pounded between two stones till they turned into something resembling dough. She ordered me to open my eyes and take her hand, and she squeezed some of the juice of this plant into my eyes. At first it felt cool to the eyes, but then it began to itch, though without pain, as though there were worms in my eyes. I wanted to rub them, but couldn't because I was being held down, so I had to suffer some discomfort until the itching died away and I fell asleep. I slept deeply for a long time, not waking till it was almost time for the afternoon prayer, and I felt a lightness in my eyes and the pain had gone. At night, she came and squeezed some more juice into my eyes, and I slept most comfortably. In the morning, she squeezed some more again, and my eyes cleared, as though they'd never been inflamed. I slaughtered a fat ram for a feast to celebrate my recovery and gave the old woman a fat young goat.

Most plants and trees fruit at the end of the "autumn," which is the summer 4.29
in our country, because they call our summer autumn and our autumn *darat*, by which they mean spring in their parlance, though our spring they call summer.[249] The only thing they agree with us on is the winter—when it's winter in their country it's also winter in ours. During the true summer, it rains where they are, and they sow their crops; the first rainfall there coincides with the appearance of the Twins, this being what they call "the sprinkle."[250] In the Crab,[251] the clouds open, there's lots of rain, and the wadis fill. It is this, you may be interested to know, that causes the rising of the Blessed Nile. That the plentiful rains where the Blacks live are the cause of the rise of the Nile in Egypt is confirmed by, among other things, the great rise in prices that occurred in Egypt in 1253 [1837–38], when an *irdabb* of wheat was sold for 150 piasters

الدليل قاضي القضاة بمملكة الواداي فأخبرني أنّه في تلك السنة قلّ القَطْر حتّى أجدبت الأرض وغلت الأقوات وأكلت الناس الجيف والكلاب وهو اتّفاق عجيب وأدلّ[1] دليل على أنّ زيادة بحر النيل من أمطار تلك البلاد ولله في ذلك حكمة لا يعلمها إلّا هو

٣٠،٤ وفي وقت الرشاش يكثر هبوب الرياح والمؤتفكات وأكثر مجيئها في أوقات العصر وإذا هبّت ترى من بعد كالسحاب فتارة تكون حمراء وقد سدّت الأفق من الجهة التي تأتي منها وغالب المؤتفكات تأتي من قبل المشرق ونادرًا أن تأتي من الجنوب وفي مجيئها من الشرق تحمل رملًا كثيرًا من القوز الذي تمرّ عليه وكلّ مؤتفكة تأتي بمعيّة مطر لأنّ قبل ذهابها يرعد الرعد وبعد الرشاش ينزل المطر برعد قويّ حتّى إنّه ربّما نزلت منه صواعق فضرّت ولقد رأيت صاعقة نزلت على شجرة هجليج فكسرت منها فرعًا عظيمًا وساخت في الأرض وأخرى نزلت على بيت فدخلت نار من خلال البيت وأصابت رجلًا فأحرقت ذراعه وساخت في الأرض وسمعت منهم أنّ من كان معه حديد لا تقربه الصاعقة وهذا خلاف رأي الإفرنج

٣١،٤ وفي فصل صيفهم الذي نسمّيه ربيعًا تكثر الزوابع ويرى السراب في الأرض ولا أعلم أرضًا يكثر فيها الزوابع والسراب كأرض السودان وأحسن المطر عندهم وأهنأه ما يقع بالليل والناس نيام وهو وإن كان يحصل فيه رعد إلّا أنّه لا يضرّ كما يضرّ الرعد الذي يأتي بالنهار ويكثر قوس قزح عندهم في وقت نزول المطر حتّى إنّه يكون في الساعة الواحدة في أربعة محالّ أو خمسة. منها ما يكون كالقوس ومنها ما يكون على خطّ مستقيم وهو قليل وأكثره يكون على خطّ منحني

٣٢،٤ والرشاش عندهم نحو خمسة عشر يومًا فيه يزرعون الدخن والذرة بأنواعه وأطول خريف عندهم ستّون يومًا غير أيّام الرشاش وأوسطه ستّون يومًا بأيّام الرشاش وأقلّه لا حدّ له وأغلبه أن يكون خمسة وأربعين أو خمسين يومًا وأقلّ من ذلك قحط

١ الأصل: ادل.

or even more, the cause being the failure of the Nile flood to rise as normal. At the time, I had no firm information as to whether the same had occurred in the Lands of the Blacks or not, and my doubt remained unresolved until 1257 [1841–42],[252] when Judge al-Dalīl, chief judge of the kingdom of Wāddāy, arrived and told me that in the year in question there was so little rain that the earth failed to produce any plants, food prices rose, and the people ate carrion and dogs. This is a remarkable coincidence and the best evidence that the rise in the River Nile is due to the rains in that country—an instance of the divine wisdom comprehensible to God alone.

At the time of "the sprinkle," strong winds and violent storms often arise, 4.30
most often in the late afternoon. When they blow, you see in the distance something like a cloud, which is sometimes red, while the horizon fills with dust in the direction of the storm. Most storms come before sunset, and rarely from the south. When they come from the east, they bring great quantities of sand with them from the Dunes, over which they pass. Every storm is accompanied by rain, because before it passes there is thunder. After the sprinkle, the rains fall, with thunder so strong it can cast damaging thunderbolts. Once I saw a thunderbolt hit a *hijlīj* tree and break off a huge branch before piercing the ground like an arrow. Another hit a house, and even before it pierced the ground the whole place caught fire and a man was hurt when his arm was burned. They told me that a thunderbolt will not go near anyone with iron on him, which is the opposite of what the Franks believe.

In their summer season, which we call spring, dust devils become frequent, 4.31
and mirages can be seen on the ground; I know no other country that has as many dust devils and mirages as the Land of the Blacks. Their best and most beneficial rain falls at night, while people are asleep; even if accompanied by thunder it does less damage than the thunder that comes during the day. Rainbows are so frequent there when the rain is falling that one may appear in four or five different places during a single hour. Some are like a bow and some a straight line, though these are few; most are curved.

The "sprinkle" lasts for about fifteen days, during which time they sow 4.32
millet and various kinds of sorghum. The "autumn," or rainy season, at its longest lasts no more than sixty days, not counting the sprinkle; the average is sixty days including the sprinkle. There is no limit to how short it can be. Most often, it lasts forty-five or fifty days; less than that means drought and crop

وجدب فهو كالعدم إلّا إن جاءت في تلك المدّة أمطار غزيرة روت الأرض ريّاً عظيماً خصوصاً عند آخر الفصل وختام الزرع وإذا طالت مدّة الخريف وكثرت أمطاره سمّوه خريف التِيمَان

٣٣،٤ وأسماء الشهور في بلاد الفور والواداي بالعربيّة فلا يعرفون الأشهر الروميّة ولا القبطيّة ولا الأعجميّة فأهل العلم منهم يسمّونها كما سمّتها العرب قديماً بالأسماء المشهورة الآن كمحرّم وصفر وربيع الخ وأمّا عوامّ الناس فيسمّون الشهور بأسماء أخر وهذه الأسماء وإن كان معناها عربيّاً لكنّها مستهجنة ويبدأون في حساب السنة بشوّال لكن باسم آخر فيسمّون شوّالاً بالفُطَر وذي القعدة فَطَرَيْن وذي الحجّة بالضحيّة ومحرّماً بالضحيّتين وصفر بالوحيد وربيعاً الأوّل بالكرامة وربيعاً الثاني بالتوم وجمادى الأوّل بالتومين وجمادى الثاني بسايق التِيمان ولم يسلم من التغيير إلّا رجب ورمضان فيقولون رجبا ويسمّون شعبان القُصَيِّر ورمضان رمضان انتهى

٣٤،٤ وبالجملة فخواصّ النبات في دارفور عجيبة حتّى أنّي أخشى إن ذكرتها يكذّبوني ولا أجد لي شاهداً على ذلك وأكثر الخواصّ في الجذور وهناك معلّمون نباتيّون لهم تلامذة عديدة أكثر أوقاتهم مسافرون يصعدون أعالي الجبال ويتخلّلون بطون الأودية يحفرون على النبات ويعلّمون تلامذتهم وهؤلاء القوم يسمّون بالمُعْراقيّين ولهم في دارفور شنآن ولهم معاندة مع بعضهم كلّ منهم يريد أن يرتفع صيته وجميع الجذور التي يأخذونها يضعونها في قرون الغنم بل وفي قرون البقر

٣٥،٤ وهي على أنواع منها ما هو للمحبّة والقبول والجذور التي لذلك تسمّى نارة وكان في أيّامنا أشهر الناس بها رجل يسمّى بَكُرْلوكو وكان مقرّه بجديد السيل وكان من عشق صبيّة وامتنعت عليه بغضاً فيه ذهب إلى بكرلوكو فأخذ منه نارة ودلك بها وجهه ويديه وذهب إلى محبوبته ومسح بيده على كتفها أو شيء من جسمها فوقع حبّه في قلبها بحيث لا تقدر تفارقه فيفعل بها ما يريد وإن خطبها وأبى أبواها فرّت معه حيث يريد وتزوّجته قهراً عنهما ومن كان له حاجة بباب الملك وخشي ألّا تُقَضَى وذهب إلى

failure. Then there is nothing, unless heavy rains come during that period and thoroughly irrigate the soil, which tends to happen especially at the end of the season, when the sowing is coming to an end. If the rainy season goes on for a long time and the rains are plentiful, they call it "Twins' autumn."[253]

In Darfur and Dār Wāddāy, the names of the months are Arabic; the Roman,[254] Coptic, and Persian months are unknown. Educated persons use the same currently well-known names that were used by the ancient Arabs, such as Muharram, Safar, Rabiʿ, etc.[255] The common people, however, use other names, which, though they have Arabic meanings, are bastardized forms. They begin the calendar with Shawwal,[256] but use another name, calling it al-Faṭur; Dhu l-Qaʿdah they call al-Faṭrayn, Dhu l-Hijjah they call al-Ḍaḥiyyah, Muharram they call al-Ḍaḥiyyatayn, Safar they call al-Waḥīd, Rabiʿ al-Awwal they call al-Karāmah, Rabiʿ al-Thani they call al-Tawm, Jumada al-Awwal they call al-Tawmayn, and Jumada al-Thani they call Sāyiq al-Tīmān.[257] Only Rajab and Ramadan have been spared change. They say Rajab, but they call Shaʿban al-Quṣayyar, and Ramadan Ramaḍān. 4.33

To sum up, the special properties of the plants of Darfur are so remarkable that I'm afraid to list them all lest people call me a liar, and I won't be able to find anyone to bear out my claims. Most of these special properties are in the roots. There are plant masters with many students who spend most of their time traveling, climbing the heights of mountains, descending deep into the bottoms of wadis to dig about for plants, and teaching their students. People of this type are called *muʿrāqī*s, and in Darfur their skills are recognized. They are always stubbornly at odds with one another, each wanting his reputation to soar higher than his rivals'. They put all the roots into goat, sheep, or even cow horns. 4.34

These roots are of different kinds. Some are for love and acceptance; the roots used for these purposes are called *nārah*.[258] The man most famous for these in our day was named Bakurlūkū; he had his headquarters at Jadīd al-Ṣayl. Any man in love with a girl who rejected his advances because she didn't like him would go to Bakurlūkū and get *nārah* from him and massage his face and hands with it and then go to his beloved and rub his hand on her shoulder or any other part of her body. At this, her heart would become so full of love for him she'd be unable to leave him. Then he could do with her as he wished: if he asked for her hand in marriage and her parents refused, she'd run away 4.35

بكرلوكو وأخذ منه قطعة من النارة ودلك بشيء منها بين كفّيه ومسح على وجهه أحبّه الملك وقضى حاجته وإن كان ضامرًا له سوء واشتهر بكرلوكو بهذا الأمر حتّى إن النساء ليغنّين به ويقلن

بكرلوكو أبًا
بنتين بسدى

ومعناه أنّ بكرلوكو إن أراد أن يرخّص مهور البنات يجعل الرجل يتزوّج بنتين[1] بسدًى[2] واحد والسدى هو عشرة أذرع غزلًا قِيامًا وممّا اتّفق لي في ذلك أنّه في يوم من الأيّام جاءني رجل معه نارة يدّعي أنّها عظيمة جدًّا وأنّه أخذها من بكرلوكو وعرضها[3] عليّ للشراء فقلت له يا هذا إنّما يحتاج إلى النارة من تبغضه النساء وأنا في شبابي هذا وتيسير حالي لو أردت ابنة الملك لما تعذّرت عليّ فكيف بغيرها ويحتاج إليها من يخشى سطوة الملك وأنا في أمن من ذلك لأنّي غريب وشريف ولي عند الملك حرمة فاعرضها على غيري فهو أولى بها منّي لأنّي أنا في نفسي نارة فما أصنع بالنارة انتهى

٣٦،٤ ومنها ما يستعمل للمضرّة وهو على أنواع نوع يستعمل لقتل العدوّ وكيفيّة ذلك أن يؤخذ الجذر الذي فيه خاصّيّة القتل ويغرز في ظلّ رأس المراد قتله ففي الحال يتأثّر ويلتهب المخّ ويبقى الشخص لا يعي شيئًا فإن لم يتدارك سريعًا بضدّ ما فعل له مات وإذا أريد إبطال عضو منه يغرز الجذر في ظلّ العضو المراد إبطاله كاليد أو الرجل ففي الحال يتألّم العضو ويلتهب وينتفخ وربّما حدثت فيه غدّة كغدّة الطاعون وإن لم يتدارك سريعًا ينتفخ وينتهي بفقد إحساس العصب وبطلان الوظائف كلّها

٣٧،٤ وإذا أريد أن يصاب بالدوار وبالقيء هناك جذور توضع على الجمر ويتلقّى دخانها ولو في كمّ الثوب ويطبّق عليه طبقًا جيّدًا ويتوجّه للشخص المقصود فيفتح كمّ الثوب

١ أضيف للسياق. ٢ الأصل: بسداء. ٣ الأصل: عرفها.

with him to wherever he wanted, and he could marry her in spite of them. Also, anyone who had business before the king's court and was afraid that it might not be seen to, would go Bakurlūkū, obtain a piece of *nārah* from him, massage some of it between his hands, and rub it on his face. He'd then discover that the king had taken a fancy to him and seen to his business, even if he had harbored ill will toward him. Bakurlūkū became so famous for these things that the women used to sing songs about him, saying:

> Bakurlūkū could make them give away
> Two girls for one *sadā*

meaning that if Bakurlūkū wanted to bring down the cost of dowries, he could have a man marry two girls for a single *sadā*, a *sadā* being ten cubits of straight yarn. Apropos of this, it happened that one day a man brought me some *nārah* that he claimed was very powerful and that he said he'd obtained from Bakurlūkū. He offered to sell it to me but I told him, "Fellow, only a man whom women hate has need of *nārah*, but I'm still in my youth as you can see, and blessed with wealth—if I wanted the king's daughter she wouldn't be beyond my reach, so how much less so other girls? The kind in need of it is afraid of the king's power, but I'm safe from that—I'm not from this country; I'm a descendant of the Prophet, and I've been granted protected status by the king. Offer it to someone else. Others need it more than I do, because I'm a love potion in and of myself!"

Other roots are used to cause harm. There's a kind used to kill one's enemies. 4.36 To do this, obtain the deadly root and thrust it into the shadow of the head of the man whose death is desired. He will feel the effects immediately, his brain will become inflamed, and he'll lose consciousness. If an antidote isn't quickly administered, he will die. If the desire is to render a particular limb of his useless, the root is stuck into the shadow of the limb, whether hand or foot, whose disablement is desired. That limb will immediately feel pain, become inflamed, and swell up. Sometimes buboes like those of the plague will appear on it, and if it isn't treated quickly, the limb will swell, eventually losing sensation in the sinews, and all its functions will be disabled.

If one wants to make someone dizzy and nauseous, there are roots that 4.37 are put on embers whose smoke is then captured, for example in the sleeve of a garment. This is then carefully folded and dispatched to the intended

ونحوه بقرب أنفه فتسطع رائحة دخان الجذر في أنفه فيقع في الحال حتّى تبقى رجلاه أعلى من رأسه فإن لم يتدارك في الحال بقي كذلك أيّاماً

٣٨،٤ ومنها جذور خاصيّتها جلب النوم وهذه الجذور تستعملها السارقون وتجعلها في قرون فيدخل السارق بالليل على المحلّ وأهله مستيقظون فيشير إليهم بالقرن الذي فيه الجذر ثلاث مرّات فيضرب الله على آذانهم فلا يعون شيئاً فيدخل السارق ويأخذ ما يريد أخذه وربّما ذبح الشاة وسلخها وشوى من لحمها وأكل ووضع في يد كلّ من أرباب المحلّ قطعة من الكبد ثمّ أخذ ما أراد وخرج وبعد خروجه من الدار يفيقون ويسأل بعضهم بعضاً عن الرجل الذي كانوا رأوه فكلّ منهم يقول رأيته ولا أدري ما فعل فإذا بحثوا في محلّهم يرون أنّه ما ترك لهم شيئاً وقد فاز بما أخذ فيعضّون أناملهم تلهّفاً وقد امتنع عليهم

٣٩،٤ وبالجملة فهذا الأمر في دارفور مشهور لا ينكر وكنت سألت عن تلك الخواصّ أستاذي الفقيه مدنيّ الفوتاويّ أخا الفقيه مالك الذي تقدّم ذكره فأخبرني أنّ الكتب المنزلة على آدم وشيث وإبراهيم وغيره من الأنبياء دفنت في الأرض وأنبت الله هذه النباتات في المحلّ الذي دفنت فيه وانتشر بزرها بهبوب الرياح في الأرض فعمّ نباتها وانتشر واستفيدت منها هذه الخواصّ بالتجربة. أقول وهذا نوع من أنواع السحر وضرب من ضروبه

٤٠،٤ ومنها نوع يعمل بالكتابة والتعزيم على الأملاك العلويّة والسفليّة ومن هذا النوع تظهر أمور كثيرة خارقة للعادة لقد أخبرني الثقات[١] بدارفور أنّ في محاربة الخليفة للسلطان عبد الرحمن كان للخليفة عدّة رجال يقوّسون بالبندق فسحرهم جماعة السلطان حتّى إنّ البارود كان يخرج من البندق كالمبلول لا يسمع له صوت ورصاصه كان لا يضرّ وبندق جماعة السلطان بعكسه في الصوت والضرر

١ الأصل: الثقاة.

victim. The latter will then open the sleeve of the garment or the like close to his nose, the smell of the smoke of the root will fill his nose, and he will straightaway fall down, legs in the air. If not treated immediately, he will stay like that for days.

There are roots whose special property is to induce sleep. These are used by thieves, who place them in a horn and at night enter a place whose occupants are awake. They wave the horn containing the root at them three times and God blocks the occupants' ears, so that they become insensible to everything. The thief then enters and takes whatever he wants. Sometimes he will slaughter a ewe, flay it, grill some of its meat, eat it, and place a piece of its liver in the hand of each person in the place, then take what he wants and leave. After he's left the house, they revive and ask each other about the man they saw, each saying, "I saw him but I don't know what he did." When they search their place, they find that he's left nothing and has succeeded in getting away with what he's taken. At this, they bite their fingertips in grief, for he's escaped and there is nothing they can do about it. 4.38

To sum up, such things are well known in Darfur and not forbidden. I asked my teacher, Faqīh Madanī al-Fūtāwī, the brother of Faqīh Mālik of whom we spoke earlier, and he told me that the books of revelation sent down to Ādam, Shīth, Ibrāhīm, and other prophets were buried in the ground; God then made these plants grow where the books were buried, their seeds were scattered by the blowing of the winds over the land so that the plants became common and widespread, and by trial and error people learned to take advantage of their special properties. I say it's all a form of magic. 4.39

Another type is the kind that uses writings and charms to invoke the upper and lower angels. This kind of magic produces many extraordinary things. Trusted sources in Darfur informed me that at the battle between the Successor and Sultan ʿAbd al-Raḥmān, the Successor had a number of men firing muskets, and the sultan's side put a spell on them so that the powder would spill out of the musket as though wet, making no sound, while the sultan's muskets, on the contrary, made lots of noise and did a great deal of damage.[259] 4.40

٤١،٤ وممّا وقع من هذا القبيل أنّ لمّا توفّي السلطان عبد الرحمن وولي ابنه السلطان محمّد فضل مكانه أبى عليه أولاد السلاطين كأولاد السلطان تيراب وأولاد السلطان أبي القاسم وأولاد الخليفة وأولاد السلطان عمر وخرجوا عن الطاعة وركبوا خيولهم وخرجوا إلى القرى وجيّشوا جيشاً عظيماً فخشي الأب الشيخ محمّد كرّا من خلل يقع في البلاد فدعا بالفقيه مالك الفوتاويّ وأعلمه بما يخشاه من غائلة هذا الأمر فضمن له أن يأتي بهم إلى بين يديه أذلّاء فأخرج الأب الشيخ محمّد كرّا جيشاً لنظر الملك محمّد دلدن ابن عمّة السلطان محمّد فضل وذهب الفقيه مالك فعمل من سحره ما عمل وكانت أولاد السلاطين في محلّ بينه وبين الفاشر مسيرة يومين فلمّا عمل فيهم السحر ركبوا خيولهم عند المساء خوفاً من الملك محمّد دلدن أن يهجم عليهم بجيشه وأرادوا البعد فعموا عن الطريق وباتوا ليلتهم تلك سارّين إلى جهة الفاشر والملك دلدن في إثرهم فما أصبحوا إلّا وهم تحت الفاشر ولمّا أصبح الصباح ورأوا أنفسهم بقرب الفاشر ندموا على سريانهم وسمع بهم الأب الشيخ محمّد كرّا فأرسل لهم وحينما وصل الجيش إليهم أطبق عليهم جيش الملك محمّد دلدن لأنّه في أثرهم ولمّا صاروا بين العسكرين انهزمت الناس الذين كانوا التفّوا عليهم وبقيت أولاد السلاطين في نفر قليل فقبض عليهم الملك محمّد دلدن وتوجّه بهم إلى الأب الشيخ محمّد كرّا فأمر بهم إلى السجن واكتفى شرّهم وكان ذلك من السحر ولولاه لجاسوا خلال دارفور وعاثوا فيها واتّسع الخرق على الراقع

٤٢،٤ والمخصوص بالأعمال السحريّة في دارفور هم قبيلة الفلّان ولقد رأيت منهم رجلاً يسمّى الفقيه تَمُرُّو بفتح المثنّاة الفوقيّة وضمّ الميم وآخره راء مشدّدة مضمومة يذكرون عنه أموراً عجيبة ويفيضون في[1] ذكرها مع التصديق لها حتّى بلغت هناك مبلغ التواتر الذي يمتنع تكذيبه فمنها ما أخبرني به الثقة من فقهاء دارفور أنّه سافر مع الفقيه تمرو المذكور من جديد كريو إلى الفاشر ورجع معه إلى جديد كريو فقال لمّا كنّا في أثناء الطريق اشتدّ علينا حرّ الشمس وكان الفقيه تمرو راكباً على جمل فأخذ ملحفته وفردها

[1] أضيف للسياق.

Similarly, when Sultan ʿAbd al-Raḥmān died and his son Sultan Muḥammad Faḍl assumed his place, the sons of the sultans, such as those of Sultan Tayrāb, Sultan Abū l-Qāsim, the Successor, and Sultan ʿUmar, refused to accept him and rebelled. They mounted their horses, rode out to the villages, and gathered a mighty army. Shaykh-Father Muḥammad Kurrā was afraid that harm might befall the country, so he summoned Faqīh Mālik al-Fūtāwī and told him of his fears regarding the havoc that might ensue. But Faqīh Mālik assured him that he would bring the sons to his feet in humiliation. Shaykh-Father Muḥammad Kurrā then dispatched an army under the command of Malik Muḥammad Daldan, nephew of Sultan Muḥammad Faḍl, and Faqīh Mālik accompanied it. He worked his magic when the sons of the sultans were about two days' march from the sultan's capital. That evening, after he'd cast his spell on them, they mounted their horses, fearing that Malik Muḥammad Daldan might attack them with his army and seeking to put distance between them. However, they lost their way and spent the night moving in the direction of the capital, with Malik Daldan in pursuit. When morning came and they found themselves close to the capital, they regretted they'd ever set off. Shaykh-Father Muḥammad Kurrā heard they were there and sent an army against them. When it arrived, the army of Malik Muḥammad Daldan closed in on them because he was right behind them. Finding themselves between the two armies, the people who'd rallied to the sons of the sultans lost their resolve, and the sons were left with a small band. Malik Muḥammad Daldan then arrested them and took them to Shaykh-Father Muḥammad Kurrā, who commanded they be sent to prison, thereby ridding himself of their evil doings. This was due to magic: without it they would have run rampant, ravaging Darfur, and the damage would have been beyond repair.[260] 4.41

The magic specialists in Darfur are the Fullān. I met one of them, a man called Faqīh Tamurrū—spelled *a* after *T*, *u* after *m*, double *r*, and *ū* at the end—of whom remarkable things were said. People there so often stated these things and affirmed their truth that they turned into one of those things that can't be denied simply because the number of those reporting them is too great for them to be colluding in a lie. For example, a holy man of Darfur whom I trusted told me that once he went with the aforementioned Faqīh Tamurrū from Jadīd Karyū to the sultan's capital and then back again with him to Jadīd Karyū. "When we were on the road," he said, "we found the heat of the sun unbearable. Faqīh Tamurrū was riding a camel, and he took his cloak, unfolded and 4.42

ثمّ رجع وضمّها بين يديه وقرأ عليها بعض أسماء ثمّ قذفها إلى أعلى فانفردت[١] على رأسه كأنّها ظُلّة وظلّلته هو وصاحبه من حرّ الشمس كأنّها ممسوكة من أطرافها بين رجلين تتبعهما أينما توجّها كالمظلّة وهذا الأمر من أغرب ما يسمع وأعجبه ومنها بينما هما سائران في سفرهما ذاك إذ نزل عليهما المطر فقال الفقيه تمرو لخادم كان معهما ائتني بقبضة من التراب فناوله إيّاها فأخذها بيده وقرأ عليها بعض كلمات ثمّ نثر التراب حول رأسه فانقشع السحاب وصار المطر ينزل عن يمينهما ويسارهما وهما يمشيان في اليبس لا تنزل عليهما قطرة وممّا بلغني أنّ المسائيط اقتتلوا مع الفلّان في بعض الأحيان وهزموهم واقتفوا أثرهم ليستأصلوهم فعمل الفلّان شيئاً من سحرهم فسحروا أعين المسائيط حتّى إنّهم كانوا يرون أثر الذهاب معكوساً كأنّه أثر المجيء

٤٣،٤ ولقد بلغني من شيخنا الفقيه مدنيّ الفوتاويّ عليه سحائب الرحمة أنّ ملك البرنو كان له كاتب جليل القدر على غاية من التقوى والصلاح فجاء إليه الوزير الأعظم وقال له إنّ الملك يأمرك أن تكتب كتاباً لفلان مضمونه كذا وكذا فأبى الكاتب عليه وقال لا أكتب إلّا أن يقول لي السلطان بنفسه أو يرسل لي علامة تدلّ على صدق رسوله فذهب الوزير إلى السلطان وأخبره بما قاله الكاتب فدعاه السلطان وقال له قد أذنتك أن كلّما قال لك وزيري هذا اكتب لكذا أو كذا على لساني أن تكتب له

٤٤،٤ وكان الخاتم الذي تختم به الأوامر السلطانيّة مع الكاتب المذكور فامتثل أمره وصار يكتب له كلّما أراد حتّى إنّه جاء إليه يوم من الأيّام وقال له إنّ الملك يأمرك أن تكتب إلى فلان الملك أن يتوجّه إلى العامل فلان ويقتله ويستصفي أمواله ويرسلها صحبة رأسه فكتب له ذلك والسلطان لا يعلم بشيء من ذلك فما راعه إلّا وقد امتلأت البطحاء بالأموال والرقيق والبقر والإبل والغنم ورأس شخص موضوعة على سنّ رمح فسأل السلطان عن الخبر فأخبر أنّ هذا رأس فلان وهذا ماله وقد قتل حسبما أمرت فأنكر السلطان ودعا بالكاتب وقال من أمر بقتل فلان واستصفاء

---

١ الأصل: فانفرد.

refolded it, held it between his hands, recited over it certain names, and then tossed it into the air. It spread out above his head like a patch of shade," and shaded him and his friend from the heat of the sun as though it were being held by a man at each end; it followed them like a sunshade wherever they went. This is one of the strangest and most remarkable things one could hope to hear. In another example, the two of them were proceeding on the same journey when it rained on them. Faqīh Tamurrū told a servant who was with them, "Get me a handful of soil." When the man handed him the handful of soil, he took it in his hand, recited a few words over it, and sprinkled the earth over his head—the clouds moved aside and the rain started falling to their right, while they proceeded in the dry, without a drop falling on them. I've been told that once the Masālīṭ fought with the Fullān and defeated them and were tracking them as they retreated, intending to exterminate them. The Fullān worked a little magic and bewitched the eyes of the Masālīṭ, with the result that they saw the tracks of those retreating back to front, as though they were the tracks of people coming toward them.

I was told by my teacher, Shaykh Madanī al-Fūtāwī, may clouds of mercy 4.43
hover over him, that the king of Barnaw had a scribe of great accomplishment, who was God-fearing and righteous in the extreme. The chief vizier went to him and said, "Our monarch commands you to write a letter to so-and-so containing the following." The scribe, however, refused, responding, "I write only when the sultan himself tells me to do so, or sends me some token to show that his messenger is telling the truth." The vizier went to the sultan and told him what the scribe had said, so the sultan summoned the man and said to him, "I hereby grant you permission to the effect that, whenever this vizier of mine tells you, 'Write such and such!' in my name, you may do so."

Now, the seal with which royal commands were sealed was in the keeping 4.44
of the scribe in question, so he obeyed the sultan's command and started writing for the vizier whatever he wanted. Then one day the vizier came to him and said, "Our monarch commands you to write to Malik So-and-so that he should go to the tax collector so-and-so, kill him, impound his wealth, and send it, along with his head." The man wrote this but the sultan had no idea what was going on and was surprised to see the courtyard filled with treasures: slaves, cattle, camels, and flocks of sheep and goats, along with someone's head on the point of a spear. The sultan inquired and was told, "This is the head of so-and-so and these are his assets. He was killed at your command." The sultan denied

أمواله فقال له أنت فقال له في أيّ وقت أمرتك بذلك قال في الوقت الفلانيّ جاءني وزيرك فلان وقال لي اكتب إلى فلان الملك[١] بالجهة الفلانيّة أن يتوجّه إلى فلان العامل بالجهة الفلانيّة ويقطع رأسه ويرسلها على رمح ويرسل أمواله كلّها فقال لم آمره بذلك وكيف مع عقلك وحسن تدبيرك أنّك كتبت له بغير استئذان منّي فقال أيّدك الله مولانا إنّك قد دعوتني في اليوم الفلانيّ وقلت لي كلّما قال لك وزيري هذا اكتب لكذا أو كذا على لساني فاكتب له فامتثلت أمرك من ذلك الوقت وصرت أكتب له كلّ ما أمرني به

٤،٤٥ فغضب السلطان وقال إنّي لم آمرك أن تكتب له في مثل هذا الأمر المهمّ بل أمرتك أن تكتب له في الأمور التي لا ضرر فيها على الدولة. أَوَمثل هذا الأمر يكون بغير استئذان فقال الكاتب إنّ مولانا لم يستثنِ أمرًا من الأمور حين أمرني بطاعته فزاد غضب السلطان وأمر بالقبض على الكاتب فلم يقدر أحد على القبض عليه وما ذاك إلّا أنّه كلّ من مدّ إليه يدًا ليقبض عليه تَيَبّس فلا يقدر أن يثنيها وتصير كأنّها قطعة خشب فلمّا رأى السلطان ذلك قال له اعف عن هؤلاء فقال لا أعفو[٢] عنهم إلّا إن أعفاني السلطان من الخدمة فأعفاه من الخدمة وعفا عنهم هو أيضًا فلانت أيديهم ورجعت كما كانت وهذا مصداق قوله صلّى الله عليه وسلّم من خاف من الله خاف منه كلّ شيء ومن لم يخف الله خوّفه الله من كلّ شيء

٤،٤٦ وممّا ينخرط في سلك هذه العجائب[٣] ما شاع على ألسنة أهل دارفور من أنّ هناك قبيلتين من رعايا الفور إحداهما تسمّى مساليط[٤] والثانية تيموركه يتشكّلان بأشكال الحيوانات لكنّ المشهور أنّ مساليط[٥] تتشكّل بشكل الضبع والهرّ والكلب وأمّا تيموركه فتتشكّل بشكل السبع لا غير وأعجب من ذا أنّ هذه القبيلة يقولون عنها إنّ الميّت منها يقوم بعد ثلاثة أيّام من قبره ويتوجّه إلى بلد آخر ويتزوّج بها ويعيش زمنًا ولقد أشيع على ألسنة أهل دارفور أنّ للسلطان طائفة من هذه القبيلة يرسلها في

١ الأصل: العامل. ٢ الأصل: اعف. ٣ الأصل: الاعجائب. ٤ الأصل: مسلاط. ٥ الأضل: مسلاط.

this, summoned the scribe, and asked him, "Who ordered this man to be killed and his wealth impounded?" "You did," replied the scribe. "When?" he asked. The scribe said, "At such and such a time, so-and-so, your vizier, came to me and told me, 'Write to so-and-so, the *malik*, in such and such a place, that he should go to the tax collector so-and-so in such and such a place, cut off his head, send it on a spear, and send all his assets.'" "I never commanded you to do that," said the sultan, "so how could you, with all your intelligence and professionalism, write to him so without seeking my permission?" "God aid our master!" the man replied. "You summoned me on such and such a day and told me, 'Whenever this vizier of mine tells you, "Write to so-and-so" in my name, do so!' I have obeyed your command from that time on and gone ahead and written everything he ordered me to."

The sultan now grew angry and said, "I never ordered you to write whatever he asked on a matter as important as this! I commanded you to write what he asked in matters of no danger to the state. Do you imagine that things of this sort can happen without my permission?" And the scribe replied, "Our master made no exceptions when he commanded me to obey the vizier." The sultan grew angrier still and ordered that the scribe be seized, but no one could lay a hand on him, for every time someone stretched out a hand to seize him, it would go stiff, its owner unable to bend it, and it would be like a piece of wood. When the sultan saw this, he said to him, "Release these men!" but the scribe said, "I will release them only when the sultan releases me from his service." The sultan released the scribe from his service, and the scribe released the men in turn, and their hands relaxed and became as they had been. This demonstrates the truth of words of the Prophet, may God bless him and grant him peace, when he said, "All things fear the one who fears God, and he who has no fear of God, God will cause to fear all things." 4.45

Also to be numbered among such wonders is the story told by the people of Darfur to the effect that there are two tribes subject to the Fur, one called the Masālīṭ, the other the Tomorókkóngá,[261] who assume the shapes of animals. The best-known version of the story, though, is that the Masālīṭ take the shapes of hyenas, cats, and dogs, while the Tomorókkóngá take the form of lions only. Even more remarkably, they say that after three days a man of this tribe who dies will rise from his grave, go to another village, marry there, and live on for a time. The Darfurians commonly say that the sultan has a group of men from this tribe whom he sends on his personal business and that they have a 4.46

مهمّات أموره وأنّ لها ملكًا حاكمًا عليها ويبالغون في هذه الطائفة حتّى إنّهم يقولون إنّها تتشكّل بجميع أنواع التشكّلات حتّى الرجل منهم إذا ضاق عليه المجال وخاف من الضبط عليه يبقى ريحًا

٤،٤٧ ولقد أدركت حاكم هذه الطائفة وكان يسمّى عليّ كُرْتَب وكان رجلًا مسنًّا ضعيف الحركة من فقراء الجند لا يظهر عليه أثر الثروة ثمّ إنّه مات وولي ابنه مكانه وكان شابًّا جسيمًا وَخْش الخلقة لكن يظهر عليه أثر الثروة وكان يركب العتاق من الخيل وله خدم وأبّهة فانعقدت بيني وبينه صحبة وذهبت إلى داره عدّة مرار وكان يسمّى عبد الله كرتب فاتّفق أنّي خلوت به في بعض المرار وسألته عمّا تقول فيه الناس من التشكّل وأنّه يسافر مسيرة عشرة أيّام في برهة فشاغلني بكلام آخر ولم يفدني بشيء فتركته في ذلك الوقت وسألته ثانيًا في وقت آخر فتبسّم وقال سبحان الله ما كنت أظنّ أنّك تصدّق هذا القول ثمّ شاغلني بغير ذلك حتّى خرجت من عنده ثمّ أنكر معرفتي بعد ذلك وصار يمرّ عليّ ولا يلتفت لجهتي وتركته أنا أيضًا لما رأيت من تنكّره ولا أعلم لذلك سببًا سوى تكرار سؤاله في هذا الشأن

٤،٤٨ ولقد سافرت للغزو مع ملك من الملوك اسمه عبد الكريم بن خَمِيس عَرمان وكان أبوه من أعظم وزراء السلطان ونقم عليه وأبّد سجنه حتّى مات وصار ولده خادمًا للدولة حتّى أرسل للغزو في الفرتيت وكان لي عليه دين فذهبت معه لأستوفاه منه فتوغّلنا في بلاد الفرتيت مدّة ثلاثة أشهر وكنّا في محلّ لا يوجد فيه شيء من البقول ولا الخضراوات[١] فدعاني ذات يوم من الأيّام فلمّا دخلت عنده وجدت بصلًا أخضر وفقّوسًا وكلّ منهما كأنّما أخذ من مقثأته الآن فسألته عنهما ومن أين وصلا له فقال من دارفور فسألته عمّن أتى له بهما وكيف بقيا طريّين مع بعد المسافة سيّما الفقّوس فإنّه كان غضًّا بالكلّيّة فقال قد جيء بهما في أقلّ زمن وانظر إلى تاريخ هذا المكتوب فأخذت المكتوب منه ونظرت إليه فإذا هو من بعض أحبابه بدارفور وتاريخه

١ الأصل: الخضروات.

malik who rules them. They even go so far as to say of this group that they can assume any shape and that if one of them finds himself in a tight spot and is afraid he'll be captured, he turns into wind.

I was there when the man in charge of this group, who was called ʿAlī Kartab, was still alive. He was old and feeble, a poor soldier in whom it was almost impossible to detect any sign of wealth. Then he died, and his son took his place. He was a well-built young man, hideous to look at but giving every sign of being well-off. He rode the best-bred horses and had servants and pomp. He and I became friends and I went to his house several times. His name was ʿAbd Allāh Kartab, and I happened once to find myself alone with him, so I asked him about what people said about his assuming different shapes, and that he could travel a ten-day journey in an instant. He distracted me with talk of other things and gave me no information, so I didn't pursue the matter on that occasion. Then, on another occasion, I asked him again and he smiled and said, "Goodness gracious, I never thought you'd believe such talk!" Then he distracted me with talk of other things, till I left his house. After this, he denied knowing me and took to walking past me without turning to look in my direction, so I too left him alone once I saw how he snubbed me. I can think of no reason for it except that I'd questioned him repeatedly about this business. 4.47

Once I traveled in a slaving party with a petty king named ʿAbd al-Karīm ibn Khamīs ʿArmān. His father had been one of the sultan's greatest viziers but the sultan had turned against him and held him in prison till he died. His son became a servant of the state and was eventually sent to raid the Fartīt. He owed me a debt, so I went with him to get it out of him.[262] We had penetrated three months deep into Fartīt country and were in a place where no pulses or vegetables were to be found. One day he invited me to eat with him, so I went into his house and found green onions and cucumbers, each as fresh as if they had been pulled that minute from their bed. I asked about them and where they'd come from and he said, "Darfur." I asked him who'd brought them to him and how they'd stayed fresh in spite of the distance, especially the cucumbers, which were as juicy as could be. He said, "They were brought in the shortest possible time. Look at the date on this letter." So I took the letter and looked at it and found it was from a friend of his in Darfur, and that the date was the morning of that very day. I was astounded and showed my amazement that such a thing could be, and when he saw how surprised I was he said, 4.48

صبيحة ذلك اليوم فبهت وصرت متعجّبًا من ذلك فلمّا رأى عجبي[1] قال لي لا تعجب فإنّ معنا جماعة من التموركه وفيهم قوّة التشكّل يذهبون إلى أبعد محلّ في أقرب زمن فقلت أريد أن تريني أناسًا منهم فقال لك ذلك

٤،٤٩ ثمّ لمّا قفلنا نريد دارفور ووصلنا إليها بتنا بظاهر بلد من بلاد التموركه نسيت اسمها ولمّا كان عند الصباح جاءنا أناس كثيرون يسلّمون على الملك وأنا جالس معه فرحّب بهم وأكرمهم وكسا رؤساءهم ثيابًا حسنة ففرحوا بذلك ولمّا أردنا الرحيل قال رئيسهم إنّا نوصّيكم إن رأيتم في طريقكم سباعًا فلا تمسّوها بسوء لأنّ جميع ما ترونه من السباع في هذه الجهة منّا فقال الملك إذ ذاك نحن نريد أن نسمع من بعض أصحابك الآن فقال سمعًا وطاعة ثمّ ندب ثلاثة أنفار منهم سمّاهم فقاموا وتوجّهوا إلى الخلاء فغابوا قليلًا ثمّ سمعنا زئير أسد عظيم أزعج القلوب وأفزع الدوابّ فقالوا هذا صوت فلان ثمّ سكت وزأر أسد آخر يقرب منه ثلاث زأرات فقالوا هذا فلان ثمّ سكت وسمع بعد ذاك زئير أعظم من الزئيرين السابقين حتّى كادت أن تخلع القلوب لسماعه فقالوا هذا صوت فلان سمّوه وأعظموا أمره ثمّ بعد قليل جاءوا على هيئتهم الآدميّة وقبّلوا يد الملك ففرح بهم وأكرمهم وحينئذ كساهم ثيابًا فاخرة وودّعناهم وارتحلنا وحينئذ قال لي الملك هؤلاء الطائفة هم الذين أتونا بالبصل والفقّوس ونحن في آخر دار فرتيت انتهى

٤،٥٠ وممّا يلحق بهذه العجائب ما يقوله الرمّالون حين يضربون تخت الرمل لأنّهم يقولون كلامًا وقع للإنسان لا يعلم به أحد إلّا الله تعالى ويقولون على أمور تقع كأنّه يراها بعينه فممّا دعاني إلى صدق أقوالهم أنّي حين أردت الانتقال من دارفور والسفر إلى دار واداي كان في البلدة التي كنت فيها رجل يقال له سالم له صهر في بلد آخر يقال له إسحاق ماهر في علم الرمل وكنت ضيق الصدر لتعسّر أمور السفر عليّ فقال لي سالم المذكور هل لك في أن تتوجّه معي إلى صهري إسحاق يضرب لك الرمل ويقول

[1] الأصل: عجابي

"Don't be surprised. There's a party of Tomorókkóngá with us and they have the ability to change their shapes and go to the farthest place in the shortest time." I said, "I'd like you to show me some of them," and he said, "And so I will."

When we'd assembled our caravan and reached Darfur, we spent the night on the outskirts of a Tomorókkóngá village whose name I've forgotten. In the morning, crowds of people came to salute the *malik*, with whom I was sitting. He welcomed them, provided them with hospitality, and gave their leaders handsome robes, which pleased them greatly. When we wanted to depart, their chief said, "We advise you, if you see any lions on your way, to do them no harm, as any lions you may see in this neighborhood are from our village." "In that case," said the *malik*, "we'd like to hear from some of your friends right now." "To hear is to obey," said the chief, and he picked out three individuals by name, who rose and went off into the open country. A short while after they'd disappeared from sight, we heard a mighty lion's roar that struck terror into our hearts and panicked the riding animals. "That," they said, "is the voice of so-and-so." Then that lion stopped, and another lion close to the first roared three times. "That," they said, "is so-and-so." That stopped, and after it a roar was heard that was so much mightier than the first two that our hearts almost leaped from our breasts on hearing it. "That," they said, "is the voice of so-and-so," and they named him and sang his praises. A little later the men came back, in their human form, and kissed the *malik*'s hand. He was delighted with them, offered them food, and gave them fine robes to wear, and we bade them goodbye and went on our way. At this point the king told me, "Those are the people who brought us the onions and cucumbers when we were on the far side of Dār Fartīt." 4.49

To these wonders may be added the pronouncements of geomancers when they perform their operations, for they speak of events that have happened to a person of which no one but God Almighty knows anything and report things as though they were occurring before their very eyes. One of the things that has made me believe in what they say is that, when I wanted to leave Darfur and go to Dar Wādday, there was in the town where I was a man called Sālim. He had an in-law in another town called Isḥāq who was skilled at geomancy. I was depressed because my travel arrangements weren't going well, so Sālim asked me, "Would you like to go with me to see my in-law Isḥāq, and have him cast the sand for you and tell you what he sees?" I accompanied him to the 4.50

لك ما يظهر له فأجبته لذلك وتوجّهت معه لبلدة صهره المذكور فدخلناها ضحى فرأيناه غائباً في زرعه فصبرنا حتّى قدم فرحّب بنا وأكرمنا وأتى لنا بغداء[1] حسن ثمّ قال له صهره سالم إن الشريف قد جاء يلتمس منك أن تضرب له رملا فقال السمع والطاعة وضرب الرمل وقال لي كلاما كنت أكذّبه فيه فوالله لقد وقع جميع ما قاله وكأنّه تكلّم من اللوح المحفوظ لم يخطئ في كلمة فمن ذلك أنّه قال لي إنّك ستذهب إلى دار واداي عن قريب بجميع أهل بيتك ما عدا امرأة أبيك فإنّها لا تذهب معك وكنت أكذّبه وأقول كيف لا تذهب مع أنّها أحوج الناس للذهاب فصدّق الله قوله فلم تذهب معنا وعملت علينا حيلة وهي أنها بقيت معنا حتّى كانت ليلة الرحيل ففرّت وتركت ابنتها بنت سبع سنين فلمّا أصبحنا طلبناها فلم نجد لها أثرا وسافرنا ولم نستقرّ لها على خبر ومن ذلك أنّه قال لي ليلة قدومك على بيت أبيك يأتونك بجارية صفتها كذا وكذا فوقع كما قال ومنها أنّه قال لي لا تجتمع بأبيك في دار واداي فكان كذلك ولم أجتمع معه الّا في تونس ومنها أنّه قال لي إن بيت أبيك حيطانه حمر كأنّها طليت بمُغْرة فرأيتها كذلك والمغرة نوع حجر لونه أحمر هشّ يسحقونه ناعماً فيطلى به البيوت ويصنعون به أيضاً الحبر الأحمر يخلط مع الصمغ في الماء ومنها أنّه قال لي إنّك تركب هناك جواداً أخضر فكان كذلك وقال لي إنّ السلطان ينعم عليك بجوار وغيرها فكان كما ذكر

٥١،٤ ومن أعجب ما وقع حين كنّا عنده أن[2] جاءته نسوة يتخاصمن مع بعضهنّ ويردن[3] أن يضرب لهنّ رملاً يظهر به مالاً ضائعاً لتعلم كلّ منهنّ من أخذه فضرب الرمل وقال قد ضاع لكنّ خرز أحمر منظوم في خيط وهو مخبّأ في رِتاج البيت الفلانيّ فقامت امرأة وأتت به من الرتاج المذكور كما قال لكن لم يقل من الآخذة له منهنّ وله في خطّ الرمل باع طويل

٥٢،٤ ومن هذا القبيل ما حدّثني به عمّي السيّد أحمد زرّوق أنّ والدي عليه سحائب الرحمة والرضوان لمّا كان صحبة المرحوم السلطان محمّد صابون في محاربة جبل تاما[4]

---

١ الأصل: بغذاء. ٢ أضيف للسياق. ٣ الأصل: ويريدن. ٤ الأصل: تامه.

in-law's town, which we entered late in the morning, only to find that he wasn't there but working his farm. We waited until he returned, when he welcomed us as honored guests and brought us an excellent lunch. Then Sālim told him, "The sharif has come to ask you to divine for him." "To hear is to obey," said the man, and he performed his divination and told me things for which I called him a liar but which, I swear, came to pass—as though he'd been reading from the Preserved Tablet: not one word he said turned out to be untrue. Among the things he told me was, "You will soon go to Dār Wāddāy with all your family except your stepmother, who will not go with you." I called him a liar and said, "How can she not go when she's the one who most needs to?" but God made his words turn out true, and she didn't go with us: she played a trick, staying with us up to the last night before our departure, then running away, leaving her daughter who was seven years old. When we woke, we looked for her but could find no trace of her, so we left without knowing what had happened to her. Likewise, he told me, "On the night of your arrival at your father's house, they will bring you a slave girl with the following characteristics," and it turned out as he'd said. Also, he told me, "You will not meet up with your father in Dār Wādday," and so it was; I only met up with him in Tunis. He also told me, "The walls of your father's house are red, as though plastered with *mughrah*," which is a type of stone, red in color and crumbly, that they crush until smooth and use to plaster houses; they make red ink from it too, mixing it with water and gum. And he told me, "Your son will ride a gray horse there," and it came to pass, and "the sultan will bestow slave women and other things on you," and it was as he said.

One of the most remarkable things that occurred when we were at his house 4.51
was that some quarreling women came to him and asked him to divine in order for them to discover the whereabouts of some property that had gone missing, and so determine which of them had taken it. He performed his divination and said, "You've lost some red beads strung on a thread, and they're hidden in the entryway to so-and-so's house." Then one of the women got up and fetched the beads from the entryway of the house in question, as he had said, but he did not say which of them had taken them. He was extremely knowledgeable about geomancy.

My uncle, Sayyid Aḥmad Zarrūq, told me something similar, to wit that 4.52
when my father, clouds of mercy and favor hover above him, accompanied Sultan Muḥammad Ṣābūn on his campaign against Jabal Tāmah, he lost a

ضاع له جمل بازل وأرسل العبيد والخدم ليفتّشوا عليه فذهبوا وغابوا طويلاً ثمّ رجعوا بالخيبة فيئس المرحوم والدي منه وكان ممّن صحبه رجل يعرف خطّ الرمل فقال له بعض الحاضرين إنّك رجل رمّال فإن كنت عارفا بيّن لنا الجمل يأتي أم لا فضرب الخطّ وقال إن الجمل هاهنا غير بعيد فقوموا وانظروه في إبل جيراننا فذهبت العبيد إلى إبل الجيران فوجدوا الجمل باركًا في وسطها وعرفوه وجاءوا به إلى محلّه وهذه غاية الإتقان في علم الرمل

ومن هذا القبيل أيضاً ما حكى لي بعض الأشراف في دار واداي أنّ جماعة من ٥٣،٤
العلماء كانوا مجتمعين في محلّ وفيهم من يعرف علم الرمل معرفة خبير وفيهم من يدّعيه فتذاكروا في علم الرمل والذي يدّعيه يقول أنا ضربت الرمل لفلان الملك ولفلان القائد وأخبرتهما بكذا وكذا فطلب منه أحد الحاضرين أن يضرب له فضرب وقال كلاماً لا يُغْني شيئاً فالتفت العارف إلى الخطّ المضروب وتأمّله ثمّ قال إنّي مبشّرك أنّك في غد تقبض من السلطان ستّين رأس رقيق وكان الأمر كما قال

وإذ[1] انجرّ الكلام إلى علم الرمل فلنذكر منه نبذة يقف بها المتأمّل على ماهيّته ٥٤،٤
وأشكاله وأسمائه والأشكال السعيدة والنحسة والمتوسّطة فنقول أمّا أشكاله فهي ستّة عشر شكلاً أوّلها الطريق وصورته هكذا  وهي جيّدة لمن أراد السفر وأجود منها لمن يسأل عن قدوم الغائب ورديّة لمن كان مريضاً فإنّها تدلّ على طريقه للقبر

وثانيها الجماعة وصورتها هكذا  وهو شكل سعيد إلّا في المريض فإنّه يدلّ على اجتماع الناس لجنازته ٥٥،٤

وثالثها اللَحيان وصورته هكذا  وهو شكل سعيد في جميع الأحوال ٥٦،٤

ورابعها النكيس وصورته هكذا  وهو شكل نحس في جميع الأحوال إلّا في الحامل فإنّها تلد ذكرًا ٥٧،٤

١ الأصل: واذا.

nine-year-old camel and sent out slaves and servants to search for it. They left, were gone a long time, and in the end returned emptyhanded, so my late father gave up on it. One of his companions was a man who knew how to divine using geomancy. One of those present said to him, "You're a geomancer. If you know, show us whether the camel will return or not." The man performed his divinations and said, "The camel is right here, nearby. Go look for it among your neighbors' camels." They found the camel kneeling in the midst of the herd, identified it, and brought it to him. This represents the acme of perfection in the science of geomancy.

Similarly, a sharif in Wāddāy told me that a group of religious scholars were gathered somewhere, one of whom had an expert knowledge of geomancy while another claimed the same but falsely. They were swapping tales of their experiences with that science, and the one who merely pretended to have that knowledge said, "I divined for Malik So-and-so and army commander so-and-so and gave them information about such and such." One of the company asked him to divine for them, which he did, saying things that made no sense. Then the man who really knew turned to the shapes that had been formed and contemplated them. Eventually he said, "I have good news for you. Tomorrow you will receive sixty head of slaves from the sultan," and it was as he said. 4.53

As our talk has turned to geomancy, let me set out an epitome that will allow the observer to contemplate its nature, forms, and names, along with its patterns, be they auspicious, inauspicious, or neutral. Its patterns are sixteen in number, of which the first is "the Road," which looks like this:  This is excellent for one who intends to travel, even better for one who is asking about the arrival of one who is absent, and bad for one who is sick, in which case it indicates the road to the grave. 4.54

The second is "the Group," which looks like this:  This is an auspicious shape, except for a sick person, in which case it indicates people gathering at his funeral. 4.55

The third is "the Jawbone," which looks like this:  This pattern is auspicious in all cases. 4.56

The fourth is "the Upside Down," which looks like this:  This pattern is inauspicious in all cases except that of a pregnant woman, when it means she will give birth to a male. 4.57

وخامسها الاجتماع وصورته هكذا  وهو شكل سعيد في جميع الأعمال ٥٨،٤
إلّا في قبض الدراهم

وسادسها العُقْلة وصورته هكذا  وهو شكل نحس إلّا في السؤال عن ٥٩،٤
الحامل

وسابعها العتبة الداخلة وصورته هكذا  وهو شكل سعيد في جميع ٦٠،٤
الأحوال فمن كان أوّل خطّه هذا الشكل أو ثانيه إن كان مغموماً زال غمّه وإن
كان مترقّبا لمجيء غائب قدم عليه سريعاً وإن كان مُعْسِرًا زال عسره

وثامنها العتبة الخارجة وصورته هكذا  وهو شكل نحس يدلّ على موت ٦١،٤
المريض وتعطيل الحاجة واضطراب الأمور وطلاق الزوجة

وتاسعها القبض الداخل وصورته هكذا  وهو شكل ممتزج يدلّ على ٦٢،٤
قبض الدراهم والظفر بالعدوّ ولكنّه يدلّ على موت المريض وحبس المطلوب
للحاكم

وعاشرها القبض الخارج وصورته هكذا  وهو شكل يدلّ على عدم ٦٣،٤
رجوع ما خرج من اليد وذهاب الآبق وإباق الرقيق لكنّه يدلّ على الخلاص
من الحبس وعلى السفر والانتقال من مكان لآخر

وحادي عشرها البياض وصورته هكذا 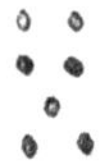 وهو شكل جيّد في كلّ الأحوال ٦٤،٤
إلّا في المريض فإنّه يدلّ على الكفن

وثاني عشرها الحمرة وصورته هكذا  وهو شكل يدلّ على إهراق ٦٥،٤
الدماء وعلى القبر للمريض لكنّه سعيد للحامل فإنّها تلد ذكرًا ويدلّ على الثياب
الحمر كما أنّ البياض يدلّ على الثياب البيض

The fifth is “the Gathering,” which looks like this:  This pattern is auspicious for all activities, except the collection of money. 4.58

The sixth is “the Knot,” which looks like this:  This is an inauspicious pattern unless the question posed concerns a pregnant woman. 4.59

The seventh is “the Incoming Threshold,” which looks like this:  This is an auspicious pattern in all cases. If one is sad and has this as the first or second pattern in his series, his sadness will vanish; if one is waiting for someone to come, he will come quickly; and if one is in hard straits, his difficulties will disappear. 4.60

The eighth is “the Outgoing Threshold,” which looks like this:  This is an inauspicious pattern indicating the death of one who is sick, postponement of the fulfillment of a need, disruption of one’s affairs, or the divorce of a wife. 4.61

The ninth is “the Incoming Fist,” which looks like this:  This is a mixed pattern that indicates collection of money and victory over one’s enemy, but also death of a sick person and imprisonment of someone wanted by the authorities. 4.62

The tenth is “the Outgoing Fist,” which looks like this:  This indicates the failure to return of what has previously left the hand, the disappearance of a runaway slave, and the flight of slaves, but it may also indicate release from imprisonment, travel, and removal from one place to another. 4.63

The eleventh is “Whiteness,” which looks like this:  This is a good pattern in all cases except for a sick person, in which case it indicates a shroud. 4.64

The twelfth is “Redness,” which looks like this:  This is a sign of the spilling of blood and, for a sick person, the grave, but it is auspicious for a pregnant woman as she will give birth to a male; it is also a sign of red garments, just as “whiteness” is a sign of white garments. 4.65

٦٦،٤ وثالث عشرها الجودلة وصورته هكذا  وهو شكل سعيد يدلّ على الفرح والسرور وأنّ الحامل تلد أنثى وأنّ الأمر يأتي على أحسن حال

٦٧،٤ ورابع عشرها نقيّ الخدّ وصورته هكذا  وهو شكل نحس ويدلّ على الشباب والعدوّ المجهول وطول المكث في الحبس وقبض روح المريض

٦٨،٤ وخامس عشرها النصرة الداخلة وصورته هكذا  وهو شكل سعيد يدلّ على النصر والظفر وقضاء الحاجة ونجاة المريض والمسجون والحامل

٦٩،٤ وسادس عشرها النصرة الخارجة وصورته هكذا  وهوشكل يدلّ على أمور حميدة إلّا في محاربة العدوّ فإنّه يدلّ على انهزام الجيش

٧٠،٤ فإذا أراد الإنسان أن يضرب الرمل المذكور يأتي برمل نظيف نقيّ ويبسطه على الأرض ثمّ ينقّط فيه بالإصبع الوسطى أربعة أسطر من غير عدد بالأسطر من اليسار إلى اليمين هكذا  ثمّ يتتبّعه زوجاً فزوجاً حتّى ينتهي إلى الآخر فإن كان الآخر زوجاً أثبته وإن بقي فرداً أثبته فيثبت ما تحصّل من السطر الأوّل أوّلاً وما تحصّل من الثاني تحته وهكذا حتّى تتمّ الأربعة أسطر فيتحصّل منها شكل من الأشكال الستّة عشر المتقدّمة ومن لم يجد رملاً ضرب الخطّ بفول أو حمّص وهو إنّه يأخذ قبضة من غير عدد ويسقطها زوجاً زوجاً ويثبت الأخير إن كان زوجاً أو فرداً

٧١،٤ وأمّا تولّدات أشكاله واتّصالاتها وما يتعلّق بها من الأسماء والحروف والكواكب والعاقبة وعاقبة العاقبة فذلك كلّه منوط بمؤلّفات علم الرمل فلا نطيل الكلام عليها

The thirteenth is "the Bed," which looks like this:  This is an auspi- 4.66
cious pattern that points to joy and happiness, that a pregnant woman will give birth to a female, and that things will turn out in the best possible way.

The fourteenth is "Pure of Cheek," and looks like this:  This is an 4.67
inauspicious pattern that is a sign of young men, unknown enemies, long imprisonment, and an invalid giving up the ghost.

The fifteenth is "Incoming Support," and looks like this:  This is an aus- 4.68
picious pattern that is a sign of support from God, victory, fulfillment of a need, and an end to suffering for the sick, the imprisoned, and the pregnant.

The sixteenth is "Outgoing Support," and looks like this:  This pat- 4.69
tern is a sign of benign matters, except where battling one's enemy is concerned, when it is a sign of the defeat of armies and failure to achieve victory.

If someone wants to "cast the sand" in the manner described above, he 4.70
fetches clean sand free of rocks and spreads it on the ground. Then, using his middle finger, he makes four rows of holes in the sand without counting the number of holes in each row and going from left to right, so that it looks like this:  Then he moves his finger along the row, going from each pair to the next, erasing every second hole until he gets to the end of the row. If the last hole is the second of a pair, he leaves it in place, and, likewise, if a single hole, he leaves it in place. Then he writes down first the total number of holes resulting from the application of this procedure to the first row, and below it the result for the second row. He continues doing this until all four rows have been so treated. From this procedure one or other of the sixteen preceding patterns will result. If he cannot find sand, he may cast the line using beans or chickpeas. He does this by taking a fistful without counting, dropping the beans or chickpeas, and moving through them two by two, leaving the last in place, whether it be a single bean or the second of a pair, as described above.[263]

As to the means of generating the different patterns and their interconnec- 4.71
tions, the names, letters, planets, and outcomes, and the outcomes of outcomes that are associated with each, these all depend on the books written on the science of geomancy, so we will not speak of them at greater length. We have provided this brief epitome so that any who peruses this travel

وإنّما ذكرنا هذه النبذة اليسيرة ليكون للناظر في رحلتنا هذه إلمام بماهيّة الرمل في الجملة ولئلاّ تخلو هذه الرحلة عن مثل هذه الفائدة والله عالم

narrative of ours may be well informed as to the nature of geomancy as a whole, and so that the work not be devoid of this useful information, though God knows best.

وقـد طبع بالحجر هذه النسخة الجليلة المنمّقة الجميلة بدار طباعة السـيّد كَيـپْلَيْنْ ١٠٥
الفاخرة الكائنة بمدينة باريز الباهرة وذلك بـرسم وخطّ السـيّد پَيْرُونْ
بنـعمة الله وعونه وكمـل طبعه على ذمّته ونظره وهمّته في سلخ شهر نونبـر
سـنة خمسين وثمانمائة بعد الألف المسيحـيّة
والحـمد لله في البدء والنهاية ونسأله من الخير بلوغ الغايـة

آمـين

Colophon

This beautiful, elegant, weighty copy was printed as a lithograph at the deluxe printing house of Monsieur Kaeplin,[264] in the dazzling city of Paris, using, through God's grace and boon, the hand and penmanship of Monsieur Perron. Production was completed—at his expense, under his supervision, and as a result of his zeal—at the end of the month of November of the year 1850 of the Christian era. Thanks are due to God at commencement and completion, and we beseech Him to grant us His most perfect benediction. 5.1

Amen.

Notes

1 The term "kings" as used here is ambiguous, referring on some occasions to the sultans of Darfur and on others to its "petty kings," i.e., the tribal and clan chieftains (see further, translator's note in volume one).

2 A form of Wāddāy (Wadai); see §3.1.2 below.

3 According to Nachtigal's editors, the term had acquired by his day "a curiously wide currency in the Middle East, where it was popularly applied to . . . the western, and sometimes also the central, Sudan" (*Sahara and Sudan*, 4:233, n. 1); by Sudan, the editors mean here the Sudanic belt of countries (see Introduction, p. xxvii), not the modern state of that name. Umar attributes this broader use to the fact that its inhabitants were the first West Africans to make the pilgrimage to Mecca (*Travels*, 209, n. 1). For more on the term, see al-Naqar, "Takrur."

4 I.e., the easternmost.

5 A Tunjūr state existed in Darfur and Wadai in the sixteenth century; however, the relationship of the Tunjūr state to the Keira state that superseded it lies, as O'Fahey puts it, "tantalisingly beyond our ken" (O'Fahey, *Darfur Sultanate*, 25; see also more generally 24–33).

6 On the identification of the Fullān as Arabs, see §2.2.29 and vol. 1, n. 150.

7 The trajectory outlined here, which can be followed on the author's map of Darfur (§3.1.12, images), runs north-northwest to south-southeast, rather than simply north to south, which explains why it ends at "the eastern limits of the Fur." A major inaccuracy in the map is that it places Rīl northwest of Jadīd Rās al-Fīl, whereas in reality it lies southwest of it.

8 Arabic *al-Ṣaʿīd*, a term also used in Egypt, where it applies to the Nile Valley from Cairo south to Nubia (i.e., Upper Egypt).

9 The title ába dimaʾng appears to predate the Keira dynasty and to be associated with the Konyunga, "the most powerful of the Fur clans after the Keira . . . according to one tradition the *takanawi*s were chamberlains to the [Keira] sultans at Turra" (O'Fahey, *Darfur Sultanate*, 118).

10 Perhaps meaning that the *dārawiyyah* are so called because they trace their origin to some *dār* (tribal territory) elsewhere.

11 Perron writes: "The shaykh had no idea of what a map was. He simply placed the localities relative to one another and not in such a way as to show the distances as one would measure them on a geographical scale. The shaykh's long stay in Darfur, as well as his intelligence, allow us to accept his information as accurate and preferable to that derived from the accounts of European travelers. None of the latter was able, as he was, to roam through the country in all directions or explore it as thoroughly" (El-Tounsy, *Voyage au Darfour*, 135, n. 2). Despite this, the map contains some major errors. To name but one, Dār Ába Umá appears in the map to the west of Jabal Marrah whereas in fact it lay to its southeast, around today's Kas (personal communication from R. S. O'Fahey).

12 The episode is recounted not in this book but in the author's account of his time in Wadai (see El-Tounsy, *Voyage au Ouadây*, chapter eight).

13 For the author's systematic presentation of the hierarchy of officeholders of the Darfurian state, see below §§3.1.50 ff., and for O'Fahey's critique of this, see n. 53.

14 Given in other sources as *abbo uumo*, which is said to mean "Lord of the Fontanelle" in Fur—despite the author's later characterization of this official as being, in military terms, "the sultan's spine"—see O'Fahey, *Darfur Sultanate*, 177–78.

15 On the association of certain titles with parts of the sultan's body, see §§3.1.50 ff. below.

16 All these places were at some time *fāshirs*, or royal compounds.

17 O'Fahey writes: "Both within and on the margins of the provinces a number of tribes, or more accurately tribal territories, preserved their identity and a degree of administrative autonomy" (*Darfur Sultanate*, 181).

18 "the Dunes" (*al-qawz*): an area of stabilized dunes with poor, light, but cultivable soil in the open wooded country that stretches from the Jabal Marrah range eastward into Kordofan (see O'Fahey, *Darfur Sultanate*, 4).

19 "saint" (*walī Allāh*): literally "a ward of God," meaning a person who enjoys God's special favor and to whom He often grants the power to perform miracles; in the literature on Sufism, the term is sometimes rendered "friend of God."

20 According to informants, *tómbol* is the generic word for "drum" in Fur.

21 I.e., Europeans.

22 It is not obvious what the author means by this. The same sentence (*wa-ammā lughatuhum fa-hiya lughatun fī-hā ḥamās*) was listed, along with other faux pas, by Aḥmad Fāris al-Shidyāq as an example of the pernicious influence of Nicholas Perron on the text (al-Shidyāq, *Leg*, 4:443, see Note on the Text, pp. xxxiii–xxxiv). Grammar, however, cannot be the issue, as the sentence is grammatically correct. Perhaps al-Shidyāq thought that this was an unsophisticated or absurd way to describe a language.

23 *kéla* means "we come"; "come!" is *béla*.

24 The author's memory may have betrayed him: according to informants, *murtá'ng* means "horse" while *yáa* means "mother of" but is not used of animals.

25 In fact, the Turkish for "he came" is *gitti*, with a hard *g*; perhaps the author assumes that because in Darfurian (and generally in Sudanese) Arabic the soft *g* replaces the hard *g* of Egyptian Arabic, the two phonemes are equivalent.

26 The French translator transcribes these as *saba*, *temâny*, *tiçâh*, presumably to represent how the Fur pronounced them.

27 Thus eleven is *wayye na tog*, and twenty *wayyenga aw* (*wayyenga* being the plural of *wayye*).

28 Cf. Q Rūm 30:23; 30:22.

29 Cf. Q Māʾidah 5:48.

30 I.e., the sultan may not be questioned as to the wisdom of his commands but a simple plea by one person on behalf of another may be entertained.

31 See §2.3.5.

32 "Grandmothers" (*ḥabbūbāt*): the word, if taken to be Arabic (plausible given its form), might be interpreted as "the Beloveds." However, Nachtigal asserts that the word (which he spells differently) means "grandmother" and implies that it derives from the Fur title *abo* and refers to "widows or aged relations of the royal house, whose land was exempt from all taxes and dues" (Nachtigal, *Sahara and Sudan*, 4:326, also n. 2). Nachtigal's glossary describes the complex usage of the word in Darfur and Wadai (*Sahara and Sudan*, 4:408).

33 Though the author uses the word *kurbāj*, which usually means a leather whip, to describe these, they must be the same as the "royal throwing irons . . . carried before the king on public processions" described by Nachtigal, which likewise were struck against one another and flourished (*Sahara and Sudan*, 4:337). O'Fahey describes "throwing knives" (*sambal*) as being "the wartime version of the common wooden hunting-stick (*safarog* or *dorma*) [for which see §2.3.8] . . . shaped like a large question mark, with sharpened edges and wings to ensure straight flight . . . carried three or four at a time in a holster and . . . a formidable weapon, [though requiring] great skill to be effective" (*Darfur Sultanate*, 194).

34 The liquid may have been wheat soaked in water and boiled (Arabic: *balīlah*) (see O'Fahey, *Darfur Sultanate*, 93, n. 26).

35 Literally "the House of Copper" (*dār al-nuḥās*).

36 Copper kettledrums were "the paramount symbol of autonomous authority throughout Darfur and beyond" (O'Fahey, *Darfur Sultanate*, 183). The sacred drums of the Keira dynasty numbered seven, some of which were regarded as male, others as female. The smallest but most sacred was that called the Victorious (al-Manṣūrah), mentioned

in what follows; others were the White and the Liar. The drums served "as a rallying point in time of war and the ultimate symbol of legitimacy" (O'Fahey, *Darfur Sultanate*, 183).

37 The Arabic translation is more or less word by word; the meaning is "So-and-so's hands are [i.e., So-and-so is] outside and humbly greet[s] you": *falān* in Perron's transliteration is equal to *fulān* (Arabic: "so-and-so").

38 The Fur does not include "even their followers and their servants."

39 See §2.2.44.

40 See §3.1.67 and §§3.1.71–75.

41 *dónga dáíng sīdī*: "(They give you) the hands, my lord." This is how the phrase is understood by modern informants; Perron may have misunderstood, since the speaker is the sultan and not the petitioner; cf. n. 37.

42 According to Nachtigal, if the sultan responded directly to a greeting, he did so "without opening his mouth with a faint drawling 'hm', or at most replied with a scarcely audible low *afia*, good health" (*Sahara and Sudan*, 4:327).

43 The festival probably took place in February or March (O'Fahey, *Darfur Sultanate*, 94, n. 29).

44 According to other sources, what follows constituted a separate feast, called the kundanga (meaning "human liver," on the significance of which see below), held three days after the drum festival, and the flesh eaten was that of a specially slaughtered wether rather than that of the bulls used to make skins for the drums. "If the 'covering of the drums' was a public affirmation of royal power in its eminent symbol, the drums, the kundanga feast was a direct and fearsome affirmation by the Keira clan of loyalty to the ruler, a kind of trial by ordeal" (O'Fahey, *Darfur Sultanate*, 95–96).

45 O'Fahey notes that evidence for human sacrifice at the drum festival is "contradictory and inconclusive," with some sources claiming that it was abolished by Sultan Sulaymān Solongdungo, the dynasty's founding father, others that it survived as late as Sultan Muḥammad al-Ḥusayn (r. 1838–73) (*Darfur Sultanate*, 96 and 96, n. 37).

46 "Mantle!" (*burnus*): the French translator understands this to mean "Protector [of the nations]!" (El-Tounsy, *Voyage au Darfour*, 168). The sultans of Bornu wore richly decorated burnooses (Nachtigal, *Sahara and Sudan*, 3:119), which suggests that the mantle was a symbol of authority elsewhere in Sudanic Africa.

47 "Breaker and scatterer of the unlevied mountains" (*firtāk al-jibāl bi-lā dīwān*): The meaning is uncertain. The word *firtāk* may be related to *fartaq* "to cut something up into tiny pieces and scatter them" (Qāsim, *Qāmūs*, art. *fartaq*). By "unlevied mountains" presumably are meant mountains whose tribes did not pay the four-yearly tribute referred

to by Nachtigal (*Sahara and Sudan*, 4:359), i.e., tribes living beyond the reach of any authority.

48 See §3.1.38.

49 Also *dilí*, according to informants. The tree is said to be important, particularly in places where rainfall is scarce, as it holds a huge quantity of water in the roots; it has not been identified.

50 Nachtigal also describes "the great drum festival," adding details not mentioned by the author, including many relating to its pagan origins (*Sahara and Sudan*, 4:338–40); for a description of this and other royal rituals that incorporates all available accounts, see O'Fahey, *Darfur Sultanate*, 92–99.

51 This "first sowing" started three days in advance of the great drum festival.

52 In the original, this section is titled "On the Offices Held by the Kings of the Fur and Their Garments and the Functioning of the Sultan's Court and So On"; however, the present section in fact deals only with offices, while the descriptions of the functioning of the sultan's court and the garments of the kings of the Fur are allocated their own sections (§§3.1.77–92 and §§3.1.93–96, respectively). The title has therefore been amended here and the sections on the court and on clothing have been given their own headings.

53 Many of the holders of the various titles listed in what follows held their offices by virtue of descent: "The Fur had come down from the mountains under a line of warrior sultans. In the course of their expansion, the lineage chiefs, ritual experts and war leaders . . . had grown into a class of hereditary title-holders" (O'Fahey, *Darfur Sultanate*, 47).

54 Elsewhere (§3.1.14) the Sultan's Face; as the author is the only source for these associations of officials with parts of the sultan's body, it is not possible to say which is correct.

55 According to Fur informants, the author is mistaken: ába poor-ii is simply an honoric title that might be given to anyone in power; "Father of the Fur" is poora'ng ába.

56 Nachtigal describes the kaamíne as "the king's shadow" (*Sahara and Sudan*, 4:326–27). He adds: "Despite his lofty title, in actual importance the *kamene* stood third in the royal household, definitely inferior to the [shaykh-father], and facetious people there called him 'the cow's vagina'. . . corresponding rather to our 'neither fish nor fowl'" (*Sahara and Sudan*, 4:328). O'Fahey characterizes *kaamíne* as a ritual title from the remote past (*Darfur Sultanate*, 113).

57 On this office, see also §3.1.9 and following paragraphs.

58 Apparently from Fur *dunggú*. The *dinqār* was made of wood (see §3.1.39); no Fur chief could possess a copper drum, for that was the exclusive prerogative of the Keira sultans, though the sultan might grant that right to a non-Fur vassal (see O'Fahey, *Darfur Sultanate*, 184).

59 On this office, see also §3.1.9 and §§3.1.11–12.

60 See, e.g., §2.2.29.

61 See also §2.2.43. Nachtigal describes the counselors as the king's confidential advisors (*Sahara and Sudan*, 4:330, 403).

62 See also §2.2.43 and Glossary.

63 "the chief of": missing in the Arabic. The French translation has "Après le soum-in-dogolah viennent les chefs kôrkoa" (El-Tounsy, *Voyage au Darfour*, 174).

64 Presumably the full title was "master of the órré bayyâ," in parallel with the "master of the órré dee" mentioned below.

65 The sultan received a regular flow of slaves as tribute (and to ensure protection from raids) from the non-Muslim Fartīt tribes, as he did from war and from raiding by his subjects, one tenth of those captured being paid to him as a tax (see further O'Fahey, *Darfur Sultanate*, 208–12).

66 According to Perron, the word originally meant "a bracelet worn above the elbow" (El-Tounsy, *Voyage au Darfour*, 176, n. 1); it probably derives from Arabic *dumlaj* "upper arm."

67 See §3.1.15.

68 Nachtigal states that "The taxes which these people had to pay consisted chiefly of tribute in the form of corn and cattle, property tax, customs dues and the so-called *diwan*," the latter being a levy imposed every four years "according to the occupations of the tribes and the yield of the regions" (*Sahara and Sudan*, 4:358–59).

69 These words, though printed in the original as prose, form a hemistich in *basīṭ* meter.

70 Browne gives the following description of what appears to be a *mooge* at a royal ceremony: "A kind of hired encomiast stood on the monarch's left hand, crying out, *à plein gorge*, during the whole ceremony, 'See the bufalloe . . . the offspring of the buffaloe, a bull of bulls, the elephant of superior strength, the powerful Sultan Abd-el-rachmân-el-rachîd! May God prolong thy life!—O Master—May God assist thee, and render thee victorious!'" (*Travels in Africa*, 213–14).

71 §3.1.59.

72 §3.1.38.

73 In standard Arabic, *khādim* means "male servant"; in Darfur, however, it means "female slave or concubine" (O'Fahey, "Slavery," 84).

74 Meaning that she had given birth to her daughter, and her daughter had given birth to the sultan. See also §2.3.4.

75 See n. 52.

76 See §2.2.30.

77 O'Fahey points out that the sultan's residence "was the Fur household writ large; the male and female entrance, the layout of the huts, the *diwan*s or places of audience, the messes . . . where men ate communally—all were features common to royal palace and prosperous households alike" (*Darfur Sultanate*, 101).

78 "Thin canes" (see Glossary). When the author speaks, here and elsewhere (e.g., §3.1.86), of "construction," he apparently has in mind specifically the roofing material used. Both Browne (*Travels in Africa*, 286) and Nachtigal (*Sahara and Sudan*, 4:260) state that the walls were made of clay, covered in the case of the homes of the better off by white, red, or black plaster (Browne, same reference), while modern sources specify that *marhabayb* is a roofing material (see, e.g., Tully, *Culture and Context*, 93–94).

79 According to Perron, on the author's authority, the *liqdābah* or *rākūbah* was an open-sided structure; if walled, e.g., with canes, it was called a *karabābah* (El-Tounsy, *Voyage au Darfour*, 186, n. 1).

80 Qāsim, *Qāmūs* (sg. *mutraq*): "light stick from a recently cut branch."

81 See §3.1.41, images.

82 Perron elaborates: "When the audience is during the day, the sultan sometimes remains mounted throughout, which is to say for perhaps one or two hours. He has for this purpose horses trained to remain perfectly still and accustomed to doing so" (El-Tounsy, *Voyage au Darfour*, 190).

83 See §3.1.40.

84 The author apparently intended to deal with construction in Wadai in greater detail later (see El-Tounsy, *Voyage au Darfour*, 192, n. 1) but the passage has not been identified in the *Voyage au Ouadây*.

85 The *Voyage au Ouadây* states that the sultan "sits for this purpose [i.e., that of holding public audience] in a room that looks out over the public square of the *fāshir*" (El-Tounsy, *Voyage au Ouadây*, 365).

86 Arabic: *ʿaqadah*. See El-Tounsy, *Voyage au Darfour*, 192, and *Voyage au Ouadây*, 365.

87 See El-Tounsy, *Voyage au Ouadây*, 366.

88 Meaning that they make their roofs with millet stalks, see §3.1.78.

89 Thus, the homestead as a whole is surrounded by an outer fence of thorny branches (*zarībah*); inside are the houses, or huts (*buyūt*), which are roofed with millet stalks and each of which is surrounded by an inner fence that serves as a dust-break (*ṣarīf*). A later reference (§4.20) indicates that subsidiary *zarībah*s for animals, here meaning circular pens fenced with branches, might be located within the larger enclosed space.

90 The significance of this addition is unclear, given that the author has already used the term *bayt* (pl. *buyūt*) to designate houses in general. It has no equivalent in the French translation.

91 According to Nachtigal, the royal dwelling "was enclosed only by a straw fence, with a thick, high, broad thorn hedge inside. This formed an oval with the longer axis running from northeast to southwest, and it took at least a quarter of an hour to go round it" (*Sahara and Sudan*, 4:261).

92 From "of the inner fence" to "millers" is absent from the Arabic and has been supplied from the French translation (El-Tounsy, *Voyage au Darfour*, 200–1). That an equivalent passage was part of the original is evidenced by the abruptness with which the sentence stops in the lithographed edition and the absence there of the expected description of the sultan's quarters. In addition, the occurrence of the phrase "as I have said" indicates that this passage in the French is not simply an elaboration of Perron's.

93 See n. 52.

94 Umar states (*Travels*, 306, n. 1) that this consisted of a copy of the Qur'an, which presumably was kept in a gilt holder or had gilt covers.

95 Lane describes the early nineteenth-century Egyptian *milā'ah* (*milāyeh* in his transcription) as "a kind of blue and white plaid" which the men "throw . . . over the shoulders, or wrap . . . about the body" (Lane, *Manners and Customs*, 32, n. 5).

96 "a couple of inches" (*qīrāṭān*): the term *qīrāṭ* (from which English "carat") is not commonly applied to cloth. Its basic sense is "one twenty-fourth part," so what is meant here may be two twenty-fourths of a pik (Arabic: *dhirāʿ*, otherwise "cubit"), a measurement of length used in the eastern Mediterranean that varied from country to country. In 1885, the Egyptian pik was equal to 26.37 inches (Baedecker, *Egypt*, 28).

97 Perron describes the *durrāʿah* as "a piece of white cloth that the Negresses place over their breasts, passing it under the armpits, tying it almost like a belt, and throwing the loose end over their left shoulder. The same piece of cloth also serves them as a cover for the body, at least to the knees" (El-Tounsy, *Voyage au Darfour*, 258, n. 1).

98 *ʿaqīq* in fact means "agate."

99 *dam-l-raʿāf* ("blood from the nose"): this voweling, specified in the lithograph edition (al-Tūnisī, *Tashḥīdh* 1850, 192), rather than the standard *dam al-ruʿāf*, may be intended to represent the Fur pronunciation, which is given in the French translation as "dengueraf" (El-Tounsy, *Voyage au Darfour*, 208, n. 3).

100 *Erythrina abyssinica*, sometimes called "lucky bean tree."

101 The author may have added this qualifier in the belief that his Egyptian readers would be more familiar with the common (fava) bean (*fūl*), which is green when fresh, brown when cooked.

102 Writing in 1937, A. J. Arkell states that such waist beads "are quite out of fashion and the younger generation will have nothing to do with them, occasionally referring to them with contempt as the jewellery of slaves" (Arkell, "Hebron Beads," 300); by that time,

all such beads had come to be known in Darfur as *manjūr* (see below) (same reference, 302).

103 Meaning "tranquil noontime sleep," implying, according to Umar, that the women who wear them "could afford to sleep most of the day without doing any housework" (*Travels*, 315, n. 1).

104 Perhaps meaning "squared off" or "chipped, nicked" (Dozy, *Supplément*); however, Arkell believes the word may have an Indian origin ("Hebron Beads," 300, n. 1). Today in Egypt, the *manjūr* is a broad leather belt to which goat's hooves have been attached that is worn by one of the musicians involved in the exorcism ceremony known as the *zār*; by shaking his waist, he produces a sound like that of maracas.

105 Perhaps meaning "crude, rough to the touch" (Qāsim, *Qāmūs*; Dozy, *Supplément*).

106 On the history of Hebron, or al-Khalīl, as a beadmaking center, see Francis, "Beadmaking in Islam."

107 From the Arabic root *kh-d-r*, related to concealment. Nachtigal writes, referring to Wadai, that they are "used as women's ornaments, worn under their clothing around the waist" (*Sahara and Sudan*, 4:201).

108 See §3.1.100.

109 Browne lists "brass wire" among the goods regularly imported to Darfur from Egypt (*Travels in Africa*, 303).

110 Specifically, *Artemisia arborescens*.

111 From the civet cat (Qāsim, *Qāmūs*); civet, as an ingredient in perfumes, is in fact taken from the perineal gland, rather than the skin, of the animal..

112 Perhaps the same as *dāyūk*, a name applying to "*Solanum spp.*" (Vogt, *Murshid*, 278).

113 The French translation explains that by "brother" the man means lover and that the lover does this "as a way of consoling himself" (El-Tounsy, *Voyage au Darfour*, 212).

114 The words are colloquial (hence the author's explanation) and mean "Girl, why is your head as ugly as that hut?"

115 "Where's that hut that's as ugly as my head?"

116 The text says, "If they knew they were strangers." Perron's translation understands this to mean the above (El-Tounsy, *Voyage au Darfour*, 215).

117 Q Baqarah 2:255.

118 Cf. Q Jinn 72:3 but also Isrā' 17:111.

119 Q Isrā' 17:111.

120 Q Ikhlāṣ 112:4.

121 Q Ṣād 38:26.

122 Perron states, presumably on the authority of the author, that Muslims believe that Adam was allowed to sleep only lightly so that he would be aware of the extraction of

Eve from his rib cage, be conscious that she was flesh of his flesh, and therefore love her more (El-Tounsy, *Voyage au Darfour*, 222, n. 1).

123 The wording mimics that used at marriage ceremonies.

124 See §3.1.113.

125 Literally "Mother Nightingale." Perron says that it is made of sprouted barley and is a fizzy wine "like champagne and very intoxicating" (El-Tounsy, *Voyage au Darfour*, 426–27).

126 The Birqid were a people living in southeastern Darfur. They rebelled under Sultan Muḥammad Tayrāb and were brought more firmly under Darfurian rule (O'Fahey, *Darfur Sultanate*, 51–52). It may be that the singer sought to flatter the author by associating him with this (by then long past) incident.

127 Barley beer (also sometimes *būẓah*).

128 A viscous cold drink of slightly fermented rice, sugar, and water that is not considered alcoholic.

129 Despite having originally made it clear that the dancers are *young* men and women (*shubbān, shābbāt*), the author proceeds, in the Arabic, to refer to them frequently throughout the rest of the section as "men" (*rijāl*) and "women" (*nisā'*). In the translation, the dancers are referred to as "boys" and "girls" throughout, for clarity.

130 Presumably because of its association with the drums of the same name; see §3.2.5.

131 Described as "a sound in the chest like the sound made by one who is being throttled or is making a great effort" (Qāsim, *Qāmūs*).

132 According to Perron, the author glossed the verse as follows: "The night passes and leaves. O my love, my treasure, you who are as dear to me as a gold piece, come, for my head is spinning with sleep; come sleep with me" (my translation). The *mutqāl* referred to in the Arabic is explained by Perron, on the same authority, as meaning "a piece of gold, or a weight used mainly to weigh gold" (El-Tounsy, *Voyage au Darfour*, 429).

133 According to Perron, the author glossed the verse as follows: "By Darfur is meant the world. For the Darfurians, Darfur is the universe . . . [*jafah*] means 'without happiness, without love' . . . [*nawā*] means 'wanting' (to sleep), meaning 'My head has need of sleep; come with me'" (my translation) (El-Tounsy, *Voyage au Darfour*, 429).

134 According to Perron, the author glossed the verse as follows: "O you whom I love, you lean toward us like a flexible branch, love sweeps us away and you make us sigh for you. You love me, you prefer me to the other girls of the village and by so doing excite their jealousy of me and attract their vengeance because they believe that you must have disparaged them to me. O you whose love reminds me of the scent of sandalwood, you grow like its sweet-smelling branches and you lean over our dwelling places to cast your shade over them (meaning, to stay with us forever). With you, happiness will also

always be here" (my translation) (El-Tounsy, *Voyage au Darfour*, 429–30). The unusual spellings *furaya*ʿ/*furay*ʿ*ā* in the Arabic may point to a Fur word that the author did not understand, perhaps *periya*, "a kind of spice cut from the twig of a tree" (informants).

135 I.e., Muḥammad *Daldan* wad Binayyah (see Glossary).

136 According to Perron, the author glossed the verse as follows: "Young Darfurians, go with brave Daldang to seek rich booty and become wealthy. Run, catch up with him! His horsemen are still at Karyū!" (my translation). Perron notes that Daldang, son of Binayyah, a princess, raided the Fartīt during the reign of Sultan Muḥammad Faḍl and returned with vast booty in the form of slaves, occasioning the composition of these lines (El-Tounsy, *Voyage au Darfour*, 430). He also notes that the "riches" are to be used by the young men to pay dowries (El-Tounsy, *Voyage au Darfour*, 233). O'Fahey regards Daldan as a typical *fāris*, or professional warrior imbued with a chivalric ethos fighting for booty, a figure common in eastern Sudanic Africa during this period (*Darfur Sultanate*, 121).

137 The translation of this song, which is entirely in Fur, goes (from Perron's French), "Children of Báási Ṭāhir, You and your father, You swore on the Qur'an, But in Kūbayh you've set, Treachery's foot by breaching its walls" (my translation) (El-Tounsy, *Voyage au Darfour*, 233–34, 431). Perron points out that the song is hardly appropriate for a wedding and is sung simply to allow people to dance.

138 See §3.2.7.

139 "The Fur compare their chiefs, their parents and their wives' parents to the sun [for] 'You cannot look them in the face'" (O'Fahey, *Darfur Sultanate*, 176). The author has already touched on this custom above (§3.1.113).

140 The expected form would be *warāniyyah*, but both *Tashḥīdh* 1850 and 1965 write it as given above. The word does not occur in Qāsim's dictionary of Sudanese Arabic.

141 "to protect him, oho" (*farajābā*): according to Perron, on the authority of the author, the word *farājābā* ("to protect him") in the Arabic text consists of *farāj*, meaning "as protection," plus the meaningless syllables *-ābā*, added to fill out the line and provide the rhyme (El-Tounsy, *Voyage au Darfour*, 434).

142 *Allāh ḥayy*, a chant used in *dhikr*.

143 See §3.2.9.

144 The first line uses the Fur forms for the names Gabriel and Michael but the second line appears to be Arabic.

145 This translation follows Perron's, which reads, "Filles de dieu, ô filles de dieu!" (El-Tounsy, *Voyage au Darfour*, 249); presumably the women singers are referring to themselves.

146 According to Perron, on the author's authority, the fasting month of Ramadan is described as God's remedy because during it "God cures souls of their faults, or corrects the defects in men" (El-Tounsy, *Voyage au Darfour*, 437).

147 According to legend, Qābīl and Hābīl (Cain and Abel) each had twin sisters, Aqlīmā and Labūdā (thus elsewhere for the second, though the name given here is Dhamīmā), each destined to be the bride of the other. Qābīl, wanting to marry his own twin, agreed to let the matter be settled by God but, when God's judgment went against him, he murdered Hābīl and married his twin (*EI2*, G. Vajda, art. *Hābīl wa-Ḳābīl*).

148 Q Mā'idah 5:27–32.

149 "his cheeks": Arabic poetic convention addresses the beloved using masculine grammatical forms, regardless of the actual gender of the addressee.

150 Attributed by Yāqūt al-Ḥamawī to Ḥafṣah bint al-Ḥājj al-Rakūniyyah (ca. 530–89/1135–91), a poet and princess of Granada, and by others to another aristocratic Andalusian poet, Walladah bint al-Mustakfī (d. ca. 484/1091), daughter of the Umayyad caliph al-Mustakfī bi-llāh.

151 By the Egyptian poet Yaḥyā ibn ʿĪsā ibn Maṭrūḥ (592–649/1196–1251), also known as Jamāl al-Dīn.

152 I.e., the orondolong, or "doorposts," who controlled access to the sultan.

153 Rūngā was in Dār Rungā, a territory south of Darfur inhabited by Fartīt, or pagan, enslaveable, people, from whom the slaves to be made into eunuchs would have come. "Gifts" probably means here "gifts for the sultan," i.e., tribute (see §3.1.60).

154 "their innocent needs" (*awṭārihinna ghayri l-khanā'*), *khanā'* being perhaps from *khanī*, meaning "foul-mouthed."

155 According to Perron, the name means in Fur "black young man" (El-Tounsy, *Voyage au Darfour*, 254).

156 I.e., the hot rainy season that occurs toward the end of the year (see §3.3.8 below).

157 According to informants, the phrase is more correctly *in attô*; however, the author apparently heard it as given (see below). The meaning is "This is the Day, this is the Day, this is the Day" (El-Tounsy, *Voyage au Darfour*, 438).

158 Q Insān 76:10, the reference being to the Day of Judgment.

159 See §3.1.103.

160 See §3.1.102.

161 "pinafore . . . apron": see §3.1.97.

162 The author tells the story of Sultan Muḥammad Ṣābūn's attack on Tāmah, in which his father was involved and on one occasion even saved the day, in his second work (El-Tounsy, *Voyage au Ouadây*, 187–210).

163 Abū Nuwās (ca. 140–98/757–813).

164 Cf. Q Baqarah 2:61 «And when you said, "Moses, we will not endure one sort of food."»

165 See §3.1.97.

166 Since leucorrhea is an exclusively female condition, the author may be confusing it with a sexually transmitted disease such as gonorrhea, which also produces a discharge in males. Elsewhere *al-ḥaṣar* is defined as "retention of the urine" (Qāsim, *Qāmūs*).

167 Literally "The Arm of the All-Capable."

168 The author commented to Perron: "The affair caused great public scandal. I knew several Fur who, more unfortunate than my friend, had cause to repent of having satisfied the desires of women who seduced them" (El-Tounsy, *Voyage au Darfour*, 263, n. 1).

169 The first line is attributed to Fayṣal ibn Muḥammad al-Jumaylī (875–965/1470–1557); the rest are attributed to Imam ʿAlī ibn Abī Ṭālib (d. 40/660).

170 I.e., by pagans. It is stated above (§3.2.38) that most eunuchs in Darfur were castrated by the Rūngā, a non-Muslim tribe living southwest of Darfur within the sphere of influence of Wadai. The term "Magian," i.e., Zoroastrian, believed to have its origins in the situation of Zoroastrians as non-Muslims living in contact with Muslims in Iraq (formerly) and Iran, was also applied to non-Zoroastrians (e.g., the Vikings, see *EI2*, art. *al-Mādjūs*) by premodern Arab writers; the same terminology was used by the Fur, who referred to pagans as *majusinga* (O'Fahey, *Darfur Sultanate*, 167).

171 See §3.1.14.

172 The Arabic reads *al-abyaḍ al-shāhiq*, literally "braying (like a donkey) white" or "breath-inhaling white"; perhaps a slip of the pen for *abyaḍ sāṭiʿ* "radiant white."

173 Cf. Q Fāṭir 35:19–21 «Not equal are the blind man and the seeing man, and the shadows and the light, and the shade and the torrid heat» (Arberry, *Koran*, 446).

174 Attributed to Qays ibn al-Muwallaḥ, known as Majnūn Laylā (first/seventh century).

175 I.e., of different kinds of galia moschata, "a perfume composed of musk, ambergris, camphor and oil of ben" (Lane, *Lexicon*).

176 I.e., even a little of the beloved's color, in the form of a beauty mark, would be enough to make a white person beautiful.

177 I.e., his saliva.

178 "Counter-poems" (*muʿaraḍah*), with which a poet attempts to contradict, or outdo, an older poem while retaining the original rhyme and meter, are an established genre (see *EAL* 1/82).

179 Al-Ṣaftī's is also a counter-poem, "outdoing" the one that opens "You've fallen for a girl who's black!" above.

180 Q Isrāʾ 17:12.

181 Q Baqarah 2:148.

182 The quotation forms a hemistich (meter: *ṭawīl*) that appears in the work of many poets and seems to be proverbial, though it is sometimes attributed, incorrectly, to Bashshār ibn Burd.

183 Literally "the father of the tongue" or "that of the tongue." Tonsillitis may be meant.

184 The literal sense is unknown; elsewhere *umm ṣuquʿ* is defined as "a swelling in the sinuses" (Qāsim, *Qāmūs*).

185 I.e., verses of the Qur'an written on slips of paper, which are then attached to relevant parts of the patient's body.

186 Quotidian, tertian, and quartan fevers are symptoms of infection by different strains of malaria; it is not clear what "time-specific fever" refers to.

187 I.e., typhoid fever.

188 The date of his visit is given in the French translation as October 1841 (El-Tounsy, *Voyage au Darfour*, 341).

189 I.e., cholera.

190 "the Frankish disease": a sexually-transmitted disease; probably syphilis or gonorrhea.

191 A kind of hoe (see §3.3.52).

192 See §3.2.51 and n. 166.

193 The same word is applied to the intense dust storms carried on weather fronts that affect Sudan, where they were first described, as well as other parts of the world, and that are known in English as "haboobs."

194 Perron believed that the malady in question was "hysteria": "Hysteria, as is well known, sometimes manifests itself in men but is frequent in women. I find it hard to believe that the lubricious habits of the inhabitants of Darfur and other regions of Sudan, the frequency of sexual intercourse, the ardor of their temperaments, and the hot climate are not sufficient causes to engender hysteria among men there much more frequently than among the men of our countries. This would explain their belief that this malady is contagious" (El-Tounsy, *Voyage au Darfour*, 285, n. 1).

195 "Causing rows."

196 Unidentified.

197 See §2.3.23.

198 Elsewhere, *ṭibb* means "medicine" (as a science and a profession); a practitioner of medicine is called a *ṭabīb*.

199 See §4.41.

200 See §4.42.

201 The author does not, in fact, refer to this elsewhere.

202 Cf. Q Naba' 78:33.

203 This dish, a stew made from rehydrated ingredients, is typically made from okra (see, e.g., Qāsim, *Qāmūs*); however, as the following shows, it may be made from a variety of ingredients.

204 Either of two bushes (*Cassia absus* and *Cassia tora*, see Vogt, *Murshid*, 294). The method of preparation is described as follows: "It is chopped, stalk and leaves, then gathered, wrapped, and placed in tightly sealed earthenware pots until it ferments and becomes as soft as dough. Impurities are then removed and it is turned into small disks and left to dry. When used, it is crumbled like a condiment or spice" (Qāsim, *Qāmūs*).

205 There is no such earlier reference.

206 On the basis of the descriptions that follow, "wild cattle" may mean any of various species of hartebeest (still found in the extreme southwest of Sudan), while by *taytal* may be meant the Bubal hartebeest, once present in North Africa but now extinct.

207 On the face of it, the text contradicts itself (people cannot have no occupation other than hunting and at the same time be smiths), and the passage is absent from the French translation; the solution may lie in the fact that smiths formed an outcaste group in Darfur as elsewhere in the Sudanic lands; below (§3.3.32), the author gives them the alternate name of Darāmidah and says they are outlaws and marry only among themselves. Thus, the hunters in question may have belonged to this group by birth but lived exclusively from hunting.

208 Perron hazards that this may be the marabou stork (*Ardea argola*) (El-Tounsy, *Voyage au Darfour*, 307, n. 1).

209 "whydahs" (*abū mūsā*): the identification is tentative and based on Cave and MacDonald's naming of the paradise whydah "abu mus" [*sic*] (Cave and MacDonald, *Birds of the Sudan*, 414).

210 Ordinarily, *ẓalīm* means "male ostrich" while *rabdā'*, a feminine adjective, means "of a grayish color." Perron explains, however, on the author's authority, that in the usage of Darfur *ẓalīm* means (of an ostrich) "having four large and four small pure-white plumes" while *rabdā'* means "having eight gray plumes" (El-Tounsy, *Voyage au Darfour*, 459).

211 *dafra* (*Echinochloa colona/frumentacea*) (voweled in the lithograph as *difrah*) is a cultivated grass (see Vogt, *Murshid*, 279; also https://en.wikipedia.org/wiki/Echinochloa_colona accessed 1 January 2016).

212 "*hijlīj* kernels": Perron transcribes the word as *serneh* and describes them as "kernels of the *hijlīj* fruit from which the bitterness has been removed by maceration in cold water" (El-Tounsy, *Voyage au Darfour*, 459). The fruit and leaves of the same tree were also eaten (see, e.g., §3.3.19, §3.3.25, §4.7).

213 I.e., gold and silver coin.

214 On the contrary, copper ore, mined at Ḥufrat al-Nuḥās in the far southwest of the sultanate, was one of Darfur's most lucrative exports (O'Fahey, *Darfur Sultanate,* 80), while Browne refers to "copper, white, in small quantity" as a regular export (*Travels in Africa,* 304).

215 See §2.2.26.

216 These were the catchment areas of the markets of various towns, as is made clear further on (§3.3.47).

217 No earlier reference has been found. According to Browne, the size, and therefore value, of these rings varied greatly: "These rings are made of so many sizes, that I have known sometimes twelve, sometimes one hundred and forty of them, pass for a given quantity and quality of cotton cloth" (*Travels in Africa,* 290).

218 The Spanish (rather than the French) dollar bore the image of two pillars, which were interpreted in Arab countries as cannons (see Lane, *Manners and Customs,* 573).

219 See §3.1.102.

220 E.g., (approximately) French *tabac.*

221 Various members of the Bakrī family, which claims descent from the first caliph, Abū Bakr al-Ṣiddīq, were prominent in Egypt as scholars, poets, and religious leaders from the sixteenth century through the seventeenth and later, and tobacco first appeared in Egypt in 1606 (Zack, *Egyptian Arabic,* 70). The author is, therefore, mistaken in attributing the poem to the ninth century AH/late fourteenth to late fifteenth centuries AD.

222 The word *ḥashshāshah* ("hoe") is an instrumental noun derived from the word *ḥashīsh* ("weeds, grass").

223 By 1830, these hoes had been reduced, as a part of their conversion into a true currency of purely conventional value, to two or three inches in length, and an observer failed to recognize them for what they were (see O'Fahey, *Darfur Sultanate,* 243).

224 For copper bracelets see §3.1.103 and for the red-and-white cylindrical beads called *khaddūr* see §3.1.102.

225 I.e., Indian corn, maize (*Zea mays*).

226 See §3.1.22.

227 I.e., "dimbi," a red-seeded cultivar of pearl millet (*Pennisetum glaucum* L., also known as "bulrush millet"); by "ordinary millet" the author probably means other, white-seeded, pearl millet cultivars (see Ali and Idris, "Germination," 1).

228 I.e., the hot rainy season that occurs in autumn (see §3.3.8).

229 See also §3.3.19.

230 See §2.2.27 and §3.1.20.

231 The last statement is contradicted by what follows, not to mention that okra is a staple of the diet in Darfur and Sudan generally. Perron corrects the author by translating as

follows: "One rarely finds these vegetables elsewhere, though an exception must always be made for okra."

232 Perron states that this canal—al-Khalīj al-Miṣrī ("the Cairo Canal") in full—which ran southwest to northeast through the center of Cairo, was about twenty feet wide (El-Tounsy, *Voyage au Darfour*, 327, n. 2); it dated probably to pharaonic times, was re-dug on several occasions, and was filled in in 1897.

233 See §3.1.101. By "a kind of bean whose pods grow below ground" the author may mean either the peanut (*Arachis hypogaea*), introduced into western Africa from South America in the sixteenth century and known in Egypt today as "Sudanese beans" (*fūl sūdānī*) or the indigenous Bambara groundnut (*Vigna subterranea*); the same applies to "the Sinnār bean."

234 See §3.1.20.

235 The nabk (Arabic: *nabq*), or Christ's-thorn jujube (*Ziziphus spina-christi*).

236 The tree denoted in Fur by the word *dalayb* (see below) is the deleb palm or toddy palm (*Borassus aethiopum*), whereas the fruit denoted by *al-jawz al-hindī* (literally "Indian walnut") is the coconut, whose seeds resemble those of the deleb palm. The term *dulab* does not occur in Arabic dictionaries; the author may have confused Fur *dalayb* with Arabic *dulb*, which, however, refers to the plane or sycamore.

237 According to Nachtigal, the people of Darfur also ate the seeds of the deleb palm (Nachitgal, *Sahara and Sudan*, 4:238).

238 *qiddīm*: perhaps a local pronunciation of or an error for *qiḍḍīm* (*Grewia tenax*) (Bakri and El Gunaid, "Plants Use," 63).

239 See §3.3.49.

240 Probably a local pronunciation of or an error for *laʿūt* (*Acacia nubica*) (Bakri and El Gunaid, "Plants Use," 63).

241 See §3.1.86.

242 Umar defines *jaʿjaʿ* as *Fadogia glaberrima*, a member of a genus of flowering plants found widely in tropical Africa (*Travels*, 451).

243 See §3.2.56 and n. 172.

244 See §3.1.46.

245 I.e., the tree comes to look like a solid object, not like an ordinary tree with branches sticking out.

246 See §3.1.109.

247 Umar identifies it as a species of *Adenium* (dogbane) (*Travels*, 453. n. 3).

248 See §3.1.18, and what follows.

249 I.e., what is called "autumn" (*al-kharīf*), the rainy season, occurs in Darfur during what in Egypt is the summer, while the hot season (*al-darat*) that follows this "autumn" in

Darfur is called the spring (*al-rabīʿ*) because it is when the plants grow, and what is called spring in Egypt, they call summer (*al-ṣayf*) in Darfur. Depending on latitude, the rainy season in Darfur starts between September and October and ends between November and December.

250 The Twins (al-Jawzāʾ) are the stars Castor and Pollux of the constellation Gemini, which appears in Darfur in late June; thus the "sprinkle" (*al-rushāsh*) is what are sometimes called "the little rains" that occur during the dry season.

251 I.e., the constellation of Cancer.

252 See §3.3.11 and n. 191.

253 Perhaps because the constellation of the Gemini is associated with the onset of the rains (see §4.29), and therefore with abundance of rain in general.

254 By the Roman (*rūmī*) calendar the author probably means the Julian calendar.

255 These old Arabic names are also the names of the Islamic calendar, hence still in use.

256 The Islamic year starts with the month of Muharram; Shawwal is the tenth month.

257 The meanings of the Darfurian names for the months of the Islamic year are (following the author's explanations to Perron): al-Faṭur (Shawwal) = "Breaking of the Fast" (because this is the month following the fasting month of Ramadan); al-Faṭrayn (Dhu l-Qaʿdah) = "Double Breaking of the Fast" (because this is the second month after Ramadan); al-Ḍaḥiyyah (Dhu l-Hijjah) = "the Sacrifice" (because the Great Feast, when animals are sacrificed, falls on the tenth day); al-Ḍaḥiyyatayn (Muharram) = "Double Sacrifice" (because this is the month after al-Ḍaḥiyyah); al-Waḥīd (Safar) = "the Lonely" (because it comes between two months that have their own, significant, names, meaning that it is a kind of orphan month); al-Karāmah (Rabiʿ al-Awwal) = "the Miracle" (because this is the month in which God first revealed the Qur'an to the Prophet Muḥammad); al-Tawm (Rabiʿ al-Thani) = "the Twin" (i.e., the month that is the twin of the month that follows); al-Tawmayn (Jumada al-Awwal) = "Double Twin" (see the preceding); Sāyiq (Sāʾiq) al-Tīmān (Jumada al-Thani) = "the Driver of the Twins" (because it follows immediately after the Twins); al-Quṣayyar (Shaʿban) = "the Short" (because, as it precedes Ramadan, it always seems too short) (El-Tounsy, *Voyage au Darfour*, 468–69).

258 The word *nārah* is not to be found in the dictionaries but is presumably from *nār* "fire."

259 See §2.3.13.

260 According to Browne, the sons of the sultans (whom he refers to as the rightful heirs of Muḥammad Tayrāb), following their defeat, "are now [in 1794] wandering about, scraping a miserable subsistence from the parsimonious alms of their usurping uncle" (Browne, *Travels in Africa*, 278).

261 The Tomorókkóngá are generally regarded as a subgroup of the Fur.

262 I.e., the author expected to recover his debt in the form of slaves captured during the raid.

263 The text in this passage is so laconic that it has been necessary, while following the Arabic as closely as possible, to draw on the French translation, which expands on it (El-Tounsy, *Voyage au Darfour*, 365–66) in the following instances: "erasing every second hole"; "and moving through them"; "as described above." Perron describes even his own translation of the text as "much too abridged" and follows it with a further explanation, some one thousand words in length, that he was given by the author orally (El-Tounsy, *Voyage au Darfour*, 366, n. 1).

264 See Volume 1, Notes to the Frontmatter, n. 80.

Glossary

Names of persons are alphabetized by the first element of the name. Names are given in the form in which they appear in the text, which generally reflect al-Tūnisī's spelling. Other spellings found in the literature (especially O'Fahey, Nachtigal, and Browne) are given in parentheses, e.g., "Fartīt (elsewhere Fertit)." The ascription "Fur" in parentheses after an item indicates that the word is used in the Fur language, but not necessarily that it is ultimately of Fur origin (many terms used in Fur are also used by other ethnic groups). The names of beads, other accessories, and perfumes are ever changing. Items (such as certain plants and diseases) that it has proven impossible to identify satisfactorily are omitted here and dealt with in the notes.

Ab Sanūn a people, also called Kodoi, related to the royal family of Wadai.

ába dima'ng (Fur) see Dār Ába Dima'ng.

ába poor-ii (Fur) according to the author, a title of the kaamíne.

ába umá (elsewhere abbo uumo*; Fur)* commander of the rearguard of the army and hereditary ruler of Dār Umá (Dar Uumo), one of the four primary provinces of Darfur, southeast of Jabal Marrah.

abbo (Fur) a title of respect.

ʿAbd al-Raḥmān al-Rashīd sultan of Darfur (r. 1202/1787 to 1218/1803–4).

Abīrīs (= Bārīs) an outlying oasis west of the al-Khārijah group, fifty-four miles from the town of al-Khārijah.

abū abāṭ Indian corn, maize (*Zea mays*).

Abū ʿAbd Allāh Muḥammad al-Wirghī (d. 1190/1776) Tunisian chancellery secretary and poet.

Abū l-Judūl an estate or group of villages near Tandaltī (El-Fasher) granted to the author's father as a fief and where the author lived during his stay in Darfur.

Abū Muḥammad Ḥammūdah Pasha Ḥammūdah Pasha ibn ʿAlī II (r. 1196–1229/1782–1814), ruler of Tunis.

Abū l-Qāsim sixth historical sultan of the Keira dynasty (r. ca. 1739–52); preceded by ʿUmar Lēl and succeeded by Muḥammad Tayrāb.

Abū l-Ṭayyib al-Mutanabbī see al-Mutanabbī.

abū ṣaffayr (so voweled in the original) jaundice.

abū l-ṣufūf pleurisy.

Abū Zaʿbal a locality north of Cairo, where the first modern Egyptian medical school was opened on February 28, 1827, attached to a military hospital; the school was transferred to Qaṣr al-ʿAynī in Cairo in 1837.

Ādam Adam, father of humankind; also a male given name.

Adiqiz (Agadez) formerly a city-state, now a region of central Niger.

ʿAdnān putative ancestor of the Northern Arabs, i.e., those who speak Arabic as it is commonly known, versus the Southern Arabs, who speak the now largely extinct South Arabian languages.

ʿAfnū Hausaland.

Aḥmad Bukur (or Bukr) (r. ca. 1700–20) third of the historical Keira sultans, associated with the second phase of Islamization of the Darfur state.

Aḥmad ibn Sulaymān a teacher in Tunis and the maternal uncle of the author's father.

Aḥmad Zarrūq an uncle of the author's; presumably a son, born in Sennar, of his grandfather Sulaymān.

al-Alfī Muḥammad Bayk al-Alfī (d. 1226/1811), a Mamluk army commander who, shortly before the events described by the author, had played a role in the failed attempt to restore Mamluk control over Egypt; his sobriquet, from *alf* ("one thousand"), means "purchased for a thousand dinars."

ʿAlī, Imam ʿAlī ibn Abī Ṭālib, cousin and son-in-law of the Prophet Muḥammad and fourth caliph (r. 35–40/656–61), famed for his wise sayings.

ʿAlī al-Darwīsh ʿAlī ibn Ḥasan ibn Ibrāhīm al-Ankūrī al-Miṣrī (1211–70/1797–1853), Egyptian poet, laureate to the viceroy ʿAbbās I.

ʿAlī al Ghurāb ʿAlī ibn al-Ghurāb al-Ṣafaqisī (d. 1183/1769), poet from Sfax, known for eulogies of the rulers of Tunis and bawdy verse.

ʿAlī Pasha I ʿAlī I ibn Muḥammad (r. 1148–70/1735–56), second Ḥusaynid ruler of Tunis.

ʿAlī wad Jāmiʿ a grandee at the court of Sultan ʿAbd al-Raḥmān and patron of Shaykh-Father Muḥammad Kurrā.

Anbūsah (elsewhere *Umm Būsa*) a slave woman belonging to Sultan ʿAbd al-Raḥmān and mother of his successor, Sultan Muḥammad Faḍl.

ʿandurāb a tree: either *Cordia monoica*, "snot-berry tree," or *Cordia sinensis*, "gray-leaved cordia."

ʿanqallū green fruit of the Jericho balm tree (*hijlīj*).

the Anṣār literally "the helpers"; i.e., the men (of the peoples of Aws and Khazraj) of Medina who supported the Prophet Muḥammad, as distinguished from the Muhājirūn or "emigrants," i.e., his Meccan followers who moved with him to Medina.

ʿaqīq round agate beads.

ʿArafah al-Dusūqī al-Mālikī Muḥammad ibn Aḥmad ibn ʿArafah al-Dusūqī (d. 1230/1815), a prominent Mālikī jurisprudent and scholar of his day.

al-Azhar the premier mosque and teaching institution of premodern Cairo, built 361/972.

báási (Fur; approx. "royal") a title originally given the brother of the sultan and later extended to apply to all his male relatives.

Bāb al-Muʿallā Mecca's most ancient cemetery.

Banī ʿAdī a town in Upper Egypt near the west bank of the Nile in the governorate of Banī Suwayf and the terminus of the so-called Forty Days Road (*Darb al-Arbiʿīn*) between Egypt and Darfur.

the Banū Ḥalbah cattle-herding nomads living south of Jabal Marrah.

the Banū Jarrār cattle-herding nomads belonging to the Fazārah group.

the Banū ʿUmrān cattle-herding nomads belonging to the Fazārah group.

al-Bāqirmah (Bagirmi) formerly, a state southeast of Lake Chad in what is now Chad.

Baradiyyah in the Wadai sultanate, a goblet drum.

the Barajūb probably, the swamps of Baḥr al-Ghazāl and Baḥr al-Jabal, south of Darfur.

the Barqū a people, originally from Wadai, with many communities in Darfur (cf. Dār Barqū, a name for Wadai).

the Bartī (Berti) a people living in eastern Darfur, formerly speakers of a now-extinct Nubian language.

al-Basūs, War of a pre-Islamic intertribal conflict fought toward the end of the fifth century AD that lasted forty years and was blamed on an old woman called al-Basūs whose camel had been killed by a member of a rival tribe.

baṭṭūm a tree: probably terebinth (*Pistacia terebinthus*).

Bawwā a wadi in northern Darfur, perhaps the same as the "Wadi Howa" on modern maps.

the Bidāyāt a non-Arabic-speaking people found in northwestern Darfur.

bindilah a kind of dance.

Bingah a Fartīt people living on the southern fringes of the sultanate.

the Bīqū (Beigo) a Dājū-speaking people of originally servile status living in southern Darfur.

Bīr al-Malḥah ("Salt Flat Well") alternative name of Bīr al-Zaghāwī.

Bīr al-Zaghāwī ("al-Zaghāwī's Well") a well on the road from Asyut to Darfur south of Laqiyyah, also called Bīr al-Malḥah.

the Birqid a people living east of Jabal Marrah and south of Tandaltī (El-Fasher) who spoke a Nubian language.

Bornu (Barnaw) from 1380 to 1893, an empire that at its height incorporated parts of what are now Nigeria, Chad, Cameroon, and Niger; in the author's day, the state immediately west of Wāddāy (Wadai).

al-Bukhārī, Muḥammad ibn Ismāʿīl (194–256/810–70) author of an authoritative collection of some eight thousand sound prophetic hadiths.

Būlāq (1) the name of two localities in Cairo, one (Būlāq Abū l-ʿIlā) being the city's port, on the east bank of the Nile; the other (Būlāq al-Dakrūr) a settlement on its west bank, in Giza; (2) a village on the caravan route from Asyut to Darfur, seventeen miles west of al-Khārijah.

al-burjuk scarlet fever.

būzah in Egypt, barley beer; elsewhere usually spelled *būẓah*.

the Caravanserai of the Jallābah (Wikālat al-Jallābah) a *wikālah* was a combined warehouse and hostel for merchants; the *jallābah* were traveling merchants drawn largely from Upper Egypt and northern Nilotic Sudan who traded between the Sudanic countries and Egypt. The greater part of their trade from Darfur was in slaves, but ivory, ostrich feathers, wild-animal parts, camels, and other merchandise were also taken to Egypt, while beads, tin, cloth, swords, coffee, paper, and more were taken from Egypt to Darfur.

counselor (Arabic: amīn, pl. umanāʾ) a confidential advisor to the sultan of Darfur.

the Dājū a people living in southern Darfur whose ancestors are said to have ruled the first Darfurian state and who were superseded in the sixteenth century by the Tunjūr.

al-Dalīl, Judge chief judge of Wadai, who passed through Cairo in October 1841 on his way to Mecca and there met with both the author and Nicolas Perron.

dallūkah set of three goblet drums.

dam-l-raʿāf (= *dam al-ruʿāf*, literally "nosebleed blood") a kind of coral bead.

damsuga (Fur) personal spirit guardian purchased from the jinn.

Dār literally "house" and, when followed by the name of a group or individual, "land of, territory of"; hence Dār Fartīt ("the Land of the Fartīt"), Dār Bagirmi ("the Land of the Bagirmi"), Dār Wāddāy ("Wadai"), Dār al-Tikináwi (Darfur's northern province, governed by the Tikináwi).

Dār Ába Dima'ng (Dar Aba Dima; Fur) literally "The Land of the Lord of Dima'ng"; an autonomous area southwest of Jabal Marrah ruled by a line of hereditary chiefs.

Dār Bandalah a Fartīt people, non-Muslims living on the southern fringes of the sultanate.

Dār Mallā (Mali) formerly (tenth to fifteenth centuries AD), a western Sudanic empire between the Upper Senegal and Upper Niger rivers.

Dār Qimir (Dar Qimr) a sultanate subject to Darfur, north of Dār Masālīṭ and south of Dār Zaghāwah, ruled by a dynasty allegedly originating from the Jaʿaliyyīn ethnic group in the Nilotic Sudan.

Dār al-Rīḥ literally the Land of the Wind; an alternative name for Dār al-Tikináwi, the sultanate's northern province.

Dār Rūngā the territory of a Fartīt (non-Muslim) people living on the south-western fringes of the sultanate.

Dār Silā (Dar Sula) a Dājū-speaking kingdom lying between Darfur and Wadai and paying tribute to both.

Dār Ṣulayḥ (also Dār Ṣāliḥ) an alternative name for (Dār al-) Wāddāy (Wadai), either because its inhabitants claimed descent from one Ṣāliḥ (of which Ṣulayḥ is the diminutive) ibn ʿAbd Allāh ibn ʿAbbās, or because its second founder, Sultan Jawdah (r. ca. 1747–75), bore the epithet al-Ṣāliḥ, meaning "the Righteous."

Dār Tāmā, Dār Tāmah an area between Darfur and Wadai in the west, never comfortably part of Darfur or of Wadai; it takes its name from the Tāmā (Tāmah) people of Jabal Tāmā.

Dār Tunbuktū (Timbuktu) a state on the Niger River, today in Niger.

darat a period of extreme heat lasting about forty days from the end of the rainy season (see *kharīf*), during which the sorghum ripens.

Darfur a formerly independent sultanate located between al-Wādday (Wadai, now eastern Chad) on the west and Kordofan on the east; since 1916, part of Sudan. The name is a contraction of Dār al-Fūr, the Land of the Fur.

darmūdī member of an outcast group of hunters and smiths.

dawdarī kind of *waykah* (q.v.) made from bonemeal.

dééng saaya (Fur) a slightly fermented drink of rice, sugar, and water (= Arabic *sūbiyā*).

dhikr Sufi ceremony that, through rhythmic movement and sound, allows the participant to achieve mystical unity with God; the specifically Fur form of the *dhikr* described by the author differs, however, from this norm.

difrah a grain; probably sawa millet.

dimlij (pl. damālij) literally "bracelet"; subchief under the authority of a *shartāy*.

dinbī "dimbi," a cultivar of pearl (bulrush) millet.

dinjāyah a mud-brick storehouse within the *fāshir* (q.v.) of the sultan of Darfur.

dinqār a large wooden drum of state.

Dongola a town on the Nile in Sudanese Nubia.

dullong (Fur) a kind of small clay pot.

al-duqrī osteomyelitis.

durdur a circular wall of mud forming the foundation of the walls of the houses of members of the elite.

durrāʿah a length of cloth wound around the upper half of a woman's body.

durzūyah a wooden pillar used to support the roof of a *tukultī* (q.v.).

emir army commander.

The Epitome (al-Mukhtaṣar) an authoritative handbook of Islamic law according to the Mālikī school of jurisprudence by Khalīl ibn Isḥāq al-Jundī (d. 776/1374).

Fallātā, Fallātah (from Kanuri, "people"; Fellata) name of a nomadic people found from Mauritania to eastern Sudan, who call themselves Fulbe (sg. Pullo); also called here Fullān (sg. Fullānī), from the Hausa.

the Fanqarū (Fongoro) a people living in southern Dār Ába Dima'ng.

faqīh (1) (used of non-Darfurians; plural *fuqahā'*) a man trained in Islamic legal science, a jurisprudent (2) (used of Darfurians; plural, anomalously, *fuqarā'*) a holy man, i.e., a man, not necessarily learned, from a family, usually of non-Darfurian origin, credited with religious charisma (*barakah*) and supernatural powers who often acted as a village schoolmaster.

the Farāwujayh (Feroge) a Fartīt (non-Muslim) people living south of Baḥr al-ʿArab.

fardah apron-like garment worn by women.

Fartīt non-Muslim peoples living on the southern margins of Darfur; they were regarded as enslaveable by the raiders from the north; despite this, it was recognized that in some way the Fartīt were related to the Fur.

fāshir the compound forming the seat of the sultan's government, in former times itinerant but from 1791 located permanently at Tandaltī (now known as El-Fasher, capital of the federal state of North Darfur); the term, which is used from Lake Chad to the Nile, is of unknown origin and seems to have referred in the first instance to the open space before the encampment of a king or chief.

the Fazārah a generic term for the cattle-owning, Arabic-speaking nomads of southern Darfur.

feathers (Arabic: rīsh) (1) "the feathers": the sultan's ceremonial fan; (2) a kind of bead.

Fezzan Libya's southwestern province.

Fullān (Fulan, Fulani, Fulbe) an alternative name for the Fallātā (q.v.).

fuqarā' see *faqīh*.

Fur the largest ethnic group in Darfur, forming about one third of the population and speaking a Nilo-Saharan language. Sultans from the Fur ruled Darfur from the mid-seventeenth century until 1916.

al-Fusṭāṭ site of the first capital of Egypt under Muslim rule, just south of Cairo.

The Glittering Ladder *The Glittering Ladder on Logic* (*al-Sullam al-murawnaq fī l-manṭiq*) by ʿAbd al-Raḥmān ibn Muḥammad al-Akhḍarī (918–83/1512–75), a well-known didactic poem on logic.

the Ḥabbāniyyah (Habbania) an Arab-speaking, cattle-herding, semi-nomadic people of southern Darfur.

al-habūb wind trapped in the lower belly.

Hadith the corpus of reports (hadiths) of the words or actions of the Prophet Muḥammad.

the Hafsids the dynasty that ruled Tunisia and eastern Algeria from 627/1229 to 982/1574.

al-Ḥājj title of Muslims who have made the pilgrimage to Mecca.

al-Ḥajjāj al-Ḥajjāj ibn Yūsuf (ca. 41/661 to 95/714), governor of Iraq, who brutally crushed several revolts against Umayyad rule.

Ḥalfāwīn a historic district of Tunis (Halfaouine).

Ḥalq al-Wād the fortified port of Tunis (La Goulette).

Ḥammūdah Pasha see Abū Muḥammad Ḥammūdah Pasha.

ḥarāz a tree: apple-ring acacia (*Faidherbia* (or *Acacia*) *albida*).

al-Ḥarīrī al-Qāsim ibn ʿAlī al-Ḥarīrī (446–516/1054–1122), Iraqi prose writer, poet, and civil servant, author of fifty immensely popular *maqāmāt* (compositions in a highly polished style), which he arranged in a work of the same name.

ḥarish a kind of bead worn by poor women and used in certain localities as currency.

Ḥasan wad ʿAwūḍah chief imam of Kūbayh under Sultan ʿAbd al-Raḥmān.

al-ḥaṣar leukorrhea.

ḥashāb a tree: gum acacia (*Senegalia* (or *Acacia*) *senegal*); elsewhere spelled *hashāb*.

ḥashshāshah a kind of iron hoe.

al-hayḍah cholera.

Ḥawwā' the first woman, the Qur'anic equivalent of Eve; also a given name.

the High Plain (al-Ṣaʿīd) the name given in Darfur to the area from Rīl south to the farthest limits of the country.

hijlīj a tree: Jericho balm (*Balanites aegyptiaca*).

Ḥillat Jūltū village in the district of Abū l-Judūl.

ḥummayḍ a tree: marula (*Sclerocarya birrea*).

al-Ḥusayn, Shrine of mosque in Cairo containing a tomb said to hold the head of al-Ḥusayn, grandson of the Prophet Muḥammad.

Ḥusayn ʿAmmārī al-Azharī Bedouin shaykh from Kordofan, known as the introducer of tobacco to Darfur.

Ḥusayn Pasha al-Ḥusayn I ibn ʿAlī al-Turkī (r. 1117–48/1705–35), founder of Tunis's Ḥusaynid dynasty.

Ibn Ajurrum's Text (al-Ājurrūmiyyah) widely used brief compendium of Arabic grammar, formally entitled *al-Muqadimmah al-Ājurrūmiyyah*, by Abū ʿAbd Allāh Muḥammad ibn Dā'ūd al-Sanhājī (672–723/1273–1323), known as Ibn Ājurrūm.

Ibn Ḥajar Aḥmad ibn Muḥammad ibn ʿAlī ibn Hajar al-Haythamī al-Makkī al-Ansārī (909/1503–4 to 973/1565–66), an influential Shāfiʿī jurist.

Ibrāhīm the builder of the Kaaba, identified with biblical Abraham; also a male given name.

Ibrāhīm al-Riyāḥī Ibrāhīm ibn ʿAbd al-Qādir ibn Aḥmad al-Riyāḥī al-Tūnisī (1180–1266/1766–1850), Mālikī jurist, chief mufti of Tunis, and poet.

Ibrāhīm wad Ramād powerful Fur clan chief and Master of the Drums during the reign of Sultan ʿAbd al-Raḥmān; his name, "son of Ashes," alluded to his illegitimacy.

the Illumined City Medina.

Imruʾ al-Qays (sixth century AD) celebrated pre-Islamic Arabian poet.

the ʿIrayqāt (Ireigat) an Arabic-speaking, camel-herding people forming part of the Northern Ruzayqāt.

irdabb a dry measure equal to 198 liters.

iyā kurī (Fur: "mother" + "power") title of the sultan's premier wife.

ʿIzz al-Dīn al-Jāmiʿī (elsewhere, al-Jāmiʿ) a judge during the reign of Sultan ʿAbd al-Raḥmān and later chief judge of Darfur and its territories; member of the Jamāwiʿah family of holy men whose ancestor came from the east and was invited to settle in Darfur by Sultan Sulaymān Solóng.

Jabal Marrah mountain range in western Darfur; homeland of the Fur and cradle of the Keira dynasty of Darfur sultans (see O'Fahey, *Darfur Sultanate*, 3, 33–36). The author refers to a specific peak within the range as "the true Marrah" and on his map of Darfur draws a Little Jabal Marrah (presumably the same) about halfway between the north and south ends of the range but slightly to the west. It has not proven possible to identify this peak.

Jabal Tāmah see Dār Tāmah.

(Jadīd) Karyū a village south of Tandaltī, on the estate of Faqīh Mālik al-Fūtāwī.

(Jadīd) Rās al-Fīl a village in southeast Darfur, northeast of Rīl; formerly a *fāshir* (q.v.).

Jadīd al-Sayl a village near Tandaltī (El-Fasher).

jallābah (sg. jallāb) traveling merchants trading between Egypt and Sudan.

Jarkū perhaps modern Jarkul, near Mellit.

jêl (Fur) kind of dance.

al-jiqqayl a sexually-transmitted disease; probably syphilis or gonorrhea.

jūghān or jūkhān a tree: jackalberry (*Diospyros mespiliformis*).

kaamíne (kamni, kamene; Fur) the "shadow sultan," an ancient ritual title of enormous prestige but little power.

kaʿb al-ṭīb literally "the best of perfumes": a perfume made from a certain root.

the Kabābīsh an Arabic-speaking group of camel nomads living between Kordofan and Sennar.

kabartū in the Wadai sultanate, officers of the law, executioners, and musicians of a low caste.

Kabkābiyyah (Fur; literally "they threw down their shields") a town ninety-two miles west of Tandaltī (El-Fasher), named in reference to the defeat of invading Wadaian forces by those of Darfur under Sultan Aḥmad Bukur.

al-Kāf a city in northwest Tunisia (Le Kef).

Kalīlah and Dimnah (Kalīlah wa-Dimnah) a book of animal fables translated by ʿAbd Allāh ibn al-Muqaffaʿ (second/eighth century) from the Persian and ultimately of Indian origin.

kalkaf a fine cotton cloth.

kamkūlak in the Wadai sultanate, a counselor attending the sultan at audience; or one of four with this title, one of whom was in charge of the administration of the sultan's palace while the other three assisted with the administration of the sultan's estates; said to mean "sweeper of the sultan's house" (same reference).

kanfūs (pl. kanāfīs) women's breechclouts.

Karakriit one of the three great sections of the Fur; the Karakriit live in and to the east of Jabal Marrah.

karbābah reed hut.

karnū a variety of jujube.

kāshif literally "uncoverer, inspector"; in contemporary Egypt, governor of a minor province, as a rule drawn from the Turkish-speaking military elite.

the Kashmirah a people living in Wadai.

Katakū (Kotoko) formerly a kingdom covering parts of modern Cameroon, Nigeria, and southwest Chad.

katkāt a kind of heavy *tukkiyyah* (q.v.) of a compact weave.

kawal either of two bushes (*Cassia absus* and *Cassia tora*) and the condiment made from their fermented leaves and stalks.

kenykenya (Fur) a kind of candy made from dried jujube seeds.

Khabīr literally "expert"; title of the leader of a desert caravan; also a given name.

khaddūr kind of bead worn by poor women and used as currency for small purchases; Nachtigal describes the beads as large and made of clay.

Khalīl [ibn Isḥāq al-Jundī] (Khalīl al-Mālikī) (d. ca. 1365), author of *The Epitome* (q.v.).

kharīf the rainy season in Darfur, which starts between September and October and ends between November and December depending on latitude.

Khāqān a title of the sultans of Darfur, as also of the Ottoman sultan.

al-Khārijah (Kharjah) a group of oases in Egypt west of Asyut.

khayriyyah an Egyptian gold coin of the value of nine piasters (see Lane, *Manners*, 573).

Khūrshīd Pasha Aḥmad Khūrshīd Pasha, Ottoman governor of Egypt from 1804 until ousted by Muḥammad ʿAlī in 1805.

kilí a tree (unidentified) producing a drink used to determine the innocence or guilt of accused persons.

kīm horn bracelets worn by women.

Kīrī a village; according to informants it is close to Qirlī at the foot of Jabal Marrah.

kitir a tree: blackthorn (*Senegalia mellifera*).

kóór kwa (Fur) literally "spearmen"; slaves with spears who stood behind the sultan as part of his bodyguard when he held audience and surrounded him when he rode out; among them were young boys who sang and made music with whistles and maracas. They were also used as messengers and for other services.

Kordofan the region from Darfur's eastern border almost to the Nile; unlike Darfur, and Sennar to its east, Kordofan never underwent a process of state formation. Today, as part of Sudan, the area is divided into the federal states of North and South Kordofan.

Kūbayh (Kobbei, Kobbé) a town, now abandoned, thirty-five miles northwest of Tandaltī (El-Fasher). Kūbayh formed the southern terminus of the trade route between Asyut in Egypt and Darfur (the "Forty Days Road"), was inhabited almost exclusively by traders, and constituted the commercial capital of Darfur; in its heyday in the eighteenth and first half of the nineteenth centuries, it may have been the largest town in the sultanate, with six to eight thousand inhabitants.

the Kūkah a people of southwestern Wadai.

kumbā (or kanbū: both occur in the text; from Fur kômbo*)* as defined by the author, a liquid extracted from the ash of the *hijlīj* tree (Jericho balm, *Balanites aegyptiaca*) and used as a salt substitute.

Kunjáara (Kunjaara, Kunyjaara) one of the three great sections of the Fur people and that to which the Keira dynasty belonged; the Kunjáara live in and to the east of Jabal Marrah.

kūrāyāt literally "grooms"; four high officials in charge of the sultan's horses and servants. The word, though presumably Fur, was not recognized by informants.

kūrayb either of two grasses that are used for fodder and as famine foods: Egyptian crowfoot grass (*Dactyloctenium aegyptium*) and dropseed grass (*Sporobolus festivus*).

kurnug a kind of house resembling a *tukultī* but whose roof is raised on four rather than two wooden pillars (see §3.1.86, images).

Kusā a region of central Darfur.

laddāy a woman's headpiece of silver wire and beads.

lanngi (Fur) a dance.

Laqiyyah (Leghea, Laguyeh, Lagia) an uninhabited oasis on the route from Asyut to Darfur, south of Salīmah and close to the northern marches of Dār Zaghāwah.

lawī a variety of the cotton known as "Indian."

liqdābah (apparently from Fur libdenga*)* a roofed, open-sided structure within the sultan's compound used as an audience hall, mess, etc.

Little Jabal Marrah (Jubayl Marrah) the author's name for the peak, probably that usually referred to on modern maps as the Deriba Caldera, that lends its name to the entire Jabal Marrah mountain range and plateau.

Lubad According to ancient Arabian legend, Luqmān the Long-lived, a pre-Islamic figure to whom wise sayings are attributed, was granted, as a reward for his piety, a life as long as that of seven named vultures (the vulture being a popular symbol of longevity among the Arabs). The last vulture was named Lubad; when Lubad died, so did Luqmān.

madīdah a broth made from pounded desiccated watermelon.

madraʿah a bead bracelet worn by women.

Majūs literally "Zoroastrian"; applied in Darfur to the pagan peoples on its southern borders.

the Maḥāmīd cattle-herding nomads of the Fazārah group.

the Majānīn Arabic-speaking camel-herding nomads living in eastern Darfur and western Kordofan.

Makk a title, equivalent to "king," used by rulers in the Nile Valley, such as the Makk of Sennar; also used by the chief of the Birgid of Darfur.

the Malanqā (also Mananqah) a subgroup of the Ab Sanūn (q.v.).

malik a title used of (1) a king; (2) a tribal chief or person related to the royal family to whom some of the accoutrements of Sudanic royalty (such as the possession of copper war drums) pertained; (3) an official in charge of a significant place or specialized group. See further Volume One, Note on the Text, pp. xliii–xliv.

Mālik al-Fūtāwī Mālik ibn ʿAlī ibn Yūsuf al-Fūtāwī (d. ca. 1820), a prominent member of the Awlād ʿAlī family of holy men and an influential vizier at the court of Sultan ʿAbd al-Raḥmān; sponsor of the author's father.

Mālikī follower of the school of jurisprudence established by Mālik ibn Anas (179/795); most African Muslims, apart from those of Egypt, are *Mālikī*s and the designation often appears in names, e.g., Shaykh ʿArafah al-Dusūqī al-Mālikī.

the Mananqah see Malanqā.

Mandarah a kingdom (ca. 1500–1893) and people in what is today northwest Cameroon.

Manfalūṭ a city in Upper Egypt on the west bank of the Nile north of Asyut.

manjūr a bead worn by women of the middle class.

manṣūṣ (literally "squashed") round, flattened amber beads.

maqāmah a short independent narration written in ornamental rhymed prose with verse insertions, a common plot-scheme, and two constant protagonists: the narrator and the hero.

al-Maqs (Macs, Maghs, Mughess) the southernmost oasis of the Khārijah complex, uninhabited in the author's day.

al-Marbūṭah a village on the banks of Wādī l-Kūʿ not far from Tandaltī (El-Fasher).

marhabayb a species of thin cane (*Cymbopogon nervatus* and/or *proximus*) with which houses are roofed; elsewhere sometimes spelled *marḥabayb*.

mārīq a generic name for sorghum.

Marrah see Jabal Marrah, Little Jabal Marrah.

the Masālīṭ (Maṣālīṭ, Mesalit) a large people with its own language living to the west of Jabal Marrah.

al-Mazrūb a well marking the northern entry into Darfur for those coming from Asyut in Egypt.

mééram (Fur) a title given to the daughter of the sultan of Darfur or to younger marriageable women of the royal family in general, as opposed to the *habbūbāt*, and to the representative of the bride and her friends at a wedding.

The Memorandum (al-Tadhkirah) see al-Qurṭubī.

the Mīdawb (Meidob) a people living on Jabal Mīdawb in far northeastern Darfur who speak a language of the Nubian group.

mīdawbī a kind of naturally occurring salt.

the Mīmah a people centered on the town of Wadaʿah east of Wādī Kuʿ in eastern Darfur.

al-Minyah a city in Upper Egypt on the west bank of the Nile.

mishāhrah a bead worn by women.

the Misīriyyah (Misiriyah, Messiria) the Brown Misīriyyah (al-Misīriyyah al-Ḥumr) are camel nomads living in northern Kordofan, the Black Misīriyyah (al-Misīriyyah al-Zurq) are cattle nomads living in southern Kordofan; both peoples have offshoots in Darfur.

mooge (singular and plural; Fur—pronounced as two syllables) jester cum eulogist cum crier who shouted the praises of his master (for example, the sultan) on public occasions, was licensed to speak audaciously, and sometimes acted as public executioner.

the Mother of the Book the Qur'an.

mudd measure of volume used for grain; Perron states, on the author's authority, that the Sudanese *mudd* was equal to the Egyptian *malwah*, i.e., 4.125 liters.

Mughulṭāy al-Turkī Mughulṭāy ibn Qalīj ʿAbdullāhi al-Bakjarī al-Miṣrī (689–762/1290–1361), Egyptian historian and Hadith scholar of Turkic origin, also known for his book on martyrs for love, *al-Wāḍiḥ al-mubīn fīman ustushhida min al-muḥibbīn* (*The Clear Exposition Concerning Those Who Gave Their Lives for Love*).

mughrah a stone from which a red pigment is obtained.

al-Muhallabī, the vizier al-Ḥasan ibn Muḥammad al-Muhallabī (291–352/903–63), administrator and general for the Buyid princes of Baghdad, and a litterateur.

Muḥammad ʿAlī (r. 1805–48) ruler of Egypt under the nominal suzerainty of the Ottoman state.

Muḥammad Daldan (Fur: Daldang) wad Binayyah (d. 1804?) Keira warlord and slave trader, styled "King" because he was a grandson of Sultan Muḥammad Tayrāb.

Muḥammad Faḍl (elsewhere usually al-Faḍl) ninth sultan of Darfur of the Keira dynasty (r. ca. 1730–39), preceded by his father, ʿAbd al-Raḥmān, and succeeded by his son, Muḥammad al-Ḥusayn.

Muḥammad al-Ḥasanī Muḥammad III ibn ʿAbd Allāh (r. 1171–1204/1757–90), ʿAlawid ruler of Morocco.

Muḥammad ibn al-Qāsim ʿImād al-Dīn Muḥammad ibn al-Qāsim al-Thaqafī (ca. 695–715), a Muslim general best known for the conquest, at an extremely young age, of Sindh and Multan.

Muḥammad al-Jallūlī Ḥusaynid governor of Sfax in Tunisia in the late eighteenth or early nineteenth century.

Muḥammad Kurrā (d. 1804) in Fur "Muḥammad the Tall"; a palace servant in the days of Sultan Muḥammad Tayrāb who rose to become, despite temporary setbacks, shaykh-father under sultans ʿAbd al-Raḥmān and Muḥammad Faḍl and, for a time, master of Kordofan. His rivalry with Muḥammad Faḍl led to his death. The author was a protégé of Muḥammad Kurrā's associate Mālik al-Fūtāwī and met Muḥammad Kurrā shortly before the shaykh-father's death.

Muḥammad al-Maḥrūqī likely the leading merchant of that name (d. 1232/1816–17) appointed by Muḥammad ʿAlī to advise his son Ṭūsūn when the latter was given responsibility for the campaign (1811–16) against the Āl Saʿūd rulers of the Hejaz.

Muḥammad al-Muknī nineteenth-century governor of Fezzan (southern Libya).

Muḥammad Órré Dungo a eunuch belonging to Sultan Muḥammad Tayrāb and a shaykh-father.

Muḥammad Shihāb al-Dīn al-Miṣrī Muḥammad ibn Ismāʿīl ibn ʿUmar (1210–74/1795–1857), known as Shihāb al-Dīn al-Miṣrī, a scholar and poet who became coeditor of the official *Egyptian Gazette* (*al-Waqāʾiʿ al-Miṣriyyah*), was associated with the royal family, and wrote much occasional verse.

Muḥammad Tayrāb (r. ca. 1752–53 to 1785) third son of Aḥmad Bukur to become sultan of Darfur; invaded Kordofan toward the end of his reign and incorporated it into the sultanate, thus creating the largest premodern state within what is now the Sudan.

mukhkhayṭ a tree: *Boscia senegalensis.*

Murād Bayk Murād Bayk al-Qazdaghlī, a Mamluk who ruled Egypt in partnership with Ibrāhīm Bayk from 1784 until the French invasion in 1798.

muʿrāqī literally "rooter"; one skilled in the gathering and use of medicinal plants.

al-Musabbaʿ brother of Sultan Sulaymān Solóng (q.v.); left Darfur for western Kordofan, parts of which his descendants thereafter ruled.

al-Musabbaʿāwī, Hāshim (fl. 1770–1800) a descendant of al-Musabbaʿ who, during the reign in Darfur of Sultan Muḥammad Tayrāb, attempted to create from his base in Kordofan a state that would rival or supplant that of Darfur.

Musāʿid (ibn Surūr) a member of the family of the Dhawū Zayd dynasty of rulers of Mecca resident in Darfur during the author's time there.

al-Mutanabbī Aḥmad ibn al-Ḥusayn Abū l-Ṭayyib al-Mutanabbī (ca. 303–54/915–65), a renowned poet of the Abbasid era.

nārah a love potion.

Nufah (Nupe) a state, founded in the mid-fifteenth century, in what is now north-central Nigeria.

Numlayh a village in Jabal Marrah, in the area inhabited by the Karakriit, a clan of the Fur (not to be confused with Nimule, a town in South Sudan).

Nūr al-Anṣārī a holy man living in Kubayh and married to the daughter of Sultan ʿAbd al-Raḥmān.

nyúlmá (Fur) sesame lees.

The One-Thousand-Line Poem (al-Alfiyyah) a popular textbook of grammar in the form of a poem of some thousand lines, by Muḥammad ibn Mālik (ca. 600–72/1203–74).

ǒrnang (Fur) the representative of the men at a wedding and organizer of hunting parties for the young men of a village; the ǒrnang may be evidence of a residual age-grade system, comparable to that of the Maasai or the Zulu, in which he acted as a war leader.

orondolong (Fur) literally "the door posts"; the highest officer of state, also known as "the sultan's face" (or "the sultan's head"). In peace, he acted as majordomo of the sultan's compound and the main intermediary between sultan and subjects; in war, he marched at the head of the sultan's army. He also governed four tribal territories.

órré bayyâ (Fur) literally "the narrow door," but generally referred to as "the women's door": the southern entrance to the sultan's compound or *fāshir*; also, in the author's usage, the superintendent of the *warrābāyah*, who supervised the eunuchs of the harem and acted as jailer and executioner.

órré dee (Fur) "the men's door": the northern entrance to the sultan's compound or *fāshir*.

órré'ng ába (Fur) a title listed by the author as that of a member of the state hierarchy who governed two tribal territories, without further explanation of the title's meaning or its holder's role.

păw (Fur) artificial coral.

Perron, Nicolas (1798–1876) the translator from Arabic into French of *The Land of the Blacks* (*Voyage au Darfour*) and other works. See Volume One, Introduction.

The Poem on Words Ending in -ā and ā' (al-Maqṣūrah) a pedagogical poem by Mūhammad ibn al-Ḥasan ibn Durayd (223–321/838–933).

pôlgo (Fur) kind of manufactured salt, sold in finger-shaped pieces.

poora'ng ába (Forrang Aba; Fur) literally "Father of the Fur"; the guardian of Fur law and custom, a ritual title dating from the Fur state's remote past.

Preserved Tablet the urtext of the Qur'an, preserved in Heaven.

the Protected City an epithet of Cairo.

qafal a tree: perhaps in this context frankincense (*Boswellia papyrifera*) or African myrrh (*Commiphora africana*); identification is tentative as the word was applied to a number of trees used in perfumes, medicines, and incense.

qanā savannah bamboo (*Oxytenanthera abyssinica*).

qaraẓ the pods of the sant acacia (*Acacia nilotica*), used for fodder.

Qimir see Dār Qimir.

Qirlī (Gurly, Gerli, Gerle) a settlement, now disappeared, that the author places between the northern end of Jabal Marrah and Kabkābiyyah on the west, site of a *fāshir* of Sultan Muḥammad Tayrāb.

The Qualities *The Prophetic Qualities* (*al-Khaṣā'iṣ al-nabawiyyah*), a work on the qualities of the Prophet Muḥammad by Egyptian historian and Hadith scholar Mughulṭāy al-Turkī.

qudānī an indigo-dyed cloth.

quffah in Egypt, a large basket.

qūqū the practice of carrying a baby by tying it to its mother's back.

al-Qurṭubī Muḥammad ibn Aḥmad ibn Abī Bakr al-Anṣārī al-Qurṭubī (d. 671/1273), author of a renowned commentary on the Qur'an and other works, including his *Memorandum on the Conditions of the Dead and Matters of the Hereafter* (*al-Tadhkirah fī Aḥwāl al-Mawtā wa-Umūr al-Ākhirah*); originally from Cordoba, Spain, he relocated to Egypt.

al-Quṣayr a port on Egypt's Red Sea coast, the point of embarkation for pilgrims going to the Hejaz.

Quss Quss ibn Sāʿidah (sixth century AD), a pre-Islamic Arabian Christian renowned for the eloquence of his preaching.

rabdā' (of an ostrich) having four small, pure-white plumes.

Rajab seventh month of the Islamic calendar; it has the epithet "the Separate" because, under the pre-Islamic system according to which no fighting was allowed during certain months, it was the only such month that was neither preceded nor followed by another sacred month.

Rās al-Fīl see Jadīd Rās al-Fīl.

al-Raṭlī Pond one of thirteen ponds or lakes that existed in Cairo until the nineteenth century.

réèka (Fur) a kind of large basket.

The Reliable Compendium (*al-Jāmiʿ al-ṣaḥīḥ*; *al-Ṣaḥīḥ*), a collection of some eight thousand sound hadiths, by Muḥammad ibn Ismāʿīl al-Bukhārī (194–256/810–70).

Rīfā a son of Sultan Aḥmad Bukur who was passed over for the succession in favor of ʿAbd al-Raḥmān.

Rīl town in southeast Darfur (Dār Birqid); formerly a *fāshir*.

Rīz a son of Sultan Aḥmad Bukur who was passed over for the succession in favor of ʿAbd al-Raḥmān.

Rizayqāt (Rizayqat, Rizeigat) a group of nomadic Arabic-speaking peoples with northern (camel-herding) and southern (cattle-herding) sections, the former living in the north and west, the latter in the south and southeast of Darfur.

rubʿ a measure of volume used for grain, equivalent to 8.25 liters.

Rūngā a town in Dār Rungā (q.v.).

ruqād al-fāqah (literally "restful sleep") a kind of large bead worn by the women of the rich.

Ṣābūn, Muḥammad sultan of Wadai (r. ca. 1805–16).

the Sacred House the Kaaba at Mecca.

al-Ṣaftī probably Aḥmad al-Sāʾīm al-Safṭī, shaykh (rector) of the mosque-university of al-Azhar in Cairo from 1838 to 1847.

Salīmah (Selima) an uninhabited oasis on the route from Asyut to Darfur, between al-Shabb and Laqiyyah.

sangadiri (Fur) a dance.

ṣanṭ sant acacia (*Vachellia* (or *Acacia*) *nilotica*).

Sarf al-Dajāj town northwest of Jabal Marrah and west of Kabkābiyyah; according to Perron, *sarf* (Fur) means "brook"; thus the name means "Chickens' Brook."

ṣarīf internal fence within a homestead acting as a dust-break for the huts.

sayāl umbrella thorn tree (*Vachellia/Acacia tortilis*).

sayyid male claiming descent from the Prophet Muḥammad; also the title of such a man, used interchangeably in this work with "Sharif."

sequin gold coin minted in Venice.

al-Shabb (Sheb) literally "alum"; a small oasis north of Salīmah on the road from Asyut to Darfur.

al-Shāfiʿī, Muḥammad ibn Idrīs (150–204/767–820) a leading jurist from whose teachings emerged one of the four canonical schools of legal interpretation, and a much-quoted poet.

al-Shaʿīriyyah a village near Tandaltī (today's El-Fasher).

Shālā a Fartīt people living on the southern fringes of the sultanate.

shallāngīn (Arabization of Fur *sagala kin*) traditional eye doctors specializing in the removal of cataracts.

shaʿlūb a vine (*Leptodenia arborea*).

sharāmīṭ literally "shreds": jerked meat.

sharif a male claiming descent from the Prophet Muḥammad; also, the title of such a man, used interchangeably in this work with "Sayyid."

shartāy (pl. sharātī) head of a *shartāyah*, one of the districts into which the provinces of the sultanate of Darfur were divided. The *shartāy* was the representative of the ruler and his village was the center for the collection of taxes, the administration of justice, and the levying of troops.

shāshiyyah in Tunisia, a rigid red felt cap similar to that called a tarboosh in Egypt.

shāw a tree: arak (*Salvadora persica*).

shawtar (pl. shawātir) a kind of camlet (a fine woolen fabric, originally of camel hair), sometimes dyed blue, and used in some areas as currency.

shaykh-father (Arabic: al-ab al-shaykh; Fur: abbo shaykh (daali)) chief eunuch and traditionally governor of the eastern region (Dār Dālī); the holder, though not necessarily himself a slave, was head of the slave hierarchy. Arabic *ab* "father" assimilates Fur *abbo*, a title of respect.

shīkah a kind of raw calico (*tukkiyyah*) of light, loose weave.

Shīth Seth, third son of Ādam and Ḥawwāʾ (Adam and Eve) and one of the first prophets.

shūsh small red seeds used to make amulets and as hair decorations for women.

shuwūr a bead bracelet worn by women (synonym of *madraʿah*).

Silā see Dār Silā.

Sinnār (Sennar) a town in the area between the Blue and White Niles now known as al-Jazīrah; home of the Funj sultanate, which lasted from 1504 until its conquest by Egyptian forces under Muḥammad ʿAli's son Ibrāhīm in 1821.

Ṣirāṭ a promontory on the coast of Tunisia between Sejnane and Tabarka (Cap Serrat).

Sodom apple a tree (*Calotropis procera*; Arabic: *ʿushar*).

soom'íng dogólá (Fur) the pages' house (literally "the children's house"). The author describes these pages or cadets as agents who oversaw the sultan's business. The *soom*, located within the *fāshir*'s public area, was also the assembly place where the people came together for conversation or for a common meal; it also functioned as a school where the palace pages or cadets were taught.

soomiit (Fur) a kind of bead.

sūbiyā in Egypt, a cold, thick nonalcoholic drink of slightly fermented rice, sugar, and water.

sudāsī (fem., sudāsiyyah) literally a "sixer": a slave measuring six handspans from heel to earlobe.

suklāyah a kind of house (see §3.1.86, images).

Sulaymān al-Azharī father of the author's teacher Aḥmad ibn Sulaymān, and the maternal grandfather of the author's father.

Sulaymān ibn ʿAbd al-Malik ibn Marwān sixth caliph of the Umayyad dynasty (r. 96–99/715–17).

Sulaymān Solóng (r. ca. 1660–80) founding father of the Keira dynasty in its historical manifestation. This sultan, generally known as Sulaymān Solongdungo (meaning "the Arab" and/or "of reddish complexion"), who ruled from ca. 1660 to 1680, though regarded as the first historically documented sultan of the Keira dynasty, is said, in Fur tradition, to have been preceded by at least three earlier sultans. With his two immediate successors, Mūsā and Aḥmad Bukur, he was responsible for the transformation of their Fur tribal kingdom into a multiethnic empire and played a major role in the Islamization of the Darfurian state.

Sulaymān al-Tūnisī the author's paternal grandfather

suspended ode (muʿallaqah) one of the seven renowned poems by seven renowned poets that (according to legend) hung in the Kaaba in the days before Islam.

al-sūtiyyah inflammation of the knee joint.

al-Suwaynah (Sweini) the first village in Darfur reached by caravans coming from Asyut.

al-Suyūṭī, Jalāl al-Dīn a prolific Egyptian polymath (d. 911/1505).

tābā tobacco.

ṭabābī a practitioner of the science of magic (*ṭibb*).

tabaldī a tree: the baobab (*Adansonia digitate*).

Tabaldiyyah a place northeast of Nyala where Sultan ʿAbd al-Raḥmān inflicted a defeat on his rival Isḥāq.

Ṭāhir a son of Sultan Aḥmad Bukur to whom Muḥammad Kurrā allegedly pledged allegiance when the latter revolted against Sultan Muḥammad Faḍl.

al-Ṭā'if a city in the Hejaz ninety miles northeast of Mecca.

takākī see *tukkiyyah.*

al-Takrūr a name used in northern Africa to designate West Africans in general; now pronounced Dakrūr.

Tāldawā a hill northeast of Nyala.

ṭalḥ a tree: red acacia (*Vachellia* (or *Acacia*) *seyal*).

Tāmā, Tāmah see Dār Tāmā, Dār Tāmah.

Tamurrū al-Fullānī a holy man known for his skill as a magician.

Tandaltī a town east of Jabal Marrah where Sultan ʿAbd al-Raḥmān established his *fāshir*, or royal compound, in 1206/1791–92. Subsequent sultans maintained the tradition; El-Fasher is now the name of the capital of North Darfur State.

Tărne (Tarni; Fur) a village southwest of Tandaltī (today's El-Fasher).

tărne (Fur) a ring of tin used as currency.

tawse (Fur) a dance, performed by slaves.

Ṭaybah a name for Medina, site of the tomb of the Prophet Muḥammad.

thawb a large wrap worn by women.

ṭibb magic.

*tikináwi (*takanawi*; in the author's spelling* takaniyāwī*; Fur)* title of the hereditary governor of Dār Zaghāwah in the sultanate's northern region (also known as Dār al-Tikináwi); the tikináwi had a position of command in the army and was known as "the Sultan's Left Arm."

tindinga (Fur) a dance.

togjêl (Fur) a kind of goblet drum.

Tomorókkóngá (Tamuurkwa; Fur) one of the three great sections of the Fur people; the Tomorókkóngá live to the west of Jabal Marrah.

the Tubū (Toubou, Tebou) an ethnic group speaking a Nilo-Saharan language that inhabits parts of today's Chad (where they are concentrated in the Tebesti region), Libya, Niger, and Nigeria.

al-Ṭughrā'ī Mu'ayyid al-Dīn Abū Isma'īl al-Ḥusayn ibn ʿAlī al-Ṭughrā'ī (453/1061 to 514/1120–21), Arab poet and administrator under the Saljuq sultans of Mosul and Baghdad.

al-Tuhāmī Abū l-Hasan ʿAlī al-Tuhāmī (d. 416/1025); poet and scholar of Yemeni origin.

tukkiyyah (pl. takākī) raw or unbleached calico; bolts of the latter ten cubits in length and one in breadth were used by poor women to make their robes and also, especially in the area around the sultan's capital, as currency.

tukultī a kind of house with a roof raised on two wooden pillars (see §3.1.86, images).

al-Tūnisī, ʿUmar ibn Sulaymān see ʿUmar ibn Sulaymān al-Tūnisī.

al-Tūnisī, Sulayman see Sulaymān al-Tūnisī.

Tunjūr a people living in central Darfur who in the sixteenth century superseded the Dājū as its rulers and as rulers in Wadai; in the mid-seventeenth century, they were themselves succeeded in Darfur by Fur sultans of the Keira dynasty.

Turqunak in the Wadai sultanate, one of sixteen freeborn men, four of whom acted as overseers of persons of the royal blood and four as captains of the sultan's bodyguard, while eight assisted the *kamkūlak*s (q.v.) in the provinces.

Turūj a generic and pejorative term applied by Darfurians to enslaveable tribes living south of Kordofan.

al-Ṭuwayshah a town close to Umm Kidādah on Darfur's border, and its surrounding district.

ʿUmar ibn Sulaymān al-Tūnisī the author's father.

ʿUmar Lēl (or Lēle) (r. ca. 1730–39), fifth historical sultan of the Keira dynasty, preceded by his father Muḥammad Dawra and succeeded by his uncle Abū l-Qāsim.

umm bulbul literally "Mother Nightingale"; a kind of barley wine.

the Victorious (al-Manṣūrah) smallest and most sacred of the royal kettledrums of the Darfur sultans.

vizier a general title (rather than an office) of high officials in the courts of Tunis, Darfur, and elsewhere.

al-Wādday (Wadday, Wadaday) Wadai, formerly a sultanate immediately to the west of Darfur, also called Dār Ṣulayḥ or Dār Ṣalīh; today part of Chad.

Wādī l-Kūʿ a seasonal watercourse running south from Jabal Sī (north of Jabal Marrah), on whose banks at Tandaltī Sultan ʿAbd al-Raḥmān built his *fāshir*.

Wārah the capital of the sultanate of Wadai.

warrāniyyah a meal eaten in addition to regular meals.

waykah a dish made from rehydrated ingredients, most commonly okra.

Yājūj and Mājūj monstrous peoples who, according to the Qur'an and the Torah (where they are called Gog and Magog), will invade the world on the last days before the Day of Judgment; they are said by some to number 400,000, by others to be nine times as numerous as humans.

Yūsuf Pasha Yūsuf Pasha al-Karamanlī (1795–1832), hereditary governor of Libyan Tripoli.

Yūsuf the Seal Bearer (Muhurdār) Yūsuf Ṣāḥib al-Ṭābiʿ (ca. 1765–1815); a slave, possibly Moldovan, bought at around age thirteen in Istanbul by Bakkār al-Jallūlī, an army commander and rich merchant of Sfax. Yūsuf was raised in the Jallūlī household and presented to Ḥammūdah Pasha, ruler of Tunis, when he was eighteen; he rose to be the latter's principal minister and the country's most powerful figure, with control over much of the economy. He was assassinated not long after his sponsor, Ḥammūdah Pasha, died.

al-Zaghāwah peoples speaking a language of the Nilo-Saharan family and living on the northern marches of Darfur and in Wadai.

al-Zaghāwī (or, Bīr al-Zaghāwī) a well on the road from Asyut to Darfur south of Laqiyyah, also called Bīr al-Malḥah.

zaghāwī a kind of naturally occurring salt.

zakat a property tax disbursed by the state in the form of alms for specified categories of persons.

ẓalīm (of an ostrich) having four large and four small pure-white plumes.

zarībah a fence of thorny branches surrounding a homestead.

al-Zarqā' a spring in Medina.

the Zayādiyyah Arabic-speaking camel-herding nomads of the Fazārah group living in the northeast of Darfur.

ẓufr literally "fingernail"; *Unguis odoratus*: fragments of the operculum, or plug, of certain kinds of mollusks, which when broken up resembles blackish fingernails and which is used in perfumes.

Bibliography

Abū l-ʿAmāyim, Muḥammad. *Āthār al-Qāhirah al-islāmiyyah fī l-ʿaṣr al-ʿUthmānī*. 3 vols. Istanbul: Markaz al-Abḥāth li-l-Tārīkh wa-l-Funūn wa-l-Thaqāfah al-Islāmiyyah bi-Istānbūl (IRCICA), 2003–15.

Ali, Siddig A. M. and Abdellatif Y. Idris. "Germination and Seedling Growth of Pearl Millet (Pennisetum glaucum L.) Cultivars under Salinity Conditions." *International Journal of Plant Science and Ecology* 1, no. 1 (2015): 1–5.

Al-Naqar, Umar. "Takrur, the History of a Name." *The Journal of African History* 10, no. 3 (1969): 365–74.

Arberry, Arthur J. *The Koran Interpreted*. Oxford World's Classics. Oxford: Oxford University Press, 1982.

Arkell, A. J. "Hebron Beads in Darfur." *Sudan Notes and Records* 20, no. 2 (1937): 300–5.

Artin, Yacoub Pacha, ed. *Lettres du Dr Perron du Caire et d'Alexandrie à M. Jules Mohl, à Paris, 1838–1854*. Cairo: F. Diemer, 1911.

Baedecker, K., ed. *Egypt. Handbook for Travellers. Part First: Lower Egypt with the Fayûm and the Peninsula of Sinai*. Second edition, revised and augmented. Leipzig: Karl Baedecker; London: Dulau and Co., 1885.

Bakri, M. Ahmed and F. Hassan El Gunaid. "The Plants Use for Traditional Treatment in East Darfour State, Sudan." *University of Bakht Alruda Scientific Journal*, no. 8 (September 2013): 56–66.

Browne, W. G. *Travels in Africa, Egypt, and Syria, from the Year 1792 to 1798*. London: T. Cadell Junior and W. Davies, 1799 [Ecco Eighteenth Century Collections Online Print Editions].

Cave, Francis O. and James D. MacDonald. *Birds of the Sudan, Their Identification and Distribution*. Edinburgh and London: Oliver and Boyd, 1955.

Clot Bey [Antoine Barthélemy Clot]. *Kunūz al-ṣiḥḥah wa-yawāqīt al-minḥah*, translated by Muḥammad al-Shāfiʿī, edited by Muḥammad ʿUmar al-Tūnisī and Nicolas Perron. Cairo: Būlāq, 1844.

De Waal, Alex, ed. *War in Darfur and the Search for Peace*. Cambridge, MA: Harvard University Press, 2007.

Dozy, R. *Supplément aux Dictionnaires Arabes*. 2 vols. Leyden: E. J. Brill, 1881 (offset: Beirut: Librairie du Liban, 1968).

EAL = Meisami, Julie Scott and Paul Starkey, eds. *Encyclopedia of Arabic Literature.* 2 vols. London and New York: Routledge, 1998.

EI2 = P. Bearman, Th. Bianquis, C. E. Bosworth, E. von Donzol, and W. P. Heinrichs, eds. *Encyclopaedia of Islam.* 2nd ed. Leiden: E. J. Brill, 1960–2009.

El-Tounsy, Mohammed Ebn-Omar. *Voyage au Darfour*, translated from the Arabic by Dr. Perron. Paris: Benjamin Duprat, 1845.

———. *Voyage au Ouaday*, translated from the Arabic by Dr. Perron. Paris: Benjamin Duprat, 1851.

Fabre, Antoine François Hippolyte, ed. *Dictionnaire des dictionnaires de médecine français et étrangers ou traité complet de médecine et de chirurgie pratiques, par une société de médecins.* 8 vols. Paris: Germer Baillière, 1840–41.

Fahmy, Khaled. "Translating Bichat and Lavoisier into Arabic," unpublished paper presented at the Middle East, South Asian, and African Studies Colloquium, Columbia University, February 9, 2015.

Al-Fīrūzābādī, Muḥammad ibn Yaʿqūb. *Al-Qāmūs al-muḥīṭ wa-l-qābūs al-wasīṭ fī al-lughah.* 2nd ed. 4 vols. Cairo: al-Maktabah al-Ḥusayniyyah al-Miṣriyyah, 1344/1925–26.

Flint, Julie and Alex de Waal. *Darfur: A Short History of a Long War.* London: Zed Books, 2005.

Francis, Peter, Jr. "Beadmaking in Islam: The African Trade and the Rise of Hebron." *BEADS: Journal of the Society of Bead Researchers* 2 (1990): 15–28.

Gray, Richard. *A History of the Southern Sudan, 1839–1889.* London: Oxford University Press, 1961.

Heyworth-Dunne, J. *An Introduction to the History of Education in Modern Egypt.* London: Luzac and Co., [1939].

Hill, Richard. *A Biographical Dictionary of the Sudan.* 2nd ed. London: Frank Cass, 1967.

Holy, Ladislav. *Neighbors and Kinsmen: A Study of the Berti of Darfur.* London: Christopher Hurst, 1974.

Hunwick, John O. and R. S. O'Fahey, eds. *Arabic Literature of Africa.* Vol. 1, *The Writings of Eastern Sudanic Africa to c. 1900.* Compiled by R. S. O'Fahey. Leiden: E. J. Brill, 1994.

Hunwick, John O. "Leo Africanus's Description of the Middle Niger, Hausaland and Bornu." In *Timbuktu and the Songhay Empire: Al Saʿdi's Tarikh al-Sudan Down to 1613 and Other Contemporary Documents*, edited and translated by John O. Hunwick, 272–91. Leiden: Brill, 1999.

Ibn Abī l-Ḍiyāf, Aḥmad. *Ithāf ahl al-zamān bi-akhbār mulūk Tūnis wa-ʿahd al-amān.* 9 vols. Tunis: al-Dār al-ʿArabiyyah li-l-Kitāb, 1999.

Lane, Edward William. *An Account of the Manners and Customs of the Modern Egyptians: The Definitive 1860 Edition.* Introduction by Jason Thompson. Cairo: The American University in Cairo Press, 2003.

Lane, Edward William. *An Arabic-English Lexicon.* 8 vols. London: Williams and Norgate, 1863–93.

Lentin, Jérôme. "Middle Arabic." In *Encyclopedia of Arabic Language and Linguistics.* General editor Kees Versteegh. Vol. 3, 215–24. Leiden–Boston: Brill, 2008.

McGregor, A. J. *Darfur (Sudan) in the Age of Stone Architecture c. AD 1000–1750: Problems in Historical Reconstruction.* Cambridge: Archaeopress, 2001.

Al-Maydānī, Aḥmad ibn Muḥammad. *Majmaʿ al-amthāl.* 2 vols. Cairo: al-Maṭbaʿah al-Khayriyyah, 1310 AH.

Messaoudi, Alain. "Perron, Nicolas." In *Dictionnaire des orientalistes de langue française*, 2nd ed. Edited by François Pouillon, 750–51. Paris: IISMM-Karthala, 2008.

Al-Mutanabbī, Abū l-Ṭayyib. *Al-ʿArf al-ṭayyib fī sharḥ dīwān Abī l-Ṭayyib.* Edited by Nāṣīf al-Yāzijī, revised by ʿUmar Fārūq al-Ṭabbāʿ. Beirut: Dār al-Arqam ibn Abī l-Arqam, n.d.

Nachtigal, Gustav. *Sahara and Sudan.* Vol. 3, *The Chad Basin and Bagirmi.* Translated from the original German, with an introduction and notes by Allan G. B. Fisher and Humphrey J. Fisher. London, C. Hurst, 1987. Vol. 4, *Wadai and Darfur.* Translated from the original German, with an introduction and notes by Allan G. B. Fisher and Humphrey J. Fisher with Rex S. O'Fahey. London, C. Hurst, 1971.

O'Fahey, R. S. and M. I. Abu Salim. *Land in Dar Fur.* Cambridge: Cambridge University Press, 1983.

O'Fahey, R. S. "Egypt, Saint-Simon and Muḥammad ʿAlī." In *The Exploration of Africa in the Eighteenth and Nineteenth Centuries*, 17–36. Edinburgh: Centre of African Studies, University of Edinburgh, 1972.

———. "Two Early Dar Fur Charters." *Sudan Texts Bulletin 1* (1979): 13–17.

———. "Slavery and the Slave Trade in Dar Fur." *Journal of African History* 14 (1973): 29–43.

———. "The Awlad ʿAli: A Fulany Holy Family in Dar Fur." In *Gedenkschrift Gustav Nachtigal, 1874–1974*, edited by Herbert Genslmayr, 147–66. Bremen: Übersee-Museum, 1977.

———. "The Archives of Shoba." *Sudanic Africa: A Journal of Historical Sources* 1 (1990): 71–83 (part one); 2 (1991): 79–112 (part two).

———. "A Prince and His Neighbours." *Sudanic Africa: A Journal of Historical Sources* 3 (1992): 57–93.

———. "Endowment, Privilege and Estate on the Central and Eastern Sudan." *Islamic Law and Society* 4 (1997): 258–67.

———. "The Conquest of Darfur, 1873–82." *Sudan Notes and Records*, New Series 1 (1998): 47–67.

———. *The Darfur Sultanate: A History*. New York: Columbia University Press, 2008.

———. *Darfur and the British*. London: Christopher Hurst, 2017.

———. "The Affair of Ahmad Agha." *Sudan Notes and Records* 53 (1972): 202–3.

Perron, Nicolas. *Al-Jawāhir al-saniyyah fī l-aʿmāl al-kīmāwiyyah*. Edited and translated by Muḥammad al-Tūnisī, Muḥammad al-Harrāwī, Darwīsh Zaydān, and Husayn Ghānim. 3 vols. Cairo: Būlāq, 1260/1844.

Qāsim, ʿAwn al-Sharīf. *Qāmūs al-lahjah al-ʿāmmiyyah fī l-Sūdān*. 2nd ed. Cairo: al-Maktab al-Miṣrī al-Ḥadīth, 1985.

Al-Qurṭubī, Muḥammad ibn Aḥmad ibn Abī Bakr Faraj al-Anṣārī. *Al-Tadhkirah fī aḥwāl al-mawtā wa-umūr al-ākhirah*. Edited by Aḥmad Ḥijāzī al-Saqqā. Cairo: Maktabat al-Kullīyāt al-Azhariyyah, [1980].

Al-Shāfiʿī, Muḥammad ibn Idrīs. *Shiʿr al-Shāfiʿī*. Edited by Mujāhid Muṣṭafā Bahjat. Mosul: University of Mosul, 1986.

Al-Sharīf, Muḥammad al-Hādī. *Tārīkh Tūnis*. 3rd ed. Tunis: Dār CERES li-l-Nashr (Centre d'Études et de Recherches Économiques et Sociales), 1993.

Al-Shayyāl, Jamāl. "Duktūr Birrūn (Dr. Perron) wa-l-shaykhān Muḥammad ʿAyyād al-Ṭanṭāwī wa-Muḥammad ʿUmar al-Tūnisī." *Majallat Kulliyyat al-Ādāb, Jāmiʿat Fārūq al-Awwal* 2 (1944): 179–221.

Al-Shidyāq, Aḥmad Fāris. *Leg over Leg*. Edited and translated by Humphrey Davies. 4 vols. Library of Arabic Literature. New York: New York University Press, 2013–14.

Al-Ṣūlī, Abū Bakr Muḥammad ibn Yaḥyā. *The Life and Times of Abū Tammām*. Edited and translated by Beatrice Gruendler. Library of Arabic Literature. New York: New York University Press, 2015.

Al-Ṭanṭāwī, Muḥammad ʿAyyād. *Aḥsan al-nukhab fī maʿrifat lisān al-ʿArab; Traité de la langue arabe vulgaire*. Leipzig: Wilhem Vogel, 1848.

Theobald, A. B. *ʿAli Dinar: Last Sultan of Darfur, 1898–1916*. London: Longmans, 1965.

Tully, Dennis. *Culture and Context in Sudan: The Process of Market Incorporation in Dar Masalit*. New York: SUNY Press, 1988.

Al-Tūnisī, Muḥammad ibn al-Sayyid ʿUmar ibn Sulaymān. *Tashḥīdh al-adhhān fī sīrat bilād al-ʿArab wa-l-Sūdān*. Paris: Benjamin Duprat, 1850.

———. *Tashḥīdh al-adhhān fī sīrat bilād al-ʿArab wa-l-Sūdān*. Edited and annotated by Khalīl Maḥmūd ʿAsākir and Muṣṭafā Muḥammad Musʿad. Cairo: al-Dār al-Miṣriyyah li-l-Ta'līf wa-l-Tarjamah, 1965.

Umar, H. S. "Al-Tunisi: Travels in Darfur. Translation, Collation and Annotation of *Tashhidh al-Adhhan bi Sirat Bilad al-Arab wa-l-Sudan*" (master's thesis, Bayero University, Kano, 1976).

Vogt, Kees. *Murshid ḥaqlī li-l-ta'arruf 'alā l-ashjār wa-l-shujayrāt al-shā'i'ah fī l-manāṭiq al-jāffah fī l-Sūdān wa-subul ikthārihā wa-fawā'idihā*. Translated by Kamāl Ḥasan Bādī. London: SOS International, n.d.

Walz, Terence. "Wakalat al-Gallaba: The Market for African Goods in Cairo." *Annales Islamologiques* 13 (1977): 263–86.

———. *Trade between Egypt and Bilad as-Sudan*. Cairo: Institut Français d'Archéologie Orientale du Caire, 1978.

Zack, Liesbeth. *Egyptian Arabic in the Seventeenth Century: A Study and Edition of Yūsuf al-Maghribī's Daf' al-iṣr 'an kalām ahl Miṣr*. Utrecht: Landelijke Onderzockschool Taalwetenschup, 2009.

List of Images

The *safrūk* §2.3.8
Tribes and Bedouin of Darfur §3.1.12
Scourges (3) §3.1.38
The *dinqār* §3.1.39
"The feathers" §3.1.40
The sultan's place of audience §3.1.41
The sultan's escort §3.1.45
The gourd of the *kóór kwa* §3.1.69
The *togjêl* §3.1.69
The *mooge*'s headband §3.1.71
The *mooge*'s stick §3.1.71
Pole for the *liqdabah* §3.1.78
Post holes for the *liqdabah* §3.1.78
Roof frame for the *liqdabah* §3.1.78
The sultan's audience dias §3.1.80
Decorative cloth for sultan's hut topknot §3.1.80
The *suktāyah* §3.1.86
The *tukultī* §3.1.86
Órré dee door §3.1.89
The sultan's fashir at Tandalti §3.1.92
Women's noserings (2) §3.1.98
Women's necklaces (2) §3.1.100
A *shūsh* amulet §3.1.101
Women's forehead ornament (*laday*) §3.1.103
Tool for treating *abū l-lisān* §3.3.4
Cauterization for diarrhea §3.3.6
Tracks of the smallpox creature §3.3.10
Cuts for treatment of pleurisy §3.3.14
Spear for hunting §3.3.33
A net for bird-hunting §3.3.35
A hoe §3.3.52
Geomancy patterns:
"the Road" §4.54
"the Group" §4.55
"the Jawbone" §4.56
"the Upside Down" §4.57
"the Gathering" §4.58
"the Knot" §4.59
"the Incoming Threshold" §4.60
"the Outgoing Threshold" §4.61
"the Incoming Fist" §4.62
"the Outgoing Fist" §4.63
"Whiteness" §4.64
"Redness" §4.65
"the Bed" §4.66
"Pure of Cheek" §4.67
"Incoming Support" §4.68
"Outgoing Support" §4.69
Arrangement of holes for "casting the sand" §4.70

Index

Ab Sanūn, §3.2.57
ába ăw mang, §3.1.52
ába dima'ng, §3.1.9, §3.1.14, §§3.1.53–54, §3.1.92, 255n9. *See also* Dār Ába Dima'ng
ába poor-ii, §3.1.51, 259n55
ába umá, §3.1.14. *See also* Dār Ába Umá
ʿAbd Allāh Kartab, §4.47
ʿAbd al-Karīm ibn Khamīs ʿArmān, §4.48
ʿAbd al-Raḥmān al-Rashīd, §3.1.38, §3.1.73, §3.1.85, §3.1.108, §§4.40–41
Abīrīs, ix
abū abāṭ. *See* sorghum
Abū Bakr al-Ṣiddīq (caliph), 270n221
Abū l-Judūl, §3.1.15, §3.3.24
Abū l-Qāsim (sultan of Darfur), §4.41
abū shalawlaw. *See* sorghum
abū ṣuffayr. *See* jaundice
abū l-ṣufūf. *See* pleurisy
abū ṭanṭarah (bird), §3.3.34, 269n208
Abū Zaʿbal, §4.19
acacia, §4.6, §4.18, 271n240
Ādam (Adam), §§3.2.1–3, §3.2.35, §4.39
Adiqiz, ix, §3.1.1
ʿAfnū, §3.2.58
Agadez. *See* Adiqiz
agate, §3.1.100, 262n98
agha, §3.2.34
Aḥmad Badawī, §3.1.32
Aḥmad al-Fāsī, §3.3.38
Aḥmad Zarrūq (author's half-brother), §4.52
alcohol, §3.1.109, 284n128. *See also* beer; wine
Alexandria, ix
Algiers, ix
ʿAlī [ibn Abī Ṭālib], 267n169
ʿAlī Kartab, §4.47
amber, §3.1.100
amulet, §3.1.94, §3.1.101, §3.2.43, §3.3.7
Anbūsah (mother of Muḥammad Faḍl), §3.2.47
ʿandurāb (tree), §4.12
anklet, §3.1.71, §3.1.103, §§3.2.10–12, §3.2.48
ʿanqallū (fruit), §3.3.28
antimony, §3.1.104
ʿaqīq (bead), §3.1.100, §3.1.103, 262n98
Aqlīmā, §3.2.35, 266n147
Arab, Arabs, §3.1.5, §§3.1.12–13, §3.1.17, §3.1.19, §3.1.21, §3.1.35, §3.1.41, §3.2.47, §3.3.7, §4.33, 267n170, 270n218
Arabic (language), §3.1.11, §3.1.23, §3.1.29, §3.1.41, §3.1.71, §3.1.76, §3.1.112, §§3.2.26–27, §3.2.29, §3.2.33, §3.2.57, §4.3, §4.33, 255n8, 257n25, 257n32, 257n34, 258n37, 260n63, 260n66, 260n73, 261n86, 262n92, 262n96, 263n107, 264n129, 264n132, 264n134, 265n140, 265n141, 265n144, 266n149, 267n172, 271n235, 271n236, 272n255
artemisia, §3.1.104, 263n110
ʿazīr. *See* sorghum

baft, §3.1.95, §3.1.97

Bakrī (family), §3.3.48, §270n221

Bakurlūkū, §4.35

baldāyā, §3.1.78

bamboo. *See qanā*

banana tree, §3.1.19, §4.7

Banī ʿAdī, ix

banquet, §3.1.33, §3.1.74, §3.1.110, §3.2.42

Banū Jarrār, §3.1.5, §3.1.12, §3.3.23, §3.3.37

Banū ʿUmrān, §3.1.5, §3.3.23

Banū Ḥalbah, §3.1.5, §3.1.12

(al-)Bāqirmah, ix, §§3.1.1–2, §3.1.96, §3.2.58

baradiyyah (drum), §3.1.83

Barajūb, §3.1.6

barley beer. *See* beer

Barnaw, §§3.1.1–2, §3.1.96, §3.2.58, §4.43

Barqū, §3.1.4, §3.1.10, §3.1.35, §3.2.57

Bartī, §3.1.3, §3.1.10, §§3.1.13–14, §3.1.35, §3.2.57, §3.3.23

baṭṭūm (tree), §4.23

bead, §3.1.33, §3.1.71, §§3.1.98–103, §3.2.43, §3.2.50, §3.3.45, §3.3.53, §4.51, 262n101, 263n104, 263n106, 270n224. *See also ʿaqīq; dam-l-raʿāf; ḥarish; khaddūr; manjūr; manṣūṣ; mishāhrah; ruqād al-fāqah; soomiit*

beans, §3.1.65, §3.1.101, §4.2, §§4.5–6, §4.70, 262n100, 262n101, 271n233

Bedouin, §3.1.12, §3.2.46, §3.3.2, §§3.3.8–9, §3.3.18, §3.3.22, §§3.3.37–40, §4.9

beer, §3.2.32; barley (*būzah*); §3.2.6; millet, §3.2.5, §3.2.28

Bidayāt, §3.3.22

bindalah (dance), §3.2.8, §3.2.11

Bīngah, §§3.1.7–8, §3.3.22

Bīqū, §3.1.4, §3.1.7, §3.1.10, §3.1.13, §3.1.15, §3.1.35, §3.2.48, §3.2.57

Bīr al-Zaghāwī (Bīr al-Malḥah), ix, §3.3.47

bird, §3.1.70, §§3.3.34–35. *See also abū ṭanṭarah*; bustard; ostrich; parakeet; parrot; sparrow; whydah

Birqid, §3.1.4, §3.1.10, §§3.1.13–15, §3.2.5, §3.2.12, §3.2.57, §3.3.9, 264n126. *See also* Dār Birqid

Black Misīriyyah. *See* Misīriyyah

black thorn, §3.1.88

black-eyed peas, §4.5

Blacks, §§3.1.1–2, §3.1.23, §3.1.76, §3.2.37, §3.2.43, §§3.2.45–47, §§3.2.57–59, §§3.3.7–8, §3.3.10, §3.3.23, §3.3.43, §3.3.48, §§4.21–22, §4.25, §4.29, §4.31

bracelet, §3.1.103, §3.3.53, 260n66, 270n244

broadcloth, §3.1.40

Brown Misīriyyah. *See* Misīriyyah

Browne, W. G., 260n70, 261n78, 263n109, 270n214, 270n217, 272n260

Būlāq (near Cairo), ix

Būlāq (oasis), ix

al-burjuk. *See* scarlet fever

bustard, §3.3.34

būzah (*būẓah*). *See* beer

Cairo, ix, §3.1.16, §3.3.11, §4.6, 255n8, 271n232

Cairo Canal. *See* al-Khalīj al-Miṣrī

calico, §3.1.97

camel, §3.1.5, §3.1.79, §3.1.110, §3.2.53, §3.3.32, §3.3.37, §3.3.39, §3.3.47, §4.42, §4.44, §4.52

camlet, §§3.1.96–97, §3.3.44

Cancer (constellation), §4.29, 272n251

caravan, §4.49

carob, §4.10, §4.15

cashmere, §3.1.94

castration, §§3.2.38–39, §3.2.55, 267n170. See also eunuch
cattle, §3.1.5, §3.1.16, §§3.1.42–43, §§3.1.65–66, §3.2.5, §3.2.22, §3.3.21, §3.3.26, §3.3.29, §3.3.31, §§3.3.37–38, §3.3.44, §3.3.54, §4.3, §4.44, 260n68, 269n206
cauterization, §3.2.55, §§3.3.6–7, §3.3.12, §3.3.17. *See also* surgery
childbirth, §3.3.19
cholera (*al-hayḍah*, "the yellow air"), §3.3.11, 268n189
circumcision, §3.1.111, §3.1.112, §3.2.28
cloth. *See* textiles
clothing, §3.1.25, §3.1.64, §§3.1.93–97, §3.2.39, §3.2.44, §3.3.37, §4.1, §4.8, §4.16, 259n52, 262n97, 263n107. *See also durrāʿah; fardah; kanfūs; milāʾah; thawb*
Constantinople, §3.2.38
copper, §3.1.53, §3.1.98, §3.1.103, §3.3.53, 257n35, 257n36, 259n58, 270n214, 270n224
coral, §§3.1.98–100, §3.1.103
coriander, §3.1.19, §4.6
cotton, §3.1.65, §§3.1.95–97, §3.2.55, §3.3.44, §§3.3.50–51, §4.16, 270n217
counselor, §§3.1.14–15, §§3.1.56–57, §3.1.80, §3.1.92, 260n61
court (of the sultan), §3.1.41, §3.1.77, §3.1.92, 259n52. *See also fāshir*; órré bayyâ; órré dee
covering the drums, §3.1.42, §3.1.46, §3.1.95, 258n44
crema, crème. See madīdah
cress, §4.6
crops. *See abū abāṭ; abū shalawlaw; ʿazīr*; beans; black-eyed peas; coriander; cress; cucumber; *dinbī*; eggplant; fava beans; garlic; Jew's mallow; *kawal; kūrayb*; long cucumber; millet; okra; onions; pepper; sesame; sorghum; squash; wheat
cucumber, §3.1.19, §4.6, §§4.48–49
currency §§3.3.41–55. *See also* bracelet; cattle; cotton; dollar; franc; *khaddūr; ḥarish*; millet; onion; piaster; *pôlgo*; sequin; *shawtar; sudāsī; tărne*; tobacco; *tukkiyyah*

Dafʿ Allāh, §3.2.31
Dājū, §3.1.4, §3.1.10, §3.1.13, §3.1.15, §3.1.35, §3.2.57
dalayb. See palm
al-Dalīl (judge), §3.3.11, §4.29
dallúka (drum, dance), §3.2.5, §3.2.8, §3.2.16, §3.2.20, §3.2.22, §3.2.28
damālij. See dimlij
Damascus, §3.1.102
dam-l-raʿāf (bead), §3.1.100, §3.1.103, 262n99
damsuga, §3.1.31, §§3.1.32–33. *See also* jinni
daqarah (plant), §§4.27–28
Dār Ába Dima'ng, §§3.1.8–14. *See also* ába dima'ng
Dār Ába Umá, 256n11. *See also* ába umá
Dār Bandalah, §3.1.7
Dār Bīngah. *See* Bīngah
Dār Birqid, §3.1.4, §§3.1.14–15. *See also* Birqid
Dār Fanqarū, §3.1.7, §3.1.8, §3.1.11, §3.3.22
Dār al-Farāwujayh, §3.1.4, §3.1.9
Dār Fartīt, §3.1.3, §4.15, §§4.24–25, §§4.48–49. *See also* Fartīt
Dār Mallā (Dār Mullā), §3.1.1

Dār Masālīṭ, §3.1.3. *See also* Masālīṭ
dār al-nuḥās. *See* Drum House
Dār Qimir, §3.1.3
Dār al-Rīḥ. *See* Dār (al-)Zaghāwah
Dār Rungah, §§3.1.7–8
Dār Silā, §3.1.11, §3.2.22
Dār Ṣulayḥ. *See* Waddāy
Dār Tāmah, §3.1.3, §4.52, 266n162
Dār (al-)Tikináwi. *See* tikináwi; Dār (al-)Zaghāwah
Dār Tomorókkóngá. *See* Dār Ába Dima'ng
Dār Tunbuktū, ix, §3.1.1
Dār Wāddāy. *See* Wāddāy
Dār (al-)Zaghāwah, §3.1.3, §3.1.7, §3.1.9, §3.1.14, §3.3.22. *See also* Zaghāwah, tikináwi
darabukkah (drum), §3.1.69, §3.1.83, §3.2.5
darat (season), §3.3.8, §4.12, §4.29, 271n249
Darfur, ix, §3.1.1, §§3.1.3–5, §§3.1.7–8, §3.1.10, §§3.1.12–14, §3.1.16, §§3.1.21–22, §3.1.27, §3.1.32, §3.1.34, §3.1.38, §§3.1.42–43, §3.1.46, §3.1.48, §3.1.50, §§3.1.74–76, §3.1.93, §3.1.95, §3.2.13, §3.2.29, §§3.2.37–39, §3.2.46, §3.2.48, §3.2.54, §3.3.3, §3.3.13, §3.3.22, §3.3.37, §3.3.43, §§3.3.47–48, §4.3, §§4.6–7, §4.9, §4.11, §4.15, §§4.24–25, §§4.33–34, §§4.39–42, §4.46, §§4.48–50, 255n1, 255n5, 255n7, 256n11, 256n13, 257n23, 257n32, 257n36, 260n73, 262n102, 263n109, 264n126, 264n133, 265n136, 266n153, 267n170, 268n194, 269n207, 269n210, 270n214, 270n231, 271n237, 271n249, 272n249, 271n250, 272n257
Darfurians, §3.1.22, §3.1.43, §4.46, 264n133, 265n136
Darmūdī, §3.3.32, §§3.3.35–36
date palm. *See* palm
dawdarī, §§3.3.26–27. *See also waykah*
dāyūq (tree), §3.1.104
dééng saaya, §3.2.6, §3.2.28
Dhamīmā, §3.2.35, 226n147
dhikr, §§3.2.29–33, 265n142
dimlij (pl. *damālij*), §3.1.63, 260n66
dinbī, §4.3. *See also* millet
dinjāyah, §3.1.91
dinqār (drum), §3.1.39, §3.1.53, §3.1.80, 289n58
disease, §§3.3.4–5, §§3.3.7–8, §§3.3.11–15, §3.3.18, §§3.3.23–24, §4.27, 267n166. *See also* cholera; dropsy; *al-duqrī*; *al-ghuzayyil*; gonorrhea; guinea worm; *al-habūb*; jaundice; *al-jiqqayl*; leucorrhea; leprosy; measles; plague; pleurisy; scarlet fever; smallpox; *al-sūtiyyah*; syphilis; tuberculosis; *umm ṣuquʿ*; vitiligo; *wirdah*
dollar, §§3.3.38–39, §3.3.44, §3.3.51, §3.3.54, 270n218
doum palm (*muql*). *See* palm
dropsy, §3.3.15
drum, §3.1.22, §3.1.34, §§3.1.38–39, §3.1.42, §§3.1.45–46, §3.1.53, §3.1.69, §3.1.70, §3.1.83, §3.1.90, §3.1.92, §3.1.95, §3.2.5, §3.2.7, §3.2.12, §3.2.16, §3.2.22, §3.2.28, §3.2.42, §3.3.29, 256n20, 257n36, 258n44, 258n45, 259n50, 259n51, 259n58, 264n130. *See also baradiyyah*; *dallúka*; *darabukkah*; *dinqar*; kettledrums; *naqāqīr*; *togjêl*; *tómbol*; the Victorious
Drum House (House of Copper), §3.1.38, §3.1.45, §3.1.90, §3.1.92, 257n35
dulab. *See* palm
dullong, §3.1.86

the Dunes, §3.1.16, §3.3.22, §4.30, 256n18
al-duqrī (disease), §3.3.15
durdur, §3.1.86
durrāʿah, §3.1.97, 262n97
dust devils, §4.31

earrings, §3.1.99
ebony (tree), §4.24
eggplant, §4.6
Egypt, Egyptians, §3.1.3, §3.1.32, §3.1.35, §3.1.42, §3.1.69, §3.1.71, §3.1.83, §3.1.93, §3.1.95, §3.1.104, §3.1.112, §3.2.6, §3.2.34, §3.3.7, §3.3.8, §3.3.11, §3.3.14, §3.3.19, §3.3.21, §3.3.48, §4.3, §4.5, §§4.6–7, §4.12, §4.17, §4.29, 255n8, 257n25, 262n95, 262n96, 262n101, 263n104, 263n109, 266n151, 270n221, 271n233, 271n249, 272n249
elephant, §§3.3.31–32, 260n70
El-Fasher, x
emir, §3.1.92, §3.2.40, §3.2.56, §3.3.26
eunuch, §3.1.59, §3.1.90, §3.1.92, §3.1.108, §3.2.34, §§3.2.37–38, §3.2.40, §§3.2.43–44, §3.2.49, §§3.2.53–55, 266n153, 267n170. *See also* castration
Europe, §3.1.21, §3.1.100, 256n11, 256n21. *See also* Franks

Fallātā (Fullān), §3.1.1, §3.1.5, §3.1.12, §3.3.18, §3.3.21, §3.3.23, §4.42, 255n6
fan. *See* feathers
Fanqarū. *See* Dār Fanqarū
faqīh, §3.1.18, §§3.1.22–24, §§3.1.79–80, §3.1.92, §3.3.18, §3.3.21, §3.3.25, §3.3.36, §4.39, §§4.41–42
al-farandīt. *See* guinea worm
Farāwujayh. *See* Dār al-Farāwujayh
fardah, §3.1.97
al-fartīt. *See* guinea worm
Fartīt, §3.1.7, §4.15, §4.25, §4.48, 260n65, 265n136, 266n153. *See also* Dār Fartīt
fāshir, §3.1.14, §3.1.77, §3.1.87, §§3.3.44–45, §4.6, 256n16, 261n65
fava beans, §3.1.65, §4.2, §4.5, 262n101. *See also* bean
Fazārah, §3.1.5. *See also* Maḥāmīd; Majānīn
feathers, §3.1.40, §3.1.72, §3.1.100, §3.3.35, §§3.3.38–39
the feathers (the sultan's fan), §3.1.40, §3.1.94
Fezzan, ix, §3.3.38, §3.3.48
franc, §3.1.76, §3.3.44
the Frankish disease. *See al-jiqqayl*
Franks, §3.1.28, §3.3.12, §3.3.19, §3.3.46, §3.3.48, §4.5, §4.30. *See also* Europe
French, §3.3.38, §3.3.44, 257n26, 258n46, 260n63, 261n90, 262n92, 262n99, 263n113, 265n137, 268n188, 269n207, 270n218, 270n220, 273n263
fruit, §4.17, §4.20, §4.29. *See also ʿanqallū*; banana trees; *baṭṭūm*; *dāyūq*; *hijlīj*; *ḥummayḍ*; jackalberry; jujube; *kilí*; *mukhkhayṭ*; pomegranate; *qiddīm*; *shaʿlūb*; *shāw*; shea; Sodom apple; *tabaldī*; tamarind; watermelon
Fullān. *See* Fallātā
Fur, §§3.1.3–4, §3.1.7, §3.1.9, §§3.1.1–12, §3.1.19, §3.1.29, §3.1.31, §3.1.33, §3.1.35, §3.1.37, §§3.1.41–42, §3.1.47, §3.1.51, §3.1.53, §3.1.59, §§3.1.67–68, §§3.1.70–73, §3.1.76, §3.1.78, §3.1.80, §3.1.82, §3.1.83, §§3.1.84–88, §3.1.97, §§3.1.104–5, §3.1.112, §3.2.4, §3.2.8, §3.2.12, §3.2.26, §3.2.29, §§3.2.33–34,

Fur (cont.), §3.2.38, §§3.2.40–41, §§3.2.57–58, §3.3.2, §3.3.23, §3.3.26, §3.3.29, §3.3.44, §§4.2–3, §4.6, §4.11, §4.28, §4.46, 255n7, 255n9, 265n14, 256n20, 257n26, 257n32, 258n38, 259n52, 259n53, 259n55, 259n58, 260n77, 262n99, 265n134, 265n137, 265n139, 265n144, 266n155, 267n168, 267n170, 271n263, 272n261
al-Fusṭāṭ, ix
al-Fūtāwī. *See* Madanī al-Fūtāwī; Mālik al-Fūtāwī

galanga, §3.2.41
garlic, §3.1.19, §4.6
geomancy, §§4.50–54, §4.71
Gemini (The Twins; al-Jawzā'), §4.29, 272n253. *See also* Twins' autumn
al-ghuzayyil (disease), §3.3.7
gold, §3.1.76, §3.1.98, §3.2.13, §§3.3.42–43, 264n132, 269n213
gonorrhea, 267n166. *See also al-jiqqayl*
gourd, §3.1.19, §§3.1.32–33, §3.1.69, §3.1.106
groom (in marriage), §3.1.105, §3.2.5, §§3.2.16–17, §3.2.19, §3.2.22, §3.2.23
groom (office) (*kūrāyāt*), §3.1.57, §3.1.90
guinea worm (*al-farandīt, al-fartīt*), §§3.3.14–15
gum arabic, §3.1.88, §4.18, §4.20
gunpowder, §3.1.33, §3.3.36, §4.17

Ḥabbāniyyah, §3.1.8, §3.3.40
ḥabbūbāt, 257n32
Hābīl (Abel), §3.2.36, 266n147
al-habūb (disease), §3.3.14
ḥarāz (tree), §4.19
harem, §3.1.107, §3.2.34, §3.2.37
ḥarīrah. See madīdah
ḥarish (bead), §3.1.102, §3.3.45, §3.3.47
Ḥasan al-Kaw, §3.2.41
al-ḥaṣar. See leucorrhea
ḥashāb (tree), §4.18, §4.20
ḥashshāshah, §3.3.12, 270n220. *See also* hoe
ḥasūw. See madīdah
Ḥawwā' (Eve), §§3.2.1–3
al-hayḍah. See cholera
Hebron, §3.1.102, 263n106
the Hejaz, §3.3.11
hijlīj (tree), §3.3.19, §3.3.25, §§3.3.27–28, §§3.3.39–40, §§4.7–8, §4.30, 269n212. *See also kumbā*
hoe, §3.3.52, 270n223
honey, §3.1.19, §3.1.101, §3.3.17, §3.3.25, §§3.3.38–40, §4.4, §4.7, §4.9
horn, §3.1.103, §3.3.29, §3.3.32, §3.3.38, §4.34, §4.38
horse, §3.1.5, §3.1.40, §§3.1.47–48, §3.1.64, §3.1.79, §3.1.90, §3.1.92, §3.1.94, §§3.2.40–41, §3.2.52, §3.3.37, §3.3.44, §3.3.54, §4.17, §4.41, §4.47, §4.50, 257n24, 261n82, 265n136
House of Copper. *See* Drum House
ḥummayḍ (tree), §4.12
hunting, §3.1.40, §3.1.50, §3.1.71, §§3.3.30–31, §§3.3.34–39, 257n33, 269n207
Ḥurmat khidmat al-khiṣyān li-ḍarīh sayyid wuld ʿAdnān. See The Prohibited Nature of Using Eunuch Attendants at the Tomb of the Lord of ʿAdnān's Descendants

Ibrāhīm (Abraham), §4.39
India, §3.1.100, §4.16, 261n104, 270n225, 271n236

indigo, §3.1.96
interpreter, §3.1.39, §3.1.41, §3.1.80, §3.1.83
Iraq, 267n170
ʿIrayqāt, §3.3.37
iron, §3.1.38, §3.3.52, §4.30, 257n33
Isḥāq ("the Successor"), §3.2.40, §§4.40–41
Islam, §3.1.109, §3.2.55, 263n106. *See also* Muslim
ivory, §3.1.103, §3.3.32
iyā kūrī, §3.1.76, §3.1.86, §§3.1.91–92. *See also* Kinānah

Jabal Marrah, x, §§3.1.10–12, §§3.1.15–17, §3.1.23, §3.1.28, §§3.1.30–31, §3.1.35, §3.3.22, §4.3, §§4.6–7, 256n11, 256n18
Jabal Tāmah, §3.1.13, §4.52, 266n162
jackalberry, §4.24
Jadīd Karyū, x, §3.1.7, §3.1.10, §3.1.12, §3.2.14, §3.3.50, §4.42, 265n136
Jadīd Rās al-Fīl, x, §3.1.7, §3.1.10, §3.1.12, §3.3.52, 255n7
Jadīd al-Sayl, x, §3.1.12, §3.1.85
jaʿjaʿ (tree), §4.24, 271n242
jalād, §3.1.104
Jalāl al-Dīn al-Suyūṭī, §3.2.55
Jarkū, x
jaundice (*abū ṣuffayr*), §3.3.7
al-jawz al-hindī, §4.11, 271n237. *See also* palm
al-Jawzāʾ. *See* Gemini
Jedda, ix
jêl (dance), §§3.2.8–9, §3.2.13
jewelry, §3.1.98, §3.2.48, §3.3.43
Jew's mallow, §4.6
jinn, §3.1.22, §§3.1.30–31, §3.1.34, §3.1.42, §3.3.7, 263n118
al-jiqqayl (disease), §§3.3.12–13, 268n190
jujube, §3.3.39, §3.3.40, §4.9, §4.14, 271n235
juri jaráng, §3.2.26

kaamíne, §3.1.14, §§3.1.51–52, §3.1.92, §3.1.94, 259n56
kaʿb al-ṭīb, §3.1.104
kabartū, §3.1.83
Kabkābiyyah, x, §3.1.12, §§3.1.21–22, §3.3.45, §4.3, §§4.6–7
Kaeplin, §5.1
kalkaf, §§3.1.96–97
kamkūlak, §3.1.83
kanfūs, §3.1.97
karbābah, §3.3.8
al-Khārijah, ix
karīr, §3.2.9, §3.2.33
karnū (jujube), §4.9
Karyū. *See* Jadīd Karyū
Kashmirah, §3.2.57
Katakū, ix, §3.1.2, §3.2.58
katkāt, §3.3.44
kawal, §3.3.28
Keira, 255n5, 255n9, 257n36, 258n44, 259n58
kenykenya, §3.3.39, §4.9
kettledrums, §3.1.34, §3.1.38, §3.1.42, 257n36
khaddūr (bead), §3.1.102, §3.3.53, 263n107, 279n224
al-Khalīj al-Miṣrī, §4.6, 271n232
kharīf (season), §4.29, §4.32, 271n249
khayriyyah, §3.3.44
kilí (tree, fruit), §3.1.46, §4.26
kīm. *See* horn
Kinānah (iyā kurī, wife of ʿAbd al-Raḥmān al-Rashīd), §3.1.74

king, §3.1.1, §3.1.4, §3.1.9, §§3.1.14–15, §3.1.17, §3.1.34, §3.1.37, §§3.1.42–45, §3.1.49, §§3.1.53–54, §3.1.56, §3.1.59, §3.1.63, §3.1.65, §§3.1.68–69, §3.1.72, §3.1.74, §3.1.80, §§3.1.82–83, §3.1.86, §§3.1.92–93, §3.1.96, §3.2.17, §3.2.27, §3.2.53, §3.2.56, §3.3.18, §3.3.23, §3.3.41, §4.35, §4.43, §§4.48–49, 255n1, 257n33, 259n52, 259n56, 260n61

Kīrī, §3.1.86

kitir (tree), §4.18, §4.20

kohl, §3.1.104, §3.2.19

Konyunga, 255n9

kóór kwa, §3.1.39, §3.1.41, §3.1.46, §3.1.47, §3.1.58, §3.1.68, §3.1.80, §3.1.90, §3.1.92

Kordofan, §3.1.1, §3.1.16, §3.3.13, 256n18

Kūbayh, x, §3.1.7, §3.1.12, §3.1.21, §3.3.22, §3.3.45, §3.3.47, §4.3, §§4.6–7, 265n137

Kūkah, §3.2.57

kumbā, §3.3.26, §3.3.28, §4.8. *See also hijlīj*; salt

Kunjáara, §3.1.11, §3.1.16

kūrāyāt. *See* groom (office)

kūrayb, §3.3.40

kurnug, §3.1.86

Kusā, §3.3.48

Land of the Blacks, §3.1.2, §3.2.58, §§3.3.7–8, §3.3.10, §3.3.23, §3.3.43, §§4.21–22, §4.29, §4.31

Land of the Fūr, §3.1.1, §3.1.9, §3.1.6

language mouth, §3.1.83. *See also* interpreter

lanngi (dance), §§3.2.8–9, §3.2.14

la'ūt (tree), §§4.19–20

lawī (cotton), §4.16

lemon tree, §3.1.19, §4.2, §4.7

leprosy, §3.3.14

leucorrhea (*al-ḥaṣar*), §3.2.51, §3.3.14, 267n166

lion, §3.1.16, §3.3.31, §4.46, §4.49

liqdābah, §§3.1.78–79, 261n79

livestock, §3.1.30, §3.1.60, §3.1.110

long cucumber, §4.6

Madanī al-Fūtāwī, §3.3.18, §3.3.36, §4.39, §4.43

madīdah (*ḥarīrah*), §3.3.19, §4.5, §4.10

madra'ah (*shuwūr*), §3.1.103, §3.2.43

Magian (pagan, Zoroastrian), §3.2.55, §4.25, 267n170

magic (*ṭibb*), §3.1.85, §3.3.18, §3.3.21, §§4.39–42

mahaleb, §3.1.104

Maḥāmīd, §3.1.5, §3.3.23, §§3.3.37–38

Majānīn, §3.1.5, §3.3.23, §3.3.37

Malanqā (or Mananqā), §3.2.57

malik, §3.1.62, §4.44, §4.46, §4.49

Mālik al-Fūtāwī, §3.3.25, §4.41

Mananqā. *See* Malanqā

Mandarah, ix, §3.1.2

Manfalūṭ, ix

manjūr (bead), §3.1.102, §3.4.43, §3.2.50, 262n102, 263n104

manṣūṣ (bead), §3.1.100, §3.1.103

al-Maqs, ix

marāhīk. *See marhākah*

(al-)Marbūṭah, x, §3.1.12, §4.6

marhabayb, §3.1.78, §3.1.86, §4.20, 261n78

marhākah (pl. *marāhīk*), §3.1.91

maribou stork. *See abū ṭanṭarah*

mārīq. *See* sorghum

market, §§3.1.18–19, §3.1.61, §3.1.91, §3.3.45, §§3.3.47–52, §§3.3.54–55, §4.27, 270n216

Marrah, x, §3.1.11, §3.1.15, §3.1.23. *See also* Jabal Marrah
marriage, §3.1.113, §3.2.3, §3.2.25, §3.2.34, §3.2.48, §3.3.20, §3.3.32, §4.35, 264n123
Masālīṭ, §3.1.3, §§3.1.12–14, §3.2.57, §3.3.23, §4.42, §4.46
master of the tax collectors, §3.1.62, §3.1.66. *See also* taxation
maṭāriq, §3.1.78
al-Mazrūb, ix–x, §3.1.3, §3.1.7
measles, §3.3.15
Mecca, ix, §3.3.23, 255n3
Medina, ix, §3.3.23
mééram, §3.1.26, §§3.2.16–17, §3.2.19
Mīdawb, §3.1.3, §3.1.12, §3.2.57
mīdawbī. *See* salt
milā'ah, §3.1.95, 262n95
milk, §§3.1.32–33, §3.3.5, §3.3.17, §3.3.25, §3.3.28, §3.3.40, §4.3, §4.11, §4.17
millet, §3.1.28, §3.1.65, §3.1.78, §3.1.86, §3.1.91, §3.1.99, §3.2.5, §3.2.28, §3.3.7, §3.3.19, §3.3.28, §3.3.37, §3.3.40, §3.3.54, §4.3, §4.5, §4.20, §4.32, 261n88, 261n89, 270n227
millet beer. *See* beer
Mīmah, §3.1.4, §3.1.10, §3.1.15, §3.1.35, §3.2.57, §3.3.23
minerals. *See* agate; amber; antimony; copper; coral; gold; iron; natron; *păw*; salt; silver; zinc
mirages, §4.31
mishāhrah (bead), §3.1.102
Misīriyyah, §§3.1.5–6, §3.1.8, §3.1.12, §3.3.23, §3.3.40
mooge, §3.1.41, §3.1.67, §§3.1.71–73, §3.1.75, §3.1.80, 260n70
mortar, §3.3.26, §3.3.49, §4.5, §4.8, §4.27
mughrah, §4.50
Muḥammad (the Prophet), §3.2.55, §4.35, §4.45, 272n257
Muḥammad Daldan wad Binayyah, §3.2.14, §4.41, 265n135, 265n136
Muḥammad (al-)Faḍl (sultan of Darfur), §3.1.17, §3.1.76, §3.2.39, §3.2.47, §3.2.54, §4.41, 265n136
Muḥammad al-Ḥusayn, 258n45
Muḥammad Kurrā (shaykh-father), §3.1.55, §3.2.39, §3.2.54, §4.41
Muḥammad Órré Dungo, §§3.2.41–42, 266n155
Muḥammad Ṣābūn (sultan of Wāddāy), §3.1.13, §3.2.44, §4.52, 266n162
Muḥammad Tayrāb (sultan of Darfur), §3.1.6, §3.1.74, §§3.2.40–42, §4.41, 264n126, 272n260
Muḥammad Taytal (maternal uncle of Muḥammad Faḍl), §§3.2.47–48
Muḥammad al-Tūnisī, §3.1.17
mukhkhayṭ (tree), §4.14
Muqaṭṭam Hills, §3.1.16
muql. *See* palm
mu'rāqī, §4.34
musket, §3.1.33, §3.3.36, §4.40
Muslim, §3.2.55, 260n65, 263n122, 267n170. *See also* Islam
muslin, §§3.1.94–95
myrtle, §3.1.104

nabk (*nabq*). *See* jujube
Nachtigal, Gustav, 255n3, 257n32, 257n33, 258n42, 258n47, 259n50, 259n56, 260n61, 260n68, 261n78, 261n91, 263n107, 271n237
naqāqīr, §3.1.42. *See also* kettledrums

nārah, §4.35, 272n258
natron, §§3.3.4–5, §3.3.14
Nile, §4.29, 255n8
non-Arabic-speaking, §3.1.11, §3.1.35, §3.1.112, §3.2.29, §3.2.33, §3.2.57, §4.3
Non-Arabs, §3.1.17
Nufah, ix, §3.1.1
Numlayh, x, §3.1.12, §3.1.18, §3.1.31, §3.3.51, §4.7, §4.27
nyúlmá, §3.3.28

O'Fahey, R. S., 255n5, 256n13, 256n17, 257n33, 258n45, 259n56, 260n77, 265n136
okra, §4.6, 269n203, 270n231, 271n231
onions, §3.1.19, §3.3.51, §4.6, §4.48, §4.49
ŏrnang, §3.1.26, §3.3.29
orondolong, §3.1.14, §§3.1.50–51, §3.1.92, §3.1.94, 266n152
órré bayyâ, §3.1.59, §3.1.77, §3.1.80, §3.1.87, §§3.1.91–92, 260n64
órré dee, §3.1.59, §3.1.77, §3.1.79, §3.1.87, §§3.1.89–92, 260n64
órré'ng ába, §3.1.14
ostrich, §3.1.40, §3.1.71, §3.1.86, §§3.3.37–39, 269n210
ostrich eggs, §3.1.86

pagan. *See* Maglan
palm, §3.1.19, §3.1.32, §3.1.38; date, §4.7, §4.11; deleb (*dulab, dalayb*) palm, §3.2.11, §4.11, 271n236, 271n237; doum (*muql*), §4.12
parakeet, §3.3.35
Paris, §5.1
parrot, §3.3.35
păw, §3.1.100
pepper, §3.1.19, §3.3.28, §4.6, §4.27
Perron, Nicolas, §5.1, 256n11, 256n22, 258n37, 258n41, 260n66, 261n79, 261n82, 262n92, 262n97, 263n116, 263n122, 264n125, 264n132, 264n133, 264n134, 265n136, 265n137, 265n141, 265n145, 266n146, 266n155, 267n168, 268n194, 269n208, 269n210, 269n212, 270n231, 271n232, 272n257, 273n263
petty king, §3.1.9, §§3.1.14–15, §3.1.17, §§3.1.43–45, §§3.1.53–54, §3.1.59, §3.1.63, §3.1.65, §3.1.68, §3.1.72, §3.1.74, §3.1.80, §§3.1.82–83, §§3.1.92–93, §3.1.97, §3.3.23, §4.48, 255n1
petty sultan, §3.1.15, §3.1.63, §3.1.94
piaster, §3.3.44, §4.29
pilgrimage (to Mecca and Medina), 255n3
plague, §3.3.8, §3.3.15, §4.36
pleurisy (*abū l-ṣufūf*), §3.3.14
pôlgo, §§3.3.46–47. *See also* salt
poora'ng ába, §3.1.14, 259n55
pomegranate, §3.1.101,§4.2, §4.26. *See also* *qiddīm*
The Prohibited Nature of Using Eunuch Attendants at the Tomb of the Lord of ʿAdnān's Descendants (*Ḥurmat khidmat al-khiṣyān li-ḍarīh sayyid wuld ʿAdnān*), §3.2.55
prophet, §3.1.30, §3.2.55, §4.35, §4.39, §4.45, 272n257
The Prophet. *See* Muḥammad

Qābīl (Cain), §3.2.35, 266n147
qafal (tree), §4.17, §4.19
qanā (bamboo), §4.25
qaraẓ pods, §4.18. *See also* sant tree
qawwārīn, §3.1.61

qiddīm (tree), §4.13, 271n238
Qirlī, x, §§3.1.11–12, §3.1.14, §§3.3.46–47, §4.7
qudānī, §§3.1.96–97
qūqū, §3.3.19
al-Quṣayr, ix

raʿāf. *See dam-l-raʿāf*
rabdāʾ, §3.3.39, 269n210. *See also* ostrich
rainbow, §4.31
rākūbah, §3.1.78, 261n79
Ramadan, §4.33, 266n146, 272n257
raqraqah, §3.2.7, §3.2.16
Rās al-Fīl. *See* Jadīd Rās al-Fīl
Rashīd. *See* ʿAbd al-Raḥmān al-Rashīd
red sorghum. *See* sorghum
religious scholars, §4.53
rhinoceros, §§3.3.31–.32, §3.3.38
Rhodes, ix
rice, §3.3.25, §3.3.40, §4.3, 264n128
Rīl, x, §3.1.7, §3.1.9, §3.1.12, §3.1.14, §3.3.50, 255n7
Rizayqāt, §§3.1.5–6, §3.1.8, §3.3.23, §3.3.40
root, §3.1.104, §3.2.53, §4.8, §4.24, §§4.34–38, 259n49, 263n107
Rūngā, §3.2.38, 266n153, 267n170
ruqād al-fāqah (bead), §3.1.102

sadā, §4.35
the Ṣaʿīd, 255n8
Salīmah, ix
salt, §3.1.43, §3.3.26, §3.3.28, §§3.3.46–47, §§4.7–8, §4.14; *mīdawbī*, §3.3.47; zaghāwī, §3.3.47. *See also kumbā*; *pôlgo*
sand dunes, §3.1.85. *See also* the Dunes
sangadiri, §3.2.8, §3.2.10
sant tree, §3.2.91, §4.18, §4.20
Sarf al-Dajāj, ix–x, §3.1.12, §3.3.45, §4.7
ṣarīf, §3.1.86, §4.20, 261n89
sayāl, §3.1.83
sayyid, §3.1.17, §3.1.41, §4.52. *See also* Aḥmad Zarrūq
scarification, §3.3.14, §3.3.17. *See also* surgery
scarlet fever (*al-burjuk*), §3.3.15
scholar, §3.1.17, §3.1.41, §§3.1.73–74, §3.1.80, §3.1.83, §3.2.33, §3.2.55, §3.3.21, §4.53, 270n221
sequin, §3.3.44
servant, §3.1.17, §3.1.23, §3.1.33, §§3.1.39–41, §3.1.107, §3.2.27, §3.2.39, §3.2.43, §3.2.52, §3.3.18, §3.3.38, §4.42, §§4.47–48, §4.52, 258n38, 260n73
sesame, §3.1.65, §3.3.28, §4.4, §4.15
al-Shabb, ix
al-Shaʿīriyyah, x, §3.3.50
Shālā, §§3.1.7–8, §3.3.22
shaʿlūb (tree), §3.1.109, §4.26
sharātī. *See shartāy*
sharif, §3.1.14, §3.1.17, §3.1.32, §3.1.38, §3.1.41, §§3.1.79–80, §3.1.83, §3.2.5, §3.3.38, §4.50, §4.53
shartāy (pl. *sharātī*), §3.1.14, §3.1.63
shāw (tree), §§4.22–23
shawtar (pl. *shawātir*), §3.3.52, §3.1.96
the Shaykh of the Mountain, §3.1.20
shaykh-father, §§3.1.14–15, §3.1.55, §3.1.59, §3.1.92, §3.2.38, §§3.2.41–42, §4.41, 259n56. *See also* Muḥammad Kurrā
shea, §4.15
shīkah, §3.3.44
Shīth (Seth), §4.39
shūsh, §3.1.101
Shūshū (shaykh), §3.3.38

shuwūr. See madraʿah

sickness, §3.1.22, §3.3.1, §3.3.23

Silā. *See* Dār Silā

silk, §3.1.80, §3.1.95, §3.1.97, §3.2.40, §4.17

silver, §3.1.20, §3.1.76, §3.1.91, §§3.1.98–99, §3.1.103, §§3.3.42–43, 269n213

Sinnār, §3.1.1, §3.2.58, §4.6, 271n233

slave, §3.1.18, §§3.1.32–33, §3.1.39, §§3.1.47–48, §3.1.60, §3.1.66, §3.1.69, §3.1.76, §3.1.80, §§3.1.90–92, §3.1.107, §§3.1.112–113, §3.2.3, §3.2.5, §3.2.8, §§3.2.11–12, §3.2.28, §§3.2.35–36, §3.2.41, §§3.2.48–52, §3.3.36, §3.3.44, §4.1, §4.44, §4.50, §§4.52–53, §4.63, 260n65, 260n73, 262n102, 265n136, 266n153, 273n262

smallpox, §§3.3.8–10

smith, §3.3.30, 269n207

sparrow, §3.3.4, §3.3.35

Sodom apple, §3.3.14, §4.17

sons of sultans, §3.1.45, §3.3.21, §4.41, 272n260

soomiit (bead), §3.1.100

sorghum (*mārīq*), §3.1.65, §3.1.99, §3.3.37, §4.3, §4.32; red (*ʿazīr*), §4.3; Syrian (*abū abāṭ*), §4.3; white (*abū shalawlaw*), §4.3

spikenard, §3.1.104

spleen, §3.3.15

the sprinkle (season), §§4.29–30, §4.32, §4.42, 282n250

squash, §3.1.19, §4.6

stork. *See abū ṭunṭurah*

sūbiyā, §3.2.6

subu jelló, §3.2.26

the Successor. *See* Isḥāq the Successor

Sudan, 255n3, 257n25, 258n46, 265n136, 265n140, 268n193, 268n194, 269n206, 269n207, 270n231, 270n233

sudāsī, §3.3.45. *See also* slave

suktāyah, §3.1.86, §§3.1.90–91, §3.1.108

Sulaymān Solongdungo, 258n45

Sulaymān Tīr, §3.1.92, §3.2.39

surgery, §§3.3.16–17. *See also* cauterization; castration; circumcision; scarification

al-sūtiyyah (disease), §3.3.15

al-Suwaynah, ix–x

syphilis. *See al-jiqqayl*

Syrian sorghum. *See* sorghum

tābā. See tobacco

tabaldī (tree), §3.3.19, §4.10

Tabaldiyyah, §3.1.7, §3.1.10, §3.1.12

ṭabbābī, §3.3.21, 268n198. *See also* magic

ṭabīb, 268n198

Ṭāhir (son of Aḥmad Bukur), 265n137

takākī. See See *tukkiyyah*

Takrūr, §3.1.2

Tāldawā, x, §3.1.7

ṭalḥ (tree), §4.18

tamarind, §3.3.17, §3.3.40

Tamurrū al-Fullānī, §3.3.21, §4.42

Tandaltī, x, §3.1.7, §3.1.12, §3.1.14, §§3.1.84–85

tărne, §§3.3.44–45, §3.3.47

Tărne, ix–x, §3.1.12

tarnga jíso, §3.2.26

tawse (dance), §3.2.8, §3.2.12

taxation, §§3.1.5–7, §3.1.14, §§3.1.61–62, §§3.1.65–66, 257n32, 260n65

tax collector, §3.1.62, §3.1.66, §4.44

taytal, §3.3.29, 269n206. *See also* cattle

textiles. *See* baft; broadcloth; calico; camlet; cashmere; cotton; *kalkaf*; *katkāt*; *lawī*; muslin; *qudānī*; *shawtar*; *shīkah*; silk; *tīkaw*

thawb, §3.1.97
ṭibb, §3.3.21, 268n198. *See also* magic
tīkaw, §§3.1.96–97
tikináwi, §3.1.9, §3.1.12, §§3.1.14–15, §3.1.54, §3.1.92
Timbuktu. *See* Dār Tunbuktū
tindinga (dance), §3.2.8, §3.2.12, §3.2.15
tobacco (*tābā*), §3.1.49, §§3.3.48–49, 270n221
togjêl (drum), §3.1.70, §3.1.83
tómbol (drum), §3.2.22, 256n20
Tomorókkóngá, §3.1.9, §3.1.11, §3.1.14, §3.1.35, §3.1.53, §3.2.57, §3.3.53, §4.46, §§4.48–49, 272n261
Tradition, §3.1.38, 255n9
tree. *See* acacia; *ʿandurāb*; banana tree; *baṭṭūm*; carob; *dāyūq*; doum palm; *dulab*; ebony; *ḥarāz*; *ḥashāb*; *hijlīj*; *ḥummayḍ*; jackalberry; *jaʿjaʿ*; jujube; *karnū*; *kilí*; *kitir*; *laʾūt*; lemon tree; *mukhkhayṭ*; palm; *qafal*; *qiddīm*; sant tree; *sayāl*; *shaʿlūb*; *shāw*; shea; *tabaldī*; *ṭalḥ*; umbrella thorn acacia
Tripoli (Libya), §3.3.48
tuberculosis, §3.3.15
Tubū, §3.2.58
tukkiyyah (pl. *takākī*), §§3.3.44–45, §§3.3.51–52, §3.3.54
tukultī, §3.1.86
Tunis, ix, §3.2.38, §3.3.7, §4.15, §4.50
Tunjūr, §3.1.4, §3.1.10, §3.1.13, §3.1.15, §3.2.57, 255n5
Turkey, Turks, §3.1.29, §3.1.71
Turqunak Muḥammad, §3.2.44
al-Ṭuwayshah, ix, §3.1.3, §3.1.16
the Twins. *See* Gemini
Twins' autumn, §4.32, 272n253.
ʿUmar Lēl (sultan of Darfur), §4.41
ʿUmar al-Tūnisī (father of the author), §3.1.17
umbrella thorn acacia, §4.18
umm bulbul. *See* wine
Umm Ḥabīb. *See* Kinānah
umm ṣuquʿ (disease), §3.3.5, 268n184
Upper Egypt, §4.12, §4.17, 255n8
ʿUthmān wad ʿAllaw, §3.3.9

the Victorious (drum), §3.1.34, §3.1.38, §3.1.45, 257n36, 260n70
vitiligo, §3.3.14
vizier, §3.1.16, §3.1.24, §3.1.41, §3.1.43, §3.1.45, §3.1.46, §§3.1.48–49, §3.1.59, §§3.1.73–74, §3.1.80, §3.1.92, §3.1.93, §3.1.96, §§3.2.16–17, §3.2.19, §3.2.39, §3.3.38, §§4.43–45, §4.48

Wāddāy (Wadadāy), ix–x, §§3.1.1–2, §3.1.11, §3.1.13, §3.1.16, §§3.1.82–83, §3.1.96, §3.2.44, §3.2.54, §3.2.58, §3.3.3, §3.3.11, §3.3.13, §§3.3.37–38, §4.29, §4.33, §4.50, §4.53, 255n2
Wādī l-Kūʿ, x, §3.1.12, §3.1.85, §3.1.92, §4.6
wajaj, §3.3.37
Wārah, §3.3.39
warrāniyyah, §§3.2.26–27
watermelon, §4.5
waykah, §§3.3.25–27, 269n203
wedding, §3.1.26, §§3.2.–5, §3.2.8, §3.2.19, §3.2.22, §3.2.26, §§3.2.28–29, §3.3.20
wheat, §3.1.21, §3.1.28, §3.1.91, §§4.2–3, §4.29, 257n34
white sorghum. *See* sorghum
whydah, §3.3.35, 269n209
wild cattle, §3.2.29, §3.3.31, 269n206

wine, §3.2.20, §4.26; metaphor for saliva, §3.2.60, 267n177; *umm bulbul*, §§3.2.5–6, §3.2.28, 264n125
wirdah (disease), §3.3.8
woman, women, §3.1.13, §3.1.18, §3.1.23, §§3.1.25–26, §3.1.32, §§3.1.37–38, §§3.1.59–60, §3.1.66, §§3.1.76–77, §§3.1.90–92, §§3.1.97–105, §§3.1.107–8. §3.1.112, §§3.2.5–7, §3.2.9, §§3.2.12–16, §3.2.19, §3.2.22 , §3.2.24, §3.2.26, §§3.2.29–30, §§3.2.32–34, §§3.2.36–37, §3.2.39, §§3.2.43–48, §3.2.50, §§3.2.52–59, §3.3.2, §§3.3.13–14, §§3.3.19–20, §3.3.24, §3.3.43, §3.3.45, §3.3.53, §§4.27–28, §4.35, §§4.50–51, §4.57, §4.59, §4.65, §4.66, 263n103, 263n107, 264n129, 265n145, 267n168, 268n194
Yājūj and Mājūj (Gog and Magog), §3.3.23
the yellow air. *See* cholera

Zabadah, §3.3.37
Zaghāwah, §§3.1.9–10, §§3.1.13–15, §3.1.35, §§3.3.22–23. *See also* tikináwi, Dār (al-)Zaghāwah
zaghāwī. *See* salt
zakat, §§3.1.65. *See also* taxation
ẓalīm, §2.3.39, 269n201. *See also* ostrich
zarībah, §§3.1.86–87, §4.20, 261n89
Zayādiyyah, §3.3.24, §3.3.37
zinc, §3.1.103
Zoroastrian. *See* Magian
ẓufr, §3.1.104

About the NYU Abu Dhabi Institute

NYU
ABU DHABI
INSTITUTE

The Library of Arabic Literature is supported by a grant from the NYU Abu Dhabi Institute, a major hub of intellectual and creative activity and advanced research. The Institute hosts academic conferences, workshops, lectures, film series, performances, and other public programs directed both to audiences within the UAE and to the worldwide academic and research community. It is a center of the scholarly community for Abu Dhabi, bringing together faculty and researchers from institutions of higher learning throughout the region.

NYU Abu Dhabi, through the NYU Abu Dhabi Institute, is a world-class center of cutting-edge research, scholarship, and cultural activity. The Institute creates singular opportunities for leading researchers from across the arts, humanities, social sciences, sciences, engineering, and the professions to carry out creative scholarship and conduct research on issues of major disciplinary, multidisciplinary, and global significance.

About the Typefaces

The Arabic body text is set in DecoType Naskh, designed by Thomas Milo and Mirjam Somers, based on an analysis of five centuries of Ottoman manuscript practice. The exceptionally legible result is the first and only typeface in a style that fully implements the principles of script grammar (*qawāʿid al-khaṭṭ*).

The Arabic footnote text is set in DecoType Emiri, drawn by Mirjam Somers, based on the metal typeface in the naskh style that was cut for the 1924 Cairo edition of the Qur'an.

Both Arabic typefaces in this series are controlled by a dedicated font layout engine. ACE, the Arabic Calligraphic Engine, invented by Peter Somers, Thomas Milo, and Mirjam Somers of DecoType, first operational in 1985, pioneered the principle followed by later smart font layout technologies such as OpenType, which is used for all other typefaces in this series.

The Arabic text was set with WinSoft Tasmeem, a sophisticated user interface for DecoType ACE inside Adobe InDesign. Tasmeem was conceived and created by Thomas Milo (DecoType) and Pascal Rubini (WinSoft) in 2005.

The English text is set in Adobe Text, a new and versatile text typeface family designed by Robert Slimbach for Western (Latin, Greek, Cyrillic) typesetting. Its workhorse qualities make it perfect for a wide variety of applications, especially for longer passages of text where legibility and economy are important. Adobe Text bridges the gap between calligraphic Renaissance types of the 15th and 16th centuries and high-contrast Modern styles of the 18th century, taking many of its design cues from early post-Renaissance Baroque transitional types cut by designers such as Christoffel van Dijck, Nicolaus Kis, and William Caslon. While grounded in classical form, Adobe Text is also a statement of contemporary utilitarian design, well suited to a wide variety of print and on-screen applications.

Titles Published by the Library of Arabic Literature

For more details on individual titles, visit www.libraryofarabicliterature.org

Classical Arabic Literature: A Library of Arabic Literature Anthology
Selected and translated by Geert Jan van Gelder (2012)

A Treasury of Virtues: Sayings, Sermons, and Teachings of ʿAlī, by al-Qāḍī al-Quḍāʿī, with the **One Hundred Proverbs** attributed to al-Jāḥiẓ
Edited and translated by Tahera Qutbuddin (2013)

The Epistle on Legal Theory, by al-Shāfiʿī
Edited and translated by Joseph E. Lowry (2013)

Leg over Leg, by Aḥmad Fāris al-Shidyāq
Edited and translated by Humphrey Davies (4 volumes; 2013–14)

Virtues of the Imām Aḥmad ibn Ḥanbal, by Ibn al-Jawzī
Edited and translated by Michael Cooperson (2 volumes; 2013–15)

The Epistle of Forgiveness, by Abū l-ʿAlāʾ al-Maʿarrī
Edited and translated by Geert Jan van Gelder and Gregor Schoeler (2 volumes; 2013–14)

The Principles of Sufism, by ʿĀʾishah al-Bāʿūniyyah
Edited and translated by Th. Emil Homerin (2014)

The Expeditions: An Early Biography of Muḥammad, by Maʿmar ibn Rāshid
Edited and translated by Sean W. Anthony (2014)

Two Arabic Travel Books
Accounts of China and India, by Abū Zayd al-Sīrāfī
Edited and translated by Tim Mackintosh-Smith (2014)
Mission to the Volga, by Aḥmad ibn Faḍlān
Edited and translated by James Montgomery (2014)

Disagreements of the Jurists: A Manual of Islamic Legal Theory, by al-Qāḍī al-Nuʿmān
Edited and translated by Devin J. Stewart (2015)

Consorts of the Caliphs: Women and the Court of Baghdad, by Ibn al-Sāʿī
Edited by Shawkat M. Toorawa and translated by the Editors of the Library of Arabic Literature (2015)

What ʿĪsā ibn Hishām Told Us, by Muḥammad al-Muwayliḥī
Edited and translated by Roger Allen (**2 volumes**; 2015)

The Life and Times of Abū Tammām, by Abū Bakr Muḥammad ibn Yaḥyā al-Ṣūlī
Edited and translated by Beatrice Gruendler (2015)

The Sword of Ambition: Bureaucratic Rivalry in Medieval Egypt, by ʿUthmān ibn Ibrāhīm al-Nābulusī
Edited and translated by Luke Yarbrough (2016)

Brains Confounded by the Ode of Abū Shādūf Expounded, by Yūsuf al-Shirbīnī
Edited and translated by Humphrey Davies (**2 volumes**; 2016)

Light in the Heavens: Sayings of the Prophet Muḥammad, by al-Qāḍī al-Quḍāʿī
Edited and translated by Tahera Qutbuddin (2016)

Risible Rhymes, by Muḥammad ibn Maḥfūẓ al-Sanhūrī
Edited and translated by Humphrey Davies (2016)

A Hundred and One Nights
Edited and translated by Bruce Fudge (2016)

The Excellence of the Arabs, by Ibn Qutaybah
Edited by James E. Montgomery and Peter Webb
Translated by Sarah Bowen Savant and Peter Webb (2017)

Scents and Flavors: A Syrian Cookbook
Edited and translated by Charles Perry (2017)

Arabian Satire: Poetry from 18th-Century Najd, by Ḥmēdān al-Shwēʿir
Edited and translated by Marcel Kurpershoek (2017)

In Darfur: An Account of the Sultanate and its People, by Muḥammad ibn ʿUmar al-Tūnisī
Edited and translated by Humphrey Davies (2 volumes; 2018)

English-only Paperbacks

Leg over Leg, by Aḥmad Fāris al-Shidyāq (2 volumes; 2015)
The Expeditions: An Early Biography of Muḥammad, by Maʿmar ibn Rāshid (2015)
The Epistle on Legal Theory: A Translation of al-Shāfiʿī's *Risālah*, by al-Shāfiʿī (2015)
The Epistle of Forgiveness, by Abū l-ʿAlāʾ al-Maʿarrī (2016)
The Principles of Sufism, by ʿĀʾishah al-Bāʿūniyyah (2016)
A Treasury of Virtues: Sayings, Sermons and Teachings of ʿAlī, by al-Qāḍī al-Quḍāʿī with the **One Hundred Proverbs**, attributed to al-Jāḥiẓ (2016)
The Life of Ibn Ḥanbal, by Ibn al-Jawzī (2016)
Mission to the Volga, by Ibn Faḍlān (2017)
Accounts of China and India, by Abū Zayd al-Sīrāfī (2017)
A Hundred and One Nights (2017)
Disagreements of the Jurists: A Manual of Islamic Legal Theory, by al-Qāḍī al-Nuʿmān (2017)
What ʿĪsā ibn Hishām Told Us, by Muḥammad al-Muwayliḥī (2018)

About the Editor–Translator

Humphrey Davies is an award-winning translator of some twenty works of modern Arabic literature, among them Alaa Al-Aswany's *The Yacoubian Building*, five novels by Elias Khoury, including *Gate of the Sun*, and Aḥmad Fāris al-Shidyāq's *Leg over Leg*. He has also made a critical edition, translation, and lexicon of the Ottoman-period *Hazz al-quḥūf bi-sharḥ qaṣīd Abī Shādūf* (*Brains Confounded by the Ode of Abū Shādūf Expounded*) by Yūsuf al-Shirbīnī and compiled with a colleague an anthology entitled *Al-'āmmiyyah al-miṣriyyah al-maktūbah: mukhtārāt min 1400 ilā 2009* (*Egyptian Colloquial Writing: selections from 1400 to 2009*). He read Arabic at the University of Cambridge, received his Ph.D. from the University of California at Berkeley, and, previous to undertaking his first translation in 2003, worked for social development and research organizations in Egypt, Tunisia, Palestine, and Sudan. He is affiliated with the American University in Cairo, where he lives.